Jane Austen at Home

Also by Lucy Worsley

LUCY WORSLEY

Jane Austen at Home

St. Martin's Press

New York

www.stmartins.com

The Library of Congress Cataloging-in-Publication Data is available upon request.

ISBN 978-1-250-13160-7 (hardcover)
ISBN 978-1-250-13161-4 (ebook)

Our books may be purchased in bulk for promotional, educational, or business
use. Please contact your local bookseller or the Macmillan Corporate and
Premium Sales Department at 1-800-221-7945, extension 5442, or by email
at MacmillanSpecialMarkets@macmillan.com.

First published in Great Britain by Hodder & Stoughton, an Hachette UK company

First U.S. Edition: July 2017

10 9 8 7 6 5 4 3 2 1

To Mark

Contents

ACT THREE:
A REAL HOME

ACT FOUR:
THE END, AND AFTER

Jane Austen at Home

Introduction

'Miss Austen's merits have long been
established beyond a question;
she is, emphatically, the novelist of home.'[1]

Richard Bentley,
publishing Jane Austen's novels in 1833

THE WORLD OF Jane Austen's novels, seen in countless feature films, is domestic, well ordered and snug. Her characters inhabit neat, genteel cottages, gentleman-like country mansions, and elegant town-houses in London or Bath.

And her life is often seen through the same lens.

It's an impression that you can't help but take away from the pretty, flower-filled country cottage at Chawton in Hampshire that finally provided Jane, her sister and their mother with a long-sought home. Jane moved there in 1809, probably expecting to live there happily until the end of her life. As it would turn out, she would not.

For Jane, home was a perennial problem. Where could she afford to live? Amid the many domestic duties of an unmarried daughter and aunt, how could she find the time to write? Where could she keep her manu-scripts safe? A home of her own must have seemed to Jane to be always just out of reach. With only a tiny stash of capital hard earned by her writing, the death of her father forced her into a makeshift life in rented lodgings, or else shunted between the relations who used her as cheap childcare.

It's not surprising, then, that the search for a home is an idea that's central to Jane's fiction. The majority of her scenes take place indoors, with people talking, always talking, in a room, which is very often a drawing room. And yet, when Jane's characters want to talk about what really matters – their feelings, the truth – they often have to go outdoors. They escape the jaws of the drawing rooms that confine their lives. 'You were sick of civility', says Lizzy Bennet in a moment of intimacy with Mr Darcy.

Young people reading Jane Austen for the first time think that the stories are about love and romance and finding a partner. But a happy home is equally as much what all of her heroines don't have, and yet desire. All of Jane's leading ladies are displaced from either their physical home, or from their family. Jane shows, subtly but devastatingly, how hard it is to find a true home, a place of safety in which one can be understood and loved. She is uniquely sensitive to a particular home's happiness – or unhappiness.

This has led people to assume that Jane herself was unhappy at home, flawed or damaged in some way. But the depressing fact is that she was just one among many spinsters of her time and position in society who had to try to feel 'at home' in unusual, meagre or unpleasant places. And it wasn't just spinsters. 'I cannot help feeling a great desire *to be at home*, however uncomfortable that home may be', wrote Jane's sister-in-law, Fanny.[2] Home to her was a cramped cabin on board her sailor husband's ship.

And so Jane's novels are full of homes loved, lost, lusted after. In her first published work, *Sense and Sensibility*, it is a death in the family that forces Elinor and Marianne out of their childhood home. In *Pride and Prejudice*, Elizabeth Bennet and her sisters will be expelled from their home at the end of her father's life. Fanny Price is sent away from her home, like one of Jane's own brothers, to live with richer relations at *Mansfield Park*. Anne Elliot misses her country life at Kellynch Hall when packed off in *Persuasion* to Bath. Even Catherine Morland of *Northanger Abbey* and Emma Woodhouse of *Emma*, young, relatively well-off and in no immediate danger of homelessness, have to choose their future domestic set-ups wisely.

In real life, perhaps contrary to expectation, Jane did not *have* to enter the 'years of danger' without a home of her own, for she was a spinster by choice. Far from lacking romance, as people often think, in her life she turned down at least one suitor for absolute certain, and in her story we'll encounter no fewer than five potential life-partners. I believe that Jane deliberately kept herself free of all that because she believed that marriage and property and a substantial home *could* be a prison.

I also hope to introduce you to Jane's everyday life at home, good days, bad days, domestic pleasures and domestic chores, the 'little matters on which the daily happiness of private life depends', as Jane put it herself in *Emma*. The idea that women of the gentry didn't 'work' is long since debunked: they either performed 'work' that society deemed virtuous, like playing the piano or reading improving books, or else they discreetly carried out – and this was the case in the Austen family – much of the actual labour needed to keep the food on the table and the clothes clean. Sometimes this meant actively supervising contract labour, sometimes rolling up their sleeves to do the domestic work themselves.

We know so much about Jane's life from day to day, even hour to hour, because she was a prolific letter writer. Despite vigorous excisions by the Austen family, Jane has left us hundreds of thousands of words, chiefly written to her sister Cassandra.

These letters, full of the mundane detail of everyday life, have often disappointed readers. The trouble has been that they do not directly comment on the French Revolution, or the great affairs of state. One of Jane's fussy relatives claimed that 'they could be no transcript of her mind', and that a reader 'would not feel that they knew her any the better for having read them'.[3] Wrong, wrong, wrong! The affairs of state are there, all right, for those who know how to read the tiny details of the changing social life of Jane's age. And her personality is there, bold as brass, bursting with life, buoyant or recalcitrant as each day required. These letters are a treasure trove hiding in plain sight.

They are also a resource that can be read in many different ways, to paint a picture of the Jane that the reader wishes to find. I am interested in them as a record of the little evasions of feminine duty that Jane must have made in order to win herself the time to write. 'I often wonder', Jane wrote to her sister, 'how *you* can find the time for what you do, in addition to the care of the House.' Well, I wonder the same thing. Jane had to fight against domestic duties to 'find the time' in a way that did not offend her family or their notions of what a spinster aunt should do. This was her battle, a grimy, unexciting, quotidian domestic battle, about who should do which chores. It's a battle that still holds women back. It's a battle that continues to this day.

'Short and easy will be the task of the mere biographer', wrote Jane's brother Henry after her death. 'A life of usefulness, literature, and religion, was not by any means a life of event.'[4] Big mistake! Jane's life contained bitterness and regret, financial deprivation and anxiety. But she and her family kept much of this from us. Above all other authors, Jane is attractive but elusive to her readers: she tantalises, hints, retracts. 'Seldom, very seldom,' she herself warns us, 'does complete truth belong to any human disclosure; seldom can it happen that something is not a little disguised, or a little mistaken.'

I've been at pains to try to place Jane in the context of the physical world of her homes, but this will inevitably be a personal, not a definitive, interpretation of her life. Every generation gets the 'Jane Austen' it deserves. The Victorians searched for, and found, a 'good little woman' who wrote her books almost accidentally, with no apparent effort, 'St Aunt Jane of Steventon-cum-Chawton Canonicorum' as she's been called. More recently, biographers have been at pains to show Jane as a much more modern woman. 'If I am a wild Beast I cannot help it', she wrote, and much has been made of her dancing, her hangovers, her anger. This version of Jane can best be summed up by the 1990s argument that Jane deliberately chose the pseudonym of 'Mrs Ashton Dennis' for writing cross letters to her publishers, enabling her to close with: 'I am Gentlemen &c &c MAD'. 'Mad was how she felt, and that was how she signed herself', argues her biographer David Nokes.[5]

While I'll try to put Jane back into her social class and time, I must admit that I also write as a signed up 'Janeite', a devotee and worshipper. I too have searched for my own Jane, and naturally I have found her to be simply a far, far better version of myself: clever, kind, funny, but also angry at the restrictions of her life, someone tirelessly searching for ways to be free and creative. I know who I *want* Jane Austen to be, and I put my cards on the table. This is, unashamedly, the story of my Jane, every word of it written with love.

But in searching for this Jane of mine, I have accidentally met a whole generation of women for whom Jane seems to speak: the governess Anne Sharp, her sister spinster Cassandra, her sisters-in-law killed by child-bearing, the female friends who cheered her on through her publishing triumphs and disasters. Jane's passage through life, so smooth on the surface, seems sharply marked by closed doors, routes she could not take, choices she could not make. Her great contribution was to push those doors open, a little bit, for us in later generations to slip through.

A sad life, a life of struggle, is at odds with the first impression given by her books: of a country parsonage on a sunny morning, with roses round the door, a spirited heroine about to meet her life-partner, a fresh romance about to unfold . . .

ACT ONE

A Sunny Morning at the Rectory

Steventon Rectory, Hampshire

I

To Steventon

'The rector of a parish has much to do . . .
his parish duties, and the care
and improvement of his dwelling.'

Pride and Prejudice

To generations of Austen worshippers, the site of Steventon Rectory is hallowed ground. They are often to be found at the side of the lane, silent and thoughtful, peering through the hedge into the Hampshire field where it stood. This is the place where she spent twenty-five years and wrote three novels. This is where it all began.

Anyone who reads Jane Austen's novels closely will notice that although we have a picture in our minds of Pemberley, or Trafalgar House in *Sanditon*, or Donwell Abbey, the details she actually gives us are very sparse. She sketches an outline; our minds then fill it in. But the houses Jane describes in the most detail are always parsonages. In *Mansfield Park*, for example, we get a much fuller physical description of Edmund Bertram's future home in his parish than we do of the great mansion of Mansfield Park itself. That's because parsonages mattered to Jane. She often visited great houses and was familiar with places like Pemberley. But Jane was most at home in a parsonage like the one she knew from growing up with her parents and brothers and sister in the Hampshire countryside. And yet, to work out what her real home, Steventon Rectory, was like, takes time, patience and imagination, because the house itself is gone.

The story of the Austens at Steventon Rectory really begins in the late summer of 1768, when a wagon heavily loaded with household goods made its way through the Hampshire lanes from nearby Deane to the village of Steventon. Its members had no notion that so many historians and biographers would scrutinise this ordinary event in the life of an ordinary family.

Although Mr George Austen (thirty-eight) and his wife Cassandra (twenty-nine) had only been married for four years, their household was not inconsiderable. It included Mrs Austen's own mother, Mrs Jane Leigh, and the couple's three boys: James ('Jemmy'), George, and Edward ('Neddy'), the latter less than one year old. There would also have been maids and manservants, of name and number unknown. They probably included Jane Leigh's servant Mary Ellis.

Although it was only a short distance of just over a mile from Deane to Steventon, their wagon crept slowly along a road that 'was a mere cart track, so cut up by deep ruts as to be impassable for a light carriage'.[1] The village of Steventon was deep in the countryside, difficult to reach if the 'rough country lanes' were muddy. Indeed, many a coachman would not take you. Once, a member of the Austen family travelling by carriage near Steventon called out to his driver to hurry up and get on with it. 'I *do* get on, sir, where I can!' came the answer. 'You stupid fellow!' was the response. 'Any fool can do that. I want you to get on *where you can't*.'[2]

Mrs Jane Leigh, the mother-in-law, had even made her will just before the journey. Now in her sixties, she feared that she was terminally ill. Her daughter, Mrs Cassandra Austen, was also far from well. She travelled along 'on a feather-bed, placed upon some soft articles of furniture in the waggon'.[3] She was 'not then in strong health', an early indicator of a lifetime of ailments, and possible hypochondria, that would alternately amuse and exasperate her family. But she does deserve some sympathy for having given birth to three children in four years. Mr George Austen's brother-in-law thought they were mad for having so many children so quickly. 'I cannot say', wrote this brother-in-law, Tysoe Hancock, who was out in India, 'that the News of the violently rapid increase of their family gives me so much pleasure.' The problem was that all these children, one of them his own godson, 'must be provided for'.[4]

Mr George Austen was a man of many cares: an ill wife, a dying mother-in-law, and his second son George's suffering from fits. Not least among his worries was his financial situation. The records of Mr Austen's account at Hoare's Bank in London show that on 6 August he had sold stock worth more than £250, presumably for the expenses of bringing the new house up to a habitable standard.[5] This sum of money represented nearly a year's income for him.

Mr Austen had in fact been in charge of the parish of Steventon for the last four years. But he had found his Rectory there so run-down and dilapidated, 'of the most miserable description', that he and his family had been living instead in a rented house in the neighbouring village of Deane.[6] This building was hardly any better: a 'low damp place with small inconvenient rooms, and scarcely two on the same level'.[7] The pokey parsonage at Deane was about the size of a coach, its various rooms the 'Coachbox, Basket & Dickey' (the box being the seat at the front for the driver, the dickey being the seat at the back for servants).

In 1764, the year George and Cassandra had married and moved to Hampshire, there had been great rains at Deane: 'the Wells in the Parish rose to their Tops, and Fish were taken between the Parsonage Yard & the Road'.[8] The other freak of nature to be seen in Georgian Deane was its enormous cabbages; a neighbour grew one 'five feet in circumference in the solid part, and [which] weighs upwards of 32 lbs'.[9] Meanwhile, down the lane in the neighbouring parish of Steventon, the high winds of February had blown down the church's timber steeple.[10]

It was an inauspicious beginning. Indeed, when the future Mrs Austen had visited Hampshire to take a look at the county in which she was to live, she had found it 'unattractive, compared with the broad river, the rich valley, and the noble hills which she had been accustomed to behold at her native home near Henley-upon-Thames'. Here her father enjoyed a comfortable life as a clergyman employed by an Oxford college. Hampshire, by contrast, presented a miserable prospect: 'the poverty of the soil in most places prevents the timber from attaining a large size'.[11] Mr Austen's new parish or 'living' would scarcely provide him with income enough from tithes to make such a life as his wife had been used to.

The couple had met in the sophisticated surroundings of Oxford, possibly in the house of Cassandra's uncle, the Master of Balliol College. Marriage to the delicate Cassandra Leigh, as she was then, must have been a slightly daunting prospect. She was a gifted writer, and a member of an old, prosperous, rambling family, the Leighs of Warwickshire. Her father had been a Fellow of All Souls before becoming an Oxfordshire rector. Her uncle, Dr Theophilus Leigh, was the Master of Balliol for more than fifty years, a chatty man 'overflowing with puns and witticisms and sharp retorts'.[12] He was rather taken with his niece's own quickness and inventiveness, naming her as 'the Poet of the Family' and a writer 'promising a great Genius'.[13] People later thought that Mrs Austen, rather than her husband, must have bequeathed Jane her talent, for she possessed 'the germ of much of the ability which was concentrated' in her younger daughter.[14]

The Leighs were a clever family, if self-regarding in the Balliol manner. They liked to embroider the stories from their long family history – they were descended from an Elizabethan Lord Mayor of London – but also to undermine them with their own dry wit. Their females were as sharp as the Oxford-educated males. 'You wish me to collect all the anecdotes I can recollect and gather of our Family', wrote Cassandra Leigh's cousin, an amateur novelist named Mary.[15] 'Prepare yrself for much oral tradition; for old Womens legends, – for Ghosts & Goblins & for being extremely tired of the prolixity.'[16] While Cassandra's own part of the Leigh family contained a large number of clerics, she also had lurking about in the upper branches of her family tree some titles and significant landed estates and fortunes, including the vast Stoneleigh Abbey in Warwickshire.

Jane Austen's mother, then, was a powerful personality. She had 'strong common sense,' wrote a relative, 'and often expressed herself, both in writing and in conversation, with epigrammatic force and point'. But these were not necessarily attractive qualities in a Georgian woman, and perhaps explain why she'd been still unmarried at what was, for a gentle-woman, the relatively advanced age of twenty-four. Another Georgian lady wrote to the *Lady's Magazine* to complain, on behalf of her sex, that if women 'dare to read anything of more importance than a play or a novel, we are called critics, wits, female pedants, &c.'.[17] To be witty was a flaw. Yet Cassandra Leigh was proud of her 'sprack wit', as she called it ('sprack' meaning quick, or lively). She was proud of her facility for words and jests and comebacks, and Jane's father was an exceptional Georgian gentleman in valuing it just as highly as she did.

In appearance, Jane's mother was striking rather than beautiful, with her dark hair, 'fine well cut features, large grey eyes, and good eyebrows'. 'She was amusingly particular about people's noses,' we're told, 'having a very aristocratic one herself.'[18]

But Cassandra Leigh, frail and aristocratic in appearance, was at her core as tough as leather. She had married her George on 26 April 1764 in the gay city of Bath. In a marriage like this, at the lower fringes of genteel life with money rather scarce, a wedding also created a business partnership. She signalled her intentions by dressing for the ceremony in a sturdy red riding habit, which would become her practical daily outfit for the early years of her married life, and which 'in due course was cut up into jackets and trousers for her boys'.[19]

Mrs Austen was no passenger; her contribution to family life would be considerable. She understood that a man like George Austen wanted – no, *needed* – a woman to keep his household running. He wasn't marrying a woman; he was marrying a lifestyle. There was no way round that. In the very opening paragraph of their daughter Jane's first published book, *Sense and Sensibility*, we're introduced to a man who likewise 'had a constant companion and housekeeper in his life': his sister. The action all springs from her death, because he can't get along without a woman to run the house, and has to find a replacement. Mr Austen, never a sentimental man, would even go so far as to refer to Mrs Austen to third parties as 'my housekeeper'.[20] And indeed, some family members thought that Cassandra had married George simply out of her own desire for a house and financial security. When Cassandra's father died, one family historian wrote, her wedding took place 'immediately afterwards', so that she 'might make a home for her mother'.[21]

So Cassandra was quite a catch: born, perhaps, to look down her sharp-bladed nose at people at Oxford dinners, but equally willing to knuckle down and work hard. Her husband, on the other hand, was much less sure of his place in the world.

The heroine of any story, George Austen's daughter Jane would write, really ought to 'have the misfortune, as many heroines have had before her, of losing her Parents when she was very young'. This was true in real life of Jane's father, both of whose own parents had died before he was nine. Indeed, his story was even more traumatic than that.

George Austen's mother, Rebecca, had died when he was a baby, and his father William, a surgeon of the town of Tonbridge in Kent, had remarried. When William Austen died too, it emerged that he had not updated his will at the time of his second marriage. This meant that George Austen's stepmother could legitimately claim that her interest in her husband's estate took priority, and that she intended not to bother any more with her stepchildren. Six-year-old George and his two sisters Philadelphia and Leonora had to leave the family home in Tonbridge. They were now under the care of their uncles.

The children went to live in London with their Uncle Stephen Austen, a bookseller at the sign of the 'Angel and Bible' in the churchyard of St Paul's, right in the heart of the printing and book-making part of town.[22] But George later claimed that this Uncle Stephen had treated the three siblings 'with neglect', and 'a determination to thwart the natural tastes of the young people'.[23] George himself was allowed to go back to Tonbridge, to live with his Aunt Betty. There he worked hard at school and made a success of himself. George Austen's fight to overcome his own precarious start in life would give him small patience for laziness or weakness in other people. Indeed, his early years hardened him, and he had 'little toleration for want of capacity in man or woman'.[24]

George was lucky enough to possess uncles in plenty. Another of them was the rich and entrepreneurial Uncle 'Old Francis' Austen, a lawyer of Sevenoaks. 'Old Francis' kept a watchful eye upon his orphaned nieces and nephew. Family stories had it that he'd 'set out in life with £800 and a bundle of pens'. Working hard in his career as an attorney, he'd amassed a 'very large fortune, living most hospitably, and yet buying up all the valuable land' around Sevenoaks. He also acquired two wealthy wives, plus many of the first families of Kent as clients. Among them was the Earl of Dorset at the great house of Knole just up the road.

'Old Francis' certainly had a gift for making money, and secured some measure of stability for his young relatives with his contacts and gifts. In an age when parents often died before their children were grown, aunts and uncles and extended kin could be just as important. 'I like first Cousins to be first Cousins, & interested about each other', Jane would later write. Among the Austens, cousins frequently married, and brothers sometimes married an older sister and then, if she died, the younger one. The pool of eligible spouses at the 'right' level in society was not large, so this was a world that was almost incestuous.

George Austen worked nearly as hard as his admirable uncle, and ended up with a cosy nook as a Fellow at an Oxford College. But when he met Cassandra and decided to marry, he was forced to give up his fellowship. It was a position intended only for single men.

And now his extended family stepped up to help him. Uncle 'Old Francis' Austen purchased the 'living' of Deane in Hampshire for George, and his distant but generous cousin, Mr Thomas Knight (the elder), presented him in 1761 with the adjacent, bigger, and better, living of Steventon. When a patron awarded a living to a clergyman, it was like giving him a franchise in a chain of restaurants: here is a parish, raise what tithes you can from your parishioners, get on with it.

You might wonder why George Austen needed two livings, and how he could preach in both churches at once. As they were close together, he could dash from one to the other, and their combined income enabled him to live like a gentleman, or as close an approximation to it as he could manage. Later on he would subcontract the work of the smaller parish to a curate.

It was a fine situation for George Austen, but perhaps less good for his parishioners, who paid their tithes but did not get his undivided attention. It was this sort of thing that was leading the Anglican Church in the later eighteenth century into stagnation, and why alternative sects such as the Methodists were gathering strength. Some young curates, known as 'gallopers', rode hard to gabble the service at each of a great number of churches every Sunday, and skimped their duties where they could. But George Austen with his two adjacent parishes was hardly acting dishonourably, or even in any way out of the ordinary. Most people recognised that population changes meant that many country parishes no longer had enough inhabitants to support a clergyman and his family.

But there were also other ways for a Georgian clergyman to supplement his income. As the Austens travelled into Steventon in 1768, the land and the fields around them were going to be just as important as the house. Steventon parish was three miles long and three-quarters of a mile wide.[25] The living included the Rectory itself, and 'glebe' lands of three acres that were to be farmed specifically for the maintenance of the parish priest. In Steventon, the former common fields of the village had been 'inclosed' and made into private farms. This meant that George wouldn't have to go through the arduous business of collecting his tithes in kind from each individual family. He would just take 10 per cent in money from the profits of his farmer neighbours. The fact that he collected his tithes directly, rather than via a landowner, was what made Mr Austen a rector rather than a plain parson. But the business of the tithes did mean that his fortunes were still very closely tied to those of the land.

'Inclosure' and the great changes to the countryside in Georgian times, affecting the lives of some for good but others for ill, would in time crop up in Jane's novels – tangentially, it's true, but always there in the background. In her work, the enormous upheavals of her age, such as the French Revolution, or the Industrial Revolution, or the agricultural revolution, are played out off stage. What she shows us instead is their subtle effect upon the hearts and minds and daily lives of individuals.

The parish of Steventon, where Jane would be born, contained only thirty families. According to one of Mr Austen's predecessors as rector, its management should give little trouble as it contained no Papists, nor Dissenters, nor any 'nobleman, gentleman or person of note'.[26] The men grew turnips and beans, while the women worked at home, spinning flax, or wool from the sheep that wandered Hampshire's hills. Or sometimes they went out hoeing the turnips themselves. One traveller reported that the female field-workers of Hampshire were 'straight, fair, round-faced, excellent complexion and uncommonly gay'. At the sight of the stranger, they 'all fixed their eyes upon me, and, upon my smiling, they bursted out into laughter'.[27]

But they did not have much to laugh about. This writer, William Cobbett, had never seen 'a more *hilly* country', and nowhere else in England were 'the labouring people so badly off as they are here'.[28] A plough that worked perfectly well in Suffolk 'totally failed in the stiff ground round Steventon'.[29] With their poor and illiterate neighbours, some young clergymen moving as Mr Austen had done from Oxford to Hampshire found their harsh new lives in rural parishes to be quite shockingly lonely. At nearby Dummer, another young clergyman 'would have given the world for one of his Oxford friends, and mourned for the want of them like a dove'.[30]

Steventon itself was a straggling community 'of cottages, each well provided with a garden'.[31] An old maple tree on the village green formed the central point where people would gather to gossip.[32] Appropriately, given the higher status of its inhabitants, the Rectory was Steventon's last house, at the junction of Church Walk and Frog Lane. The site appears today to be isolated, but that's because the other cottages, like the Rectory itself, have also disappeared.

The Rectory stood 'in a shallow valley, surrounded by sloping meadows, well sprinkled with elm trees'.[33] Unfortunately this valley-bottom site made the house prone to flooding. Cobbett makes the landscape of Hampshire sound almost malevolent, even in August: 'the clouds, coming and settling upon the hills, sinking down and creeping along, at last coming out again in springs, and those becoming rivers'.[34] So the Austens' wagon in 1768 drew up in front of a building as damp as it was substantial.

Traces have been found to indicate that the Rectory's site was occupied as long ago as the fourteenth century. But the core of the farmhouse dated from the late seventeenth century, when it had 'two bays of building' with a cellar. Although in 1768 the Rectory had been recently refurbished for the family, it was nevertheless still a little rickety, constructed as it was from a hodgepodge of local materials: 'Brick Brick Pannelled and Tiled except part of the South side Plaister and Weather Tiled'.[35] The finishes were not fine. 'No cornice marked the junction of wall and ceiling' and 'the beams which covered the upper floors projected into the rooms below in all their naked simplicity, covered only by a coat of paint or white-wash'.[36] The windows were old-fashioned casements, except for a 'patched-on bow' (the pet hate of General Tilney in *Northanger Abbey*) stuck onto the back of the house. Because Mr Thomas Knight, who owned the house, didn't live in it or get rent from it, and because George Austen would only have use of it for the length of time that he would serve as parish priest, no one had much incentive to improve the Rectory.

But parsonages very often had a higgledy-piggledy, piecemeal appearance, and Deane was the same. Their limited funds meant that clergymen could usually only afford to add the odd new room or window, rather than investing in major improvements. George Austen and his fellow clergymen did, however, often feel a moral responsibility to maintain their houses at their own expense, if they could, because they held their properties in trust for their successors.

This idea that a house and land were not owned by a family, but held on behalf of others, would permeate Jane's novels. She always praised a landlord for reinvesting, working for the community, and not selfishly enriching himself alone. In fact *Mansfield Park*, her novel most concerned with ownership and stewardship, is really about who had looked after England best, and who therefore deserves to inherit it. One of Jane's characters in *Northanger Abbey* hankers after the 'unpretending comfort of a well-connected parsonage', and what elevated you into the status of 'gentility' was not so much your grand house, but your way of living: hospitable, responsible, civilised.

Over time, Mr Austen would be a good steward to the Rectory. As the years went by, he 'added and improved' many features, enlarging the house 'until it came to be regarded as a very comfortable family residence'.[37] Jane would often show her fictional clergymen, Dr Grant and Edmund Bertram, as well as the horrible Mr Collins, devoting care to this very eighteenth-century clergyman's concern of the 'improvement of his dwelling'. Noblemen improved their country houses and parks; clergymen improved their rectories. It was something of a duty: according to Mr Collins, a clergyman 'cannot be excused from making [his home] as comfortable as possible'.

And George Austen was a man in the right place at the right time. Over his lifespan, country clergymen would become better and better off, because technological improvements to agriculture would allow them to extract more money from their glebe lands and tithes. The consequence of all this was that the Church became increasingly attractive as a profession to the younger sons of landowners. One of Mr Austen's grandsons would, through a few lucky breaks, become a fully paid-up member of the landed gentry. He nevertheless followed in his grandfather's footsteps as rector of Steventon. But for him the old house would not do. The whole building would be pulled down in about 1825 and replaced on higher ground, out of the reach of those troublesome floods.

Steventon Rectory, as Jane's parents knew it, had a carriage drive, or 'sweep', at the front to bring in vehicles off the road, an important mark of gentility. There was a pond, and a 'screen of Chestnuts & firs'. To the sunny south side of the house, behind a thatched mud wall, was 'one of those old-fashioned gardens in which vegetables and flowers are combined'.[38]

The house itself had a three-storey main block, with two projecting wings at the back. More than a thousand nails were recovered from an archaeological investigation of the site in 2011, which solved a long-standing dispute about which of two inconsistent drawings of the house is the more accurate: it is the one that shows the house as larger rather than smaller.[39]

As the family walked inside and began to open the doors, they discovered that the ground floor contained the two parlours, the 'best' and the 'common', and two kitchens, as well as Mr Austen's study.[40] A member of the Austen family reported later that the front door opened immediately into the common parlour, where Mrs Austen could be found seated, 'busily engaged with her needle, in making or repairing'.[41] But the 2011 excavation of the Rectory site, under the leadership of Debbie Charlton, shows that in fact a long passage ran front to back, so that you could walk right through to the gardens at the rear. The best, or dining parlour, just over seventeen feet square, was to the left of the door, with two casement windows looking out at the carriage sweep.[42] The two kitchens to the right were identified as 'back' and 'front'. In the former, the real cooking took place, while the 'front' one was probably used for crockery storage, and perhaps the making of morning tea and toast.

The stuff of Jane's childhood was recovered in fragmentary form when a multitude of household items emerged from that 2011 excavation of the Rectory's site. There were pieces of the family's blue willow-pattern china, for example, of cheaper British rather than Chinese manufacture. There were teacups like bowls, lacking handles, intended to stand in deeper saucers than we would recognise today. Other discoveries included a candle-snuffer and an egg cup, nine wine bottles, and fragments of the family's Wedgwood creamware dining service.[43] This home-grown product of the Potteries was fashionable but affordable: 'it is really amazing how rapidly the use of it has spread almost over the whole Globe', wrote creamware's inventor, Josiah Wedgwood, in 1767.[44] It's fun to try to guess which other finds might tie in with Mr Austen's account at the local house-furnisher: the pieces of a heavy ceramic dish recovered from the earth, for example, could be the very same 'pudding boul' he bought for two shillings and sixpence in Basingstoke in 1792.[45] These finds from the Rectory, everyday things from an ordinary life, are too strangely poignant, because to me they prefigure the way that Jane would later take ordinary people and their lives, and use her imagination to make them extraordinary.

The Rectory's most pleasant-sounding room was Mr Austen's study, with its bow window over the garden. This was his 'own exclusive property safe from the bustle of all household cares'.[46] Although the study housed hundreds of books in Hepplewhite cases, Mr Austen was not pretentious enough to rename it as a 'library', as many a more ambitious clergyman might have done.[47] The study had the great advantage that his parishioners could reach it without entering the other rooms. A 'heavy step' in the passage let other members of the family know that an outsider was in the house.

Our own idea that home is separate from work, a private place for resting or socialising, simply does not apply to the Georgians, whose homes were places of hard labour. The sheer physical effort of keeping such a house clean and functioning must not be underestimated. The washing of clothes, the cooking, cleaning: all were arduous and time-consuming.

In fact, Mr Austen would also share the agricultural labours of his parishioners. 'In this country', pontificated an MP in 1802, every parish priest is 'in some degree, an agriculturist; he is, *ex officio*, in part a farmer'.[48] As well as his glebe land, Mr Austen had the use of a farm of 195 acres, named Cheesedown, and attempted to make money from it. The Austens therefore lived with the rhythm of the country year, the festivals at sheep shearing and harvest home.

Mr Austen's 'factotum', John Bond, particularly enjoyed the 'dissipation' of the annual harvest festival.[49] It was his job to manage Mr Austen's rented farm. John Bond had no book learning, but would chalk the farm's accounts upon his oak table, in figures nobody else could read.[50] Following country custom, he'd marry his wife Ann only after their first daughter was born. But this little girl, Hannah, would die in infancy, to be buried by Mr Austen.[51] Master and servant over time grew close. Mr Austen clubbed together with a neighbouring gentleman farmer to buy sheep, and 'that all might be fair it was their custom to open the pen, and the first half the sheep which ran out were counted as belonging to the rector'. John Bond would sneakily ensure that the best sheep ran out first. 'I see'd her the moment I come in', he said of the finest one, 'so when we opened the pen I just giv'd her a "huck" with my stick, and out a' run.'[52] Mr Austen, and John Bond: rector, and huckster.

And Mrs Austen as well as her husband could call herself a farmer. Once she'd recovered from the journey upon the feather bed, she would become the manager of a small business, producing food and supplies from the garden and glebe to feed her large family. The outbuildings gathered to the right, or west, of the Rectory included the washhouse, the 'garden tool house', the granary, the brew house and the barn. There was a yard for poultry, and a dairy for making butter and cheese. ('I was as cool as Cream-cheese' would become a stunning simile of Jane's.[53]) The poultry yard would end up as the home of turkeys, ducks, chickens and guinea fowl, while Mrs Austen became very attached to her cows, which she kept in the Rectory field: 'My little Alderney one turns out tolerably well, and makes more Butter than we can use.'[54] In time, she would acquire a bull and no fewer than six cows, but only little ones. 'You would laugh to see them,' she writes, 'for they are not much bigger than Jack-asses.'[55]

Mrs Austen also liked to work in the garden herself. 'My flesh is much warmer,' runs one of the jokey verses she loved to write, 'my blood freer flows / When I work in the garden with rakes & with hoes.'[56] She was a skilled cultivator of potatoes, imports from the New World that were still considered to be outlandish novelties in eighteenth-century Hampshire. They met with a warm reception when once she served them to a tenant's wife. 'Mrs. Austen advised her to plant them in her own garden,' we're told, but the suggestion fell flat: 'No, no; they are very well for you gentry, but they must be terribly *costly to rear*.'[57] The clergy wives of Hampshire were Ladies Bountiful to their parishioners, dispensing advice and material goods. The vicar's wife in the next parish along spent her time inoculating hundreds of people against smallpox, leaving off only 'till the Harvest is over as it would be inconvenient to the poor people to have a stiff arm for some days in this busy season'.[58]

In later years, the Austen family entered into a kind of collective conspiracy to cover up their humble origins, and to make their famous aunt's life look easier, more genteel, less hard work than it really was.

'I feel it must be a difficult task to dig up the *materials*, so carefully have they been buried out of our sight by the past generation', wrote one of them to a projected biographer.[59] Mrs Austen's granddaughter Anna (a gifted writer herself) produced a celebrated description of her grandmother at Steventon Rectory sitting and waiting for company. Anna places Mrs Austen indoors, forever at leisure, 'seated' in the 'entrance parlour', ready to put her needlework aside and welcome visitors.[60]

In reality, though, she was more likely to have been out overseeing the milking of her cows, or the stocking of the barn. Even when visiting the grandest houses in the land, Mrs Austen took a great interest in the practical arrangements such as the deployment of the staff and the quality of the cheese. Add in frequent confinements, and you get a life of hard work.

At least the Austens had a water supply of their own, which meant that it did not have to be carried along the lane by hand as was the case for their neighbours in the cottages. There was a well, possibly with a pump attached, remains of which survive in the field. The washing was done once a week by contract staff such as 'Dame Bushell' or 'John Steeven's wife'. ('She does not look as if anything she touched would ever be clean,' Jane wrote, 'but who knows?') In the similar household of the Georgian diarist, Parson Woodforde, they did a great clothes-wash only once every five weeks, when two specialist washerwomen moved in for two days to help the parson's own servants with the work. Including the ironing, the job took a total of four days.[61] The Austens possessed a couple of 'Mahogany Convenient stools', seat-less stools for placing over a chamber-pot.[62] These made relieving oneself more comfortable. Even so, any bathwater had to be carried from the pump into the house by hand, and those chamber-pots still needed to be emptied.

On a sunny day, though, the Rectory could be charming. Directly outside Mr Austen's study window was the 'grass walk bordered with strawberry beds' that led up to the sundial.[63] And wherever you walked in the garden, you would hear 'the scrooping sound' of the weathercock, twisting on its tall white pole in 'the summer breeze'.[64] Not everyone liked this: some visitors thought that the weathercock's groans made 'such a noise' that it disturbed their sleep.[65]

Beyond and behind the Austens' new house, they would over the years cultivate two walled gardens, one lined with 'cherry and other fruit trees', the other the 'square walled-in cucumber garden'.[66] Here, wooden protective frames were installed to provide cosy conditions for cucumbers and melons. 'I remember this sunny cucumber garden well,' Mrs Austen's granddaughter recalled in later life, 'its abundance of pot-herbs, marigolds, etc. – Oh! me! we never saw the like again.'[67] The later destruction of Jane Austen's childhood home accounts for some of this romantic, elegiac tone. Life within was not always quite so sunny and appealing.

But the Rectory's most famous garden feature of all was further south still. This was a grassy green terrace, the likely original of the one at Catherine Morland's home in *Northanger Abbey*. You can still see its shape in the soil when the sun is low. In the novel, the boyish young heroine takes great delight in 'rolling down the green slope at the back of the house'.[68] Presumably the little Austens did the same.

Once the Austens were settled into their Rectory, they found that visitors from the outside world were infrequent. Time passed slowly, but smoothly. Mrs Austen got used to the sleepy pace of rural life. In London, she wrote, everyone was always rushing about: 'tis a sad place, I would not live in it on any account: one has not time to do one's duty either to God or Man'.[69]

But there were some changes. Mrs Austen's mother was right to suspect at the time of the move to the new house that she was very ill indeed. She survived arrival for only a few days. She was replaced, though, by even more children, come to join their brothers in rolling down the 'green slope'. Henry was born in 1771. In 1773 came the first girl, named Cassandra for her mother. He was 'sorry to hear' of it, wrote Mr Austen's gloomy brother-in-law, for Mr and Mrs Austen 'will find it easier to get a family than to provide for them'.[70] In Hampshire, though, his advice was ignored, for next, in 1774, came Francis or Frank.

And then came Jane.

2

Enter Jane

'We have now another girl.'

Mr Austen, 1775

SEVEN YEARS AFTER the move, by the middle of December 1775, Mrs
Austen was heavily pregnant with her seventh baby. She'd been carrying
the child for a whole month longer than she'd expected. But at least this
one seemed to be small: she found herself 'more nimble and active' than
'last time'.[1]

It was an unusually harsh winter in Hampshire. The naturalist Gilbert
White, who lived in the nearby village of Selbourne, reported that by
26 November it was a 'very dark season: dark within doors a little after
3 o'clock in the afternoon'. The weather was damp, 'with copious
condensations on the walls, wainscot, looking-glasses, &c. of houses, in
many places running in streams'.[2] As November turned into December,
still the baby did not appear. By 13 December, White noticed that in
ponds the 'ice bears: boys slide' and he heard that 'the country people,
who are abroad in winter-mornings long before sun-rise, talk of much
hard frost'.[3] A great freeze was on its way.

For her previous births, Mrs Austen had summoned female relatives for
help, either Mr Austen's sister Philadelphia, or his cousin. But this seventh
time no such provision seems to have been made. Perhaps Mrs Austen
called for the local midwife, but certainly she felt no need to trouble an
expensive physician from Basingstoke. In later life, she would assist in delivering her own grandchildren, and then, there were always the neighbours.
Indeed, at nearby Manydown Park, another clerical wife, Jane Bigg, was
promised that the local women would certainly come to help her in the
hour of her travail. I think that her husband's clerk hoped to be reassuring
in writing this, but his poetical offering reads as rather an alarming threat:

> The good Wives of the Parish, obsequious all,
> Will attend your Commands as oft as you call;
> As oft as Occasion requires they'll march forth,
> Of your beautiful Babes to assist at the Birth![4]

At Steventon, Saturday 16 December passed just as usual. That night, when at last Mrs Austen's 'time came', it was 'without a good deal of warning'.[5]

Nevertheless, 'everything was soon happily over', Mr Austen reported with relief. 'We have now another girl, a plaything for Cassy and a future companion. She is to be Jenny.'[6] In this letter sharing the news of Jane's birth, Mr Austen casually mixed it up with local affairs as if the arrival were not that big a deal; it was feared a local ploughing match might have to be abandoned because of the hard frost.[7] But then, his playful, diminutive names for his children, the idea that the new baby would be the 'plaything' of her elder sister Cassy, show him to be an up-to-date, 'tender' father, not the harsh disciplinarian of decades past. This was a man who cared about his children, and let them know it. Nearly all his children would go on record as loving him profoundly in return.

He also reported that his wife – 'thank God' – was perfectly well.[8] Mrs Austen would have been revived after her ordeal with caudle, a kind of alcoholic porridge. One Georgian cookery book tells you to make it by boiling water with oatmeal, allspice, half a pint of beer, and a glass of gin.[9] She and her baby lay on that feather mattress transported from Deane, beneath the marital bed's four-poster canopy. The room also contained a dressing glass and a bedside carpet but little else, perhaps a chest of drawers.[10]

Contemporary doctors were trying to prevent women from following the traditional practice of shutting themselves up in bed for weeks of recovery after giving birth, and argued for the introduction of light and air into the bedchamber. 'The curtains should not be close drawn,' they recommended, 'that the effluvia may have the liberty of escaping.' But in rural Hampshire, in this unusually cold weather, Mrs Austen would have followed the old ways, keeping 'the curtains drawn round the bed, and pinned together, every crevice in the windows and door . . . stopped close, not excepting the key hole', the windows 'guarded not only with shutters and curtains, but even with blankets'. Mrs Austen herself was presumably not suffered to put 'her nose out of bed, for fear of catching cold' and was perhaps 'constantly supplied out of the spout of a tea-pot with large quantities of warm liquors'.[11] In later life, Mrs Austen's new daughter would disparage a woman with a poorly managed lying-in: 'she has no dressing-gown to sit up in; her curtains are too thin'. The cold of the Georgian countryside easily penetrated the interior of a house. It was not unknown that 'the Water above Stairs in the Basons froze in a few Minutes after being put there'.[12] Hopefully Mrs Austen and baby Jane stayed snug.

Everyone must have been greatly relieved that the baby had come at last. 'You have doubtless been for some time in expectation of hearing from Hampshire,' Mr Austen wrote to a relative, 'and perhaps wondered a little we were in our old age grown such bad reckoners.' Mrs Austen had certainly 'expected to have been brought to bed a month ago'.[13]

Were they such bad reckoners as all that? Mr and Mrs Austen were experienced; they had six children already. It could well be that their calculations were entirely accurate, and that Jane was among the 5 per cent of babies who spend longer than forty-three weeks within the womb. The risk, with such babies, is that the placenta stops working properly, and they don't get enough nutrition, resulting in a wasting away of the tissues of their bodies. A 'late' baby like this often has a very long body (like Jane) and is frail and ill for the first few weeks of his or her life. Such babies are sometimes described as 'difficult' by their mothers, and in need of extra care.[14]

A book of advice for nursery-maids suggested that a very small baby 'may be very comfortably laid upon a cushion, where it can be in no danger of falling', and that 'someone should sit by it, and divert and cheer it, if necessary, and take it up instantly, when it expresses the least dissatisfaction'.[15] Did Mrs Austen 'divert and cheer' her baby as they lay in bed together for these first few weeks of Jane's life? Or was she not feeling up to it? Long in body, late in arrival, Jane would always have an uneasy relationship with her mother. Her fiction is full of bad mothers: Mrs Dashwood and Mrs Bennet, who lack sense, Mrs Price, who lacks attention, and the absent Mrs Woodhouse and Mrs Elliot, both dead when the story starts. Perhaps the trouble began right at the beginning.

Jane in rural Hampshire would have been swaddled, which means to be wrapped snugly in a cloth to prevent her from rolling away. At this point, historians writing about Georgian childhood customarily quote Jean-Jacques Rousseau's innovatory book *Emile, or Treatise on Education* (1762) to suggest that the practice of swaddling was coming to an end. Rousseau is thought to have revolutionised child rearing with his suggestion that babies should be left at liberty, free from tight swaddling, and breast-fed by their mothers rather than servants. The latest fashion in baby wear was the 'foundling dress', a pinless garment tied on with strings, invented for use at the Foundling Hospital in London where a large number of infants needed to be dressed with 'convenience and dispatch'.[16] But Mrs Austen in Hampshire, with all her other children to think about, would have been far too busy to read a modish, metropolitan author like Rousseau, or acquire fashionable baby clothes. She was more likely to have got her knowledge, if any of it came from books at all, from volumes like the *Nurse's Guide* of 1744, which takes the form of a didactic dialogue between a pompous surgeon and a humble nurse ('Sir, I thank you for the Advice, and shall rely on your Authority'[17]). This surgeon was already insisting, long before Rousseau, that 'breast was best', and he also had his doubts about swaddling, suggesting instead 'clouts' (a nappy) and a blanket. But the listening nurse probably knew, as I know from friends who are historical re-enactors, that swaddling a baby is comforting, and soothes him or her into sleep.[18] Quite simply, it is practical. Jane was probably swaddled in the old way.

January and February of 1776, the first two months of Jane's life, remained icy cold. Cart and even horse travel was impossible for a fort-night, even on the very best roads. Towards Oxford, 217 men were employed to clear the turnpike road, and then came the ice, 'very dangerous, like driving on glass'.[19] The Thames in London was frozen solid. The conditions were so severe that it was not until 5 April 1776 that Jane was taken the short distance up the lane from the Rectory to be baptised in her father's church.

Steventon Church today stands at the top of a quiet, rising lane, running through fields, then woods, which are studded in spring with primroses. 'The chief beauty of Steventon', claims Jane's nephew and early biographer, 'consisted in its hedgerows. A hedgerow, in that country, does not mean a thin formal line of quickset, but an irregular board of copse-wood and timber . . . under its shelter the earliest primroses, anemones, and wild hyacinths were to be found.'[20] A footpath lined by such hedges – 'The Church Walk' – ran up from the Rectory towards Mr Austen's stone-built, twelfth-century church. Jane would become familiar with its yew tree, thought to be 900 years old, and its absolutely enormous door key.

Next to the church stood the manor house of the Digweed family, who'd been settled there for more than a century. Their house incorpor-ated part of a ninth-century Saxon cross, and had been a Norman dwelling until 1560 when it was pulled down and rebuilt. The manor was actually owned by the non-resident patron of Steventon's living, Mr Knight, of Godmersham, in Kent, and the Digweeds were his tenants. Their four boys would become playmates of the Austen children.

This Mr Thomas Knight of Godmersham, another of George Austen's helpfully rich relatives, was one of those Georgian gentlemen who seemed born lucky. A succession of estates simply fell into his lap through inher-itance. He had changed his birth name of 'Brodnax' to 'May' upon inheriting one estate. Then, when he inherited another, from his second cousin Elizabeth Knight of Chawton in Hampshire, 'May' became 'Knight'. As each name-change required an Act of Parliament, one MP

was heard to mutter that as 'this gentleman gives us so much trouble
. . . the best way would be to pass an Act for him to use whatever name
he pleases'.[21]

Since Mr Knight also owned more than half the land of the parish,
yet lived far away in Kent, Mr Austen was the representative of the local
landlord as well as of God. George Austen was the most important person
in the village, and to be Miss Austen certainly meant something.

Although Jane's was the first generation of the Austen family to be
born at Steventon, her first biographer makes the place sound ageless
and timeless. He wrote that the church's

> solitary position, far from the hum of the village . . . has something solemn
> and appropriate to the last resting-place of the silent dead. Sweet violets,
> both purple and white, grow in abundance beneath its south wall. One
> may imagine for how many centuries the ancestors of those little flowers
> have occupied that undisturbed, sunny nook, and may think how few
> living families can boast of as ancient a tenure of their land.[22]

The flower-strewn England of Jane Austen, well known to us from
countless Hollywood adaptations, doesn't come from the sharp, acid
novels of Jane herself, which are free of such saccharine descriptions of
the countryside. Instead they stem from this writer, Jane's sentimental
Victorian nephew. The rural idyll of Steventon, with its 'sloping meadows'
and 'fine elms', owes much to James Edward Austen-Leigh, the son of
Jane's eldest brother James. Writing more than fifty years after his aunt's
death, he was satisfying a new curiosity that people were beginning to
feel for detail about the little-known life of his celebrated aunt. James
Edward paints a powerful, charming picture, but we must take it with
a pinch – no, a wagonload – of salt. At Jane's christening the frozen
countryside presented a cold welcome to the latest member of the Austen
family. James Edward Austen-Leigh eliminated much of the mud, the
boredom and the hard work from his picture of Georgian rural life.

Once the family had trailed back home down the hill after the christening, Jane was not to stay much longer in the relative comfort of home.
Like her siblings, she was sent to be dry-nursed in the village. Her
probable foster-mother was Elizabeth Littleworth at Cheesedown Farm.
This was not traditional wet-nursing, where the nurse provided breast-
milk. Mrs Austen kept her babies at home until they were weaned. But
then she had formed the habit of sending them to spend both days and
nights with their nurse, returning to the Rectory when old enough to
walk. Mrs Littleworth, or Littlewort, would have fed the babies upon

'pap', a word that meant both the breast itself, and a baby food consisting of 'bread and water boiled and sweetened with brown sugar'.[23] Cheesedown Farm was a sociable place, for Mrs Littleworth also had her own children: Anne or 'Nanny' (who would grow up to become Jane's hairdresser) and Bet, 'playfellow' of Jane's older brother Edward. Nanny and Bet were practically part of the Austen family. When Jane's brother Frank wanted some attention but knew that he really ought to be in bed, he would poke his head around the door and say, 'Bet, my be not come to bide', in the Littleworths' Hampshire accent. Indeed, the Austens' way of spelling the title *Northanger Abbey* as 'North-hanger' suggests that they too had the Hampshire vocal habit of breathing out the letter 'H'.[24]

According to family tradition, whichever infant-Austen was at the Littleworths, he or she 'was daily visited by one or both of its parents, and frequently brought to them at the parsonage'. But still, the cottage at the farm 'was its home, and must have remained so till it was old enough to run about and talk'.[25] There was nothing unusual, or hard-hearted, about a Georgian mother sending a baby off for specialist care. For the Georgians, child rearing was the business of a much wider group than just the nuclear family, and they often 'turned to sisters and brothers, their own parents, and nurses and servants to distribute the labours'.[26] Mrs Austen's practice of outsourcing the care of her very small children worked well. Unlike most eighteenth-century families, where poor hygiene or illness carried off a distressingly high proportion of children, there is no indication that the Austens ever lost a baby.

However, this pragmatic use of childcare meant that the bonds between Mrs Austen and her children were indubitably weakened. When Mrs Austen herself was absent from Steventon, her husband wrote, her children hardly noticed. They 'turn all their little affections towards those who were about them and good to them'. This 'may not be a pleasing reflection to a fond parent,' Mr Austen mused, 'but is certainly wisely designed by Providence for the happiness of the child'.[27]

Jane's earliest biographers, members of her family, were keen to stress that life in the Rectory was tightly knit, self-contained and constantly harmonious. But more recently, historians have pointed out that with her early nursing elsewhere, and followed by time away at school, Jane was to spend nearly five of her first eleven years away from her home and mother. Put like that, it casts a new light on the famously familial Austens. It might also help to explain something of the later coldness that can be detected between Jane and her mother.

Mrs Austen gave birth to her last baby, Charles, on 23 June 1779. She was forty. Although she had given birth eight times, she had in fact spaced out her pregnancies rather cleverly to preserve her health. But now her family was finally complete. When Jane came home from Cheesedown Farm, she settled into her place as its least important member, the youngest girl, the plaything of her motherly elder sister Cassandra. She had chubby cheeks that tended to flush, and was the opposite of talkative, finding 'a sure refuge in silence'.[28] In later life, Jane regretted how shy she had been as a child. She wrote with jealousy about the self-possession of one young friend: 'a nice, natural, openhearted, affectionate girl, with all the ready civility which one sees in the best Children of the present day; – so unlike anything that I was at her age, that I am often all astonishment & shame'. Her brother Henry noticed that Jane 'never uttered either a hasty, a silly, or a severe expression', preferring, if she had nothing to say, to say nothing at all.[29] Good at watching, and waiting, she must have been a slightly disconcerting presence to her busy, over-occupied mother.

But beneath this shyness lay powerful feelings. As Jane grew up, it was to her sister that she turned for intimacy, as if Cassandra were a second mother. Substitute mothers would appear often in Jane's novels; it was a role with which she was very familiar, and would play herself in due course to younger women. In these Rectory years, the two sisters forged an unbreakable bond. 'Their affection for each other was extreme', their relatives noticed. 'It passed the common love of sisters; and it had been so from childhood.'[30]

Yet the two were not quite one. Cassandra had the colder, calmer disposition, her family noticed as the girls grew up, while Jane was more serene and biddable. Cassandra, it was said, 'had the *merit* of having her temper always under command', but 'Jane had the *happiness* of a temper that never required to be commanded'.[31] This, as the critic Marilyn Butler notes, is a rare instance when their family considered Jane and Cassandra as two separate individuals.[32] The Austens were now so many, so merry, and they valued family cohesion so much, that they forced the two to become almost one. Mr Austen called his daughters 'the Girls', as in 'Where are the Girls?' or 'Are the Girls gone out?'[33]

But the remark about Jane's placid temper, which comes from the Austen family themselves, reveals a total, almost deliberate, misunderstanding of her character. You could not think her lacking in temper once you have seen her private letters to Cassandra, which crackle, sometimes, with wickedness and rage. 'The best writers have often been the worst talkers', wrote one fellow novelist who knew Jane, in a passage musing on her qualities.[34] She was so private that even members of her own family did not know her.

Cassandra in her very old age would share an early memory that reveals strong feelings of both longing and love on the part of the supposedly passive Jane. Cassandra had been away from Steventon staying with cousins in Bath. Years and years later, she recalled one very particular occasion: her 'return to Steventon one fine summer evening'. Mr Austen had travelled to Andover to collect his daughter from the hands of her uncle, and brought her home in a hired carriage. But then, when they were almost home, Mr Austen and Cassandra met upon the road 'Jane & Charles, the two little ones of the family, who had got as far as New down to meet the chaise, & have the pleasure of riding home in it'.[35]

You must know, as Jane died so young, that this story of her life does not end happily. But do please fix in your mind this sunny scene, when she was six-and-a-half, because in this beginning there is also much that prefigures our devastating end. Imagine Jane happy, if you will, life before her, running through the Hampshire fields on a summer's evening, eager to see Cassandra once again, and to bring her home.

3

Boys

'Men have had every advantage of us in telling their own story.
Education has been theirs in so much higher a degree;
the pen has been in their hands.'

Persuasion

I T SEEMS ODD that Jane, the quintessential writer about women, grew
up in a world of boys, but so it was.

The house-move, and their growing family, stretched the finances of
the Austens. This remained the case after Mrs Austen inherited money
from her mother; even after the couple borrowed money from Mrs Austen's
brother, James Leigh Perrot; even after Mr Austen sold further stock in
the South Sea Company.[1] This must have hurt him. George Austen's
financial advice to others was: 'keep an exact account of all the money
you receive or spend, lend none but where you are sure of an early repay-
ment'.[2] The Austens 'were not rich', yet they lived among rich people,
landed squires and well-educated clergymen.[3] They belonged to what's
been called the 'pseudo-gentry', aspiring to a genteel lifestyle without
having quite enough cash to pay for it. Members of the 'pseudo-gentry'
did not own land, but were still 'gentry of a sort, primarily because they
sought strenuously to be taken for gentry'.[4] They thought of themselves
as being above 'the middling sort', who were connected with trade and
enterprise, and, ironically, often richer than the Austens.[5] And way 'below'
both groups lay the vast sea of the labouring ranks of society.

Despite the cash shortage, there was solid wealth in the background
of both the Austen and the Leigh families. Whether or not any of it
could come the Austens' way through inheritance would create a series
of sores that poisoned family relations for the whole of Jane's life.

Mrs Austen's mother's family, the Perrots, were extremely rich. When
her great-aunt, Anne Perrot, had died, she left Mrs Austen and her sister
Jane £200 each. Very nice. But their brother James did much better. He
inherited a significant fortune, so significant that he changed his name
to Leigh Perrot in gratitude. His sisters might have expected their brother
to share the loot. 'We must not all expect to be individually lucky,' says

a character in Jane's novel *The Watsons*, 'the luck of one member of the family is luck to all.' But share his fortune James Leigh Perrot did not. Their sixteen-year-old brother's getting that money placed him above his sisters in terms of both material standards of living, and social consequence, for the rest of their lives. What a difference a few more thousand pounds could have made to life at the Rectory. And what a message for Mrs Austen as a girl to learn: that she was literally not worth as much as her younger brother.

Both Mr and Mrs Austen had inherited about £1,000 each from their families. When he first came to Steventon, Mr Austen was able to get about £200 a year from his parishioners, but would later manage to increase this to nearly £600. He benefited from the Napoleonic Wars, which caused a bump in agricultural prices because they created food shortages. And on top of the tithe money, he made nearly £300 from his farm. So, after a painstaking climb to the height of his prosperity, he ended up making nearly £1,000 a year.

But what did these sums mean? To the Georgians themselves, this information would have immediately indicated a certain standard of living. Jane in her novels uses income as a shorthand for status, and expects her readers immediately to know what kind of household she is talking about when she says a family has £500, or £1,000, a year. Five hundred pounds annually was about the lower limit at which a family could aspire to 'gentility'. It's the income that Jane gives the four Dashwoods in *Sense and Sensibility*, who struggle. A thousand pounds a year was another significant point because it was the level at which one became able to run a carriage, with all its costs of stabling and staffing. The Austens would have their own carriage for a while, but found it too costly and had to give it up.

The gentry and pseudo-gentry would instantly pick up upon the nuances of dress and lifestyle that each extra £100 a year of income would provide. So the ability to stretch one's income as far as possible was a valuable skill. Jane's sharp, shrewd character Lucy Steele, for example, had the enviable knack of being able to make £500 a year look like £800.

According to Samuel and Sarah Adams, a couple of retired servants who wrote a book about household management, a family with an income of £600 a year could afford to employ three females and one man, namely a cook, a housemaid, and a nursery-maid, with 'a Boy as Groom, and to assist in the House and Garden. A Gardener occasionally.'[6]

An establishment of this size makes the Austens sound wealthy, but compare Mr Bennet in *Pride and Prejudice*, who had £2,000 (albeit a few decades later). Mr Bennet had only five children instead of Mr Austen's eight. He did live on a grander scale than the Austens, employing a cook and a butler, which they did not, and the five Bennet daughters, unlike Jane, never had to do any work in the kitchen. But even on £2,000 a year Mr Bennet failed, like Mr Austen, to save up any surplus to create dowries for his daughters.

And so, feeling the pinch of genteel poverty, the Austens decided to take advantage of the Rectory's spaciousness by opening a kind of informal boarding school.

It was a good idea. George Austen was an experienced teacher, for in his younger days he'd been a 'second master' in his own old school in Tonbridge. He sounds like a talented educator, combining 'classical learning' and a 'highly cultivated taste for literature in general' with 'gentleness of manners'.[7] At least, that's the official story: his eldest son James was able to write nevertheless of the 'unfortunate propensity which the old and the young have ever discovered to differ as much as possible'.[8]

From 1773, then, the boarding pupils provided the Austens with extra income, of about £35 per year for each one. In return George Austen prepared them for university, while Mrs Austen grew vegetables, kept the cows and dispensed dollops of a certain rough maternal kindness. It worked well: the couple would end up looking after boys for the next twenty-three years.

Their pupils all came from 'good' families. Among them was George Nibbs, whose father, James, born in Antigua, had been a fellow student and friend of Mr Austen's at St John's College. James Langford Nibbs became godfather to George Austen's eldest son. In return, Mr Austen became a trustee of Nibbs' plantation in Antigua. This is how Jane's own father became involved in the management of an estate, like Sir Thomas Bertram's in *Mansfield Park*, that depended on the labour of slaves.[9]

Then, at various times, there was the baronet Sir William East's son, and the Fowle brothers, offspring of a clergyman from Kintbury. There were less successful pupils such as the little Lord Lymington, future third Earl of Portsmouth, who was 'very backward for his Age', and eventually was taken away for 'his mamma began to be alarm'd at the Hesitation in his Speech'.[10] Mrs Austen helped with the boys' pastoral care. When one of them, Gilbert East, took an extended leave of absence, she wrote him a poem to lure him back:

> Your Steventon Friends
> Are at their wits ends
> To know what has become of Squire East;
> They very much fear
> He'll never come here
> Having left them nine weeks at the least . . .

She describes Steventon Rectory as the 'mansion of learning' where the pupils 'study all day, (Except when we play)', and:

> So we send you this letter
> In hope you'll think better,
> And reflect upon what we have said,
> And to make us amends
> Pray return to your Friends,
> Fowle, Stewart, Deane, Henry & Ned![11]

Where on earth did all these boys sleep? Well, there were no fewer than seven bedrooms upstairs, and three attic rooms peeping out of the rooftop storey above that. But sleepers must have shared rooms, even beds. Jane and Cassandra shared a room, which they liked, and later continued to do so by choice. With Mrs Austen so occupied elsewhere, they must have formed a little female alliance against a sea of boys.

Mr and Mrs Austen would probably have relished a description of life at the Rectory by a Leigh cousin that makes it sound liberal and intellectual. Mr Austen, this particular account runs, 'educates a few youths of chosen friends and acquaintances', and at Steventon, 'the simplicity, hospitality, and taste which commonly prevail in affluent families among the delightful valleys of Switzerland ever recurs to my memory'.[12] The Georgians thought Switzerland to be an egalitarian, forward-thinking country; Steventon, then, was a little republic of the mind. And yet, there would still be a clear pecking order in the family, parent to child, master to servant, brother to sister. The business of daughters in a large family was obedience and compliance and domestic duty.

What of Jane's own blood brothers (and betters)? James ('Jemmy'), Edward ('Neddy') and Henry Austen formed the elder group among the siblings, while Jane and Cassandra fitted in better with their younger brothers Francis ('Frank') and Charles.

It's worth spending some time with Jane's brothers, for her relationships with them would be among the most important of her life. A sensitive portrayer of sibling love in *Mansfield Park*, she comments that 'children of the same family, the same blood, with the same first associations and habits' will stand together for life. Thus it would be with Jane and her brothers. Jane was beholden to them emotionally, and, it would turn out, financially. But it is also certain that she liked some of her brothers better than others.

Her relationship with her eldest brother, James, was slightly vexed. Everyone thought that he was the most literary member of the family, a composer of essays and poetry, and this persisted even after his sister became published. In this role of the family's author, he's often given credit for having encouraged and inspired his sister as a writer. In his youth he was lively and high-spirited: as his sister Jane could write, 'A ball is nothing without *him*.' But there were depths to James, and in later life he would grow morose, difficult and disappointed. Nor would he find success as an author. No wonder he found it difficult being Jane's brother.

Yet Jane was only three-and-a-half when James went away to college. The point of Oxford in those days was to train future clergymen, and that's what 60 per cent of the students became. Jane was the daughter of a clergyman, and among her brothers both James and Henry (after a few detours) would end up as parish priests. There were four more clergymen among Jane's cousins; it was something of a family business. James was entitled to free tuition at his father's old Oxford College, St John's, as he could claim through Mrs Austen to be 'Founder's Kin'. Sir Thomas White, a former Lord Mayor of London, had founded the College in 1557. His descendants could apply for one of six free places, funded by the College in compensation for White having endowed the institution instead of his family.

St John's College was a den of die-hard Tories, some of whom had never even accepted the Protestant outsider, King George I of Hanover, as sovereign of Great Britain when he took the throne in 1714 in place of the Catholic heirs of the deposed James II. The Austens described themselves as quietly Tory, and Jane, so far as women were allowed to have political views, was presumably Tory too.[13] This did not mean that they belonged to a formal political party; such things did not exist.[14] And politics were not often mentioned at home, being 'rather taken for granted I suppose, than discussed', according to one family member.[15] But the Austens' self-proclaimed Tory views imply a general tendency to support the Church, the gentry and the old ways, and to oppose the reforming tendencies of the Whigs, with their veneer of new money, and association with industry and religious dissent.

The impact of the French and the American Revolutions on society seems, at first glance, to be remote from Jane's work and concerns. But in fact the question of the rightful ordering of society, and how this might be achieved when virtue and hierarchy were at odds, bubbles away vigorously beneath the surface of her stories. Jane followed her father and brothers in dispensing paternalistic Tory platitudes in scribbles in the margins of the family's copy of Goldsmith's *History of England*: 'How much', she wrote, 'are the Poor to be pitied, & the Rich to be blamed!'[16]

James was joined in Oxford by the brother generally thought to be

Jane's favourite. Henry, sprightly and joyous in personality, took life far more lightly than the lugubrious James. 'Most affectionate & kind', Jane wrote in later life, Henry was the best of company: 'he cannot help being amusing'. This sunny character was 'the handsomest of the family', and perhaps his blithe confidence came from 'the opinion of his own Father' that he was 'the most talented' of the Austen boys, with his 'perpetual sunshine of the mind'. But then, some people found Henry *over*-confident, and thought his brilliance lacked depth: 'his abilities to be greater in shew than in reality'.[17] This would prove to be the case.

The brothers at St John's received visits from their female relatives, including their elegant cousin Eliza. This young lady was the daughter of Mr Austen's sister, Philadelphia Hancock, and she had spent a sophisticated youth touring the continent. She nevertheless liked her country cousins, and their Oxford College, and on her visit was 'mightily taken with the Garden & longed to be a Fellow that I might walk in it every Day'. Typically for the fashion-loving Eliza, the clothes appealed: 'I was delighted with the Black Gown & thought the Square Cap mighty becoming.'[18] Henry Austen, like Eliza, was blessed with the gift of style, and perfectly looked the part as an Oxford student. 'I do not think you would know Henry', Eliza wrote to another relative, 'with his hair powdered & dressed in a very tonish style, besides he is at present taller than his Father.'[19] Henry's hairpowder indicated that he was a Tory, and that he held no truck with the plain, cropped hairstyles sported by the revolutionaries in France. Remember this beautiful cousin, Eliza, admiring the stylish undergraduate in the gardens of Oxford, for we will hear more of her later.

While he was at Oxford, James became the first of the Austen children to venture into literary life. He became the brains behind a monthly magazine, *The Loiterer*, which was full of gentle (and not always successful) satire. 'Of all the chymical mixtures,' he wrote in his editorial capacity, 'ink is the most dangerous'. A person 'who has once dipped his fingers in it', James continued, could never escape from its clinging influence.[20]

Running for some sixty issues, *The Loiterer* was an admirable and professional project for a student endeavour, kept up from January 1789 until March 1790. It was distributed in London by the publisher Thomas Egerton, whose firm would in due course become best known to history as the first to publish James Austen's little sister.

But Jane's brother Edward was not destined to join James and Henry at Oxford. Back in Steventon, in the summer of 1779 when Jane was three, a pair of visitors turned up, to kick into motion a total transformation of Edward's prospects. He'd end up being catapulted – with typical

Georgian unpredictability – into a life in the upper echelons of the landed gentry.

The Rectory received a visit from another of Mr Austen's many cousins, Thomas Knight of Godmersham the younger. He was the son of the rich and many-named Mr Knight who had given George Austen the living of Steventon in the first place. Mr and the new Mrs Knight – he had just married – were well worth knowing. They owned a fine estate at Godmersham Park in Kent, three days' journey from Hampshire, along with a mansion at Chawton, not far from Steventon, that was usually let out to tenants. A third estate lay near Winchester.[21]

The Georgians did not go on 'honeymoons': the word referred to the first month, or moon, of marriage, rather than a holiday. But they often undertook a wedding journey to visit relations. One of the highlights of Mr Thomas and Mrs Catherine Knight's own wedding journey was their meeting at Steventon with the twelve-year-old Edward Austen. He was a nice-looking boy, and they 'were first attracted by his personal beauty'.[22] But he also had a delightful personality, possessing the 'spirit of fun and liveliness'.[23] Jane's own view was that her brother Edward 'talks nonsense . . . delightfully'. And so the Knights took him with them as they continued on their journey. It's not as odd as it sounds: Mr and Mrs Austen, for example, had likewise begun their own married life with a temporary foster-son, a child entrusted to them by a family friend, the celebrated Warren Hastings of India. Sadly that little boy had soon died of a 'putrid sore throat'.[24] Once you were married, society saw you as a parent figure, whether for your own children or someone else's.

Edward came home to his family after his wedding tour with the Knights. But as the years passed, and as their marriage remained childless, the Knights invited Edward to stay with them from time to time. Mr Austen, the schoolmaster, was reluctant to let Edward go, worried as he was about 'a probable falling behind in the Latin Grammar'. But Edward's mother looked further into the future, and saw what might be gained from the rich, childless couple. Gradually it became clear that the Knights wanted to keep Edward. Family lore records Jane's parents' discussions about their son, which concluded with Mrs Austen's gentle words to her husband: 'I think, my Dear, you had better oblige your cousins, and let the Child go.'

As a result, young Edward went to Kent, 'riding all the way on the Pony which Mr Knight's Coachman, himself on horseback, had led from Godmersham for his use'.[25] By degrees 'it came to be understood in the family that Edward was selected from amongst themselves as the adopted son and Heir of Mr Knight'[26] And in his new family he was welcomed and loved. 'As our adopted Child', wrote Mrs Knight, 'I have felt for you the tenderness of a Mother.'[27]

'Let the Child go,' Mrs Austen had said, just a 'few simple words' that, at least in the memory of her granddaughter who gives us this evidence, 'gently turned the scale' of the decision. But they were fateful words, for Neddy, riding boldly off on his pony, would never really come back home again. And unlike his better-educated brothers, of whose brilliance great things were predicted, Edward would become the steadiest and wealthiest of the family, and the one best able to support his mother and sisters in later life.

Edward's 'beauty', his 'fun and liveliness', which had led to the Knights selecting him from among his brothers, had literally been his fortune. In this he was more like Lizzy Bennet than a conventional Georgian gentleman. Edward's great luck seemed to some observers too good to be true: it was maliciously put about that he wasn't just the adopted, but 'the illegitimate son', of Mr Knight. But the record of Edward's birth in the Deane parish register makes that seem impossible, and these reports were generally hushed up.[28] The final adoption – 'he was taken more entire possession of' – took place when Edward was sixteen, in 1783. A poignant silhouette portrait of the occasion shows Edward literally being handed over. Next time his brothers and sisters saw him, he would look decidedly different from them. There survives at Chawton House Library today a green velvet suit for a teenage boy, which is thought to have been Edward's. It's far grander than the woollen frock coat and breeches of a genteel but impoverished clergyman's son. What's more, the suit is lined with taffeta of gold.

As she grew up, the Cinderella story of her brother would become a theme of Jane's fiction. The idea of the transplanted child occurs time and time again, in Frank Churchill; Fanny Price; even Anne Elliot, who goes to live with her substitute mother, Lady Russell. Mrs Austen's words – 'let the Child go' – were well enough recorded to take their place in family history, and perhaps Jane had heard of them often enough to flip them in *Mansfield Park*, the tale of a rich family who take in a poorer relation. 'Let us send for the child,' says Lady Bertram, kicking off the action to everyone's eventual advantage. Jane also has Isabella Knightley in *Emma* give another slant on the story: 'There is something so shocking in a child's being taken away from his parents . . . To give up one's child! I really never could think well of any body who proposed such a thing.' At first sight it's painful to think of Jane's mother, who had 'let her Child go', reading this sentence. But on second reading you realise that Isabella is a stupid character, a gushingly maternal yummy mummy, and that she often says stupid things. One hopes that Mrs Austen had the subtle sense of humour necessary to see her daughter's joke.

Edward Austen's new parents completed his education not with a college degree but with a Grand Tour. His travel journal shows that in 1786 he spent a month in Switzerland, and then made a second trip in the summer of 1790 to Italy, Switzerland, Germany and the Netherlands.[29] He wrote his journal in a jolly, ironic style, rather like Jane's, to entertain and amuse the relations who would read it once he was home again. For example, while they might well have expected him to be lolling upon the lap of luxury, he wrote instead of having enjoyed an unusually long sleep one night in Switzerland 'not withstanding the badness of the beds, the closeness of the room, and the quantity of the fleas'.[30] After his tour, Edward returned to live with his new family at Godmersham Park, Kent.

The two littlest brothers, Francis and Charles, were their sisters' 'particular' playthings. Like other surplus sons in families of moderate means – but unlike any previous Austens – they were sent off to the Royal Naval Academy in Portsmouth.

In his own words, the youthful Frank Austen was 'rather small in stature' but he possessed 'great activity of body'.[31] His whippy little body earned him the nickname 'Fly'. He was a firm, dependable character, possessing 'a strong sense of duty, whether due from himself to others, or from others to himself'.[32] In fact, he was made for life in the Navy, and his men would come to admire and follow him willingly.

In the Steventon of Jane's youth, Frank had early proved that he enjoyed the headlong, thrusting pursuit of glory: on the hunting field. His very first cloth suit was remade from that old scarlet hunting habit of Mrs Austen's. His small red figure must have made a remarkable sight on the pony that he bought, aged seven. 'Squirrel', Frank called his mount, which was a bright chestnut colour, but his envious brothers called it 'Scug'. Frank rode Squirrel for two hunting seasons before selling the animal at a profit.[33] His canny transaction presaged a life as the maker of good financial deals alongside his 'official' career at sea.

Despite his diminutive size, Frank would rise to the very top of his profession as a sailor, achieving more work-related success than the rest of his brothers. In training at Portsmouth, Frank was praised for his 'uncommon' assiduity, and for having 'completed his plan of Mathematical learning in a considerably shorter time than usual'.[34] He was only fourteen when on 23 December 1788 he set sail for the first time, for the East Indies.

While Frank would excel in his profession, and revel in doing his duty, recent scholarship has found that not all of his achievements were entirely squeaky clean. At least part of his future income as a naval officer was to come from doing favours for the East India Company, such as running silver bullion in '93 chests' from China to Madras. He was to be mentioned more often and more favourably than any other officer in the Royal Navy in the secret minutes of the board of the East India Company.[35] In due course, Frank became a loving and domesticated father, happy, when at home, to make wooden toys upon a lathe, or to create fringes for the curtains. In fact, he could almost be his sister's industrious and home-loving character Captain Harville in *Persuasion*. But Frank could also, without comment, order the sort of violent punishment that was getting the Royal Navy an increasingly unfortunate reputation for its cruel treatment of old England's jolly tars. On 14 January 1796, for example, Frank impassively noted in his ship's log that he had 'punished sixteen seamen with one dozen lashes each for neglect of duty in being off the deck in their watch'.[36] And, while the Navy's captains were able to grow rich from the rewards they won for seizing enemy ships, the pay of the sailors had not risen for 140 years.[37] Frank, then, is a conundrum, admired and loved by his sister, but possessing an inner streak of steel.

Charles, the youngest brother, had a baby-of-the-family's malleability and charm. A weaker character than Frank, he possessed 'a sweet temper and affectionate disposition', which in later life would make his sailors love him, and he too would rise high in the Navy.[38] But he never had Frank's knack of making money.

Amid all this masculine ambition and excitement, it would be Jane and Cassandra's lot to stay at home. They 'were brought up in the most complete ignorance of the World & its ways', wrote one of the Austens of the next generation. Recent historians have rightly emphasised – contrary to this claim – that Jane was born into a dynamic, expanding Georgian world, with family connections spanning continents and empires. There was more to her life than the quiet of the Rectory, the dripping of the trees in the garden, the walks to visit the same neighbours over and over again.[39] But despite Jane and her sister knowing people who had actually been to the slave plantations of the Caribbean, to the markets of India where Mr Austen's brother-in-law was trying to earn a fortune, and to the common rooms of Oxford, the fact does still remain that they spent most of their time deep in the rainy countryside, writing stories because there was nothing else to do.

Jane herself was certainly conscious of what the girls were missing, and was jealous of her brothers. 'Edward & Frank are both gone out to seek their fortunes,' she wrote, 'the latter is to return soon & help us seek ours.' Finding a fortune was much harder for the girls than the boys. Girls of lower social rank might 'be made mop-squeezers or mantua-makers', but Jane and Cassandra as members of the 'pseudo-gentry' would have found such practical employment impossible. While 'sons can easily make their way in the world', the girls' only hope was to marry.[40]

Having got this far through the family, though, the observant will have noticed that I have missed one brother off the list. Where was George, who had come from Deane to Steventon in 1768, and who has not been heard of since?

Well, George was missing from home. When it became clear that he would never outgrow his propensity to 'fits', his parents decided to send him away to live permanently with a foster-family. There was precedent for this, because Mrs Austen herself had a disabled older brother, similarly treated. The two of them, the uncle and the nephew, ended up living together with the same family of carers, the Cullums, in a village north of Basingstoke called Monk Sherborne. The household there forms a curious, shadow version of the family back at Steventon.

A great deal has rightly been made by recent historians of the Austen family's silence on the subject of George, the defective child sent away. The stigma of illness meant that he was missed out of early family histories, along with any record of disagreement, or of Aunt Jane's love affairs.

So much of what we know comes through this Austen family filter that the information they *have* allowed us to access needs careful scrutiny and assessment. As Jane herself put it in *Persuasion*, 'facts or opinions which are to pass through the hands of so many . . . can hardly have much truth left'. In the case of George, the bias against him is horribly easy to spot. When Jane's nephew wrote that major profile of his aunt for publication in 1871, the work that introduced Jane Austen to her readers as a personality, he described Edward as the 'second' brother although he was in fact the third, skipping George altogether.[41] The omission was confirmed by *Jane Austen's Sailor Brothers* (1906), another significant history written by family members: 'In a family of seven all turned out well, two rose to the top of their profession, and one was – Jane Austen.'[42] Poor George, not only did he fail to turn out 'well', but he was forgotten altogether.

Was George loved? It's been speculated that Jane, who was able in later life to 'talk with her fingers' with a deaf man, had likewise communicated with a brother who lacked the ability to hear. But she could hardly have known him. George was definitely gone from the family home by 1770, when he returned on a visit. At that point he seemed 'pretty well' although he had just had another fit after a break of nearly a year.[43] 'God knows only', his father wrote, how far George would recover. But 'we have this comfort', Mr Austen continued, that 'he cannot be a bad or a wicked child'.[44]

George's intermittent 'fits' sound like epilepsy, a disorder that the Georgians still believed to be linked to the moon. A couple of centuries earlier, it's likely that the doctors who examined George would have thought him possessed by the Devil, and that his treatment would consequently have been much less compassionate. But now, with the Enlightenment, physicians were starting to consider illnesses such as epilepsy as physical disorders, rather than evidence of divine anger. In his book *Cases of the Epilepsy* of 1746, the doctor John Andree wrote that despite the old view that 'Gods, Devils and Witchcraft, and other supernatural causes' created epilepsy, it was in fact caused by 'a local Disorder in and about the Brain'.[45]

Mr Austen too, with his remarks about George's freedom from 'wickedness', clearly saw his son's suffering as physical rather than a divine punishment. And this change in the Georgian understanding of disease brought with it a new hope that it could be cured, rather than simply endured.

George's treatment has caused outrage among recent Austen historians, not least because he gradually fades from the family record to the extent that his own mother even neglects to mention him in her will. But the handling of George's illness was not out of the ordinary for the time.

Dr Andree, that contemporary expert on epilepsy, argued that patients were better off kept under special care, because they were 'in Danger of doing themselves a Mischief' by 'violent Concussions' during a fit.[46] If, as Andree suggested, fits could be triggered by gluttony, passion, fright, grief or anger, then epileptics were best kept apart from society. It was still believed that epilepsy might be contagious, like rabies.[47] So by sending George to live with other epileptics the Austens were following the best contemporary medical practice. There, his keepers the Cullums might have induced him to vomit at the dangerous time of the full moon. They might have treated him with mistletoe, valerian, opiates or the other recommended drugs, or given him a calming 'Milk Diet'.[48]

However, the shame of George's illness remained. As well as the danger of contagion, the experts also believed that 'epilepsies are sometimes hereditary either from the Father or Mother'.[49] As Mrs Austen's brother was likewise affected, the disease did seem to run in the family. To have their brother's illness known would have raised questions about the health of Jane and Cassandra themselves, and would have reduced their potential value on the marriage market.

All this meant that there were secrets lurking behind a busy, noisy, boy-filled life at the Rectory. Perhaps the lasting effect of all of this was a roughness, or toughness, in Jane, and a reticence about expressing her emotions. We never know what she was really thinking because she was expected, like her brothers, to join in with Mr Austen's austere literary enthusiasms, and Mrs Austen's 'sprack wit'. Romantic love, relationships, were not often topics of conversation at Steventon. Of course people should not marry for love, wrote her brother James, cynically, because then there would 'be no such thing as Divorces', and that would be terribly unfortunate for lawyers.[50]

It is true that Jane and Cassandra were unusual, and lucky, to grow up in a family that valued the intellect. But they were also left conscious that they could never enter the republic of the mind with the freedom given to their brothers and the pupils. The intellectual values of Steventon forced them to pay respect to the important work that the boys were doing in learning ancient languages for future lives as magistrates, clergymen and squires, while they themselves helped Mrs Austen in the kitchen.

It must have been confusing. What were Jane and Cassandra to prioritise as they learned to become young ladies?

4

A Little Learning

Henry Tilney: 'You were a good little girl,
working your sampler at home!'
Catherine Morland: 'Not very good, I am afraid.'

Northanger Abbey

GIRLS LIKE JANE and Cassandra would usually have been educated at home, under the supervision of their mother. Although their father was also their teacher, and although they lived in a school, society still insisted that Georgian girls weren't supposed to be clever, or demand too much attention. And Jane all her life would be interested in ordinary, unexceptional girls and what might happen to them. Her quietest heroine of all, Fanny Price, had 'no glow of complexion, nor any other striking beauty', while Catherine Morland had 'nothing heroic' about her, and was 'occasionally stupid'. Jane's great achievement would be to let even the ordinary, flawed, human girls who read her books think that they might be heroines too.

Mrs Austen doubtless found the time to teach her daughters how to read and write, a mother's traditional role. A set of bone counters inscribed with the letters of the alphabet, just the sort of thing that would have been used to teach children to read, was handed down through the Austen family, and you can see it at Lyme Regis Museum today.

According to her granddaughter, though, Mrs Austen's own education had not been 'much attended to'.[1] But despite any 'school room deficiencies', there was 'plenty of sparkle and spirit in her talk', and Mrs Austen could also 'write an excellent letter either in prose or verse'.[2] It was the special duty of a mother to teach her daughters to write the kinds of chatty, deceptively light-hearted letters that bound together the diverse members of the Austen and Leigh families into such a strong network spanning the shires. In this, Mrs Austen certainly succeeded.

Mrs Austen was also good at making things with her hands, the craftwork that was the perpetual duty of any well-born young lady. To hear that any Georgian young lady is 'working' means that she is doing needlework, and Jane was especially good at plain sewing. 'We are very busy making Edward's shirts', she wrote. 'I am proud to say I am the neatest worker of the party.' She was good at fancy work too, turning out items in her celebrated satin stitch embroidery. A sampler made by a 'Jane Austen' – probably in truth a member of the Kentish branch of the family – features a quotation from *The Book of Common Prayer* dated 1787. 'In the Time of trouble I will call upon the Lord and he will hear me', it reads, in tiny neat cross-stitches, a praiseworthy double-whammy celebration of the submission of both the fingers and the mind. While it wasn't Jane's sampler, it was the sort of thing that she was expected to make. Even if she 'agreed to none of it in private', like Emma Woodhouse she 'denied none of it aloud'.

It may seem to us that there is more to life than cross-stitch, but to make things neatly was a real pleasure to the Austen ladies. 'My Mother is very happy', wrote Jane, 'in the prospect of dressing a new Doll.' The whole family also spent time making and trimming paper hats. The fallback use of any spare moments was to make clothes for local paupers. This was time well spent. There was self-interest, here, too, for while stitching, ladies' 'thoughts could be their own', rather than at the beck and call of other people.[3]

Music, one of the standard accomplishments of many young ladies, was a real passion of Jane's, although characteristically she held her ability 'very cheap'.[4] At the Rectory, she had the benefit of a teacher, the assistant organist of Winchester Cathedral, who would visit private pupils in Steventon and other villages. 'I practice every day as much as I can', Jane wrote, 'I wish it were more for his sake.' Her novels give perfect insight into the mind of a musician, like Emma Woodhouse, who is good, but also good enough to appreciate that others are better.

The Austens at first only borrowed an instrument, but eventually purchased 'a piano forte in a handsome case'. Upon it, Jane played the family's 'large collection of music'.[5] She also played often 'from manuscript, copied out by herself – and so neatly and correctly, that it was as easy to read as print'.[6] Her family were proud of this as further evidence of the industriousness, so pleasing in young ladies, that Jane displayed. Friends would swap tunes, writing them out from each other's printed sheet music, just as people swap playlists today.

There was, however, a vigorous contemporary debate going on about the nature of these feminine 'accomplishments' such as writing neatly, sewing and playing. 'In the present age it is hazardous to mention accomplishments', wrote Jane's brother Henry, warily.[7] He recognised that what had once been a practical necessity – making clothes for a family – had for some well-off Georgians gradually become a decorative and slightly pointless activity, busy-work rather than real work.

Some, like Mary Wollstonecraft, grew to be quite vociferous opponents of such activities for girls, deeming them a waste of time. It would be better to cultivate moral and intellectual virtues instead. For Wollstonecraft, learning accomplishments to impress men prevented women from becoming rational creatures. Others, like the well-known evangelical Christian educator Hannah More, thought that 'this phrenzy of accomplishments' made a young lady unwholesome, too polished, too professional: 'the morning is all rehearsal, and the evening is all performance'.

Jane would go on to illustrate this debate in *Pride and Prejudice*, drawing the bookworm Mary as an unattractive character overly proud of her hard-won accomplishments. It seems awfully unfair to us now that Mary gets a kicking for having taken up music and reading in order to have something to offer instead of the good looks she lacks. But Jane's point, easy to miss today, was that Mary's accomplishments lacked heart. Mary quoted from great literature, but she did not understand it. She played, but her performance did not move the listener. Hannah More concluded that ultimately accomplishments were pointless because they wouldn't help a girl find a husband. 'It is a companion whom he wants, not an artist . . . one who can assist him with his affairs, lighten his cares, soothe his sorrows, purify his joys, strengthen his principles, and educate his children.'[8] Jane was not quite so dead set against accomplishments, and took pride in her own. But we can deduce from her novels her belief that one particular accomplishment trumps the rest. She has Mr Darcy explain that the most important accomplishment of all is for a lady to improve her mind 'by extensive reading'.

Recent scholarship, however, has also emphasised that Georgian 'accomplishments' weren't just for the ladies. Jane's brother Frank was obsessed, as were many Georgian gentlemen, with turning out small wooden items on a lathe: he 'is so delighted with the employment, that he is at it all day long'. And Jane herself would in later life treasure the gift of a footstool embroidered by a nephew. 'I long to know what his colours are,' she wrote when she heard it was in progress, 'I guess greens & purples.' The fact was that young men of the leisured classes needed hobbies simply to pass the time. Mr Austen had, for the education of his children, 'an 18-inch terrestrial globe'.[9] It must have been of practical benefit to his two sons who went on to join the Navy, as was his 'Compass & Sun-Dial' in a black horse-skin case. Less immediately useful, though, was the Rectory's 'microscope',[10] which instilled in none of them a professional interest in natural history. But, as a respectable hobby, an interest in natural history was nevertheless a worthy 'accomplishment' for Georgian men.

The Rectory was also well stocked with books for the children to read, 'above 500 Volumes' in total. Family tradition has Jane's older brother James down as a voracious consumer of books. 'We love, & much enjoy with ivory knife / To sever the yet damp & clinging leaves of some new volume', ran one of his poems.[11] We're told that Jane's brother had 'a correct taste' and 'a large share in directing her reading'.[12]

But in reality James Austen wasn't a great novel-reader. In fact, he was still writing diatribes *against* novels even after his sister had become a published novelist. His snootiness about novels wasn't particularly unusual. The novel was still young, an art form that had only emerged in the last few decades. Many Georgian readers looked down upon prose fiction as frothy and feminine, possibly even degrading and dangerous. It was safer, it was thought, if girls read 'books of piety and cookery' instead.[13]

It was Mr Austen who had a slightly unconventional love of novels, and who passed it on to his daughter. He relished an evening spent with a 'horrid' book like *The Midnight Bell*, enjoying scenes like this: 'the girls came running down the stairs, with terror painted on their countenances, and the elder of them exclaimed – that her Uncle's bed was all over blood!'[14] It was surely Mr Austen who later encouraged his daughter to write her spoof horror story, *Northanger Abbey*.

Jane's own books included *The History of Little Goody Two-Shoes* as well as a French grammar. Probably, like Catherine Morland, she read John Gay's *Fables*. But alongside this saccharine stuff aimed at kids, Jane also had adult tastes. Although there were 'Locks to the Book Case',[15] no one seems to have stopped her from reading books for grown-ups. 'At a very early age', her family remembered, 'she was enamoured of Gilpin [. . . her] favourite moral writers were Johnson in prose, and Cowper in verse.'[16] Indeed, the poet William Cowper is quoted more often than any other author in her novels and letters.

It seems that Jane and Cassandra were for once allowed to share the boys' lessons when it came to history, for Jane writing to her brother Frank years later mentions the 'Ghosts' of 'Gustavus-Vasa, & Charles 12th, and Christina, & Linnaeus', as if recalling a particular session on the history of Sweden. Perhaps they studied together in the Rectory dining parlour where, over the chimneypiece, a painting showed a skirmish between the Swedes and the Poles in 1565.[17]

The children probably had to read a certain number of pages of history each day, for the Austens' copy of *The History of England, from the earliest times to the death of George II* by Dr Goldsmith has dates marked in its margins to chart their progress, for example, '23rd August' on page fifteen.[18]

Jane would have loved today's *Horrible Histories*, for she produced her own extended spoof version of Goldsmith's *History of England*. It still survives in a notebook. In Jane's parody, the whole period from 1421 to 1649 was recounted afresh by 'a partial, prejudiced and ignorant Historian'.[19] It is highly personal and highly amusing. In *Northanger Abbey*, Jane's heroine Catherine complains that there are 'hardly any women' in history, nothing but 'the quarrels of popes and kings', with 'wars or pestilence on every page'. But Jane herself put this right in her own retelling. She made sure to include Joan of Arc, and Lady Jane Grey, and Anne Boleyn, excusing the latter for her misdeeds on account of 'her Beauty, her Elegance, and Her Sprightliness'. Oliver Cromwell, meanwhile, is a 'Detestable Monster!'[20] History gave Jane her 'strong political opinions, especially about the affairs of the sixteenth and seventeenth centuries. She was a vehement defender of Charles I and his Stuart grandmother, Mary Queen of Scots'.[21] Jane nursed a violent affection for the glamorous and doomed house of Stuart, writing that they were 'a family who were always ill used Betrayed or Neglected – whose virtues are seldom allowed while their errors are never forgotten'.[22] (Another member of the Austen family, Tories all, later wrote beneath this: 'Bravo Aunt Jane'.)

Jane's text was carefully and lovingly illustrated by Cassandra, who produced cameo portraits of all the protagonists. Cassandra shows England's monarchs not in historical dress, but in the contemporary clothing of the Austen girls' own childhood. In an ingenious piece of detective work, historians and medical experts have superimposed the various surviving portraits of real-life members of the Austen family onto these drawings by Cassandra. Hey presto! It looks like her family themselves provided Cassandra with her models.[23] Perhaps Jane herself was the young and beautiful Mary Queen of Scots, while her mother was a formidable, older, Queen Elizabeth I.

In Jane's book, the two women, both dressed in the style of the 1790s, face each other across the page: the youthful and beautiful Mary, boldly standing up to the glare of the malign and crone-like Elizabeth I. It's perhaps another glimpse of a combative, disagreeable relationship between their two models, Jane and her mother. 'I like the Gown very much,' Jane once wrote of a new dress, '& my Mother thinks it very ugly.' They simply could not agree. This notebook with the drawings, which ended up in the possession of Jane's brother Frank, was kept hidden from later

generations of the Austen family, perhaps specifically so that the unflat-
tering portrait of Mrs Austen remained unseen. Also hushed up were
the inevitable family quarrels of which only tiny clues survive. 'Mothers
angry fathers gone out', Jane wrote, aged eight, in her French book.

She also scribbled in her book the schoolgirl's timeless complaint: 'I
wish I had done.'[24] Lessons with Mr Austen never were done; Mrs Austen
mentions the household's daily reading of Virgil, 'two lessons each day'.[25]
But the girls were excluded from the Latin and Greek. Indeed, Mr Austen
would have been most odd if he had thought ancient languages necessary
to his daughters' educations. 'I should not like any woman the better for
understanding Latin and Greek', wrote another clergyman about another
little girl who *was,* reprehensibly, being indulged with lessons in the
classics. It was the same old story. 'I know not where this will end,' he
grumbled, 'but it is not a likely mode to get her well married.'[26]

So, what sort of moral education would Mr Austen have given to his
Georgian daughters? You didn't have to believe that girls were inferior
to boys to believe that their education should be different. It's worth
taking into account the views of the bluestocking Catherine Macaulay,
who did actually believe in the parity of men and women. *Even so*, she
argued, it was necessary 'to form the female mind to the particularity
of its situation'.[27]

And that situation was subordinate. Hannah More, for example, put
it thus: 'Girls should be led to distrust their own judgement; they should
learn not to murmur at expostulation; they should be accustomed to
expect and to endure opposition.' What they needed to develop was a
'submissive temper and a forbearing spirit'.[28] Jane, with her waspish
temper, her occasional rages, would struggle with this attitude all her
life. 'Imbecility in females', she wrote, witheringly, in *Northanger Abbey*,
'is a great enhancement to their personal charms.'

'Women are adapted by nature to regulate the (apparently) minor
affairs of life', wrote another Georgian hack. '*Details* fall under their
direction; these necessarily demand a training different from that which
enables men to contend with and overcome the difficulties which they
encounter in the world.'[29] Jane Austen herself might have concurred with
such a view. Yet in years to come she would write about these 'minor
affairs of life' in a brilliantly subversive way. In her fiction, she'd use small
things, domestic '*details*', to make powerful people see the world and
themselves anew.

Mr Austen was a careful, considerate father, giving most of his children
the priceless gift of confidence. When Frank went away to sea, his father
wrote him a loving letter of advice with prudence as its theme. 'Consider

what she directs!' he implored, before concluding that Frank should never forget that he had 'not upon earth a more disinterested and warm friend' than his 'truly affectionate' father.[30] Frank treasured his letter, and kept it about him for years.

Mrs Austen also had – and presumably read to her daughters – a treasured letter of advice, penned in her case by her aristocratic great-grandmother. This family relic was written in 1686 in Constantinople, where Elizabeth Chandos had travelled as the wife of an ambassador to the Turks. It gives maternal advice to a daughter that was considered valuable enough to be handed down between generations of Leighs until it reached the hands of Jane's mother.

'Ye best use that can be made of fair weather', Elizabeth Chandos wrote, 'is to provide against foule', and a commendable young woman was 'housewifly & frugal'. Elizabeth warned her daughter, one of eight children, that she must not expect much in the way of a fortune. Mrs Austen must have expressed many of the same thoughts to her own daughters. Alongside that love of novels from her father, this, too, was Jane's inheritance: an inclination to be thrifty, a good housewife, to wear good but not showy clothes. Such are the desires and values revealed again and again in Jane's letters, and in her novels too.

The Austen girls' lifelong interest in recipes, in groceries, in the storage of household goods and the management of servants stamps them as coming from society's middling ranks, not the rich. 'Habits of domestic management', runs the household manual *The Complete Servant*, 'are now generally precluded in the education of young ladies of the superior class', but happily, 'those of less exalted rank' are still taught 'the more rational, solid and lasting pleasures, of a social and comfortable home'.[31] Jane's diaries in later life would reveal her habit of totting up her income and expenditure for the year, so it was likely that Mrs Austen taught her, as *The Complete Servant* advised, 'the business of examining and keeping accounts, – and a few other of the leading points in the management of a family'.[32]

So what Jane and Cassandra really learned at home was to be prudent, to fulfil expectations. They were not taught to run after life and to gulp it down, but to be wise, to endure. These were the Tory qualities that would prevent them from going out and earning a living; these were the Tory qualities that would turn their lives inward, to their home.

At the same time, though, they must also have played and romped outdoors. Another little girl, growing up in Somerset in the 1780s, found great pleasure in the fields, 'where in haymaking time we had a delightful hidden bower round the bole of a large tree . . . we always ran home after the load of hay that we might ride back to the field on the empty wagon'.[33] Jane – and her novels – spring from a newly self-confident and less deferential generation of gentry folk, people who would challenge the stiff, formal manners of the established nobility in these years of the French Revolution. Jane in her stories is often on the side of the tomboy against the good girl, of truth rather than decorum, of the new against the old. Perhaps Jane too, like Catherine Morland, ran 'noisy and wild'.

That is, until she was sent away from home to be made civilised.

5

The Abbey School

'Girls might be sent to be out of the way
and scramble themselves into a little education.'

Emma

A T THE AGE of seven, in 1783, Jane was sent from Steventon to go
to boarding school. After periods of attendance at two different
schools, she came home again for good just as she turned eleven.

Why did Jane leave home at such a young age? Only recently have
the possible reasoning, and results, been explored. Certainly all the Austen
children were sent away as babies, for nursing, just as Jane was, before
returning to their mother. James and Henry went off to Oxford aged
fourteen and seventeen. The younger boys, Frank and Charles, were sent
away from home at the painfully young age of twelve to the Royal Naval
Academy at Portsmouth. Yet Jane left home aged only seven; again there
is this hint that she was in some way difficult, that she was sent, like the
girls at Mrs Goddard's school in *Emma*, 'to be out of the way'. Her
extreme youth calls to mind her disabled brother George, shuffled out
of the family pack as defective before he was four years old.

Later members of the Austen family would be zealous in claiming the
credit for having 'created' Jane. It was 'at Steventon that the real foun-
dations of her fame were laid', asserts her nephew.[1] But, as Marilyn Butler
notes, Steventon could not have created her entirely: because for three
significant years of her childhood she wasn't there.[2]

Was Jane happy to go? The scanty evidence suggests not. According
to Austen family tradition, Jane's being sent to school was a consequence
simply of her refusing to be parted from Cassandra: she was 'too young
to make her going to school at all necessary, but it was her own doing;
she *would* go with Cassandra'. Indeed, we hear that 'if Cassandra's head
had been going to be cut off Jane would have hers cut off too'.[3]

One historian has argued that there was a very simple reason why
Jane was sent away: economics.[4] The Rectory was growing too small for
all the boys her father hoped to entice to his school. Jane's eldest brother
James was packed off to college just a week after the birth of her youngest,

Charles, almost as if the two events were linked. In 1782, the year before the girls left for school, the house slept as many as twelve people: five Austen children, their parents, five or six pupils. It cost Mr Austen £70 a year for his girls to board. With the girls out of the way, he could perhaps pack three boys into their bedroom and make a profit.

We also know that in later life, Jane would reveal great sympathy for a little girl forced to live away from her parents: 'she did not like the idea of it at all', she wrote, 'Poor little Love'. Then, Anne Elliot in *Persuasion* had 'gone unhappy to school'; a view is expressed in *Lady Susan* that 'school must be very humiliating', and in *The Watsons*, one character says she 'can think of nothing worse' than to be a teacher in a school. Overall, if fiction can ever be an accurate pointer to reality, then Jane's experience of school was pretty miserable.

At least the two little girls, Jane seven and Cassandra ten, were joined by a third, Mrs Austen's sister's child. As well as being a cousin, twelve-year-old Jane Cooper was the girls' 'dear friend'. The destination for the three of them was Mrs Ann Cawley's school in Oxford. Now, in one sense, this was hardly a great step, because Mrs Cawley was an aunt-by-marriage. She was Jane Cooper's father's widowed sister, and her late husband had been the Principal of Brasenose College in Oxford. Mrs Cawley's establishment was not particularly formal or academic: it was just the sort of place, like Mrs Goddard's establishment in *Emma*, where girls could 'scramble themselves into a little education'. Mr and Mrs Austen perhaps thought the girls would benefit from a more feminine environment, and come home a little more refined and therefore marriage-able than would be possible among so many strapping boys at home.

Oxford was a good choice of destination, for James Austen was there as well, to look out for his sisters, and to take them about to see the city. But was the outing a success? Oxford contained 'many dismal chapels, dusty libraries, and greasy halls', wrote an anonymous contributor to James's student magazine, a satirical girl, who was spoofing the pompous, serious concerns of male undergraduates. 'I am sure I never wish to go there again.' It seems likely that this was James's little sister Jane going into print for the first time.[5]

But the 1783 experiment in boarding school ended in complete disaster. In the summer, Mrs Cawley moved her school to Southampton, appar-ently to avoid an outbreak of measles in Oxford. The extraordinary thing is that she did this without informing the girls' parents. But they escaped one disease only to encounter another, because Southampton was in the grip of an epidemic of 'putrid fever', or endemic typhus. Also known as 'jail fever', it was spread – rather horribly – by the faeces of the human body louse, and took hold when people lived in cramped, insanitary conditions. 'Nothing can surpass the dirt and bad smells of the bye streets' of Southampton, wrote one visitor, and rather too many houses had been squeezed in between the encircling medieval walls that protected it from the sea. The same writer described how the tide left 'putrescent quagmires all about the lower parts' of the town.[6] And now typhus, with its fever, chills and delirium, infected all three of the girls. However, Mrs Cawley did not worry too much. While the disease was extremely serious, and often fatal, in adults, it was generally much milder in children.[7]

It does seem very odd, though, that she again neglected to tell the girls' parents. Perhaps she thought that in any case it would have been impossible to send the girls home: they would only have infected the other children at Mr Austen's school. Whatever the reason, it was only when Jane Cooper wrote to her mother that Mrs Cooper and Mrs Austen realised what was going on. The sisters swooped down on Southampton to rescue their daughters, but Mrs Cooper paid a high price. She caught, and died of, the disease. She was only forty-seven.

What were her family going to do with the poor, now-motherless Jane Cooper? The answer was to send her away again. In 1784, she went at thirteen to the Ladies Boarding School, sometimes called the Abbey House School, in Reading. The following summer, in 1785, Cassandra and Jane came to join her. I was once a pupil at the Abbey School myself, and Jane Austen was our most famous ex-student.

Mr Austen paid extra for Jane and Cassandra to be parlour boarders. This meant eating breakfast and supper with Mrs Latournelle, the head-mistress, in her parlour. The privilege was not extended to the normal pupils, who paid less than half the parlour-boarding fee. Another new pupil remembered being welcomed into the headmistress's 'wainscoted parlour, the wainscot a little tarnished', with 'several miniatures over the lofty mantelpiece'.[8] This other new girl was delighted by the parlour breakfasts: a 'huge plate of toast and butter'. As she'd never been allowed to eat toast and butter at home, 'nor to come near a fire', she thought herself 'supremely happy under this new order of things'.[9]

The school occupied the old gatehouse of Reading Abbey, plus an adjoining two-storey building. This crumbling construction had an atmos-phere of decayed grandeur, and its most striking feature was the 'gateway with rooms above, and on each side of it a vast staircase, of which the balustrades had been gilt'. There were also 'many little nooks and round closets, and many larger and smaller rooms and passages'.[10] It sounds much more monastic than Jane's disappointing *Northanger Abbey*.

Outside was the Forbury, a green used for games by the boys from

Dr Valpy's school next door, but the school's best feature was at the back. This was a private 'beautiful old-fashioned garden, where the young ladies were allowed to wander, under tall trees, in hot summer evenings', surrounded by the Abbey's 'magnificent ruins'.[11] As no one really bothered with what the girls were doing, they 'gossiped in one turret or another', and had plenty of leisure time to frighten each other with ghost stories.[12] These probably included tales of the Abbey ghosts, which included its founder Henry I, buried there minus his eyes. At the Abbey's Dissolution its monks had hidden away an important relic, the mummified hand of St James. The shrivelled hand's rediscovery by workmen during Jane and Cassandra's time as pupils must have provided further Gothic thrills.[13]

In the house itself were dormitories for sixty or seventy girls, two to a bed. Downstairs was the schoolroom, for prayers, lessons and dinner, and the ballroom for dancing and acting. The school possessed globes, maps, and a magic lantern to show plates of historical scenes.[14]

Jane's very smart future sister-in-law attended a rather smarter school in London, the 'Ladies Eton' in Queen Square. This establishment had an old coach in a back room for the young ladies to practise getting in and out elegantly.[15] We don't hear of any such frills at the Abbey, and indeed many people thought it was unnecessary to have a dancing master to tell a girl 'to pull up her bosom and become nothing but "a very pretty puppet"'.[16]

But even if deportment was relatively neglected at the Abbey School, it was hardly an academic hothouse. Mrs Latournelle, now nearing fifty, had originally been Esther or Sarah Hackett or Hackitt. She had joined the school as a French teacher, though apparently she 'never could speak a word of French'. She took the name because having been engaged as a French teacher (presumably a rather ineffective one) 'her employers thought it right to introduce her into the school under a foreign name'.[17] She was ageless in appearance: 'her white muslin handkerchief was always pinned with the same number of pins, her muslin apron always hung in the same form'.[18] She wore the cuffs and ruffles of the 1780s on into future decades, 'a stout woman . . . but very active, although she had a cork leg. But how she lost its predecessor she never told.'[19]

One of her pupils thought her fit for not much more than 'giving out clothes for the wash, making tea, ordering dinner and, in fact, doing the work of a housekeeper'. But these were important qualities for looking after girls, and Mrs Cawley could well have paid heed. 'Hers was only an every-day, common mind,' it was said, 'but a very useful one; for tea must be made, and dinners ordered, and a house would soon tumble to pieces without these very useful every-day kind of people.'[20]

Mrs Latournelle's curriculum did include French, music, drawing, writing, needlework and 'speaking'. Her pupils learned spelling, but not punctuation. Perhaps too, they were supposed to imbibe the insubstantial notion of 'polish'. According to Edmund Burke, female beauty 'always carries with it an idea of weakness and imperfection. Women are very sensible of this; for which reason they learn to lisp, to totter in their walk, to counterfeit weakness, and even sickness.'[21] But the enduring reason for Jane's popularity today is that she seems born outside her time, to be more like *one of us*, for she lifelong expresses the opposite point of view: in favour of vitality, strength, independence. And in later life she would write of 'the ignorant class of school mistresses', as if she didn't think much of them.

In *Persuasion*, Jane Austen sends her heroine Anne to a school in Bath, and she probably had in mind the well-regarded Belvedere House. A pupil there recorded the daily round: up at six, prayers at half-past seven, breakfast at eight. Then came the writing master, who also taught arithmetic. At four they sewed, and at six, drank tea. Then they learned their lesson for the next day, or played with their dolls, until bread, cheese and beer came in at seven-thirty. Eight o'clock prayers were followed by bed. There was drawing on Tuesdays and Fridays, while Wednesday 'was dancing day'. The plain, stout teacher, Miss Fleming, 'taught the Minuetts, and figure dances', sprinkling lessons with her repeated injunction: 'Now ladies, do credit to Bath.'[22]

But Mrs Latournelle's schedule was much more lax, and pupils remembered the 'ease and liveliness of the mode of life' at the Abbey.[23] Their headmistress very likely came from a theatrical background, for she spoke often 'of plays and play-actors, and green-room anecdotes, and the private life of actors'.[24] Within the Abbey, the 'great dancing-room' was 'fitted up as a regular theatre, with foot-lights and everything else complete' including 'Scenes for Theatrical Exhibitions'.[25] The audience at the end-of-term plays included the boys from Dr Valpy's school next door, and the girls presumably went in return to see their performances. Dr Richard Valpy, an actor manqué, had his boys stage Shakespeare's *Henry the Fourth Part Two*, for example, carefully pruned of its 'indelicate speeches'.[26]

It's traditional to state that Jane learned her skill as a writer from her father, his library, and the great male role models of the eighteenth century: Joseph Addison, Samuel Johnson and Richard Steele. But more recently historians have pointed out the influence of other teachers, more fun and more feminine. The critic Paula Byrne has argued that Jane's writing shows a love of plays and the stage,[27] perhaps instilled by the thespian Mrs Latournelle, while Marilyn Butler points out that Jane's fiction bears the mark of the magazines that the pupils would have read at the Abbey School. The *Lady's Magazine*, for example, produced from 1770, boasted that it offered something for every reader from duchess to housemaid. About a third of the magazine was made up of fiction sent in by the (female) readers, and it very often involved relationships between a man and a woman of uneven rank: in other words, it was romantic. This was the feminine, perhaps slightly trashy food upon which Jane fed, as well as the polished masters of Georgian prose. And perhaps her earliest stories of all were made up to entertain the other girls during those sunny Abbey afternoons. In later life, despite her disparaging comments on teachers in general, Jane wrote of an amusing incident that she 'could die of laughter at it, as they used to say at school'.

But whatever Mr Austen's hopes might have been for making a profit, the expense of Jane's schooling seems to have brought back an old problem: lack of money. In the spring of 1786, Cassandra and Jane stopped being parlour boarders and joined the rest of the cheaper, common herd. Their father's account at Hoare's bank shows that his payments to Mrs Latournelle fell into arrears, and he made the very last one after the girls had left the school altogether, and returned to Steventon, in December.[28]

The adventure was over. There had been fear, but also fun and freedom, and maybe even early forays into fiction. The return to the Rectory bears something of the clang of the prison door, for never again would Jane live for so long away from her mother.

6

The *Freindship* of Women

'Yes Madam, it is the wretched Eliza herself.'

Jane Austen's *Henry and Eliza*

A T THE SAME time as Jane came home from school in December 1786, Steventon Rectory also gained three exotic new inhabitants. They were her twenty-five-year-old cousin Eliza, Eliza's baby boy, and Eliza's mother, Aunt Philadelphia. Despite the protestations of the Austen family that her closest male relatives formed Jane's taste and aspirations, it's recently been proved that the love and friendship of a number of older women would be equally – if not more – important for her future career. And let us not doubt that Jane's career would be important to her – much more so than the 'oh, it happened by accident' story that her male relatives liked to tell.

Eliza, the first of these women, was utterly, distinctly, outrageously foreign. Steventon was remote and quiet, but strong threads linked the Austens of Hampshire to the world beyond, and to the great concerns of Georgian Britain. These threads led to India, Antigua, France . . . the world was shrinking. It had experienced the Seven Years' War, often called the real 'First World War' as it affected so much of the globe, and Britain's Navy ruled the waves. From the East, merchants were importing tea, opium, wallpaper, parasols, porcelain, muslins, spices and bamboo furniture.[1] Turquoise blue, rose pink and shimmering yellows were the coming, highly becoming, colours. Meanwhile, from the West Indies came sugar, and concerns about the treatment of slaves. Eliza brought a whiff of all this novelty with her to rural Hampshire.

When Jane's character Willoughby in *Sense and Sensibility* speaks of 'nabobs, gold mohrs, and palanquins', he must have been using words that Eliza made familiar, for her own colourful life story begins in India. Her mother, Mr George Austen's sister, was named Philadelphia but often known as Phila for short. We left Phila, along with her somewhat shadowy sister, Leonora, living with their Uncle Stephen, the bookseller, in London, while their brother George went off to school. When Uncle Stephen died, he apologised in his will for not being able to leave anything to his two nieces.[2] And while the promising young George was given an education, the wider Austen family were much less interested in his sisters. Phila was apprenticed in 1745 at fifteen to work as a milliner in Covent Garden, a career choice that was often synonymous with sex work.[3] 'Milliners . . . mantua-makers . . . haberdashers . . . they are actually seminaries of prostitution', claimed Charles Horne in his *Serious Thoughts on the Miseries of Seduction and Prostitution* (1783). There is nothing to prove definitively that Phila's employer, Hester Cole, was anything less than respectable, but in London's red light district, Covent Garden, a milliner was often a front for other businesses. In the pornographic story published in 1748 named *Fanny Hill, or Memoirs of a Woman of Pleasure*, the heroine falls into the hands of another Mrs Cole, 'a middle-aged discreet sort of woman'.[4] In Mrs Cole's fictional shop 'sat three young women very demurely employed on millinery work'. But as soon as evening began, 'the shew of the shop was shut' and the 'mask of mock-modesty was completely taken off'.[5]

A real milliner named Cole recorded in 1745, and a fictional milliner/madam named Cole in the same district in 1748: it's a striking coincidence of names. The truth is probably that Phila's employer was neither entirely one thing nor the other. Eighteenth-century sex workers − as many as one in five of the female population, it's sometimes argued − could be 'amphibious', dipping in and out of respectable employment according to their changing fortunes. Even in the unlikely event that Phila's Mrs Cole *was* totally respectable, millinery, where profit margins were small, where the labour was hard, and where looking pretty and stylish was part of the job, was a precarious occupation.

But there was a surer way for a pretty young woman to find a future. 'Old Francis' Austen, the rich lawyer uncle, now intervened. He suggested that Phila should take the boat out to India where British administrators, soldiers and public servants needed wives. Risk still remained, for it was commonly acknowledged that this voyage out placed a girl in great danger of losing her reputation. 'I would rather you had no acquaintance with the ladies who have been to India,' Lord Clive of India wrote, 'they stand in such little esteem in England.'[6] Yet 'Old Francis' Austen had a client in India, a surgeon named Tysoe Saul Hancock. Six years older than Phila, he needed a wife; Phila might suit. She was taken from her life among the bonnets, and, along with eleven other ladies, put onto the boat east.[7] Suit she did, and she seemed to have a firm footing in life at last. Hopefully Hancock would return with both wife and an Indian fortune to London, there to enjoy a life of leisure. After all, it was surprising to come across an Anglo-Indian in British society who was short of money, and everyone could recognise that 'ostentation which in general characterises a Nabob'.[8]

Jane, hearing at least some of this, was by now old enough to find her Aunt Phila's life story troubling. She put it into an early work of fiction. 'Do you call it lucky', asks a serious girl called Catharine in a story of the same name, 'for a girl of genius and feeling to be sent in quest of a husband to Bengal, to be married there to a man of whose disposition she has no opportunity of judging till her judgement is of no use to her?' The man she was to marry 'may be a tyrant or a fool or both'.

And Aunt Phila may well have questioned her luck in ending up with Tysoe Saul Hancock, who was not in the successful 'nabob' class as a businessman. But Mr Hancock did open doors for his wife to make money on her own account. He was acquainted in India with the great administrator Warren Hastings, who ended up as the ruler of Bengal. Hastings also knew Mrs Austen's family from his childhood in the Cotswolds; his father's home had been at Daylesford, next door to Mrs Austen's family's home at Adlestrop. This connection accounts for the fact that Warren Hastings had sent his young son (the one who died) to be looked after by Mr and Mrs Austen in the early days of their marriage.

Phila in India almost certainly became Warren Hastings' mistress, and her daughter Eliza's father was almost certainly Hastings himself rather than the complaisant Hancock. Eliza was recognised as Hastings' 'god-daughter', a fudge that nevertheless caused irritating gossip. Hastings may have been governor-general of Bengal, but he wasn't above the reach of rumour. 'In no circumstances whatever keep company with Mrs Hancock,' warned Lord Clive, 'for it is beyond a doubt that she abandoned herself to Mr Hastings.'[9] In Hastings' Bengal, as Mr Hancock himself claimed, 'debauchery under the polite name of gallantry is the reigning vice'.[10]

Jane tells us that Warren Hastings 'never *hinted* at Eliza in the smallest degree'. But he nevertheless remained closely involved in his 'god-daughter's' life and education. 'Neither French nor Dancing will disqualify a Woman for filling the Duties of any Sphere in Life', Hastings decreed, and Eliza was indeed brought up to display a glamorous, man-pleasing manner. And, in due course, Hastings settled the substantial sum of £10,000 upon her. He reassured himself that with a dowry like this, his 'god-daughter' would not 'be under the Necessity of marrying a Tradesman, or any Man for her Support'.[11]

Mr Hancock himself did make a fortune, it is true, but it turned out to be rather too small to live upon happily ever after. When the family returned to London in 1765, they must have hoped it was for good, but high living soon caused the money to run out. Hancock was dispatched back East, further to plunder the subcontinent, from whence he lugubriously sent back generous presents to his wife and indeed, to his wife's family. In Steventon, Mr Austen received neckcloths of Indian muslin and Mrs Austen a handkerchief of Indian silk. But a famine in India meant that earning a second, more satisfactory fortune proved harder than expected, and Mr Hancock's letters recount exotic hardships and extreme situations. On behalf of the East India Company, Mr Hancock had the job of touring India to see 'every place where our people are employed'. This was work of great danger: in one region, boat travel was hazardous, for swimming 'Tygers' sometimes took men 'out of their Boats. We have unfortunately lost eight Men by these terrible Beasts.'[12] Despite all his efforts, he would ultimately be unsuccessful on this second trip to India. 'All my expectations', he wrote, 'are vanished like a dream & have left me astonished.'[13] And on 5 November 1775, he died in Calcutta.

Meanwhile, Aunt Phila had regularly been turning up at Steventon. She had come to help out at Mrs Austen's confinements with both Henry and Cassandra, astonishing the Hampshire residents with her feckless ways. After one typically disorganised visit in 1770, her trunk fell off the back of the carriage in the middle of a heath. She sent her servant back along the road to look for it. But then, growing nervous about waiting all alone, Phila got 'frighted' and took refuge at a nearby farm, rather idiotically leaving all the rest of her possessions in the vehicle and leaving its door wide open. She was lucky not to be robbed.[14] 'Oh Phila', sighed her long-suffering husband in India. If she had spent less time on 'dissipations', he wrote, and more on 'acquiring the necessary and most useful knowledge of Accounts', happy would it have been for them both.[15]

Phila and her daughter Eliza were the despair of their more sensible relatives, leading their lively life, not worrying too much about money, and enjoying themselves almost indecently much. With her dodgy dowry to boot, Eliza as she grew up was rich meat, 'a clever woman', it was remarked, and not entirely approved of in Hampshire. Damningly, she exuded continental chic, being 'highly accomplished, after the French rather than the English mode'.[16]

Eliza acquired this French polish of hers in the winter of 1777. When Jane was nearly two years old, the now-widowed Phila Hancock and her daughter of fifteen went off to tour the continent. Eliza had a high old time in Paris, writing to her country cousins that she and a great crowd had seen Monsieur Blanchard bravely go up in his hot air balloon, setting out 'alone for the aerial regions' and ascending to the height of 1,500 fathoms.[17] And then, 'we were a few days ago at Versailles', she wrote, in 1780, '& had the honour of seeing their Majesties & all the royal family dine & sup'. Of Marie Antoinette Eliza reported that 'The Queen is a very fine Woman, She has a most beautiful complexion.'[18] She made a close analysis of the queen's outfit: 'Petticoat of pale green Lutestring [silk], covered with a transparent silver gauze, sleeves puckered & confined in different places with large bunches of roses.' There was just one note of simplicity, 'her neck was entirely uncovered & ornamented by a most beautiful chain of diamonds'.[19] This was valuable information. Despite the rivalry between the nations, the British were forced to concede that the French were better dressed. Each year a little 'doll' dressed in miniature versions of the latest fashions was sent across the Channel so the ladies of London could see what was being worn in Paris. The 'doll' was so important that it made its journey even during times of war between the two countries.

Eliza's own skin was dark – she mentions 'the native brown of my complexion'[20] – and a miniature portrait painted during this time in France shows her with high, powdered hair, enormous dark eyes, and a snub little nose, rather like those of the fashionable pug dogs she loved. 'Bewitching animals,' she wrote, 'I shall joyfully receive as many more Pugs as you can procure for me. You would laugh to see me consulting my Doctor about my Dog, and administering Vapour Baths which he has prescribed for him.'[21]

Eliza in Paris met a dashing fellow named Jean François Capot de Feuillide, a count and an officer in Queen Marie Antoinette's own regiment. She was swept away by the slavish French devotion lavished upon her by her new suitor. 'It is too little to say he loves, since he literally adores me', she wrote. 'The whole study of his life seems to be to contribute to the happiness of mine.'[22] She started to think seriously about marrying him. One advantage would be that she could call herself a Countess, although, when looked at closely, de Feuillide's right to his title was a little dubious.

But she faced considerable opposition from the trustees of the money settled upon her by Warren Hastings, among them George Austen. 'Her Uncle Mr Austen', we're told in a family letter, doesn't 'approve of the Match'. Back in the sensible world of Steventon, Mr Austen was 'much concerned at the connection which he sais is giving up all their friends their Country, and he fears their Religion'.[23] But Eliza cleverly presented her decision to go ahead with the marriage anyway with the irreproachable female argument that her mother had advised her to do it: 'It was a step I took much less from my own judgement than that of those whose councils & opinions I am the most bound to follow.'[24]

At first all seemed well after the headstrong, nineteen-year-old Eliza married her dodgy Count. He whisked her away to the south of France near Nérac, where he had been granted an area of marshland, by royal favour, on the understanding that he would pay no taxes on it for twenty years if he drained and cultivated it. He built himself a small villa, Le Marais. Writing from the rented house they occupied while it was finished Eliza proudly told her family that the drainage works had freed people thereabouts from 'the pernicious exhalations of such an extent of stagnant Water', to the extent that her husband was 'looked upon as the Benefactor of a whole Province'.[25]

When Eliza became pregnant, though, her husband wanted to send her home to England. 'Should a Son be in store for M. De Feuillide', she wrote, 'he greatly wishes him to be a native of England.'[26] It was wise to make sure that Eliza's trustees would know and learn to love this little boy and heir to her fortune. The Count was unable to leave his land-reclamation works, so Eliza and her mother set off together for London in May 1786. Her feelings towards the Count were by now cooling. One of her cousins observed that despite expressing many warm feelings towards her husband, Eliza 'confesses that Love is not of the number on her side, tho' still very violent on his'.[27]

And Mrs Phila Hancock, as usual hopeless at planning, did not quite manage to get her daughter home to England in time. The baby was born in Calais on 25 June. Warren Hastings' £10,000 had purchased him the right to have his illegitimate grandson named after him, so the little boy was named Hastings. In July, Phila, Eliza and baby ('very fat . . . very fair & very pretty'[28]) arrived in London. Just like Warren Hastings before her, who had sent his own son to the Austens, Eliza now thought of Steventon as a healthy place to bring up a baby. She was perhaps already a little worried about young Hastings; his health did not quite seem secure. And so, in time for the Christmas holiday, the small family made the move to Hampshire.

By now Mr and Mrs Austen were entering into middle age, and their life of hard work was taking its toll. Mr Austen was 'quite white-haired', and Mrs Austen had 'lost several fore-teeth which makes her look old'.[29] Yet the family were usually 'all in high spirits & disposed to be pleased with each other'.[30] Their sense of being a unit must have been slightly off-putting to outsiders, but Eliza was warmly welcomed.

Eliza entertained the Austens with both her French tales, and her musical talents. 'We have borrowed a Piano-Forte,' wrote Mrs Austen, 'and she plays to us every day, on Tuesday we are to have a very snug little dance in our parlour . . . Five of my children are now at home, Henry, Frank, Charles & my two Girls, who have now quite left school.' She concludes her Christmas newsletter with a flourish: 'Every one of our Fireside join in Love, & Duty as due and in wishing a happy 87 to our dear Friends.'[31] All was right with the world, 'the girls' had come home, and there was a new baby in the house to play with.

And how could the eleven-year-old Jane not have been impressed by the twenty-five-year-old Eliza, who had seen the French court at Versailles, and lived an independent life? Eliza, who took marriage so lightly, and described her own wedding as 'a very stupid business'?[32] Eliza would declaim with feeling that she wouldn't lose her 'peace of mind for any male *creature breathing*'.[33] And yet, a need for flirtation and admiration was an essential weakness in her character. She believed she could not help it, claiming that 'if weak women go astray, Their stars are more in fault than they'.[34] Nevertheless, there was something irresistible about her, and her French-ness. To persuade a reluctant bachelor to marry, says Eliza's fictional doppelgänger, Mary Crawford in *Mansfield Park*, 'you must have the address of a French-woman'.

During her holiday at Steventon Rectory, Eliza revelled in the flirtations that she began to conduct there with Jane's handsome elder brothers, especially as they all took to the stage. The Austen family had for some years made a habit of performing plays at home. Now, under the leadership of Eliza, who took 'the principal part', it flourished. The dining parlour was their stage. James Austen, the family's writer, penned special 'prologues and epilogues' to be appended to standard works. His relations thought them 'very vigorous and amusing'.[35]

As time went on, the 'Steventon Theatricals' grew even more ambitious, and moved from the house into one of the outbuildings. The family had acquired, or perhaps made, a 'set of theatrical scenes'.[36] 'My uncle's barn is fitting up quite like a theatre,' wrote one of the Austen nieces, '& all the young folks are to take their part.'[37] The following Christmas, Eliza tried to persuade this absent cousin, another Philadelphia, to come and join in, grandly reassuring her that 'we shall have a most brilliant party & a great deal of amusement, the House full of company & frequent Balls'.[38] The only requirement was that all guests must be willing to act. The Rectory was too full to take any mere spectators, and 'My Aunt Austen declares "She has not room for any idle young people."'[39]

It was not unusual for gentry families to stage theatricals at home. 'We still continue Play Mad', wrote one Eugenia Wynne, who with her own friends was 'rehearsing very ill and enraging the manager', although the performance eventually 'went off with great éclat and much applause'.[40] But not everybody approved of young ladies cavorting upon a stage. Jane herself would later read, and enjoy, Thomas Gisborne's

Enquiry into the Duties of the Female Sex, which categorically stated that theatricals were sinful, because of their opportunities for 'unrestrained familiarity with persons of the other sex'.[41] One stern Scottish Methodist minister claimed that should his daughter even *visit a theatre*, let alone act, he would 'mourn the day that made me a parent – her soul is polluted, and that is the essence of prostitution'.[42]

But Jane, inspired by the Steventon Theatricals, would grow up to become an inveterate playgoer. One of the reasons that her novels work so well on the screen as feature films is because she conceived them like plays, scene by scene, with dialogue propelling the story forward.[43] And the theatricals in *Mansfield Park* recapture some of the mixed excitement, pleasure and pain that the Steventon Theatricals probably aroused.

The plays performed at Steventon in the barn, by Jane's brothers, her cousin – and perhaps even Jane herself – quite often featured battles between the sexes. In 1790 the play chosen was *The Sultan*, with its female heroine. A new epilogue, written by James, included the lines:

> Lord help us! What strange foolish things are these men
> One good clever woman is fairly worth ten![44]

In 1787, the year following the sisters' return home from school, the Austens and their friends chose a remarkable play called *The Wonder*, by Susanna Centlivre. *The Wonder* itself is that a woman *can* keep a secret, when she wants to, and the theme of the play is women's position in society. 'We are little better than slaves to the Tyrant Man', declaims one female character.[45] Eliza, playing the part of Violante, spoke some more hopeful verses written for her by James:

> But thank our happier stars, these days are o'er,
> And woman hold a second place no more.[46]

The flirtatious Eliza by now had both James and his brother Henry firmly under her thumb. Henry Austen was given lines to say about Queen Elizabeth and the Christmases of old, a couple of them pregnant with flirtatious meaning:

> Nor yet in lov'd Eliza's golden reign
> Did Christmas ever claim its rites in vain.

In a couplet that was ostensibly about Queen Elizabeth I, Henry was also announcing, in character, that he loved his spirited cousin. Or was this the hidden meaning of James, as the author of the lines? Or did they both love the elegant and exotic Countess?

It is certain that both were highly tempted. James had the advantage of age – he was twenty-three, while Henry was still in his teens – but James had also, just two weeks before Christmas, been ordained as a clergyman. He really should have known better. However, the quiet and watchful Jane knew better too, for her observations had revealed to her which brother Eliza really preferred.

Among her youthful writings is a 'novel' (really a story) called *Henry and Eliza*, in which a couple elope. They leave a letter reading simply: 'MADAM We are married & gone. Henry and Eliza'. Indeed, although at this point Eliza was still married to her French count, and flirting with Henry's brother, this story of young Jane's would prove strangely prescient.

Back during that first Christmas holiday home from school, Jane's birthday present from Eliza, received on 16 December 1786, was a book of plays intended to help children learn French. 'Pour dear Jane Austen' was her cousin's Franglais dedication. Eliza, who could 'read French easily',[47] probably now became Jane's teacher. A real French book provided by a real French countess was far better than the imaginary French of Mrs Hackitt-turned-Latournelle. Her family later recalled that one of Jane's favourite songs ('the song that I heard her sing oftenest'[48]) would be a French song of love:

> *Que j'aime à voir les Hirondelles*
> *Volent ma fenêtre tous les ans . . .*

> I love to see the swallows
> At my window every year,
> Coming to give me news
> Of the approach of sweet springtime!
> The same nest, they say to me,
> Is going to see again the same loving.
> It is only to faithful lovers
> That they announce happy days.[49]

And it was 'To Madame la Comtesse DE FEVILLIDE' that one of Jane's very earliest literary works, one of the numerous stories of her teenage years, was dedicated.

We have a pen-picture of Jane at the age of twelve, as she was in the summer of 1788. As she reached double figures in age, Jane would have been put into her first pair of stays, a rite that marked a girl's passage into adolescence. Another little girl remembers standing upon the window seat to be measured for her first set, which 'in consideration of my youth, was to be only what was called half-boned . . . notwithstanding, the first day of wearing them was very nearly purgatory'.[50] Girls grew used to the pressure over time, and the stays themselves actually changed and narrowed the shape of their soft and still-growing ribs.

The memories of another of Jane's cousins, the rather priggish twenty-seven-year-old Philadelphia Walter, reveal that Jane at twelve-and-a-half was still acutely shy. This Philadelphia liked Cassandra, and thought her very pretty, (and, tellingly, very like herself). But she thought Jane 'very prim, unlike a girl of twelve'. 'The more I see of Cassandra,' wrote their cousin, 'the more I admire.' But 'Jane is whimsical & affected'.[51]

Jane's whimsy, though, was tolerated, even admired, among the clique-ish Austen siblings. Perhaps there was a good reason that Jane never strayed far from her family circle: her brothers and sister were good company. Their conversation, we're told, had 'abundance of spirit and vivacity, and was never troubled by disagreements even in little matters'.[52]

And Austen fun was often intellectual. James Austen's magazine *The Loiterer* of 1789 contains a spoof anonymous letter from 'Sophia Sentiment', a noisy, sloppy satire of a girl whose self-indulgent sentimentality comes from reading trash. For some decades, 'Sophia's' letter has been posited as the work of a very young Jane Austen. The case is bolstered because this particular edition of *The Loiterer* was the only one ever to be advertised in *The Reading Mercury*, a newspaper that was read in Steventon. It looks like a matter arranged as a surprise so that the young author could see her own words in print for the first time.[53]

And what did Sophia/Jane have to say? Well, in eight issues of *The Loiterer*, Sophia complains, there has been 'not one sentimental story about love and honour, and all that. – Not one Eastern Tale full of Bashas and Hermits, Pyramids and Mosques.' *The Loiterer* has had 'no love, and no lady in it, at least no young lady; and I wonder how you could be guilty of such an omission'. There should be a tale with a hero who 'fled into France . . . or you might have let him set fire to a convent, and carry off a nun, whom he might afterwards have converted, or any thing of that kind, just to have created a little bustle, and made the story more interesting'. This is surely the writer of *Northanger Abbey* speaking, in the very voice of Isabella Thorpe.

However, it does seem rather too polished for a girl of thirteen. The very name 'Sophia Sentiment' was taken from a character in rather a

grown-up play, *The Mausoleum*, published in 1783, about a widow senti-
mentally devoted to her late husband, although she eventually gets over
her fine feelings and marries someone else. So, if Jane really was 'Sophia
Sentiment', did James help her? Did Mrs Austen give a hand? It looks
like a family affair.

And the Austens were united in their wish to present to history their
image of a family who never disagreed, working, playing and writing
together. Yet even its individual members may find a clique oppressive.
The Austens carefully suppressed the traces of the arguments that must
also have taken place at the Rectory, but just occasionally we can catch
them at it. Mrs Austen could be querulous, Mr Austen impatient. 'All
things were done in a hurry by Mr. Austen', wrote one of his grand-
daughters, '& of course this is *not a fact* to be written and printed.'[54]

But Jane also had her friends outside her family. Her preternatural
cleverness meant that her closest friends, beyond Cassandra, tended to
be women significantly older than herself. Also, she did not lack role
models in the form of females who were published writers.

One of these was 'Madam' Lefroy, whose husband was the rector of
Ashe, only a mile's walk away by the fields. You could easily get to
Steventon from Ashe through 'the short cut across the meadows and down
the avenue . . . and so into the lane almost close to the Rectory gate'.[55]
Mrs Anne Lefroy zipped around the Hampshire countryside in her little
donkey-cart. Described as a woman of 'luminous virtues',[56] she'd been a
published poet in her youth. Her husband's Huguenot family name was
the official reason that everyone called her 'Madam' Lefroy, but in reality
the French title was a nod to her sophistication and intelligence.[57]

She was a fantastic mentor for a future writer, having 'a warm and
rapid poetical genius; she read voraciously; her apprehension was like
lightning'.[58] While Jane would never write fondly or wistfully about her
own mother, it is different for Madam Lefroy. In later life, Jane remembered 'her smile of love'.[59]

Madam Lefroy had practical as well as literary gifts, dispensing charity
around the neighbourhood, and inoculating 'upwards of 800' poor people
with the cowpox vaccine newly discovered by Dr Jenner to prevent
smallpox.[60] Her brother was an even more prolific published writer, a
rather pompous novelist named Sir Egerton Brydges, who became a
tenant for a while at Deane Parsonage. He'd come here to live near his
sister, and recorded that her house at Ashe 'was always full of company'.[61]

Madam Lefroy may have been 'one of the happiest beings I ever saw',
one person said, 'she laughed almost the whole time'.[62] But Anne Lefroy
also had her demons. She was a clingy, possessive mother, unable to let

her children go, micro-managing their careers, telling them how melancholy she felt at home without them. As she herself admitted: 'I have so placed all my worldly hopes & happiness upon my Children loving me, that I am too easily hurt, if in the slightest degree I suspect I am lessened in their opinion.'[63] Jane was something of an extra, substitute child, perhaps a crutch to make Madam Lefroy feel better about herself, rather than being truly loved for her own qualities.

And Austen biographers cannot agree upon Madam Lefroy: sometimes she is a charismatic mentor, sometimes a spiteful, divisive figure. She was in reality a bit of both. Despite her charity and her teaching of literacy to local children, she was socially ambitious, and was very upset when her brother failed to win a lengthy legal struggle to claim a peerage. This brother of hers, Sir Egerton, takes rather a condescending line on the little girl whose fame would so much eclipse his own. Yes, he writes, he had known his sister's friend Jane as 'a little child: she was very intimate with Mrs Lefroy and much encouraged by her'.[64]

Sir Egerton was the first novelist whom Jane Austen knew personally, but she also knew that he wasn't very good. She picked up on the fact that even Mrs Lefroy was 'ashamed' of her brother's work, because he had cruelly mocked her friends round Ashe and Steventon in *Arthur Fitz-Albini, a novel* (1798).[65] Sir Egerton, therefore, was helping to teach her to form her own opinion of novels. 'My father is disappointed', Jane admitted, when the pair of them came to read one of Sir Egerton's works, but '*I* am not, for I expected nothing better.'

Jane also had two published novelists less geographically close, but both of them actual members of her extended family. Mrs Austen's first cousin, Cassandra Cooke, published a historical novel in 1799, while a more distant relative in the Leigh family, Cassandra, Lady Hawke, was 'never seen without a pen in her hand; she can't help writing for her life'.[66] A novel of hers was described as 'love, love, love unmixed'. It did not appeal to the astringent Austens.

Looking beyond the books of her neighbours and family, Jane Austen was becoming a consummate novel-reader. Jane had what the critic Claire Harman calls a good 'consumer's understanding' of the form in which she was to work.[67] She was not alone in forming this new habit of voracious novel reading. In each decade from the 1760s to the 1790s the number of novels by women being published jumped by 50 per cent.[68] It was widely believed to be a form in which female authors could excel. 'The best novels', wrote the actress, classy courtesan and feminist writer Mary Robinson, 'have been produced by women'.[69]

Another novelist among the friends of the family was Jane's favourite,

Frances Burney, who had written *Evelina* and *Cecilia*, and who now was publishing her novel *Camilla* by subscription.[70] A bit like crowd-funding today, subscribers got the privilege of having their names listed in the front of the finished book. The list for *Camilla* reads rather like a sister-hood of Georgian female novelists, because so many of them supported their fellow author. It includes a Mrs Radcliffe, and Miss Edgeworth (author of *Belinda*) and indeed a nineteen-year-old 'Miss J. Austen of Steventon', whose guinea must have been paid for her by her father. When Jane mounts her famous defence of 'the novel' in general in *Northanger Abbey*, it is Frances Burney's *Camilla* that she names. A lady who is 'only' reading a novel, Jane says, 'only' reading *Cecilia*, or *Camilla*, or *Belinda*, is 'only' reading a work 'in which the greatest powers of the mind are displayed, in which the most thorough knowledge of human nature, the happiest delineation of its varieties, the liveliest effusions of wit and humour are conveyed to the world in the best chosen language'.

'Only' a novel, then, could be a forceful thing. Mary Robinson called for female writers – 'neglected, unsought, alienated from society' – to stand together. 'How powerful might such a phalanx become', she imagined.[71] And, in years to come, Jane would in *Northanger Abbey* step forward to stand beside her. 'Let us not desert one another', she wrote, addressing her fellow novelists. 'If the heroine of one novel be not patronised by the heroine of another, from whom can she expect protec-tion and regard?'

Back in Steventon, Jane was dreaming of becoming a member of this happy band, and of becoming published. Three notebooks survive containing her early work. Called 'Volume the First', 'Volume the Second' and 'Volume the Third', they contain between them twenty-seven pieces of writing, some 90,000 words deemed worthy of preservation, and written out neatly.[72] The notebooks themselves were gifts from Jane's father, and the expensive paper was not inconsiderable evidence of his encouragement: for two shillings, the weekly wage of a housemaid, you got only forty-eight sheets, or two quires, of paper.[73]

The high-quality paper, the neat handwriting, the carefully made fair and final copies of earlier plays and stories: these three notebooks were the work of someone who was already 'an author', someone who wanted her words to be preserved and cherished. The titles of the volumes, the first, the second and the third, suggest that the whole was a body of work, something substantial. They were made as much as possible to look like real, printed books. One of the stories, called 'Catharine, or the Bower', even begins with a fulsome letter from a craven author to a patroness, claiming that earlier works published with her support have found 'a place in every library in the Kingdom, and run through three-score Editions'. Harman argues that this is early evidence that Jane would become a hard-headed, professional writer, thinking ahead about sales even before she had completed a full-length novel.[74]

There was just one obstacle to Jane's dream, but it was a big one. With all those published writers among her family and friends, and with her brothers publishing their work in *The Loiterer* as well, Jane must have gained the impression that it was quite an easy thing to get into print. When she later came to dispense advice to a niece who had written a novel of her own, both of them took it as a matter of course that the work would be published. In her own teens, Jane must have assumed that she could, *would*, become a novelist. It must have been surprising and chagrining to Jane, as she grew older, that it would take her so long. The problem was that she was too original. Her novels would be too unusual – indeed too 'novel' – for publishers to realise at first just how good they were.

But while Jane was looking out, towards a world of future readers, she was also looking in. Fourteen of the pieces of writing are dedicated to members of the Austen family or circle, and there's a sense that they were intended to be read aloud communally, perhaps even acted out in the manner of the Steventon Theatricals. And Jane could write stories as gifts to friends and family: they cost her nothing but paper and time. The family allocated lucky Charles the future ownership of one of the notebooks, as some of the pieces in it were 'written expressly for his amusement'.[75] Jane dedicated another piece to her friend Martha Lloyd as 'a small testimony of the gratitude I feel for your late generosity to me in finishing my muslin Cloak'.[76] This Martha, along with her sister Mary, would in due course become family as well as friend.

And what did all these early mentors, family and female friends, encourage Jane to write? Her stories do place rationality above emotion, not surprising for a girl who lived in a house of boys training to become classical scholars. All her life she would be on guard against gushing. In one story, 'The Beautifull Cassandra', the object of love is not, as one might expect, a bewitching young man, but instead a wonderful hat. Jane tells us the story in a succession of 'chapters' each about the length of a tweet, an entirely novel format in which not a word is wasted. 'When Cassandra had attained her 16th year,' the story begins, 'she was lovely & amiable & chancing to fall in love with an elegant Bonnet.' Her milliner mother had just made the bonnet by order of a Countess, but Cassandra 'placed it on her gentle Head and walked from her Mother's shop to make her fortune'. What a superb beginning.

In a love letter to the luxuries of London, Jane then let her heroine taste its pleasures. The 'Beautifull Cassandra' ignored a handsome viscount in favour of going instead to a pastry-cook's, where she devoured six ice creams. Asked to pay for them, she simply 'knocked down the Pastry Cook & walked away'. Next, she rode in a hackney carriage all the way to Hampstead, and when the coachman wanted his fare, she put the beautiful bonnet on his head and ran away. Finally, after an absence of seven hours, Cassandra came home, and was 'pressed to her Mother's bosom'. But even in the maternal embrace, 'Cassandra smiled & whispered to herself "This is a day well spent."' What wickedness! What brilliance!

This early story, ridiculously set out in its twelve 'chapters' each merely a sentence long, is the perfect introduction to Jane Austen's satirical, sparkling naughtiness. Jane's nephew, in his influential early biography, would depict his maiden aunt as full of virtue, kindness and meekness. 'There was in her nothing eccentric or angular,' he thought, 'no ruggedness of temper; no singularity of manner.'[77] Well, the evidence of her early writings suggests otherwise. They are simply packed full of utterly eccentric and angular girls doing bad deeds.

As well as Beautifull Cassandra, we have Sophy, who can 'toss off a bumper of wine', Sophia, a brazen thief, who 'majestically' removes a banknote from her cousin's desk and acts all outraged when caught, and Kitty, a comedienne, who regrets the loss of her much-loved governess, Miss Dickens. Kitty tells us, full of tragedy, that she will never forget how Miss Dickens disappeared. '"My dear Kitty," she said, "Good night t'ye." I never saw her afterwards.' Having created a suitably melodramatic moment, Kitty pauses theatrically to wipe her eyes before revealing what had actually happened to Miss Dickens: 'She eloped with the Butler the same night.'

As one of the best writers on Jane Austen, Virginia Woolf, put it, there's something strikingly satirical about these early stories of *Love and Freindship* (as one of them is titled) and horror and farce. 'What is this note which never merges in the rest, which sounds distinctly and penetratingly all through the volume?' she asks. 'It is the sound of laughter. The girl of fifteen is laughing, in her corner, at the world.'

And Jane's notebook was like a real book in that it got a real review. Her father annotated his daughter's 'Volume the Third' with his own opinion, which was spot on. These were 'Effusions of Fancy', he wrote, 'by a very Young Lady consisting of Tales in a Style entirely new'. 'A Style entirely new' was Jane's greatest gift. But it would also be her greatest obstacle to getting her work published for real.

7

The Wars

'What calm lives they had . . .
No worries about the French Revolution,
or the crushing struggles of the Napoleonic wars.'

Winston Churchill on *Pride and Prejudice*

JANE NEVER WENT to France. In her lifetime, the furthest north she travelled was Staffordshire; she possibly went as far west as Wales, and definitely to Ramsgate in easternmost Kent. Critics used to comment, often, that she couldn't be a 'serious' novelist because she didn't write about the French Revolution, Napoleon, or the great events of her lifetime. France itself is only mentioned three times in all her novels.[1] But in reality nothing could be further from the truth. Jane and her family simply couldn't disentangle themselves from the country just across the Channel from Hampshire, and particularly from the effects of its Revolution. It would be Jane's unique contribution to illustrate the effect of these seismic events indirectly, as they played out in the tiny details of the day-to-day life of ordinary people. She made the political into the personal.

Despite her knowledge of their language, and her admiration of Eliza's glamour, Jane is ambivalent about the French. You can even identify a subtle thread of *anti*-French feeling running through her novels. There is the nasty Mr Hurst in *Pride and Prejudice*, who likes French cookery, and the slippery Frank Churchill in *Emma*, who sprinkles his conversation with words like '*naïveté*' or '*outrée*'. Mr Knightley condemns Frank, and the French, with a damning use of French of his own: Frank, he says, 'can be amiable only in French, not in English. He may be very "amiable", have very good manners, and be very agreeable; but he can have no English delicacy towards the feelings of other people.'[2] In Jane's novels, the French, and Frenchness, do not come off well. But she's far too subtle to condemn them out of hand.

Of course even before the Revolution began, the French and English nations had long been at odds. Jane's favourite novelist Frances Burney surprised even herself by her decision to marry 'a *French* man'. 'No wonder upon Earth', she wrote, 'can ever arrive near my own in having

found such a Character from that Nation.'[3] But the Austens felt themselves to be above casual racism. Jane knew all about Burney's marriage,
and mentioned it in *Northanger Abbey* when she had a notably stupid
character refer to Burney as 'that woman they made such a fuss about,
she who married the French emigrant'. As James wrote, it was 'inconsistent with the liberality of the human mind' to laugh at the French
'*Monseers*' as lousy devils eating 'fricasseed frogs'.[4]

In 1789 many Britons had indeed welcomed the news of the storming
of the Bastille and the end of the absolute French monarchy. 'How much
the greatest Event it is that has ever happened in the World!' gasped
Charles James Fox.[5] But within a year, doubt had set in as the consequences became clearer. How would the gentlemen of Britain, asked
Edmund Burke in the House of Commons, like to have their own
'mansions pulled down and pillaged, their persons abused, insulted, and
destroyed; their title deeds brought out and burned before their faces,
and themselves driven to seek refuge in every nation throughout Europe'?[6]
As the poet Anna Seward put it, once she'd decided that her own earlier
enthusiasm for the Revolution was mistaken, 'O, that the French had
possessed the wisdom of knowing Where To Stop.'[7]

Jane was thirteen in 1789, and like everyone of her generation her
life was shaped by the Napoleonic Wars to follow. She was, in fact,
through Eliza, and her sailor brothers, even more closely connected to
them than many. Buried beneath the surface of her novels are strong
currents of feeling aroused exactly by this question of knowing Where
To Stop. 'The welfare of every Nation', states a wise character in Jane's
early story 'Catharine', 'depends upon the virtue of its individuals', and
to offend against 'decorum and propriety' is to hasten a kingdom's ruin.
In one sense, Jane's novels are a bulwark against tumultuous change. In
another, they deal with a far more important question than who would
win the Napoleonic Wars. They're concerned with how to live life well
in the peace to follow, which was what the fighting was actually *for* in
the first place.

After her flirtatious Christmases at Steventon Rectory, Eliza had
returned to France and her husband, only to be forced once again to
leave. On 7 July 1789, just in the nick of time to escape the devastation
in Paris, the Hancock family arrived in London. On 14 July, the storming
of the Bastille began.

The next key event took place on 26 January 1793, when the French
killed their king, Louis XVI. According to another country parson, poor
Louis had been 'inhumanly & unjustly beheaded on Monday last by his
cruel, blood-thirsty Subjects. Dreadful times I am afraid are approaching.'[8]

Mr Austen probably took just the same view. For the British, despite their support for liberty, this was going too far. A month later, they declared war on the French.

War would soon affect life at Steventon. The various wars grouped together as 'Napoleonic' began properly when Jane was seventeen, and did not end until she was thirty-nine. This meant that in total she only experienced thirteen years of peace out of the forty-one she lived. It also meant that she had the misfortune to come to maturity in a general drought of marriageable men, as the Napoleonic Wars would see military casualties at an average of 20,000 a year.

'War has not only been declared,' declaimed Pitt in the House of Commons, 'it is at our very door.'[9] Because the county included the vulnerable Channel coast and the dockyard at Portsmouth, Jane's Hampshire became a kind of Home Front. It bristled with soldiers and sailors, while the county's roads brought them their supplies. In Winchester, the royal palace left incomplete by King Charles II became home to thousands of captured French prisoners, who were punished for misdemeanours in their prison's 'Dark Hole'.[10] There were 6,000 troops stationed in Winchester too, with 8,000 more in camps near Andover and Basingstoke. 'Nothing was heard', wrote one memoirist of this time, 'but the dread of Buonaparte, and the French invasion. Beacons, Martello towers, camps, depots, and several species of self-defence alone occupied all minds.'[11] Jane observed all of this. Obviously the officers make a huge impact on the lives of the Bennets in *Pride and Prejudice*, but not only socially. They bring the violence of the battlefield home to the village, just as Kitty and Lydia bring home the gossip: 'several of the officers dined lately with their uncle, a private had been flogged, and it had actually been hinted that Colonel Forster was going to be married'. The casual slipping-in of the flogging, as if it were just part of normal life, doubles the insensitivity of these silly girls.

The nature of the Hampshire countryside changed as French block-ades raised the price of grain, putting further pressure on the landowners to inclose their fields, fertilise their soil, and keep out both the people and animals who'd wandered, and eaten, there before. To *enclose* meant to put up a fence, but to *inclose* was to change the land's legal status, removing former rights to graze or forage. Traces of evidence of this painful change in countryside life would pop up time and again in Jane Austen's novels, from the man who mends a hedge (the symbol of inclosure) in *Mansfield Park*, to the hungry gypsies who might have stolen Highbury's poultry in *Emma*.[12]

The most immediate impact of the war upon the Austen family came when Henry Austen decided to enlist. Republican France declared war on 1 February 1793, and Henry responded two months later by becoming a lieutenant in the Oxfordshire Militia. 'The political circumstances of the times 1793', he explained later, called upon 'every one not otherwise employd to offer his services in the general defence of the Country'.[13] Henry would now serve for five years as a militiaman. All over the nation other young men were doing the same sort of thing, servants as well as masters. 'Our Boy Tim Tooley,' recorded a Norfolk parson, 'supposed to have been gone to bed was not to be found . . . it is thought he is gone to Norwich to enlist himself, as his Head has long run on a Soldiers Life.'[14] Such was the general enthusiasm that even those who could scarcely be called suitable were signed up to fight, including the poet Samuel Taylor Coleridge. Coleridge entered the 15th Light Dragoons under an alias, but it was soon noticed that his equipment was rusty and his riding skills inadequate. After only three months he was discharged as 'insane'.[15] It is noticeable, though, that like Lieutenant Wickham in *Pride and Prejudice*, Henry signed up to the militia, which was a defensive force, rather than seeking active service overseas. His martial ardour was tempered by a love of home comforts. He also managed, through sickness and leave, to miss the most exciting events that befell his regiment (a mutiny, a riot), although he was present for a shipwreck.[16]

When the French decided in August that the whole nation should serve in the army, calling a *levée en masse*, it inspired a similar response in Britain. A correspondent to *The Gentleman's Magazine* claimed that 'the military fever has so far seized on several young and beautiful females as to make them submit to be drilled and exercised (privately of course) by a common serjeant'.[17] Jane acquired herself a military-style cockade of egret feathers from the Nile Delta to wear upon a turban, just like the cockades her sea-captain brothers would have worn upon their hats as they fought Napoleon's navy.[18] She also borrowed an Egyptian-style 'Mamalouc cap' (something like a fez) to wear to a ball in 1799 to celebrate Nelson's victory at the Battle of the Nile. Eliza was even more eager both to dress, and act, in a military manner: 'I went out to bespeak my regimentals,' she wrote, 'and be *drilled* without delay.'[19]

One worries what Eliza really meant when she asked to be '*drilled* without delay'. In spring 1791, she remained in England, visiting Margate for the health of her poorly little boy, and nursing her mother Aunt Phila, who was, it had become clear, suffering from breast cancer. Young Hastings had started to suffer from fits, and Eliza's fears were 'of his being like poor George Austen . . . he cannot use his feet in the least, nor yet talk'.[20] Despite Eliza's flaws and levities, it was generally agreed that she was deeply devoted to her dying mother and vulnerable son. Her smug cousin Philadelphia, jealous of Eliza's high life, wrote rather a horrible letter about her eventual bereavement: 'Poor Eliza must be left at last friendless & alone. The gay and dissipated life she has long had so plentiful a share of has not ensur'd her friends among the worthy . . . I always have felt concerned and pitied her thoughtlessness.'[21]

Where was Eliza's husband? The supposed Count, 'a strong <u>Aristocrate</u> or Royalist in his Heart', had found Revolutionary France to be contrary to his taste, and came over to Britain.[22] But long before Eliza had finished grieving for her mother, he was off back home, for he had been informed that 'if he still continued in England he would be considered as one of the Emigrants, & consequently his whole property forfeited to the Nation'.[23]

So Eliza found herself drawn back to Steventon, and to Jane, in 1792. Mr Austen was now the closest she had to a parent. Eliza would often sit with him, tracing her dead mother's features in his, until, as she wrote, 'my Heart overflows at my Eyes'. 'I always tenderly loved my Uncle,' she concluded, pitifully, 'but I think he is now dearer to me than ever.'

Eliza had good practical reason to be grateful to Mr Austen, for as trustee of her £10,000, he had refused to release it and allow the unreliable Count to invest it in France. It turned out to be a wise move; Eliza was still rich. She had also been more careful with her money than appearances might suggest, never contracting debts, paying for everything up front. Startlingly for one so addicted to fashionable life, she did not gamble, and under no circumstances touched cards.[24] She relished the quiet of Steventon, where she found comfort with Cassandra and Jane, 'equally sensible, and both so to a degree seldom met with'. But Eliza did have a favourite: 'My Heart gives the preference to Jane, whose kind partiality to me, indeed requires a return of the same nature.'[25]

A few short miles away across the Channel, her husband's Royalist sympathies were getting him into trouble. In 1794, he was accused of trying to help a Marquise escape a charge of conspiring against the Republic. De Feuillide was detected in the payment of bribes to aid her, and unfortunately the Committee for Public Safety discovered the very receipt for the money in the Count's trouser pocket. His and Eliza's French house and possessions were placed under the care of their black servant, *la citoyenne* Rose Clarisse, and their housekeeper, *la citoyenne* Joubert.[26]

The Austens in England heard tales that the 'Count', who had talked up his rank until the Revolution, now made a bold but desperate attempt to escape the guillotine. He cunningly claimed to be a valet, who had murdered, and impersonated, the real Count. For all this, he was sent, on 22 February 1794 (or the fourth day of the windy month of Ventôse, as the Republicans called it in their new calendar), to be guillotined.[27] This claim that he wasn't really a Count after all would make it extremely hard for his widow, Eliza, to reclaim his estates. What a terrible mess, even if it was all rather romantic.

In 1798 Britain joined a new coalition against Napoleon, and Mr Austen went off to a meeting in Basingstoke Town Hall to discuss the Defence of the Realm Act, intended to prepare the country for fighting. Across England, surveys were undertaken, and people were asked the question 'would you be willing to serve?' This prompted answers of 'yes' and 'no', but also more colourful responses such as 'I will give Boneypart a mungle turn' and 'I will crip the wings off the French frog eaters.' These returns showed that Steventon was able to muster a Dad's Army of thirty-nine capable men between the ages of fifteen and sixty. They didn't have any proper weapons such as swords, pistols or pikes, but the 'Implements they can bring' included sixteen axes, twelve spades and four shovels.[28]

On into the new century, Hampshire folk really did believe they could be invaded at any moment. 'We were alarmed last night by the sight of a great fire', wrote Jane's friend Madam Lefroy. 'I was afraid it was some signal to give notice that the enemy was off the Coast & went to bed very uncomfortable.' In fact, it was a Basingstoke malthouse burning down by accident.[29] Madam Lefroy wasn't sure whether to worry more that the French would come in flat-bottomed boats or in hot air balloons.[30] Indeed, a drawing survives in the British Library of an extraordinary 'French Raft as intended for the Invasion of England', with a castellated fortress upon it, and driven by paddle wheels powered by windmills.[31]

Meanwhile Eliza was left as the orphaned single parent of a disabled child. And here her behaviour towards her son does throw into sharp relief the Austens' treatment of Jane's brother George.[32] It's not that unusual that George Austen was sent away from the family unit to be cared for by strangers. But that sort of treatment was not good enough for Eliza's own little boy. She kept him with her and constantly sought a 'cure' for his fits. Hastings would not be sent away.

But Eliza clearly needed help, a partner to share the burden of looking after her son. She was still 'an extremely pretty woman' at thirty-four, and we hear that 'during her brief widowhood [she] flirted with all her Steventon cousins'. She had preferred Henry in the carefree Christmas holidays of old, but now James Austen was in more obvious need of a mate. Since Eliza had performed his lines in the Theatricals, he had married then lost to illness a wife of his own. He now also had a child, his own little girl, who needed a mother. James had become his father's curate, living at Deane Parsonage and looking after the secondary parish on Mr Austen's behalf. A second marriage to Eliza must have made perfect sense. But now, rather caddishly, he 'hesitated between the fair Eliza' and Jane's friend Miss Mary Lloyd. To add insult to injury, Eliza was pretty, whereas poor double-chinned Mary Lloyd had been scarred by smallpox, which had 'seamed her face dreadfully'.[33] Mary's snappish temper, humiliatingly well recorded by Austen family historians, may have appeared to them to be larger than life because of the lingering belief that outward appearance matched inward mind. If her face was scarred, then so must be her personality.

But the lugubrious James finally plumped for homely, pragmatic Mary. For her part, though, Mary could never forgive the delay while he had dithered. When James and Mary finally got together, the net result was that Eliza was banned from Steventon. They were 'not on terms' and Mary refused to have her in the house. Indeed, to the last days of her life, Jane's sister-in-law Mary Austen née Lloyd 'continued to dislike & speak ill' of Eliza.[34] Mary's strengths were dependability, frugality, practicality. They were utter opposites, the frivolous Eliza, and Mary, who liked to superintend other people's domestic arrangements, '& abuse them for expense'.

Jane, though, had no need to fear that James's choosing Mary over Eliza would mean that she'd lose contact with her glamorous cousin, whose indefinable 'Frenchness' caused so much trouble at home. Resourceful Eliza had other means of infiltrating the Austen family.

8

Cassandra's Romance

'They are perfect Beauties and of
course gain "hearts by dozens".'

Their cousin Eliza on Cassandra and Jane (1791)[1]

IN 1791, WHEN Jane was fifteen, Eliza de Feuillide described her and her sister as 'two of the prettiest Girls in England'.[2]

Cassandra was the easier to get on with, and her siblings thought her 'the most tender-hearted of the family'. As she reached her teens Cassandra started receiving 'much homage' from 'gallant gentlemen',[3] and Eliza – who knew all about such things – thought that she was very likely to marry, with her prettiness and her complaisant character. She was attractive enough for her lack of a dowry to seem a surmountable problem.

Cassandra and Jane had probably begun to menstruate around the average age of fifteen, higher than today, because Georgian diets were less nutritious. The Georgians did not like to discuss such womanly problems in writing, but they certainly had to deal with them. One doctor recommended treating period pains with valerian, or, more simply, 'a bladder, two-thirds filled with hot water . . . kept applied to the lower part of the belly'.[4]

The ache in the belly indicated that the time was coming for marriage and childbearing. But unlike today the Georgian recipe for a happy relationship had an extra stage that preceded falling in love and getting married. That stage, probably carried out by your parents, was a financial check on any putative husband. Sometimes the falling in love bit was missed out altogether, or it was hoped that it would come along later, after marriage. Cassandra, though, was coming to maturity at an interesting time in the history of love. People had of course long believed that love and marriage must be inextricably linked. But in Cassandra's lifetime there was a noticeable shift towards thinking that social and financial status, still important, were *less* important than compatibility.

Until this point, the path towards Shakespeare's 'marriage of true minds' was usually strewn with impediments, in the form of family obligations, financial arrangements, and the physical ability of the woman to bear children (the man's ability to do his part of the process was usually taken for granted). And until the Enlightenment, your duty to God was more important than your duty to find a soul mate for your personal self-fulfilment.

A century before Jane and Cassandra grew up, Lord Halifax wrote his celebrated *Advice to a Daughter* (1688), warning her not to even think about choosing her own partner. 'Young women', he advised, 'are seldom permitted to make their own choice; their friends' care and experience are thought safer guides to them than their own fancies.' The seventeen editions that his book went through, right up to 1791, show that his views appealed to the book-buying public throughout the eighteenth century.

To this end, the well-ordered Georgian family like Mr Austen's would interfere in the matrimonial affairs of its young people to an extent that would seem quite extraordinary today. In fact, this business of the organising of matches would create the very genre in which Mr Austen's daughter Jane would excel. In 1741, a printer named Samuel Richardson brought out a manual for letter writing, *Letters Written to and for Particular Friends on the Important Occasions*. Among its 150 or so sample letters made available as models to copy were many letters of advice both for and against proposed marriages. My favourite is no. 70, a model letter for a father to send to his daughter advising her 'against a frothy, French Lover'. But rather more sinister is the letter advising a daughter that she *really must* marry a suitor rather older than herself, and a follow-up insisting that she do so despite her disinclination. And then there's the letter to be sent to a male friend considering a late-life second marriage, advising him not to be a fool.

The most famous letter in the whole collection is no. 88, which is from 'A Father to a Daughter in Service, on hearing of her Master's attempting her Virtue'. This letter started off something far more significant and wonderful. It gave Richardson, who would become much better known as an author than a printer, the germ of the plot of his best-known novel. *Pamela,* a story told in letters, sets out a scenario of a maidservant threatened by the lascivious attentions of her young master. As you follow her adventures through a million or so words, though, you realise that everything's going to work out well for Pamela. Although her master traps her and tricks her and does everything he can to seduce her, she holds hard onto her virtue. Eventually, impressed by her purity of mind, he genuinely falls in love with his servant, and marries her. Like *Pride and Prejudice*, which followed in Pamela's wake, this is love triumphant across a class divide. We see the transformation of a wealthy but unpleasant gentleman through the love of a good woman, resulting in a perfectly matched couple.

Where love lead, then, for this new generation of Georgian novel readers, prosperity would follow. You had to look for virtue, not money.

Pamela's subtitle, fittingly, was *Virtue Rewarded*. It was books like these that guided Jane and Cassandra as they reached the age for romance. These were stories that would encourage Jane to argue, in her own novel *Northanger Abbey*, that 'when any two young people take it into their heads to marry, they are pretty sure by perseverance to carry their point, be they ever so poor, or ever so imprudent'. These were not sentiments you would have found in a novel of the 1750s. This was new.

But *Pamela* wasn't Jane's favourite of Richardson's novels; that privilege was reserved for his last work, *Sir Charles Grandison*. This was a story full of — as the novelist Carol Shields puts it — 'adultery, drunkenness, rape, eroticism [and] fortune hunting'.[5] It was a novel generally considered to be far too raunchy for nice young ladies, yet Jane read it so often that its leading ladies 'were as well remembered as if they had been living friends'.[6] Another million words again take us inside the mind of a young lady, and this time the heroine Harriet clearly holds her own against men. When she receives a proposal from the right man, she doesn't shilly-shally in a maiden-like manner, but cries out: 'Sir — I CAN — I DO', before he kisses her 'in so fervent a way' as to warm the blood.

Fervent kissing was in the air at Steventon Rectory, as one by one the Austen siblings started tying the knot, for love as well as for money. Jane's brother Edward had married late in 1791. His bride was Elizabeth Bridges, also from Kent like his adoptive Knight family, and the couple went to live at Rowling, a house provided for them by the bride's parents. Four children would be born to them in that house, and an impressive seven more later on. Only three months after Edward's wedding, James had married his short-lived first wife, the heiress Anne Mathew, who'd accepted him in the teeth of her father's suggestion that she should marry 'an old friend of his own'. The slender, aristocratic Anne observed, archly, that 'she did not want a father, but a husband'.[7] James did well out of the deal, for Anne's money paid for him to have a pack of harriers and a carriage.

Later in the same year, 1792, the family weddings continued thick and fast. December saw the marriage of Jane's cousin Jane Cooper, to Captain Thomas Williams of the Royal Navy. Motherless since the typhus incident in Southampton, and also having recently lost her father, Jane Cooper 'was married from her uncle's house at Steventon'.[8]

Officiating at this particular wedding was the Reverend Tom Fowle, who was now a rather impoverished young clergyman. Jane had known him since she was four. In 1779 Tom had arrived from his home in Kintbury, Berkshire, as a new pupil at Mr Austen's school. The son of a parson himself, Tom would live with the Austens for five years, becoming a general favourite, and playing parts written for him by his good friend

James in the Steventon Theatricals. In *Sense and Sensibility*, it is at Mr Pratt's school in Devonshire that Edward Ferrars falls in love with Lucy Steele, and so it was at Mr Austen's school likewise that Tom Fowle fell in love with the headmaster's daughter.

Now twenty-eight, Tom returned to his old school to perform the wedding ceremony of Jane Cooper, his fellow performer from the Theatricals. And during this winter of 1792, when Steventon Rectory was full of girls' talk of marriage and the future, twenty-year-old Cassandra found herself engaged to Tom.

It was love; indisputably love. But, like the sensible young people that they were, they agreed that marriage itself would have to wait until they had somehow found some more cash. Tom had no 'private fortune'. Yet they had high hopes that they wouldn't have to wait long, for 'he had a prospect of early preferment from a nobleman with whom he was connected both by birth and by personal friendship'.[9]

This was Lord Craven, to whom Tom was related through his mother. Indeed, Lord Craven gave Tom a living in Wiltshire upon his engagement, but it was only a little one, not likely to provide enough money for a family. Although many Georgian parishes could support a fairly lavish lifestyle, there was enormous variation. 'We must eat', wrote one struggling young clergyman in 1803, describing the difficulties of life on £60 a year. 'I can truly say that I often pretended to have had enough [food], that there might be more for my small family.'[10] But Lord Craven had other livings within his gift, and was willing to give a second, in Shropshire, to Tom as well. It was just necessary to wait until the current incumbent died.

Despite his generosity to her sister's fiancé, Jane did not approve of this Lord Craven. He had 'very pleasing' manners, but the one 'little flaw of having a Mistress'. (Eliza, predictably, got on with him very well.) This mistress was the celebrated career courtesan Harriette Wilson, who was only fifteen when Lord Craven picked her up. Highly ambitious, Harriette got so bored with Lord Craven that she eventually dumped him. His second mistress would also be well known. Miss Brunton, 'belonging to Covent-Garden-Theatre', was 'a lady of great personal beauty and attractions', famous enough to appear in tourist guidebooks.[11] In a very pleasing twist, she would later become a fan of Jane Austen's novels, being particularly (and appropriately, for a girl who bagged an earl) fond of *Pride and Prejudice*.

So Tom and Cassandra were left in limbo, delaying their marriage until an unknown Shropshire clergyman died, or until Lord Craven could extricate himself from his love life long enough to find another way to be generous to them. It would not have been surprising if Mr Austen had counselled Cassandra against Tom as an imprudent match. But no such evidence exists: Mr Austen, like his daughters, had read his Richardson. The engagement was allowed to stand.

What did Jane feel about her sister's romance? She was doubtless daunted by the prospect of life without Cassandra by her side. Jane always found it difficult when people she had known as singletons become part of a couple, and it pleased her if the newly married were cool about each other: 'I was afraid he would oppress me by his felicity & his love . . . this is not the case', she wrote with pleasure of one new husband, while a young bride's letters were 'very sensible & satisfactory' when they made 'no *parade* of happiness'. She even thought her own brothers too much in thrall to their wives.

As Frances Burney did before her, Jane surely dreaded the loss of the evenings in their Rectory bedchamber when the sisters exchanged confidences like Lizzy and Jane in *Pride and Prejudice*. Burney wrote to her own sister just before her marriage: 'There is something to me at the thought of being so near parting with you as the Inmate of the same House – Room – Bed – confidence – life, that is not very *merrifying*.' And then, after the wedding: 'O my dear Susy, if I was but to tell you how I miss you at Home!'[12] Jane's response to her sister's engagement was to write a poem. A joyful epithalamium might have been in order, but what Jane actually produced was an 'Ode to Pity' and 'disappointed love'. It might have seemed almost amusingly inappropriate.

And yet, marriage, romantic love, was what these girls had been taught to dream of. In her father's church up the lane, Jane had played around with the blank marriage forms at the back of the parish register, filling them in with the details of imagined unions between herself and a series of husbands ranging down from the highly aristocratic *Henry Frederic Howard Fitzwilliam*, of London, to *Edmund Arthur William Mortimer*, of Liverpool, and then down the social ladder once again to the plebeian-sounding Jack Smith: 'This marriage was solemnised between us, *Jack Smith & Jane Smith late Austen*.'[13] She could see herself marrying either a rich man, or a pauper. Romance novels had taught her that she might find true love in unexpected places. She could probably not imagine Cassandra turning Tom down.

But she did not have to lose her sister just yet. The saving grace was that the couple had to wait. They needed to wait until Tom could find a second living upon which – literally – to live.

Three years later, Tom and Cassandra were still waiting. A long engagement could undoubtedly be difficult. Mrs Jennings in *Sense and Sensibility* was dismayed upon hearing that Edward Ferrars and Lucy Steele were to 'wait for his having a living':

> Ay, we all know how *that* will end: – they will wait a twelvemonth, and finding no good comes of it, will set down upon a curacy of fifty pounds a year . . . Then they will have a child every year! and, Lord help 'em! how poor they will be! I must see what I can give them towards furnishing their house.

The impatient wait for financial affairs to resolve themselves was found at all levels in society. One young Irish aristocrat grew exasperated by the slow work of his trustees upon his marriage settlement, but then, he conceded, they were 'not so eager for a f-k as I am'.[14]

But Lord Craven eventually came up with another solution. He was also a Lieutenant Colonel of 'The Buffs', a unit of British forces that had seen active service in the West Indies. In fact, the specific reason that Harriette Wilson left him was his overlong descriptions of the precise whereabouts of his soldiers, the enemy's soldiers, and 'the cocoa trees, &c.'. 'O Lord! O Lord!' Harriette would say to herself. 'Lord Craven has got me into the West Indies again . . . not that there was any particular harm in the man beyond his cocoa trees.'

So, in January, Tom accepted Lord Craven's offer of travelling with him to the West Indies as his chaplain. An ambitious young clergyman might hope, sailing with his patron upon his private yacht, to strengthen the connection between them, and get more patronage more quickly.[15]

On 10 October 1795, Tom Fowle made his will, and in January he and Lord Craven departed. 'By this time they are at Barbadoes I suppose', Jane wrote in mid-January 1796. Cassandra herself went to stay with her prospective in-laws, where she tried to make a good impression. 'I hope you will continue to give satisfaction', remarked Jane, tartly, when Cassandra reported that they seemed pleased with her. Everyone thought that Tom would be back in May.

But he never came. Instead, news of the very worst nature came from Santo Domingo, the capital city of what's now the Dominican Republic. Gradually the tidings spread across the shires, numerous Austen relatives hearing 'from Steventon where they are all in great Affliction'.[16] 'He was expected home this Month,' ran a letter of Eliza's, 'but Alas instead of his arrival news were received of his Death.'[17]

It turned out that Tom had actually died of yellow fever back in February, and his corpse consigned to the Caribbean waves. For several weeks his fiancée had been living in blissful ignorance of the fact that she had lost him. It was a heavy blow: 'a very severe stroke to the whole family', wrote Eliza, 'and particularly to poor Cassandra for whom I feel more than I can express'.[18]

Cassandra Austen has a lasting reputation for being a bit cold and buttoned-up, and a lot of this comes from Jane's report on how well, how rationally, she now handled her grief. Cassandra 'behaves', Jane reported to Eliza by letter, 'with a degree of resolution & Propriety which no common mind could evince in so trying a situation'.[19]

A young woman, having lost the man she was to marry, displaying 'propriety'? It seems odd to us that anyone cared about such a thing at such a time. And yet this is how Cassandra, 'very lady-like but very prim', got through life.[20] Cassandra, with her 'starched notions', became a role model for Jane, who likewise tended to conceal her emotions. Who knows what they really thought and felt behind the façade of propriety? The only evidence we have is that they experienced it, whatever it was, together. As their family put it, 'they alone fully understood what each had suffered and felt and thought'.[21]

There was only one bright spot in the whole tragedy for Cassandra. It was Tom's will. Proved in London in May 1797, its very first clause left her the sum of 'one thousand pounds . . . to be paid to her as soon as conveniently may be'. Invested, this would now give her an income of about £35 a year: not a king's ransom, by any means, but a vital piece of financial independence. It was about the salary of a governess, and she wouldn't have to lift a finger to earn it.

Jane, meanwhile, possessed neither a lover, nor a dead lover, nor a penny of her own.

9

Youth and Beauty

'. . . it was her business to be satisfied'.

Pride and Prejudice

THE AVERAGE AGE for women to marry in the 1790s was twenty-four.[1] But it was lower in the gentry circles to which the Austens were admitted, even if they did not quite belong. Here, expectations of marriage would have started from the age of seventeen. Indeed, in *Pride and Prejudice* Jane Bennet gets her first suitor at fifteen, and seventeen was the age at which Jane's heroine Catherine Morland both meets and accepts the proposal of her future husband in *Northanger Abbey*.

So Jane, as she reached her twenties, could have been expected to take herself off her parents' hands and find herself a home elsewhere. But no offers came her way. Despite Eliza's jokey praise of her beauty and irresistibility, shy Jane seemed 'doomed', as she had an early heroine put it, to waste her 'Days of Youth and Beauty' living quietly at home, with no husbands on the horizon.

Cassandra was often absent from Steventon on one visit or another to friends, and during these periods Jane would write to her. These letters, our best single source for Jane's life, begin to mention the trials of life as an unmarried daughter; a woman who is starting to be conscious, perhaps, of being a burden upon her family. Jane had to keep her expenditure on travel, clothes, presents, charity . . . everything except board and lodging, within the £20 a year doled out in quarterly payments by her father. Twenty pounds a year was not an insignificant amount of money. It was a reasonable year's income for a farm labourer, for example. But the problem lay in expectations. Jane went to balls; she danced with the sons of noblemen; she aspired to gentility. In those circumstances, it was not much upon which to manage.

Life at Steventon Rectory was likewise far from being uncomfortable. But it was nevertheless still just a bit of a struggle. The Austens aimed not at a luxurious lifestyle, but at elegance, neatness, sufficiency. One imagines Mr and Mrs Austen taking pride and pleasure in living within their means: 'the household business going on regularly, like a good clock;

– and every thing being kept in its proper place. No scolding in the kitchen or servants'-hall . . . the food plain and in season, and sent up well dressed.'[2] Jane in her novels is very alert to domestic *discomfort*, a house badly run, servants rude, resources wasted. Jane Austen's notable trio of married sisters in *Mansfield Park* are characterised by their different housekeeping styles, all of them flawed: Mrs Norris begrudging and mean, her sister Mrs Price disorganised and wasteful, Lady Bertram hardly aware of anything at all as she dozes, as if drugged, on her sofa. Jane knew, indeed women knew, all about the politics of housework and household management. But no one before Jane had turned them into art.

The year after Cassandra lost Tom, Jane had to watch the run of sibling marriages continue. Eliza, having seen James snatched away from her, began to worry about the future. An alliance with her cousin Henry Austen, most enduring of all her flirtations, began to grow more attractive. And so at last she accepted him. It was a partnership rather than a submission. They agreed to continue to address each other as 'cousin'. 'I have an aversion to the word *husband*,' Eliza admitted, '& never make use of it.'[3]

Touchingly, the balance in favour of Henry, the showy, slightly shallow, militiaman, was tipped for Eliza because of his 'Affection for my little Boy'.[4] It's ironic that while Henry didn't spend time with his own disabled brother, he did end up looking after a disabled stepson. Eliza continued to be devoted to Hastings, who died at the age of fifteen. She would arrange that her son, her mother and herself would all be buried together in Hampstead. Jane must have observed that these, not her husbands, were the most important relationships of Eliza's life. Nevertheless, on the very last day of 1797, Henry and Eliza were married in Marylebone. She informed Warren Hastings, and Mr Austen was so pleased when he heard that he gave Henry and his fellow army officers £40 (twice his daughters' annual allowance) to buy drinks to celebrate.[5] Now all the Austen siblings were wed except George, and 'the girls'.

What was Jane like at the age at which society judged her ripe and ready to marry? It's a little difficult to describe her appearance as a young adult, because no one can agree what she looked like. Was she pretty, or was she not? The only undisputed fact is that she was tall, 'a tall woman', as Jane put it herself, half a yard taller than her mother. 'Rather tall and slender' was her nephew's view.[6]

An analysis of a brown silk pelisse (a light overcoat to be worn either in or out of doors, this one closed with a belt) strongly associated with Jane Austen shows that it fitted a woman with a bust of thirty-one to thirty-three inches, a twenty-four-inch waist, thirty-three- to thirty-four-inch hips, and a height of about five feet seven inches tall. Yes, if this really was her pelisse, Jane was a 'tall woman' indeed, at a time when the average height, deduced from skeletons, was just five feet two inches. And she was thin too. It's not often that one can turn against any biographer who has taken the trouble to write about Jane Austen, but David Nokes does annoy when he claims, on the basis of a sketch by Cassandra, that Jane was a 'plump, dumpy woman' in a blue gown that disguises 'a somewhat ample figure beneath'.[7] What he sees is an ordinary woman's figure at rest, sitting casually upon the ground, and wearing voluminous Regency clothing. What he means, in describing her as 'dumpy', is that she doesn't look like a twentieth-century film star.

This very interesting brown silk pelisse, subject of intense study by the fashion historian Hilary Davidson, dates stylistically between 1812 and 1814, and was cut to fit a woman with a cylindrical torso, rather than the elliptical shape of today. This would have been the result of Jane's wearing those constricting stays, especially before she had finished growing. Stays made the waist appear smaller from the front view (though thicker from the side), and worn lifelong permanently altered the shape of the ribs.[8]

Another problem in knowing exactly what Jane looked like is that the only secure image of her face produced in her lifetime is a sketch by her sister Cassandra, who was only moderately talented as an artist. In it, Jane looks grumpy, with what's often been called a 'mean' mouth. When Jane became a successful author, and people wanted to know what she looked like, this image had to be prettified up to meet expectations.

Jane's nephew thought she was *not* pretty, but instead he considered her lively, full of 'health and animation'. 'In complexion', he records, 'she was a clear brunette with a rich colour; she had full round cheeks, with mouth and nose small and well formed, bright hazel eyes, and brown hair forming natural curls close around her face.' She was 'not so regularly handsome as her sister', he concludes, and yet her face 'had a peculiar charm of its own'.[9]

But then he never knew his aunt when she was young. Others described her as decidedly pretty. 'Pretty – certainly pretty', wrote one kind friend, with 'a good deal of colour in her face – like a doll, no, that wd. not give at all the idea, for she had so much expression – she was like a child, quite a child, very likely and full of humour – most amiable, most beloved'.[10] The neighbourhood's conclusion, in these Steventon days, was that 'she was established as a very pretty girl'.[11]

And yet Jane herself set little store by prettiness. Her heroines are scarcely described at all in terms of their appearance; we don't know what Lizzy Bennet looks like apart from the fact that she has 'sparkling eyes', and is less pretty than her sister Jane. Anne Elliot had been pretty, but her 'bloom had vanished early'. Catherine Morland gets the fullest description of any Austen character, but Jane dwells upon her 'thin awkward figure' and 'sallow skin'. Indeed, even the blessed Emma Woodhouse is 'handsome' rather than 'pretty'. But Lady Susan, the heroine of one early story, simply doesn't care whether she is pretty or not. 'If I am vain of anything,' she said, 'it is of my eloquence. Consideration and esteem as surely follow command of language as admiration waits on beauty.'

Jane does, however, give us perfect insight into the condition of being not-quite-pretty, and perhaps that was the true state of things for her. She writes, in *Northanger Abbey*, that 'To look almost pretty is an acquisition of higher delight to a girl who has been looking plain the first fifteen years of her life than a beauty from her cradle can ever receive.' Meanwhile, Anne Elliot in *Persuasion* is pleased and relieved to recover her prettiness when she is reunited with her long-lost love.

In January 1799, Jane's letters make their first mention of what would be a recurring health problem: conjunctivitis, or an infection of the eyes. 'Weakness in one of my eyes for some days', she wrote, 'makes writing neither very pleasant nor very profitable, and will probably prevent my finishing this letter myself.' A viral infection like this, giving its victim 'red eye', can be both painful and unpleasant to see. Poor Jane would suffer again and again from the condition, which was then untreatable, but tended to clear up naturally in four to six weeks. As one of Jane's nieces recollected, at certain times 'she suffered from weak eyes and could not work or read for long together'.[12]

Because this attack of 1799 was the first of many, one medical historian has suggested that Jane's extra time in the womb, her being a 'post-mature' baby, may have injured her immune system. Against this stands the argument that an eighteenth-century baby with a deficient immune system could hardly have survived the many infections and diseases of childhood. But life in a remote village like Steventon may have kept Jane safely out of the way of epidemics.[13]

Now that Jane was all grown up, she couldn't have failed to notice that all around her women were not only marrying but also giving birth. She sometimes assisted her father by filling in the register for baptisms he conducted in the church up the lane. Jane treats the matter of childbirth lightly in her writings, but consistently gives the impression that it should be feared. 'Mrs Coulthard and Anne, late of Manydown, are both dead, and both died in childbirth', she noted when she was twenty-two. Jane's sister-in-law Mary Austen, formerly Lloyd, was pregnant herself at the time, so, not surprisingly, Jane admits that 'we have not regaled Mary with this news'. Between 1750 and 1799, a woman bore on average an astonishing seven children (not including miscarriages or stillbirths). If childbirth did not kill a woman, her number of children might well reach double figures before the menopause.[14] Indeed, the papers in 1798 announced that Mrs Banting, of Gloucestershire, 'was safely delivered of a daughter, being the thirty-second child by the same husband'.[15]

Couples wishing to limit the size of their family might have used an animal gut condom (sewn up at one end, tied on with a ribbon, and washed after use) but these items were associated with vice and protection against venereal disease. Withdrawal or abstinence from sex altogether were the most common methods of family planning. Thomas Papillon, a relative of the Knight family, received a letter of advice on the birth of his fourteenth child. 'It is now recommended to you', the letter ran, 'to deprive Yourself of the Power of Further Propagation. You have both done Well and Sufficiently.'[16] This coincided with Jane's private thoughts about an acquaintance, Mrs Deedes, who had gone through eighteen pregnancies: 'I wd recommend to her & Mr D. the simple regimen of separate rooms.'

Jane's mother, who had given birth eight times, and who had delivered her second grandchild herself, was also growing tired of the pain and anxiety involved. When Mary was finally 'brought to bed last night, at eleven o'clock', Jane wrote, she had 'a fine little boy'. But 'my mother had desired to know nothing of it before it should be all over, and we were clever enough to prevent her having any suspicion of it'. Jane would later write a mini-drama portraying an experienced mother, Mrs Denbigh, and her horrified reaction when her practical friend, Mrs Enfield, deals pragmatical with her new baby's nappy rash. 'Ah Nurse,' says Mrs Enfield, 'his shirt sticks! Do bring me some warm water & a rag.' Mrs Denbigh finds it all disgusting: 'I shall faint if I stay.' But Mrs Enfield insists that stay she must. 'How unfeeling', Mrs Denbigh thinks.[17]

Mary Austen's experience, just up the road at Deane Parsonage, did not encourage Jane to long for babies. 'Mary', she wrote of her sister-in-law, 'does not manage things in such a way to make me want to lay in myself.' 'Poor Woman!' she wrote of another friend, 'how can she honestly be breeding again?' Lord Brabourne, Jane's great-nephew, did a good deal to sanitise and bowdlerise and idealise his great-aunt's image. He did not like this line at all, finding it much too earthy, and obliterated it from the page when the letter ended up in his hands and he published it. But he did not do his obliterating firmly enough to avoid the sentence being deciphered by future scholars, so Jane's views remain on record.

Jane's family remembered how 'she always said her books were her children, and supplied her sufficient interest for happiness'.[18] Jane would even refer to *Sense and Sensibility* as her 'sucking child', and once told a new mum, 'As I wish very much to see your Jemina, I am sure you will like to see my Emma, & have therefore great pleasure in sending it for your perusal.' Jane's claim that her books were her children is cliché of clichés for the childless lady-writer, but it has also been powerfully pointed out that she had no choice other than to present her achievement in such terms. There wasn't much else that women were congratulated for doing.

People often long to know if the eternal spinster Jane Austen ever had sex with a man. The answer is almost certainly not. Again, it comes back to her tricky position in society. Women lower down the social scale would have sex before marriage almost casually, often indeed as a test-run for a legal union to follow. It's been estimated that one-third of the brides in eighteenth-century marriages were already pregnant.[19] Those in the aristocratic empyrean above Jane's rank took affairs and adultery pretty lightly.[20] But for a female member of the gentry, or pseudo-gentry, a pregnancy outside marriage would have been world shattering.

Did Jane ever have lesbian sex? Here the stakes would have been much lower. Yes, it was frowned on by society. But this was an age where women very often shared beds, and Jane herself frequently records sleeping with a female friend. People were much less worried about lesbian sex in general. It wasn't pursued in the law courts, or policed against by the matrons of polite society. This was not least because many of them didn't quite believe that it was even possible. So that door of possibility may remain ajar. But only by the very tiniest crack, and only in the absence of evidence either way.

Despite not partaking herself, Jane was certainly very familiar with the consequences of heterosexual sex. Indeed, she knew more that many people realise about what was considered at the time to be deviant sex. Because her novels are so polished (and to some readers, prissy) and because the delicate nuances of class and manners are so central, they often exist in readers' imaginations in a strait-laced Victorian setting.

But in reality, Jane was a writer of the late Georgian period, a much bawdier age. Her early story *Lady Susan* is about 'the most accomplished coquette in England'. When the Austens acted out Fielding's bawdy burlesque version of *The Life and Death of Tom Thumb the Great* in Steventon Barn, it's possible that a twelve-year-old Jane herself took the diminutive title role. The play may not be thought fit for twelve-year-olds today, with lines such as:

> Oh! Huncamunca, Huncamunca, oh!
> Thy pouting breasts, like kettle-drums of brass,
> Beat everlasting loud alarms of joy;
> As bright as brass they are, and oh, as hard;
> Oh! Huncamunca, Huncamunca, oh![21]

And even in her teens, Jane was quite willing to make jokes about sodomy. In her *History of England*, she includes a pun about James I's favourite Robert Carr being the king's pet (his *Carr*-pet), and praises the king for his 'keener *penetration* in discovering merit than many other people'. Then, there's the famous joke Jane gives to Mary Crawford in *Mansfield Park* about the dissolute household of her sailor uncle. 'Certainly, my home at my uncle's brought me acquainted with a circle of admirals', Mary says. 'Of *Rears*, and *Vices*, I saw enough. Now, do not be suspecting me of a pun.' Indeed, it's only Jane's reputation for primness that has left some readers incredulous that she could make such a rude joke. 'Rears' and 'vices' were in fact no joking matter for Jane's naval brother Frank, who'd had sailors on his ship lashed for 'the unnatural crime of Sodomy'.[22] *Mansfield Park* also contains Jane's most striking incidence of phallic symbolism. Trapped by the park palings, Maria Bertram tries to climb over them under the supervision of Henry Crawford, the man with whom she will eventually elope. 'You will hurt yourself on those spikes!' calls out Fanny. And Maria does, in every sense.

Meanwhile, while children were being made and born all around Jane, life at the Rectory ticked steadily on. Presenting herself as wife material meant that altering, refurbishing and remodelling clothes took up a good deal of Jane's time. To dress appropriately on a limited income was labour of both head and hands. The first choice was the purchase of the fabric, something to be agonised over as price and practicality must be heeded. As 'Sophia Sentiment' puts it in the play that perhaps gave Jane her first pseudonym, the colour of a dress signalled availability:

> Here is, first, a cold brown—in this gown I was nice,
> And repell'd my warm swain with the chillness of ice;
> But growing more soft, in this azure attire
> I allowed him with hope to enliven desire;
> In this pale lilac lutestring he found me relent;
> And this rose-colour'd silk was the blush of consent.[23]

In the mornings, Jane wore a practical 'plain brown cambric muslin', and in the afternoon a 'coloured gown', ideally the 'very pretty yellow and white cloud' that she dreamed of buying. A 'cloud' was a dress of muslin so fine that it floated, and the fabric had to be worn in layers so as not to be transparent. Muslin of British manufacture was now cheaper than that of the original Indian make.

Jane and Cassandra dressed similarly, and their young niece particularly remembered 'their bonnets: because though precisely alike in colour, shape & material, I made it a pleasure to guess' which was which.[24] In her letters Jane describes a constant stream of alterations and improvements to outfits. This was probably because, like the Bennet girls comparing themselves to the Bingleys, she felt that there were standards that must be reached, but that she lacked sufficient resources to reach them comfortably. Sometimes panic or desperation set in. When Cassandra was away from home, Jane actually cut up some of her clothes in her absence: 'I took the liberty a few days ago of asking your Black velvet Bonnet to lend me its cawl,' she wrote (a cawl being a kind of veil), 'which it very readily did, & by which I have been enabled to give a considerable improvement of dignity to my Cap.'

Jane writes as if a judgement of 'good enough' was all she aimed for with regard to her clothes. The ideal was 'a very useful gown, happy to go anywhere'. A really smart cloak was inappropriate, 'too handsome to be worn, almost too handsome to be looked at'. Even less successful was an exercise in dyeing. 'How is your blue gown?' Jane asks. 'Mine is all to peices. – I think there must have been something wrong in the dye . . . there was four shillings thrown away.' There is no note of vanity in all this; indeed vanity is constantly laughed at. 'My hair', she writes, 'was at least tidy, which was all my ambition.' And yet Jane knew she would be judged on her clothes. So did her characters, and here she took the flights of fantasy that she could not take in real life. One early protagonist lies in bed, affecting but affected, dressed far too carefully for real illness in a 'muslin bedgown, a chambray gauze shift, and a French net nightcap'. Meanwhile, *Northanger Abbey's* stylish Miss Isabella Thorpe 'always' wears a beautiful, impractical white gown.

Such fancy items were out of place at the Rectory, as was fine food. Mrs Bennet in *Pride and Prejudice* boasts that she can afford to employ a good cook, and that her daughters have 'nothing to do in the kitchen'. Even if Jane and Cassandra were technically supposed to be likewise 'above' the active preparation of food, they sometimes just had to muck in. Jane had dreams of endless food. One of her early stories, 'Lesley Castle', contains a scene where a wedding is called off because of a serious injury to the groom, but the fantastically heartless heroine's main concern is for the wasting of the pre-prepared provisions. 'I had the mortification', she complains, 'of finding that I had been Roasting, Broiling and Stewing both the Meat and Myself to no purpose . . . the best thing we could do was to begin eating them immediately.' Meanwhile, the bride, 'her face as White as a Whipt syllabub' after the fracturing of her intended's skull, lies on the bed having convulsions and cannot be persuaded to take even just 'a Wing of Chicken'.[25]

Living close to the land, the Austens would not have readily wasted food, and relished every part of a slaughtered animal. Georgian cookbooks remind us that even the 'eye is esteemed a great delicacy and may be taken out with the point of a knife'.[26] 'We are to kill a pig soon', Jane reports with satisfaction, and draws a pleasant picture of herself 'devouring some cold Souse'. By this, she means the flesh boiled off the head of a pig, compressed into a coarse pâté, and pickled.

Jane's biographer nephew was later at pains to point out that the family at Steventon rarely entered their kitchen: the boys breakfasted there only on early hunting mornings; and Jane's nephew declared himself 'sure that the ladies there had nothing to do with the mysteries of the stew-pot or the preserving-pan'. Pure Victorian whitewash, aimed at making his aunt seem more genteel than she really was. The recipe books of the Austen family and their friends show a detailed, hands-on understanding of cooking, and no wonder. Somehow the household, whether defined as servants or family or both, had to produce its own bread, cakes and pies, its milk, butter and cream, and to preserve the summer glut of fruit and vegetables for eating in winter. This meant pickling and jamming. 'Good luck to your jamming!' writes a friend in Jane's friend Martha Lloyd's cookbook.[27] As Martha ended up living with Jane and Cassandra, the recipes in her collection were probably Austen family favourites too. The Austens being their word-loving selves, one of them even wrote out the recipe for a pudding as a poem:

> first take two pounds of Bread
> Be the crumb only weigh'd,
> For crust the good house-wife refuses;
> The proportion you'll guess,
> May be made more or less,
> To the size that each family chuses.
> Then its sweetness to make
> Some currants you take
> And Sugar of each half a pound

Be not butter forgot
And the quantity sought
Must the same with your currants be found . . .

And so on, for four more verses, in which cloves, mace, rose water, eggs and milk are added.[28] Jane's married cousin, Jane Williams neé Cooper, was now annoyingly keen to show off her matronly credentials by dispensing her own recipes for Muffins, Broiled Eggs and Gooseberry Jam.[29] The ladies of Hampshire also swapped recipes for household cleaning products, and Martha's recipe book includes tips for making 'Ink', 'Varnish for Tables', a concoction 'To clean gilt things', and another 'To clean white silk stockings'.[30]

As well as labour, a Georgian home also contained danger. Madam Lefroy, for example, had a sister who was burned alive. A poker, red-hot from the fire, came into contact with the woman's dress, 'which being of cotton covered with a very full wide muslin apron was instantly in a blaze'.[31] Jane was twice in her life to watch a town burn, fearing for her possessions, and forced 'to think of what I should do, if it came to the worst'. During one of these fires, in Southampton, a neighbour, panicking that his house would go up in flames, actually gave away 'all his goods' to anyone who would take them.

But the very devil of the housework for Jane lay not so much in actually doing it, but in supervising its being done by others. Cassandra actively enjoyed this, and shared her mother's interest in food production and household management. 'There is so much amusement', she said, in 'attending a Farm in the country.'[32] But Jane did not. When forced by Cassandra's absence to pick up her domestic duties, she was full of jokey complaints. 'I am very grand indeed', Jane writes when temporarily promoted by her mother's illness to the role of principal housekeeper. 'I had the dignity of dropping out my mother's Laudanum last night, I carry the keys of the Wine & Closet; & twice since I began this letter, have had orders to give in the Kitchen.' Of course she hides her efforts behind teasing: 'Our dinner was very good yesterday, & the Chicken boiled perfectly tender, therefore I shall not be obliged to dismiss Nanny on that account.' The message is that this was trivial, that it wasn't her role; that she shouldn't have to be doing it. She would rather be writing.

While Jane might mock and subvert her duty as a housekeeper, the weight of the responsibility was nevertheless made very clear in cookery books like Maria Eliza Rundell's. 'The mistress of a family', Mrs Rundell intoned, 'should always remember that the welfare and good management of the house depend on the eye of the superior; and consequently that nothing is too trifling for her notice.'³³ In 1798 Jane wrote to Cassandra claiming that 'my mother desires to tell you that I am a very good housekeeper'. But really, Jane is 'very good' for all the wrong reasons: 'I always take care to provide such things as please my own appetite . . . I have had some ragout veal, and I mean to have some haricot mutton tomorrow.'

Jane's letters reveal that she knew full well that her housekeeping would be assessed and possibly found wanting by others. 'Mr Lyford [the doctor] was here yesterday,' she wrote, 'he came while we were at dinner, and partook of our elegant entertainment. I was not ashamed of asking him to sit down to table, for we had some pease-soup, a sparerib, and a pudding.' Mary Russell Mitford, growing up in nearby Alresford, complained about the scrutiny female housekeepers experienced when guests called unexpectedly. At her house, her mother would 'try all that could be done by potted meats and omelettes, and little things tossed up on a sudden'. But very often these efforts were without success: 'no shallots to the rump steak; no mushrooms with the boiled chicken; no fish; no oysters; no ice; no pineapples'.³⁴ It was all much harder when 'the unfortunate hostess lives five miles from the market town'. In *Pride and Prejudice*, when Mrs Bennet hears that Mr Bingley is to drop in for dinner, she panics and immediately has to confer with her housekeeper. 'Good Lord! How unlucky!' she says, 'there is not a bit of fish to be got today. Lydia, my love, ring the bell. I must speak to Hill this moment.'

Jane's own impressive effort for Mr Lyford of soup, meat and pudding sounds like a three-course meal, but actually it would have been served all at once, with eaters helping each other from a spread of serving dishes rather like a modern buffet. For the whole of Jane's lifetime, food was served like this, at the table itself. The modern idea of everyone eating the same thing in a succession of different courses would only come in later. It sounds wasteful, but it wasn't really, for whatever was left on the big dishes would go to the servants, or even to paupers who might call at the house. Sometimes in grand Georgian houses what was called the first course – really the first spread of dishes – might be removed, and replaced with a second, so when Jane's character Elizabeth in *The Watsons* says, 'you see your dinner', she means that there is no more to come. In fact, despite her protestations, she did have a roast turkey waiting in the wings, for genteel dinners were to be talked down yet eaten up.

Running Steventon Rectory involved what we might call 'line-managing' several people. It's been speculated that the Austens had live-in servants, but that is to make the mistake of thinking that life in a Georgian townhouse was replicated in the countryside. Yes, servants in towns often lived in, as they did in large country houses too, but in a farmhouse like the Rectory most of the help probably came in from the village, by the day or by the hour. In 1798, in letters that span not much more than one month, Jane mentions or names no fewer than nine different servants.[35] The laundry was to be handed over from Mrs Bushell to Mrs Steevens; there was a new maid: 'we have felt the inconvenience of being without a maid so long, that we are determined to like her'.

Under the circumstances, servants had to turn their hand to anything. 'You and Edward will be amused, I think,' Jane told Cassandra, 'when you know that Nanny Littlewart dresses my hair.' This is another spelling of 'Littleworth', the foster-parents of the young Austens, so 'Nanny Littlewart' was not quite the witch her name suggests. She was really Anne Littleworth, who named her own daughter Eliza-Jane after Jane, and asked Jane to be godmother.[36] Neighbours might be employees, or objects of charity, or both, as Jane tells us: 'I have given a pr of Worsted Stockings to Mary Hutchins, Dame Kew, Mary Steevens & Dame Staples; a shift to Hannah Staples, & a shawl to Betty Dawkins.'

And getting them all to do their work properly was, of course, a skill to be learned. 'It was the remark of an old domestic', runs a passage in *The Complete Servant*, that the worst mistresses are young married women. 'They are unreasonable', the author claimed, 'in their commands; they expect too much; nor do they rightly know when to commend, or when to blame.'[37] An absence of encouragement would wound, for 'it is very disheartening to a poor servant to be continually found fault with'.[38]

So Jane, anxiously trying to do her duty, is worried that one maid who did live in, another Nanny, found life at Steventon 'very dull' while the Austens were away. She frets again when Nanny falls ill 'these three or four days, with a pain in her side and fever, and we are forced to have two charwomen, which is not very comfortable'. No wonder, despite the powerful myth that genteel females had plenty of leisure time, that Jane thought it a 'luxurious sensation' to 'sit in idleness over a good fire in a well-proportioned room'.

Jane Austen is sometimes criticised for not including enough people from the 'lower orders' in her novels. The truth is that Jane's early readers, unlike us, would have known that servants were present in many of the scenes even if Jane doesn't specifically mention them. A good servant was scarcely noticed by his or her employer. To serve is to wear a cloak of invisibility, as it is in *Persuasion*:

'Did you observe the woman who opened the door to you, when you called yesterday?'

'No. Was it not Mrs Speed, as usual, or the maid? I observed no one in particular.'

In this scene, Mrs Smith reveals to Anne the hidden spy network of servants, nurses and maids that brings her all the Bath gossip. Like Mrs Smith, Jane would notice more than most people did about the invisible people who kept households running.

And even if contemporary readers failed in real life to notice servants as individuals, they would have registered a general presence. At meals Jane's fictional families know that they are being overheard. In *The Watsons*, Elizabeth tells the family's servant, (yet another) Nanny, that she and her sister will serve themselves, so that they 'shall lose no time' in getting Nanny out of the room in order to go over the gossip from the ball the night before. Georgian ladies would be accustomed to have servants witnessing their most vulnerable states: undressed, unhappy. In *Sense and Sensibility*, Marianne writes a desperate letter early in the morning, 'kneeling against one of the window-seats' to catch the dawn light because, unusually, she was out of bed 'before the house-maid had lit their fire'.

Georgian readers would have been well able to spot the clues Jane gives us to reveal, through their treatment of their servants, whether characters are kind or cruel. We know that Colonel Brandon in *Sense and Sensibility* is a good man because he goes to visit a former servant in a 'spunging house', the halfway house to a debtors' prison, where those who owe were detained by their creditors. Brandon's mercy mission reflected well on his qualities as a master. Meanwhile the bumptious Mrs Elton in *Emma*, for example, boasts objectionably of having too many servants to remember them all: it is merely 'one of our men, I forget his name' who has the job of bringing the post.[39]

Jane even includes a handful of revolutionary moments when we hear something of the servants' side of the story, such as housekeeper Mrs Reynolds' unexpected praise for Mr Darcy. In *Mansfield Park*, Baddeley the butler – most satisfyingly – puts the noxious Mrs Norris in her place.[40] Baddeley reports that Sir Thomas Bertram has summoned Fanny. Mrs Norris cannot believe that he wishes to see such a lowly creature and assumes that she is wanted instead. 'No, Ma'am', Baddeley says, '"it is Miss Price, I am certain of its being Miss Price." And there was a half-smile with the words, which meant, "I do not think *you* would answer the purpose at all."' That 'half-smile' is a glimpse of what the servants in the novels, and in real life, might have actually thought of their employers. And it doesn't bode well. The servants, too, would have to make up their minds about what the French Revolution meant, and whether they too should rise up against their employers.

'Servants Extravagant,' wrote a farmer in 1793, 'The French War may Alter Them.'[41] And despite Jane's sensitivity to servants' lives, the Austens were not really upon the side of those who worked for them. 'Show the utmost humanity to your servants', ran one conduct book, 'but if you make them your confidants, you spoil them, and debase yourselves.'[42] Ultimately Jane agrees. She thinks it is demeaning when Lydia Bennet rushes off 'to shew her ring and boast of being married, to Mrs. Hill and the two housemaids'. The Austens were perhaps just a little bit more enlightened than most employers. They weren't ashamed to perform the farce *High Life Below Stairs*, for example, in their barn, a play about a household in which the servants ape their aristocratic masters. Its message was that everyone, regardless of status, is a servant, and that no one is better than anyone else:

> Nature made all alive, no Distinction she craves,
> So we laugh at the great World, its Fools and its Knaves.
> For we are all Servants, but they are all Slaves.[43]

The pace of life at the Rectory was deeply determined by the weather. It affected Jane's ability to walk about the countryside. A freeze was to be welcomed, because it made the muddy lanes solid enough to walk upon, and allowed Jane a little independence even in winter: 'I enjoyed the hard black Frosts of the last week very much, & one day while they lasted walked to Deane by myself. – I do not know that I ever did such a thing in my life before.' Strikingly, although Jane was a good walker, Deane was only just over a mile away. It shows just how rarely young ladies wandered about unaccompanied.

But wet weather was miserable. It made the lanes 'too dirty' for exercise, and confined young ladies 'to each other's society from morning till night, with very little variety of Books or Gowns'. Jane, who had been shy at twelve, was no more extrovert at twenty-four. Staying with her friend Martha at Ibthorpe, they found themselves curiously unable to return a call paid by noisy clerical neighbours, for 'it is a not uncommon circumstance in this parish to have the road from Ibthorpe to the Parsonage much dirtier & more impracticable for walking than the road from the Parsonage to Ibthorpe'.

Nice young ladies generally wore useless footwear, and even Lizzy Bennet's travelling shoes were not suitable 'to encounter the remains of a white frost'. But Jane was usually sensibly shod, saying, of her shoes, that 'at any rate they shall all have flat heels'. She and Cassandra were sometimes seen in the lanes of Steventon wearing pattens, wooden clogs or overshoes held on over normal shoes by an iron ring. Their niece Anna remembers the sight of the sisters walking in their pattens 'in wintry weather through the sloppy lane'.[44] Pattens were ungainly, and also chimed out loudly against hard ground, so churches might contain a sign like this one from Bath, which read: 'it is requested by the church-wardens that no persons walk in the church with clumsy pattens on'.[45] Jane and Cassandra's niece defends the use of pattens – 'worn even at that time by Gentlewomen' – but I don't think Eliza would have been seen dead in them.

Jane was an amusingly 'desperate' walker when pitted against an athlete of similar ability. 'Mrs Chamberlayne is very capital,' she wrote of an acquaintance, 'I could with difficulty keep pace with her – yet would not flinch for the World.' Her heroines, too, are bold, courageous walkers; Lizzy Bennet leaping hedges to reach her sick sister, Emma Watson repelling a stupid aristocrat who thinks that ladies should ride instead of walking. Emma smartly tells him that riding is far too expensive. 'Female Economy will do a great deal, my lord,' she says: 'but it cannot turn a small income into a large one.'

It is pale, slight Fanny Price, easily done in by a walk, or stooping in the sun, who is the weakest of Jane's heroines. Her lack of strength reminds us that being strong and healthy was the lucky exception rather than the rule before vaccinations, modern dentistry and aspirin. And yet there is also a fascinating argument that Jane's portrait of Fanny in fact depicts a young lady suffering from the then-common condition of chlorosis.[46] Today we would hardly think of this as a disease, so easily is it cured: a deficiency of iron in the diet brings about debility and pale-ness. Then, it was known as 'green sickness' or 'the virgin sickness'. But it wasn't entirely physical. The thought that young ladies might suffer from it, becoming feeble and immobile, may have become a self-fulfilling prophecy. Historians of medicine are quick to point out that people in the past did not experience exactly the same diseases as we do today, for much of a disease's definition lies in contemporary language and context. But Helen King, historian of green sickness, does draw some parallels between it and the modern condition of anorexia.[47] 'When a woman speaks of her great strength,' runs one Georgian self-help book for women (written by a man of course), 'her extraordinary appetite, her ability to bear excessive fatigue, we recoil at the description in a way she is little aware of.'[48] Maybe Fanny was all too well aware, and her physical frailty was caused by the pressure of other people's expectations.

As the Rectory emptied itself of Jane's brothers and boy pupils, Mr Austen began to turn his attention to improving its grounds. The Georgian nobleman could aspire to having Lancelot 'Capability' Brown design him a landscape garden, sweeping away the formal Baroque layouts of his parents' generation. The Georgian rector, on the other hand, might aim for the more modest goal of a shrubbery. Mr Austen, too, made the modish decision to turn some of the arable land of the glebe fields near the house into a shrubbery walk.

This was a frequent choice for the clergyman who wanted to uphold the Enlightenment ideal of 'improvement' (which also happened to be a fun hobby) but who lacked the resources for anything more significant. 'Improvement' had moral as well as practical value, and Jane for example makes Edmund Bertram in *Mansfield Park,* an admirable character, plan to give his future parsonage 'the air of a gentleman's residence'.

But Edmund will only be satisfied if he can achieve his ends 'without any very heavy expense', and he was quite correct to worry that 'improvement' might get out of hand and become a wasteful self-indulgence. As Jane's favourite William Cowper put it in poetry, 'improvement', 'the idol of the age' was 'fed with many a victim'. There were the villagers whose homes were destroyed when noblemen swept them away to improve the views from their mansions. There were productive fields flooded by a sea of beautiful but unproductive green lawn. Cowper wished that 'the honest vicar, instead of indulging his genius for improvements, by enclosing his gooseberry bushes within a Chinese rail', would spend his money on his church instead.[49]

Jane observed all this in miniature in her own garden. 'Our Improvements have advanced very well,' Jane told an absent Cassandra in 1800, 'The Bank along the Elm walk is sloped down for the reception of Thorns & Lilacs.' A wandering, serpentine walk through the woods, surrounded by plants and passing the occasional tempting bench, allowed the walker to 'wilder' or to get lost (hence 'bewildered') and feel a closer, almost Romantic engagement with nature. But sadly for the Austens' elm walk, a storm that November brought down several beautiful trees.

Mr Austen, however, never spent money he didn't have. In 1784, he'd felt prosperous enough to purchase a carriage. During this high-water mark of the family's prosperity, their vehicle would have bumped the Austen ladies along the lanes on social calls when the horses could be spared from the farm, radically transforming their freedom of movement.

It continued in use until 1798. But then it fell victim to the increasing taxes being imposed by a government at war. Jane wrote in November of that year that 'we laid down the carriage'.[50] Towards the end of the decade, standards at the Rectory were on the decline.

In the middle of all this detail, was Jane happy at home? Jane's mother knew that there was something strange and wild about her younger daughter. She looked forward to the time when Cassandra would surely be steadily married, but she expected Jane to go off somewhere unknown, in a manner matching her character: 'the Lord knows where'.[51]

Even with a comfortable home like the Rectory, it was mind numbing to visit the same neighbours; help the same paupers; cultivate the same garden, over and over again. One response to boredom was to be ill. Jane's mother on medical advice took '12 drops of Laudanum' at bedtime. It would certainly have knocked her out, for laudanum was made up of 10 per cent opium, dissolved in alcohol, delivering a hefty dose of morphine, codeine and other opium alkaloids. 'She is tolerably well', Jane reported of her mother on one occasion. 'She would tell you herself that she has a very dreadful cold in her head at present; but I have not much compassion for colds.' Mrs Austen had her illnesses, just as whenever Mrs Bennet in *Pride and Prejudice* was discontented 'she fancied herself nervous'. Mrs Bennet lived only 'to get her daughters married', her consolation for disappointment being 'visiting and news'. Would the same fate be Jane's?

But it was the very tedium of the Rectory that forced Jane to take her daily life and turn it into art. One of her early literary admirers, Julia Kavanagh, would see through Jane's jokes to the quiet desperation beneath. Jane, wrote Kavanagh in 1862, 'seems to have been struck especially with its small vanities and small falsehoods' of life. 'If we look under the shrewdness and quiet satire of her stories,' she continued, 'we shall find a much keener sense of disappointment than of joy fulfilled.'[52] No wonder ladies turned to laudanum.

10

Novels

'. . . of all the chymical mixtures, ink is the most dangerous'.

James Austen, in *The Loiterer*

THE BORING BUSINESS of rural life in wartime Hampshire had the great advantage of allowing Jane time to write. In June 1793, aged seventeen, she finished copying out her three volumes of early works, and turned to her next project.

Elinor and Marianne was the title she chose for this early draft of the book that would end up being called *Sense and Sensibility*. The work started life as an epistolary novel. It was '*first* written in letters', according to Cassandra, '& *so* read to her family'.[1] The story was probably complete enough for Jane to read out loud to the assembled Austens in 1795, and they must have provided an appreciative audience.

It's easy to imagine the Austens clamouring of an evening for the next instalment of *Elinor and Marianne*, perhaps for the next 'letter'. For Jane's first full-length effort, an epistolary novel, following models like Richardson's *Pamela,* was an obvious choice. But it was one that she would later regret and reverse, as she reworked the book over many years. By the time *Sense and Sensibility* was published, when Jane was thirty-five, the idea of a story told in letters had not been in fashion for several decades. The reworking must have been extensive, for if they were always writing to each other, Marianne and Elinor must have been frequently apart in the original version of the plot. In *Sense and Sensibility,* on the other hand, they spend most of the time together. This major shift is early evidence of how carefully Jane would work away at her writing, drafting, rejecting and polishing her words.

In the 1790s, though, letters provided Jane with a natural medium for entertainment. Practically all Georgian gentlewomen wrote letters, and correspondence was one of the things that structured their lives. In the absence of having a lively social life to write about, Jane's own letters usually present tiny events as great ones. They are full of jokes, and stand up to reading after reading, for each time you find a new meaning.

Jane's letters to her sister fall into a category that the critic Deborah

Kaplan has called 'double-voiced'. At first sight, they look respectable, almost boring. It would be quite safe, for the most part, for Cassandra to have read aloud one of Jane's letters to the party at the breakfast table in whatever friend's house she was visiting. But at the same time, the letters can also be secretly, subtly, subversive about rank and society and gender. They contain what Kaplan calls 'intermittent *sotto voce* comments meant for women's ears alone'.[2]

This 'double-voice' of the letters also appears in the finished *Sense and Sensibility*, a story that can be read in two ways. At first glance it seems like a didactic tale: the over-emotional Marianne is taught a lesson and learns to control her feelings, while sensible Elinor is rewarded for holding hers in check. But at a second glance, it is much more of a close-run thing. Marianne, although socially wrong, is also a speaker of truth.

Of all Jane's books, *Sense and Sensibility* is often modern readers' least favourite. That's partly because it's the one that has most in common with the other novels of its time, and is therefore the most alien to us. And it's partly because it's written 'against' something that we no longer understand: the contemporary cult of sensibility.

Known as The English Malady, 'sensibility' had by the middle of the eighteenth century become a fashionable affliction for the well off. It was a classy kind of problem from which to suffer, for your nerves only became dangerously 'sensitive' if you had plenty of leisure time, and therefore lots of money, to indulge them.

Being subject to sensibility opened you up to all kinds of other serious complaints, such as melancholy, or a broken heart. This supposed susceptibility to both feelings and illnesses was deeply annoying to those who did not indulge in it, and Dr Johnson called the vogue the 'fashionable whine of sensibility'. But if you did want to appear delicate, full of sensibility, refined, it was a good idea to start by reading novels. And as people started to read more novels, with their high-blown, elevated notions about love and romance, they actually began to write to their own real-life lovers in the same sensitive, romantic terms. The cult of sensibility had reached its fullest, finest moment in Jane's youth. Hannah More, for example, the improving female writer, conflated sensibility with virtue, in *Sensibility: A Poetical Epistle* (1782):[3]

> Sweet Sensibility! thou keen delight!
> Thou hasty moral! sudden sense of right!

But as time went on, More began to think that sensibility, feelings, got in the way of duty and action. Mary Wollstonecraft also thought that sensibility was actually harming women, causing them to be soft, marsh-mallow-y creatures lacking purpose and firmness. As the critic John Mullan puts it, paraphrasing Samuel Taylor Coleridge, 'the woman of fashion will weep with the emotionally afflicted hero of Goethe's novel *Young Werther* or the helplessly sensitive young woman in Richardson's *Sir Charles Grandison* (1743–4), but forget that the sugar in her tea comes from slave plantations'.[4]

By the end of the eighteenth century, people had had quite enough of sensibility. In 1799, a spoof letter appeared in a magazine, apparently the complaint of a mother whose daughter does nothing but read novels, morning to night. 'One week she will read in the following order: *Excessive Sensibility, Refined Delicacy, Disinterested Love, Sentimental Beauty*, etc. In the next come *Horrid Mysteries, Haunted Caverns, Black Towers, Direful Incantations*, and an endless list of similar titles.'[5] And the heroines of these books were all quite useless. The modern woman, wrote Mary Robinson, crossly, 'disdains to be strong-minded, because she fears being accounted masculine; she trembles at every breeze, faints at every peril, and yields to every assailant'.[6]

Among Jane's important innovations as a novelist would be her deci-sion to make her heroines less than perfect, but much more than weak-minded. Indeed, they could, by contemporary standards, be posi-tively brash. They fizz with purpose and energy, they make mistakes, they learn. Marianne, this character Jane was creating in her late teens, is so eager to *feel* that her emotional vulnerability becomes pitiful. She falls in love with the caddish Willoughby precisely because he displays wonderful sensibility of his own. He speaks to her of poetry and novels they've both read, of landscape, of music. But when Marianne falls in love, indulges her sensibility, it makes her physically sick: her head aches, she is 'unable to talk, and unwilling to take any nourishment'. At first it's just an immature reaction to heartache. But finally, when Willoughby really breaks up with her, and she takes a despairing walk in the rain, it takes a more serious turn. She falls genuinely and dangerously ill. 'Sensibility' has put her life at risk.

To us, today, the mawkish Marianne perhaps arouses more sympathy than Jane's earliest readers would have been able to summon up. For in truth, apart from throwing tantrums what other means does Marianne have of objecting to the society that limits her life choices so completely? Once she's dumped by Willoughby, Marianne's friends decide that she should marry the boring but steady Colonel Brandon instead. As the critic Tony Tanner put it, in an influential argument, the 'muffled scream from Marianne at the heart of the novel' is a symptom of the sickness of society.[7] In some ways, she is *right* to scream. How else can she make her needs and feelings known? Jane hated the namby-pamby behaviour of Marianne's passive predecessors. 'Pictures of perfection', she wrote, 'make me sick & wicked'.

Hand in hand with her love of sensibility, Marianne raves about anything 'picturesque', just like Jane with her fondness for William Gilpin, one of the concept's originators. But again Jane shows that you can take a passion for wild landscape too far. She has her hero, Edward Ferrars, take a more pragmatic view. Marianne might call a hill 'bold', but Edward calls it 'steep'. She might find a landscape 'strange and uncouth', but he thinks it 'irregular and rugged'. Edward does 'not like ruined, tattered cottages': 'I am not fond of nettles, of thistles . . . a troop of tidy happy villagers please me better than the finest *banditti* in the world.' Eventually even Marianne admits that a passion for untamed, romantic landscape may 'become a mere jargon. Everybody pretends to feel and tries to describe with the taste' of a Gilpin, but fails miserably. Sensibility and the picturesque: these, then, were the vogue words of the 1790s that Jane attacked in her first full-length novel. *Elinor and Marianne* was rooted very firmly in its own particular moment of creation, and knowing the background makes reading it even more rewarding.

In 1794, probably with *Elinor and Marianne* in progress, an important event took place at Steventon Rectory. It showed that Jane's writing was becoming rather more serious than just another accomplishment. In December, for her nineteenth birthday, Jane's father bought her a 'Small Mahogany Writing Desk with 1 Long Drawer and Glass Ink Stand Compleat'.[8] There are several compartments within the desk, which can be folded up and locked. You can lift the leather, sloped writing surface to slip papers beneath it, or else use the secure drawer in the side. This meant that Jane now had some private space – small in dimension, but very significant – which was all her own, not her mother's, her father's, or her sister's. And it was to be followed by further encroachments onto other people's territory. The next year, she obtained a room of her own.

For Marianne in *Sense and Sensibility*, one of the great advantages of marriage to Willoughby was that it promised her a lovely room, a:

> remarkably pretty sitting room up stairs; of a nice comfortable size for constant use . . . it is a corner room, and has windows on two sides. On one side you look across the bowling-green, behind the house, to a beautiful hanging wood, and on the other you have a view of the church and village.[9]

It takes her rational sister Elinor to point out that until Marianne is formally engaged to Willoughby, and until the house's owner dies and leaves it to him, she really shouldn't delight so much in his real estate. To do so reveals far too much about her expectations.

Jane, growing up in a house full of boys, must have been well able to understand the longing for a pretty feminine sitting room. To her heroines, it's always a life goal to be happy and 'at home', particularly in a drawing room, the stage upon which most of social life's transactions are performed. Fanny Price in *Mansfield Park*, for example, is seen at first more often in the attic, on the stairs, or in the window recess, until she eventually grows in confidence enough to come downstairs, to make herself at home in the drawing room, and eventually even to dance there: 'she had hardly ever been in a state so nearly approaching high spirits in her life . . . and was actually practising her steps about the drawing-room'. At the start of Anne Elliot's story, *Persuasion*, Captain Wentworth makes his first appearance in the drawing room for only 'a few minutes'; he hardly speaks to her. Anne observes him dallying at the window. Only at the end of the story is he firmly and fully present in the room, all his attention directed towards her, writing her a letter as if his life depended upon it. Both of these heroines edge closer and closer to a house's beating heart, and both end up with drawing rooms of their own. The only heroine who feels no need to skulk in corners is the magnificent Emma Woodhouse, who is already queen of her own drawing room, and who eventually invites her successful suitor, Mr Knightley, to move in and share it with her.[10]

In 1795, when Jane was nineteen, a major improvement to her life in the Rectory at Steventon took place. One of the bedchambers over the dining room was repurposed into a private chamber, 'a sort of Drawing room' for 'the grown up young ladies'. The room became known as 'the Dressing room', and it communicated 'with one of smaller size' where Jane and Cassandra slept. It had only been possible for them to expand their territory in this way after the contraction of the household with the departure of their brothers and the pupils.

The real stuff of Jane's life is to be found recorded in the pages of her father's account with the furniture depot run by Mr John Ring in the nearby market town of Basingstoke: his red-brick premises still survive there today. Mr Ring's clerk recorded a seemingly endless succession of items, both small and large, going off to the Rectory over the years. They range from a 'meat screen lined with tin' to 'a Neat Japand Rack for Dry Toast' and a 'Red Leather Carpet Broom'.[11] And it's through this account book that we also know a good deal about the furnishing of the room where Jane wrote at least the first draft of her first three novels.

Mr Ring's accounts give early clues to the environment the sisters would inhabit for the rest of their lives: a simple, cheaply furnished interior garnished with small but treasured items. Mr Austen, who paid for everything, would cut corners where possible. On the same day that he purchased a 'Large Wilton Carpet' for one of the downstairs rooms, for example, he also bought '3 Remnants' of carpet for the Rectory's less important spaces.[12] Mr Ring had items to suit all comers, such as fine furniture for noblemen, whom he allowed to run up credit. And yet when James Austen came to furnish the parsonage of Deane for his new wife in 1792, Mr Ring was happy to lend him a second-hand sofa.[13]

'I remember the common-looking carpet', a family member would later recall about the sisters' new room, 'with its chocolate ground . . . a painted press, with shelves above for books, that stood with its back to the wall next the Bedroom, & opposite the fireplace; my Aunt Jane's Pianoforte'.[14] Mr Austen had ordered the bookcase from Mr Ring, along with the blue-stripe window curtains (old curtains washed and made up anew), the chocolate-coloured paint, the blue wallpaper, and the yellow deal cornice.[15]

But the most important items in the room ('above all' else, in the recollection of Jane's niece) stood beneath a mirror 'on a table between the windows'. These were '2 Tonbridge-ware work boxes of oval shape, fitted up with ivory barrels containing reels for silk, yard measures, etc'.[16] The workboxes suggest that the room must have been used for the endless dressmaking and cap-trimming mentioned in Jane's letters. At Winchester Museum, you can still see an item that might have lived inside Jane's workbox: a delicate, tubular ivory case with a lid marked 'JA', displayed as Jane's, and possessing a good provenance. She used it for storing wound silk thread. Alongside it is a tiny blue purse of beads that Jane, by tradition, is said to have made herself. It was typical of the little handmade articles and gifts that came out of these workboxes, inexpensive but nevertheless highly significant physical reminders of relationships. For example, Jane made and gave a little 'housewife', or fabric bag containing needles, to her friend Mary Lloyd upon Mary's leaving the neighbourhood, with a note recording its significance:

> And as we are about to part
> 'Twill serve another end,
> For when you look upon the bag
> You'll recollect your Freind. – Jan.ry 1792[17]

Of course, as Mary ended up as Jane's sister-in-law, they would not be parted for very long, and their close relationship would continue to the very end of Jane's life.

These workboxes, then, were rich in private meaning for the ladies, enabling them to make and give gifts. 'I thought them beautiful', their niece Anna admits, '& so perhaps in their day, & their degree, they were.' They were also – like the rest of the room – attractively private. There were no boys here; it was a private realm for talking and dreaming. 'The charm of the room,' it was later said, 'with its scanty furniture and cheaply papered walls must have been . . . the flow of native home bred wit'.[18]

In the bedroom beyond were the sisters' two beds, bought for them the previous year of 1794 by their father, once again from Mr Ring. Perhaps, until this point, they had even shared a bed, like so many other Georgian people (especially servants). Jane was happy to spend a night with her friend Martha, for example, in a fold-out bed that 'did exceedingly well for us, both to lie awake in & talk till two o'clock, & to sleep the rest of the night'. But Jane liked best to share with Cassandra, or else to be by herself. When Jane was away from home, she once wrote of 'the pleasure of writing from my *own* room . . . with everything very comfortable about me'.

Mr Ring kept his customers' records in enormous, leather-bound books, with a separate index covered in a rather beautiful, French-grey patterned piece of Georgian wallpaper. That's how we know that Mr Austen in 1794 had placed an order for his daughters' '2 Tent Bedsteads on Casters' with turned posts and 'Maho-Nobs' (mahogany knobs!). Each bed cost £1.4s.0d, not a vast sum, but then there were the fabric elements to purchase as well: forty-two yards of cotton, in blue and white check; sixty-nine yards of blue and white diamond lace; ticking, or tough fabric, to encase goose and hen feathers for the bolsters. The costs of thread and labour brought the total for the two beds to £21.1s.0d.[19]

The historian Edward Copeland points out that this was careful, moderate expenditure, as befitted Mr Austen's careful, moderate station in life. In the same account book, a richer customer, Sir Henry Paulet St John Mildmay, bought a similar bed, but with 'the best goose feathers' and more expensive, lined curtains of white dimity, which came to £25.16s.10d. The baronet's bed therefore cost more than £25, as opposed to the clergyman's daughters' beds at just over £10 each. But it's also noticeable, in Ring's ledgers, that Miss Mainwarring, a teacher 'At the School', paid just £1.5s.0d for her bed. She had no extras, flounces, curtains or accoutrements at all. As a schoolmistress, she had to get such things second hand.[20] Mr Austen himself, to save money, traded in used furniture for credit with Mr Ring, handing over an old bed for credit of £1 and 18 shillings.[21]

That detailed description of the dressing room, the holy of holies, comes from Jane's niece Anna, who was often at Steventon, and who now enters our story. In May 1795, Anna's mother, James Austen's first wife Anne, fell ill at Deane. James described having heard a curious knocking at the parsonage door, as if Death were seeking admittance.[22] Die Anne did, leaving James as a widower with a little girl. Young Anna caused so much pain by 'constantly asking and fretting for "Mama"' that her father could not bear it, and sent her away to Steventon to be taken care of by her Aunts Cassandra and Jane.[23]

When James remarried, there was a certain satisfaction in his choosing Jane's friend Mary Lloyd, because Mary and her sister Martha had been kicked out of Deane Parsonage to make way for James to live there with his first wife. Mary, efficient, often even officious, insisted that her very small dowry should be spent on paying James's debts when she returned to her old home as his wife. She was the sort of person who was 'delighted' with a gift of a mangle, when Jane at the same time got pink shoes. But despite her gift for organising things, Mary could not get on with her stepdaughter, and as a consequence Anna continued to be much at Steventon with her aunts.

Anna, seventeen years younger than Jane, is nevertheless an important witness to her aunt's early life. Unlike some other members of the family, Anna was scrupulous not to embroider or talk up her recollections. 'I look back to the first period', she admitted later, 'but find little that I can grasp of any substance, or certainty: it seems now all so shadowy!'[24]

And so Anna was too young, and too truthful, to be able to tell us much about Jane's first recorded romance, which unfolded soon after the move into the dressing room. But luckily, and despite the Austen family's efforts to hush it up, there are other sources who can tell us more.

11

'My Irish friend'

'She began to curl her hair and long for balls.'

Northanger Abbey

O NE OF THE challenges of uncovering Jane's romance over the New Year of 1795–6, when she was twenty-one, is that her relatives don't want us to know about it. 'I think I need not warn *you* against raking up that old story', one of them writes.[1]

And another obstacle lies in the difficulty of discovering what the various emotions we feel today actually felt like two hundred years ago. Jane Austen's biographers tend to treat her like just another modern person, reacting to the situations in exactly the same way as the writer would him or herself. But untangling the history of emotions – a relatively new field of historical study – has to be undertaken with care. Consider falling in love, for example. To Jane, to fall in love, to embark upon a romance, would have felt rather more daring and risky than it might today. Despite the innovations of Samuel Richardson and other romantic novelists, Jane's family and friends would still have placed much more emphasis on practicality, feasibility, and the financial viability of a match than we would now when we're told, above all things, to 'follow our hearts'.

But fall in love she did. And we do know something of Jane's own views on the vital importance of romance in a relationship from her later role as an agony aunt to her own young nieces. In 1814, she wrote to her twenty-one-year-old niece Fanny, counselling her against marrying just any young man who happened to come along. 'When I consider how few young Men you have yet seen,' Jane advised, 'and how full in temptation the next 6 or 7 years of your Life will probably be', she thought that Fanny really should take her time.

The years between twenty-one and twenty-eight, Jane considered, form 'the very period of Life for the *strongest* attachments to be formed'. And it was just after she had turned twenty-one herself that she formed the relationship that's intrigued posterity the most.

But just how close was Jane's relationship with this elusive lover? Many of her biographers, anxious to rescue her from accusations of coldness, long to imagine that she did fall in love and had her heart broken, and have gone to extraordinary lengths to argue that this is what happened. Unfortunately, the facts don't completely add up because, as always, *Jane was joking.*

As well as telling the story of Jane and Tom, in this chapter we'll see how far we can really penetrate into Jane's heart.

In 1795, Tom Fowle was still alive, Cassandra was getting married; Jane would marry too. It was inevitable. The first step towards marriage was to go to balls. As Jane knew, and as she had her fictional ladies of Meryton put it, 'to be fond of dancing was a certain step towards falling in love'. Jane herself danced with a vengeance. At their balls of the 1790s the gentlefolk of Hampshire did not see Jane Austen, the serious, committed novelist. Instead, some of them saw 'the prettiest, silliest, most affected husband-hunting butterfly'.[2]

The 'butterfly' had an excellent instructor in the art of 'husband-hunting', in the form of her cousin Eliza. 'Let me have', Eliza would imperiously declare, 'a full & particular account of all your <u>Flirtations</u>.'[3] Of each suitor, she wanted to know 'is he tall or short, fair or brown, & particularly are his eyes <u>black</u> or <u>blue</u>?'[4] All this would have given an apoplexy to the sermon-writer James Fordyce. 'I have known women of considerable merit', he warned, balefully, 'who have remained uncon-nected, and become forlorn, for no other reason but . . . the allurements which they scattered, without discrimination or choice, amongst all the men of their acquaintance.'[5] Jane didn't care for his sermons, and in *Pride and Prejudice* she would use them to make Lydia Bennet yawn.

'There were twenty Dances,' Jane wrote of one ball, '& I danced them all.' Each party was closely analysed afterwards for its success or otherwise as a marriage mart: 'There were 31 People & only 11 Ladies out of the Number, & but five single women in the room.' Good odds. Jane even managed to wear out Eliza, who complained from Steventon Rectory in 1792 that she had missed two balls because confined to bed by a 'feverish Attack'.

These two particular balls were 'a private one in the neighbourhood' of Steventon, and 'a Club Ball at Basingstoke'.[6] The backbone of Hampshire's dancing season was formed by the public balls at Basingstoke Town Hall, held monthly on Thursday nights. The county's gentry families would travel miles to dance, sometimes staying overnight at each other's houses for convenience.

The Basingstoke balls were organised by Mrs Martin, the landlady of the Maidenhead Inn. An advert like this one from January 1793 would appear in the *Reading Mercury* newspaper: 'THE next ASSEMBLY will be at the Town Hall, on Tuesday January the 22d'.[7] The balls were to 'begin precisely at nine o'clock', and were open both to subscribers, and to non-subscribers willing to pay the higher one-off fee.[8] This meant that they weren't all that exclusive. An ambitious young man was well advised not to 'lose [his] senses by dancing with the Belles of Basingstoke'.[9]

The excitement of the evening began with dressing, the moment when 'the first Bliss of a Ball began'. As Jane would put it in *The Watsons*, female camaraderie was important for getting up one's courage. This was the time when strange girls, thrown upon each other's company by the vagaries of family friendship or shared transport, ended up 'dressing in some measure together' and growing 'unavoidably better acquainted'. Jane's family recipe book includes instructions for the preparations they used, such as Lavender Water, Coral Tooth Powder and Soap for Hands.[10] Rouge or blusher was tarty, and therefore to be avoided, but Jane had the great advantage of naturally red cheeks. Dancers would certainly dress up as much as they could: one lady, after a Basingstoke ball in 1773, lost 'A DIAMOND PIN, set in the Form of a Rose; supposed to be dropt in the Hall, or on the Stair Case', and offered a guinea reward for its return.[11]

When everyone was ready, there would be dinner, and a carriage ride to the venue, whether the Town Hall, a private house, or – as in *The Watsons* or *Emma* – an inn. In *The Watsons*, the dancers arriving at the inn had their senses excited by 'the bustle, noise & draughts of air of the broad Entrance-passage . . . the first Scrape of one violin' coming towards them down 'the wide staircase'.

The Watsons also allowed Jane to reveal some of the tricks employed by provincial assembly-goers to make the best of an evening out. A mature lady, dressed in 'one of the two Sattin gowns which went thro' the winter', would turn up early 'to get a good place by the fire', while a pushy young man would lurk about 'in the Passage' in order to make an entrance alongside, as if a member of, the party of the only nobleman to attend.

You didn't actually need all that much space to hold a ball, and a large domestic drawing room or inn parlour would do; indeed a dinner party might turn into an impromptu dance afterwards if someone present could play the piano. Length was more important than width, as demonstrated by the ballroom at the Dolphin Inn in Southampton, where Jane danced on her eighteenth birthday. At least four times as long as it is wide, this space worked well for the country dance, where participants form two lines in a long set. Its origin was not in fact as rural as its name suggested: it's a corruption of the *contre-danse*, or French minuet. Dancers were not yet clasping their arms around their partners, as they would do in the Regency waltz. Instead, man and woman approached, joined hands, and parted again, in an elegant, stately, sober pastiche of seduction.

Jane herself was 'fond of dancing, and excelled in it'.[12] Although there is no mention of her having a teacher, she could well have learned from her friends Mary and Martha Lloyd. These two had been sent weekly to a dancing school in Newbury for 'a whole day of dancing. They began in the morning . . . had another dancing lesson in the evening, and after tea the carriage fetched them home.' This was essential training for the scary moment when Mary or Martha should be called upon 'to open the Newbury Assemblies with a minuet'.[13]

After the dancing came more eating: a good ball could boast both 'plenty of Gentlemen & a very elegant supper'.[14] The supper might begin with the celebrated 'white soup' mentioned by Mr Bingley in *Pride and Prejudice* as an essential ingredient for a party. 'White soup' started out as a seventeenth-century French dish called 'Potage à la Reine' containing ground almonds boiled in bouillon. It eventually made its way into English cookery, appearing in William Verral's cookbook of 1759 under the name of 'Queen's Soup'. By the end of the century, it still contained the almonds and the stock, but also, perhaps, cream, egg yolk, white bread and anchovies.[15]

Jane also danced in private mansions, like Manydown Park, or Deane House, where balls were held on the night of the full moon so people could see their way home. 'It was a delightful evening', wrote Mrs Lefroy after one party at Steventon Rectory itself, and 'the nightingales in full song serenaded us as we passed through the grove'.[16] That night she was home by eleven, but her letters show she quite often stayed out at balls until two, three, even six o'clock in the morning.

And during the strange, unsettling period when Cassandra was engaged to Tom, it was at a ball at Deane House that Jane met and danced with a Tom of her own. Over the course of two more balls, at Manydown Park, and at Ashe Rectory, she seems to have fallen in love with Thomas Langlois Lefroy.

Who was this young man who has intrigued generations of Janeites? Three weeks younger than Jane, he too had just turned twenty-one. His portrait gives him a prominent nose and chin, but a kindly, amused face with dark eyes and eyebrows. He was a young law student from Limerick who had studied at Trinity College, Dublin, before coming to London for further training. He brought with him across the Irish Sea a fine reputation. 'No young man has left our College with a higher character', wrote his Trinity tutor, 'I feel for him as a son or brother.'[17]

Tom would need his many fine qualities, for he had quite a challenging path through life already mapped out clearly before him. He was one of eleven children from an imprudent marriage. His father, Anthony Lefroy, of Huguenot descent, had ended up serving in Ireland as a Colonel of the Dragoons. There he had fallen in love with Ann, the daughter of an Irish squire, and secretly married her. They hoped for a boy, but their first five children were girls. Perhaps Tom's five older sisters gave Jane the idea for the family circumstances of the Bennets in *Pride and Prejudice*.

Tom, the eldest son, became the favourite of his rich great-uncle Benjamin Langlois, who had paid for his education at Trinity College. Uncle Benjamin may have been 'fatiguingly ceremonious, with abilities not much above the common', but he was the only member of the family with any money.[18] And he must therefore be obeyed. Tom's great drawback as husband material was that he had just so many family obligations: to please Uncle Benjamin, to make a career, and to help his ten siblings.

So Tom was under pressure. As a result he'd worked rather too hard during his studies at the Middle Temple. He strained his weak eyes, and even Uncle Benjamin told him to slow down, recommending 'the propriety of his reading for some time as little as may be by candle-light'.[19] A holiday was needed; Hampshire was chosen. Tom's recuperation and Christmas break took place at the Rectory of his uncle Mr Lefroy, rector at Ashe.

And so Tom came to stay with Mr and Madam Lefroy at Ashe Rectory, 'scarcely a mile' from Steventon by the meadow path, and so he came to dance at Deane, and at Manydown Park. At that particular ball, Jane fought off the attentions of the assiduous John Lyford in order to accept the dance invitations of this attractive new young man who was quite fresh to the over-familiar Hampshire dancing scene.

One reason that Tom Lefroy looms so large in the story of Jane Austen's love life is that it is precisely from the moment of his arrival in Hampshire that Jane's surviving letters begin. Cassandra was away from home, staying with her future in-laws the Fowles, and in need of all the Steventon gossip. In the first sentence of her earliest surviving letter, dated 9 January 1796, Jane congratulates her sister on her twenty-third birthday, and hopes that she will live twenty-three years longer. And why should Cassandra not? The sombre undertone was that they both knew that as soon as she was married, she would probably run the risks of childbirth. And in the second sentence is a mention of Tom Lefroy, the gentleman of whom Jane herself had hopes.

To Cassandra, then, Jane writes that 'we had an exceeding good ball last night . . . I am almost afraid to tell you how my Irish friend [that's Mr Lefroy] and I behaved.' The young people could indeed have an outrageous time at balls: on another occasion, Jane admitted, 'I drank too much wine last night . . . I know not how else to account for the shaking of my hand to day.'

Jane in these letters shows herself to be predatory and confident, just like the heroines of her early stories. After three balls, she tells us, she felt well able '*to be particular*' with Mr Lefroy. Indeed, everyone knew that she was after him. When she visited him at Madam Lefroy's house, she tells us, he was feeling 'so excessively laughed at' about her that 'he ran away'. And indeed, all of Jane's fictional characters who win the interest of sexy men – Marianne Dashwood, Lydia Bennet, Maria Bertram – knew exactly what they were up to; the gold-digger Mrs Clay in *Persuasion* perhaps most of all. All this despite Samuel Richardson's view that for a girl to chase a boy was technically impossible: 'an heterodoxy which prudence, and even policy, must not allow'.[20] But Jane knew of course that this was rubbish. In *Northanger Abbey* she would make Catherine Morland fall fairly and squarely in love with a young man who did not appear to return her feelings.

This rapacious self-confidence is another side of Jane's character that was later hushed up by her pious relatives. 'I can indeed bear witness', wrote her nephew in years to come, 'that there was scarcely a charm in her most delightful characters that was not a true reflection of her own sweet temper and loving heart.'[21] A sweet temper, a loving heart. The latter is exhibited in her letters, but not always the former. And I don't think James Edward Austen-Leigh would have wholly approved of the young lady who, in 1796, attracted attention with Tom Lefroy at balls by 'everything most profligate and shocking in the way of dancing and sitting down together'.

Three balls later, though, there was to be only one final opportunity for Jane and Tom to make a spectacle of themselves. 'I *can* expose myself . . . only *once more*,' she writes to Cassandra, 'because he leaves the country soon after next Friday, on which day we *are* to have a dance at Ashe.' More seriously, she tells her sister that Tom is 'a very gentlemanlike, good-looking, pleasant young man'.

During the build-up to this final ball before Tom was due to leave Hampshire, the tension was ratcheted even higher by a visit from the hero himself to Steventon Rectory. 'After I had written the above,' Jane reported in a blow-by-blow account, 'we received a visit from Mr Tom Lefroy . . . he has but *one* fault . . . it is that his morning coat is a great deal too light'. What's wrong, one might ask, with a light-coloured morning coat? Well, every girl knows the phenomenon of the 'fixer-upper' boyfriend, who presents promising material, but who is just a little *wrong* in the shoes or the trousers. Blue, not white, was the fashionable colour for coats, as worn by the hero of *The Sorrows of Young Werther* (1774); Lydia fantasises about Mr Wickham in his blue coat in *Pride and Prejudice*. Jane pretends to imagine that Mr Lefroy, an admirer of *Tom Jones*, wore a white coat to emulate the novel's hero, similarly palely attired.²² She didn't like Tom Lefroy's coat, but she did like the fact that they'd read and could talk about the same books.

The day of the much-anticipated dance at Ashe at last arrives. 'I look forward with great impatience to it,' Jane confides to her sister, 'as I rather expect to receive an offer from my friend in the course of the evening.' Oh! It's just like a novel! Surely it will reach the expected climax of a proposal?

But then, Jane's letter goes on to undercut it all, revealing that, as usual, she is not taking things very seriously. 'I shall refuse him,' she says, 'unless he promises to give away his white Coat.' So she didn't mean it. Or did she? 'At length the Day is come', she sighs, 'on which I am to flirt my last with Tom Lefroy, & when you receive this it will be over – My tears flow as I write, at the melancholy idea.'

They did dance that night at Ashe, but no proposal came. Jane's letter about the flowing tears has been read as evidence of a broken heart, but the tricky thing is that Jane – as always – *was joking*. She could play many different roles at the same time. For one thing, she was also flirting with Charles Fowle, brother of Cassandra's Tom. For another, she spent her whole life playing a game with Cassandra in which she pretended to be irresistible, and her suitors unstoppable. Listen to this. On one visit to a Hampshire neighbour, she

> was shut up in the drawing-room with Mr Holder alone for ten minutes.
> I had some thoughts of insisting on the housekeeper [. . .] being sent for,
> and nothing could prevail me to move two steps from the door, on the
> lock of which I kept one hand constantly fixed.

Only a lady of perfect self-confidence can make jokes like this. In time to come Jane would go on in the same vein to jest about her plans to marry the local rector Mr Papillon for his excellent sermons, or the poet George Crabbe for his beautiful poetry. And when at last she fell for a military man, Captain Pasley of the Engineers ('the first soldier I ever sighed for'), it was not because she had met and danced with him; it was because she had enjoyed his book on *The Military Policy and Institutions of the British Empire* (1810).

Among the songs and music copied out by Jane, and surviving today at the Jane Austen House Museum, lies a song with the chorus 'there's none can love like an Irishman'. It sounds like a wistful, poignant song of longing, which maybe Jane transcribed with Tom in mind.[23] But when you come to sing it, you realise that it is pure comedy. The song makes a tour of the world, and rejects the lover-like properties of the Turks, the French, the Spanish and the Italians, all in favour of the Irish. It lingers on the ridiculously high notes that were the speciality of the tenor comic for whom it was written. It was *a joke*.[24]

So Jane's torrents of tears were not literal. She was presenting herself as one of the heroines of the mushy novels that she loved to hate. 'It is no creed of mine', Jane wrote, 'that such sort of disappointments kill anybody.' And indeed, she's soon to be found saying of Tom Lefroy that she did 'not care sixpence' for him.

We need to turn to Tom himself if we want evidence that there was any more to this romance than a great deal of teasing. And there, surprisingly, we find it. While Jane may well have been making the running, causing him embarrassment, he did enjoy it all: the flirting, the joking, the fuss. He was a person, his descendants thought, of 'great shyness'.[25] But he admitted later that he was in love with her too, with 'a boyish love'. Boyish, he said, but it was 'love' nonetheless.[26]

So why didn't he propose that night at Ashe, when Jane expected (or at least, *joked* that she expected) him to? Why did he leave the next day?

According to private family letters, Tom Lefroy's departure was no accident. It was deliberately engineered to break off a growing romance. 'It was a disappointment,' this source runs, 'but Mrs Lefroy sent the gentleman off . . . that no more mischief might be done.'[27] Tom had all those brothers and sisters to think about, and he could not afford to marry a penniless parson's daughter. According to this source, matters had not progressed as far as an offer of marriage: 'there was *no* engagement, & never *had* been'.[28]

But in the most romantic of all Jane's novels, her last completed work, *Persuasion*, she writes about a young couple parted by the supposedly wise words of the heroine's older friend before gaining an unexpected second chance at love. And it's all too tempting to believe that the story of Tom and Jane likewise doesn't end there.

The spring of 1796 must have been a terrible one at the Rectory. The dancing was over, and both Toms gone. Tom Lefroy was back in London; Tom Fowle was dead. Some months later, the Austens had recovered enough spirit to feel the need for diversion, and her brothers took Jane to London on a jaunt. 'Here I am once more in this Scene of Dissipation & vice,' she wrote back to Cassandra on 23 August, 'and I begin already to find my Morals corrupted.' In the company of Frank and Edward, Jane set out to enjoy the city. Any hint of a broken heart is well hidden. 'We are to be at Astley's to night,' she says, meaning Astley's Amphitheatre with its circus show, 'which I am glad of . . . I must leave off, for we are going out.'

One historian, Jon Spence, has constructed a highly elegant house of cards by suggesting that Jane's motivation for going to London was – still – to chase after Tom Lefroy. When she writes of 'Dissipation & vice', he argues, she was referring to what she was getting up to with him. It is a striking suggestion. Tom's great-uncle Benjamin Langlois lived on Cork Street, the address given in Jane's letter. There were no hotels on Cork Street, and the Austens knew no one else who lived here. Spence's ingenious argument runs that Jane and her brothers must have stayed with Uncle Benjamin – after all, the Lefroys were practically family – and that there, in Cork Street, she was reunited with Tom once again.[29]

Sadly for those who long for Jane to have had the chance of a night of passion as she stayed under the same roof as Tom Lefroy for the first and last time, Jane's visit to London took place in August. It wasn't term-time at the Inns of Court. Tom would most likely have gone home to Ireland.[30]

Besides, even if Jane had been up for 'dissipation', the opinion of his tutors suggests that Tom wasn't. 'Of his [Tom's] conduct in London, however seducing its idleness and its evils, you need not have the slightest doubt', it was said. 'He is, in his religious principles . . . fortified in every place.'[31]

Indeed, his tutor gives the impression of Tom Lefroy as a goodie-goodie, devoted to his studies, and unlikely to have led Jane on. Uncle Benjamin, too, thought he had 'a good heart, a good mind, good sense'.[32] And Tom's own family papers suggest that he was emotionally committed elsewhere even before he'd arrived in England. He was already acquainted with one Miss Mary Paul, a sister of his friend from Trinity College, Dublin.[33] He would become engaged to her in 1797.

Once he had finished his studies and returned to Dublin, the intelligent and hardworking young barrister made quite a stir. After only two years, Tom Lefroy beat Jane into print by getting published. His *Proceedings by Elegit for recovery of Judgement Debts* doesn't sound like a page-turner, but it was described as a 'solid' and 'perspicuous' work.[34]

Tom's letters to Mary, now his wife, also tended towards the stolid

and sermonical. One wonders how she took his advice about the desir-
ability of devoting every spare moment to Bible reading or else to
'detecting the lurking-place of sin'. One wonders how Mary viewed her
marriage itself, when Tom told her that earthly affections 'should not
form the stay, and hope, and prop of life'.[35] Poor Mary, to be told that
she was not the stay, and hope, and prop of his life! And perhaps, lucky
Jane, ultimately, to avoid this pompous, Puritanical bore. Certainly it was
lucky for us, for as Mrs Lefroy she would have given birth to babies,
not books.

And yet. Time went by, for Jane, and the time for joking was over.
Tom had moved on but she had not. Back in Hampshire, she was 'too
proud', as she put it, to ask Madam Lefroy what he was up to. In
November 1798, there was news at last: 'Mrs Lefroy did come last
Wednesday . . . of her nephew she said nothing at all . . . I was too
proud to make enquiries; but on my father's afterwards asking where he
was, I learnt that he is called to the Bar and means to practise.' Jane's
father had the sensitivity to ask what his daughter could not.

Despite the deliberate lightness of heart, there is certainly a glimpse
of pain there, with Jane not daring to ask where Tom had gone, for fear
of looking as if she were still in love with him.

This is traditionally the end of the story of the romance of Tom Lefroy,
with uncertainty and regret trailing in its wake. But there is more. In
this same letter of November 1798 Jane mentions another young man,
who was a second, and perhaps more serious, suitor for her hand.

This was a Reverend Samuel Blackall, of Cambridge, a 'tall, overbearing
personage', frightening to some little girls. But he was chatty and outgoing,
and the little girls gradually came to like him: his 'good humour banished
our natural fear'.[36]

We hear that in 1798 he wrote to Mrs Lefroy of the 'particular pleasure'
he would find in getting to know the Austen family better, 'with a hope
of creating to myself a nearer interest'. This must surely mean a marriage
proposal. He sounds awfully like Mr Collins, writing to propose himself
for a visit, and being privately determined that he would, while he was
there, marry one of the family's daughters. And yet Reverend Samuel
Blackall lacked Mr Collins' admirable persistence. Perhaps it was money,
perhaps there was some other factor, but he wasn't quite yet in a position
to get married: 'at present I cannot indulge any expectation of it'.

Jane, when she heard about this non-proposal of marriage, seemed
not at all distressed. 'This is rational enough', she says, 'there is less love
and more sense in it than sometimes appeared before, and I am very
well satisfied. It will all go on exceedingly well, and decline away in a

very reasonable manner.' By now she had adopted that guarded, cynical air that would characterise her views on men and marriage as she grew older and tougher. 'It is therefore most probable', she concluded, 'that our indifference will soon be mutual.'

It's utterly impossible to know if this is pride speaking, or just Austen acid. Certainly Madam Lefroy made no comment on Reverend Blackall, but then, as Jane herself says, maybe Madam Lefroy was sick of playing Cupid, having made a mess over Tom Lefroy: 'perhaps she thinks she has said too much already'. However, despite appearances, that is not quite the last we will hear of Reverend Blackall.

And how did Tom Lefroy end up? He did well in life. He became Chief Justice of Ireland, outliving Jane by more than fifty years. As time went on, and Jane's fame grew, he was inevitably asked about his association with her in their youth. In his extreme old age, he would still sometimes speak of her. He was heard to say, cryptically, that she was 'one to be much admired, and not easily forgotten by those who had ever known her'.[37] *That* was the verdict for public consumption, but the private family letters of Jane's niece reveal a little bit more: that he had mentioned Jane just before he died, and that 'to the last year of his life she was remembered as the object of his youthful admiration'.[38]

So Jane's 'Irish friend' wasn't quite the reckless, passionate, perfect life-partner snatched from her by cruel fate that a casual reading of her letters might suggest. Tom himself was a rather dull law student who made a prudent marriage under family pressure, accidentally tossed to our attention by the sweeping tail of Jane's fame.

But he had also been a little in love, and been loved a little in return. And he's given us the gift of being able to see Jane, clearly, for the first time as a human being: with her pride bristling up, and her defences down.

12

First Impressions

'I have in my possession a Manuscript Novel,
comprised in three Vols.'

George Austen to the publisher Thomas Cadell

WHILE BALLS WERE attended, and marriages made, a new novel
was being created from scratch in that new private dressing room
upstairs at Steventon Rectory. Called *First Impressions*, it was the story
that would eventually end up published as *Pride and Prejudice*.

As well as recreating the very believable experience of being on the
marriage market, the takeover of the Rectory dressing room also found
its way into Jane's best-known book. The two sisters had encroached
upon formerly male territory by expanding the Rectory's female
domain with their dressing room. In *Pride and Prejudice*, something
similar happens when Charlotte Lucas after her marriage to Mr Collins
gradually takes over the running of his house, and stealthily achieves
what one historian has called a 'quietly aggressive redistribution of
space at Hunsford Parsonage'.[1] Charlotte picks a small chamber to be
'the room in which the ladies sat', deliberately choosing a cramped
and less pleasant room to make it less likely that her husband will
come in. Subtle and manipulative, this was the way to stake a claim
to domestic space.

According to Cassandra, Jane began her work on *First Impressions* in
the October of 1796, and finished it in August 1797. This indicates a
fairly rapid rate of progress on a book that would end up at 120,000
words, and that was after a good deal of it was cut. How did Cassandra
know the dates so exactly? Biographer Claire Tomalin has cleverly
suggested that it must have been because Jane wrote them down in a
now-lost diary. The implication is that steady, daily work was underway,
the work of someone committed to becoming a novelist. As with *Sense
and Sensibility*, there would be years of reworking, 'alterations & contrac-
tions', before *Pride and Prejudice* was eventually published.[2]

Her brother Henry described Jane's novels, with their many drafts, as
'gradual performances'.[3] And *Pride and Prejudice* was written for a more

literal type of 'performance', too: as entertainment for the family circle. This novel – indeed, all Jane's novels, with their extended and theatrical dialogue sections – works particularly well when read aloud, as was the custom on quiet evenings in the country. The Austens did their best to limit the number of candles they lit after dark. To light a room abundantly was a sensation that felt, quite literally, like burning money (hence the expression, 'the game's not worth the candle'). The Austens probably favoured the cheaper tallow, or animal-fat, candles instead of wax. 'Wax candles in the school-room! You may imagine how desirable', says Jane's character, Mrs Elton, of a particularly opulent household. So, if there were no guests, perhaps only a couple of candles were lit, the family gathered, one of them read, and the others listened. Even Jane's niece little Anna heard the story being read 'in the parsonage at Dean – while I was in the room, & not expected to listen'. But:

> Listen I did, with so much interest, & with so much talk afterwards about 'Jane & Elizabeth' that it was resolved, for prudence sake, to read no more of the story aloud in my hearing. This was related to me years afterwards, when the Novel had been published; & it was supposed that the names might recall to my recollection that early impression.[4]

Frances Burney's novels were also Rectory favourites, including *Cecilia*, which provides the general plotline and even the title for *Pride and Prejudice*. Claire Harman points out that even the most famous sentence in *Pride and Prejudice* is the daughter of a sentence of Burney's: '[It is] received wisdom among match-makers, that a young lady without fortune has a less and less chance of getting off upon every public appearance.'[5] And *Pride and Prejudice* sizzles with the feelings of a young lady living at home as one of many daughters without an attractive dowry. What astonishes – but what also helps explain Lizzy Bennet's believability – is the thought that Jane wrote her first draft when she was exactly the same age as her heroine, 'not one and twenty'.

At the time that Jane was writing *First Impressions*, Hampshire was awash with military officers like those with whom the Bennet girls dance and flirt. From 1794, Jane must have encountered the South Devonshires in Basingstoke, as well as her own brother Henry's unit, the Oxfordshire Militia, which was also billeted for a while in Hampshire. The officers in Jane's novel spelt trouble, and so did their real-life equivalents, leaving behind them a trail of bad debts and the consequences of drunkenness. Henry Austen's own Oxfordshire Militia had run wild and riotous in the town of Newhaven on the south coast back in April of 1795, drinking and stealing meat for two days. The two ringleaders of the revolt were then forced to kneel upon coffins before being shot by ten of their comrades, a horrific punishment that Henry Austen had to witness.[6]

The war and the soldiers provide essential background to *Pride and Prejudice*, but perhaps it was painful emotion even closer to home that gave Jane the impetus to show Lizzy Bennet, sharp-tongued, proud, and suffering in love. After Tom Lefroy's relations 'saved' him from an imprudent match, a waspish, disappointed note enters even her early letters. 'I do not want People to be very agreable,' she wrote, 'as it saves me the trouble of liking them a great deal.' At least the fictional Elizabeth and Jane, unlike the real-life Jane and Cassandra, might live happily ever after.

What did Jane do with *First Impressions/Pride and Prejudice* once it was finished? According to Henry, 'an invincible distrust of her own judgement induced her to withhold her works from the public, till time and many perusals had satisfied her that the charm of recent composition was dissolved'.[7] Indeed, he thought her far above writing for money: 'neither the hope of fame nor profit mixed with her early motives'.[8]

Henry was wrong, or at least in denial, about that. 'I write only for fame,' Jane admitted, early on, 'without any view to pecuniary Emolument.' But later, as she realised just how hard life would be without money of her own, that 'pecuniary Emolument' would become increasingly important too.

It was Mr Austen who took practical action to get his daughter's work published. He had read enough novels himself to know, by the autumn of 1797, that *First Impressions* was worth publishing. He took it upon himself to become his daughter's literary agent; we do not know whether this was with or without Jane's own blessing.

He wrote, on 1 November 1797, to offer *First Impressions* to a publisher named Thomas Cadell, asking him what sum his firm might advance for it, and indeed asking what the price would be for it to be published 'at the author's risk'.[9] This was generous. Mr Austen was proposing an arrangement where he himself would pay for the printing of his daughter's novel. If it didn't sell, he would bear the loss. Just as Mr Austen had written endlessly to admirals on behalf of his naval sons, he also did his best by his younger girl.

But Mr Austen did not go about his work as a literary agent in a very effective manner. He described the work as consisting of three volumes, 'about the length of Miss Burney's *Evelina*'.[10] This reference to *Evelina* was a mistake: it had been popular twenty years previously. He also gave no hint of who had written the novel, or even why the publisher should be interested. *First Impressions* was rejected by Cadell immediately, and

Mr Austen's letter came back to him with a note saying it was 'declined by Return of Post'.

I hope that he hadn't told Jane what he was doing, so that she did not have to face the instant rejection. For a novelist, this was a bad beginning indeed.

13

Godmersham Park

'I shall eat Ice & drink French wine
& be above Vulgar Economy.'

Jane on a visit to Godmersham Park

M R DARCY'S PEMBERLEY, Lady Catherine's Rosings Park, even Mr
Bingley's Netherfield Park so close to home, are all much grander
mansions than the house where Lizzy Bennet grew up. When she visits
these places, she becomes an outsider, uncharacteristically self-conscious
about her status (or lack of it). She gains self-knowledge; we gain an
unfolding drama.

There's a notable coincidence of dates between the writing of the first
draft of *Pride and Prejudice* and a visit Jane paid in the summer of 1796 to
a smart house where life was lived on a much grander scale than at the
Rectory. Rowling, in Kent, was her brother Edward's home now that he
was married. He had risen into the ranks of the genuinely landed gentry;
there was no longer anything 'pseudo' about him. The evidence suggests
that Edward himself was nothing but kind and welcoming to his sister.
But once she got home to Steventon, Jane straightaway created the snooty
characters of Mr Darcy and Lady Catherine. A visit to Edward's new
universe involved an adjustment of values, and Marilyn Butler argues that
Pride and Prejudice reveals Jane's 'instinctive reaction against Kentish hauteur'.

In August 1798, Mr and Mrs Austen, Jane and Cassandra all went to
visit Edward again, in an even more spacious, gracious house than
Rowling. Godmersham Park, about eight miles to the southwest of
Canterbury, was, and still is, a magnificent Palladian mansion. You could
catch glimpses of it for the whole of the last mile of the journey as you
approached along the old drive through a wooded park 'well stored with
deer'. Once you were out of the trees, the 'seat rises in the midst of a
delightful lawn'.[1]

It's easy to imagine Jane and her family bowling up to the entrance
by carriage after their long journey from Hampshire, 'very dirty, very
noisy', ready and eager for entertainment and high living. The scene
conjures up all the National-Trust big-house lovely-dresses glamour of a

Jane Austen feature film. From these films, many people might imagine that Jane spent all her time dancing at balls or drinking tea in houses like Godmersham. But it wasn't really her world. Jane spent months of her life *staying* in grand and stately homes, but she never really *lived* in any of them. She was always a guest, and an onlooker, and a judge.

Jane's visits to great houses would teach her, in her novels, how to characterise a textbook's-worth of architectural styles. We're left with the impression that she could easily have drawn us a floor plan of Mansfield Park or Pemberley if we were to ask for it. But she never bothers to spell out the exact layout of a house. She only gives us what we really need, the few details that most vividly characterise a place. Northanger Abbey, for example, a former real abbey much improved by its owner, has Gothic windows but a completely up-to-date heating system. By contrast, Donwell Abbey has been left unaltered to reflect the reliable, unpretentious values of its owner Mr Knightley. Sotherton is Elizabethan, brick-built, 'heavy, but respectable looking'. Although it is dignified and noble, its foolish and fashion-conscious owner thinks it looks like 'a dismal old prison'. Pemberley, a 'large, handsome, stone building', dates from the early 1600s, while Uppercross is from the other end of the same century, the William and Mary period. But Mansfield Park itself is in the eighteenth-century Palladian style, just like Godmersham Park.

This particular summer visit of 1798 was occasioned by Edward's having moved into the big house. After his adoptive father Mr Knight died, Mrs Knight decided to relocate to Canterbury and let Edward have the mansion. This was 'out of her love and affection' for him, as the legal transfer put it. He would, in turn, provide her with an income of £2,000 a year.

Mrs Knight's action was generous, but perhaps not as generous as it first seems, for Edward now had to shoulder the burden of managing the estates. Indeed, he might, if things went badly, have to make up the difference on Mrs Knight's income himself.[2] She bequeathed him the heavy responsibilities of a major landowner and put him in charge of a demanding business. But Mrs Knight had chosen well. Edward enjoyed it, and was good at it. He was 'more his own "man of business" than is usual with people of large property', a niece considered, and 'it was his greatest interest to attend to his estates'.[3]

Godmersham Park was built in 1732 without the help of any particular architect. The south front was of red brick with none-too-fine stone dressings. But the north front was much more ambitious. In 1780 Mr Knight had added flanking wings of five windows each, one side the library, the other side offices. There was history here. Each generation had made its mark. To inherit an estate like this was more than a matter of bricks and mortar. Edward had also inherited a set of Tory values, the feudal idea that with privilege came a responsibility of care.

Behind the house there were the pleasure grounds, and before it, the sleepy curve of the River Stour. There was a hill topped by a little temple. It was the sort of place that got included in tourist guides. One, published in 1793, calls it 'a modern building of a centre and two wings; one of which, the Eastern, contains a most excellent library'.[4]

Into this house Edward's wife brought more and more children. Elizabeth Austen née Bridges, who'd been taught at school how to get in and out of a carriage nicely, was 'a very lovely woman, highly educated, though not I imagine of much natural talent. Her tastes were domestic.'[5] But this slightly sneering opinion comes from her more intellectual, less gregarious, Hampshire in-laws. Elizabeth's own extensive family helped make up the lively social whirlwind that blew in and out of Godmersham Park on an almost daily basis. Among her ten siblings was a brother, Edward, who took a fancy to Jane, making an offer of marriage and being refused: 'I wish you may be able to accept' an invitation from Lady Bridges, Jane wrote to Cassandra on one occasion, 'though *I* could not her son Edward's.' He had a try with Cassandra, and failing there too, eventually contented himself with another lady.

Unlike Jane and Cassandra, the family at Godmersham were very sure of their place in the world and their welcome in any society. They ooze entitlement. Edward's eldest daughter Fanny described her brothers and sisters as 'a numerous and joyful race of children; all born to bask in the brightest sunshine that fond & wealthy Parents could spread around them'.[6] But not all children at Godmersham were equal. It's noticeable that their poorer cousins, the children of James Austen, visited Godmersham only rarely, and did not quite fit in. James's little daughter Caroline, daughter of his second wife Mary, remembered her visit in Fanny-Price mode: 'I don't think I <u>was</u> very happy there, in a strange house. I remember the model of a ship in the passage, and my cousins' rabbits out of doors, in or near a long walk of high trees. I have been told it was the lime-tree walk.'[7] Caroline was described as less 'headstrong or humoursome' than her Godmersham cousins. After he or she had got over the loving, jolly, wealthy welcome that Edward and his family provided, more than one visitor felt this subtle sense of alienation.

But there was much for Jane to enjoy in the arrival itself. Her nieces Fanny and Lizzy 'met us in the Hall with a great deal of pleasant joy', she wrote of another visit paid without Cassandra. That hall, paved in black and white, still has its light, bright and spectacular plasterwork. It gave onto the drawing room and dining room to left and right. Ahead lay the stairs, and on that particular visit, Jane was given the luxurious solitude of the Yellow Room: 'it seems odd to me to have such a great place all to myself'. She unpacked her trunk that first night. It became her practice to present her hosts with a gift over the next morning's breakfast: once, a handmade rug, 'which was received most gratefully, and met with universal admiration'. This was the sort of present, representing the labour of many hours rather than the expenditure of many guineas, that the unmarried aunts were expected to provide.

A day '*a la* Godmersham', as Jane described it, got off to a slow start. 'It has struck ten; I must go to breakfast', she wrote. And then, if she could, it was back to her luxurious big room. 'I enjoy my apartment very much,' she told Cassandra, '& always spend two or three hours in it after breakfast.' Sometimes she invited a favoured niece to join her. 'I remember', wrote one of the others, 'that when Aunt Jane came to us at Godmersham she used to bring the manuscript of whatever novel she was writing with her, and would shut herself up with my elder sisters in one of the bedrooms to read them aloud.' Marianne, this niece, felt excluded. 'I and the younger ones used to hear peals of laughter through the door, and thought it very hard that we should be shut out from what was so delightful.'[8]

The family lived in the library, breakfasting in it in hot weather, having a fire lit there in spells of summer cold. During the day, when they dispersed to their various activities, they left it free for Jane to use, 'in warm & happy solitude'. This was the best of Godmersham. The deserted library was a wonderful place for just one bookish person. 'I did not mean to eat,' she once wrote, 'but Mr Johncock [the butler] has brought in the Tray, so I must . . . At this present time I have five Tables, Eight & twenty Chairs and two fires all to myself.' The billiard table elsewhere was to Jane a great advantage: 'it draws all the Gentlemen to it whenever they are within, especially after dinner', leaving the library 'in delightful quiet'.

This library contained a collection of books even bigger than Mr Austen's. Its handwritten catalogue still survives, marked in gilt letters: GODMERSHAM PARK LIBRARY CATALOGUE.[9] It shows that Jane could have read books ranging from *Letters written by a Peruvian Princess* by Françoise d'Issembourg d'Happoncourt de Graffigny to her favourite novels by Richardson. Some books especially favoured by the family were marked in the catalogue as having been 'Removed to the Drawg. Room', and these, in due course, would include all six of Jane's novels.[10] But the Kentish part of the family had different tastes to the novel-reading Hampshire Austens. Lady Bridges, Edward's mother-in-law, thought Miss Edgeworth's to be 'very foolish books'.[11]

Library aside, Jane found that life at Godmersham could be oppressively social. There were many duties, and much making of small talk, to be done by the diligent houseguest. 'In this House there is a constant succession of small events,' she complained, 'somebody is always going or coming.' That very morning they'd had an unexpected visitor 'to breakfast with us'.

Jane ('of course') offered to help look after Elizabeth's multitudinous children, not least by hearing the little girls practise their reading. Her brothers and sisters-in-law began to use her more and more for unpaid childcare; it so clearly fell among the duties of a spinster aunt. It was 'races & merriment' with her nephews George and Henry, and 'Battledore & Shuttlecock' with their younger brother William: 'we have frequently kept it up *three* times, & once or twice *six*'. Jane was also known for her skill at spillikins, a game of dexterity learned at Godmersham. Two rival sets of delicate spillikins, each said to be hers, survive today, made out of bone, and looking more suitable for dolls than human beings.[12] Jane considered her own family's set to be 'a very valuable part of our Household furniture, & not the least important Benefaction from the family of Knight to that of Austen'.

But Jane did not always relish her aunt duties. She wrote that a cute little boy would inevitably turn into 'an ungovernable, ungracious fellow', and paints an unforgettable picture in *Sense and Sensibility* of Lady Middleton's spoiled children, full of 'mischievous tricks' to play upon visiting young ladies, whose sashes were 'untied, their hair pulled about their ears, their work-bags searched, and their knives and scissors stolen away'. These were indeed juvenile delinquents in search of weapons. Jane was in favour of smacking, writing of one great-nephew that he was 'terribly in want of Discipline. – I hope he gets a wholesome thump or two.' All the new Rousseau-esque freedom and liberation for children could turn them into monsters.

And the Godmersham children themselves were able to detect that Jane secretly thought them brats. 'Of the two Sisters', their niece Anna wrote, 'Aunt Jane was generally the favourite with children, but with the young people of Godmersham it was not so.' They liked her 'as a play-fellow, & as a teller of stories, but they were not really fond of her. I believe that their Mother was not.' The reason, in Anna's mind at least, was the sense of inferiority that Jane inspired among the lively Godmersham set, where sportiness was valued over braininess. 'A little talent went a long way' with this family, '& <u>much</u> must have gone a long way too far.'[13]

There was one exception to this rule. For Jane was truly close to her oldest niece, Fanny. 'I wish my dear Fanny many happy returns of this day,' she wrote to Godmersham on one birthday, 'and that she may on every return enjoy as much pleasure as she is now receiving from her doll's-beds.' This Fanny would grow up to be described by Jane as 'quite after one's own heart'. Becoming something of a second mother to her ten younger siblings forced Fanny to mature quickly and become more of her aunt's equal. 'You are inimitable, irresistible', Jane told her in one letter. 'You are the delight of my Life.' They got up to some ridiculous antics together, such as playing at housemaids to a male guest after 'a mistake in the [real] Housemaids Preparations'. 'I wish you had seen Fanny & me running backwards & forwards with his Breeches,' Jane wrote, 'in the greatest of frights lest he should come upon us before we had done it all.'

While Jane preferred to remain 'quietly & comfortably' enjoying the library, the gentlemen of Godmersham and their visitors spent their days hunting, or riding out on farm business such as going to see a pond being dragged. Agriculture was the basis of the family's wealth and Edward was, after all, the birth child of a pair of farmers. Back in Hampshire, the Austens took a great interest in his activities: 'My mother wants to know whether Edward has ever made the hen-house they planned', and 'My father is glad to hear so good an account of Edward's pigs.' Mr Austen himself was as keen a pig-breeder as his contemporary Parson Woodforde, who once made the mistake of letting his pigs drink some beer so they got 'so amazingly drunk by it, that they were not able to stand and appeared like dead things'.[14] Edward, though, had little toleration for other people's pigs. He complained in the local paper that damage had been done to his woods 'by the number of Hogs turned out to feed on acorns'. If it happened again, Edward warned, their owners would be 'sued for the trespass'.[15]

Edward's huge house meant that he could often offer hospitality to his brothers and sisters and their children, and it was his natural inclination to do so. But each of the Austens had different patterns of visiting.[16] Frank and Charles came whenever they could leave their naval duties, and indeed Frank in 1806 would spend his honeymoon at Godmersham. Henry made short visits for occasions like Twelfth Night, and maybe for an autumn shooting party; Eliza, less willing to blend in with the horsey atmosphere, was a much less frequent guest. James only visited twice, and although Jane and Cassandra both made long visits, Cassandra's were more frequent. Perhaps Jane and James, often at odds but in many ways alike, were both too proud to enjoy being the poor relations. 'Kent is the only place for happiness,' Jane wrote drily, 'everybody is rich there.'

And yet there were compensations. She certainly relished the luxury. Godmersham dinners were late, at six rather than the unfashionable half-past three of the Rectory. 'I shall eat Ice & drink French wine,' she insisted during one visit, '& be above Vulgar Economy.' She also received regular financial gifts from generous old Mrs Knight – 'Her very agreable present will make my circumstances quite easy' – and certainly there was 'not much to try the patience or hurt the Spirits at Godmersham'. Despite enjoying the ice cream and 'Orange Wine', though, Jane pointedly praised the pleasures of home as including items missing from Godmersham: 'Friendship, of unreserved Conversation, of similarity of Taste & Opinions'.

Years later, even Jane's beloved niece Fanny would turn traitor, forgetting the fun she'd had with Aunt Jane, and rewriting the past with a deeply unattractive snobbery. Fanny later claimed that it was Mrs Knight who'd made Jane fit for polite society. 'Aunt Jane', Fanny thought, was 'too clever not to put aside all signs of "commonness" (if such an expression is allowable) & teach herself to be more refined'. 'If it had not been for Papa's marriage,' Fanny continued, 'which brought them into Kent', Jane and Cassandra 'would have been, tho' not less clever & agreeable in themselves, very much below par as to good society & its ways'.[17]

It's a passage from a letter that could have been written by one of Mr Bingley's sisters. It's striking, too, that Godmersham Park has much in common physically with that other magnificent but unwelcoming Palladian mansion, Mansfield Park, where grandeur lives but compassion does not.

But of course the mansion wasn't just home to Edward, Elizabeth and their children. The household also included 'the governess and 19 servants', some of whom became Jane's friends.[18]

The Complete Servant recommended that a gentleman of Edward's income should employ eight female and eight male servants: a cook, lady's-maid, two housemaids, a nurse, a nursery-maid, kitchen-maid and laundry-maid, with a butler, valet, coachman, two grooms, footman and two gardeners.[19] Edward, additionally, needed a governess for his many children, and somehow also acquired two more surplus servants on top of that. He was expected to provide bed and board as well as wages for all these people. It was likely that he allowed the men 'a Pot of Ale per day, and the Women a Pint, besides table-beer'.[20]

These masses of servants put Jane into a quandary: she could not afford to give them the tips that they expected. 'I am in great Distress,' she admitted to Cassandra, 'I cannot determine whether I shall give Richis [a maid] half a guinea or only five Shillings when I go away.' On another visit, feeling herself 'very poor', she guiltily gave the nursemaid Susannah Sackree only ten shillings. Sackree, also known as 'Caky', nursed the children for so many years that she became almost part of the family. But Jane's impecunious state was known and forgiven below stairs. Mr Hall, the visiting hairdresser, did Elizabeth's hair for five shillings. Yet he only charged Jane and Cassandra half that amount for a cut. 'He certainly respects either our Youth or our poverty', she wrote.

Jane considered that Mr Hall was lucky to work at Godmersham, for as well as dressing hair, he had the pleasure of the company of Mrs Salkeld, the housekeeper, and Mrs Sace (or Sayce), the lady's maid, who was the niece of nursemaid Mrs Sackree. Mrs Salkeld's was a position of dignity within the household, as her honorific 'Mrs' suggests, and she had budgetary responsibility for obtaining provisions and paying bills. As Jane's family did not, could not, employ a housekeeper, it was Mrs Salkeld, and then her successor Mrs Driver, who must have provided Jane with the inspiration for her own fictional housekeepers, Mrs Whitaker at Sotherton, Mrs Hill at Longbourn, Mrs Hodges at Donwell Abbey and Mrs Reynolds at Pemberley.[21] Other servants at Godmersham included Richard Kennet, the groom, and Mrs Kennet, the laundress.

Jane took them all seriously, just as Lizzy Bennet thinks that an opinion on a person's character is well worth having if it comes via the observations of an 'intelligent servant'. She would remain in touch by letter with Susannah Sackree for years, even after the Godmersham children were grown up. Sackree herself never married, living on and on at Godmersham, where she 'saw and played with many of the children of her nurslings, and died in 1851 in her ninetieth year'.[22] She ended up with the status of a treasure like Sarah, the children's old nurse in *Persuasion*, the only character in the entire combined households of the Musgroves who really cares for the injured Louisa. Sackree did much for the children, but it would be misleading to see the Godmersham household as dividing cleanly into 'upstairs' and 'downstairs' or to think that the children's mother skimped on her duties. Historian Joanne Bailey describes the Georgians as believing in 'household-families', whereby everyone under one roof, related or not, all had a role in caring for the young.[23]

This is where Jane, and aunts in general, fitted in, as part of the wider 'household-family'. And Jane did make one firm friend at Godmersham at a point on that continuum from upstairs to downstairs that lay almost equal to her own. The governess Miss Anne Sharp worked at the house between 1804 and 1806. Well-born boys had had 'governors' for centuries, but the role of 'governess' had only emerged since the 1770s. *The Complete Servant* advises, when one hires a governess, that she should 'be able to conduct herself in such as manner, as never to render an apology necessary for her presence at family parties'.[24] Yet while the governess could be *with* the family, she was not *of* the family. 'I sit alone in the evening, in the schoolroom,' complained Georgian governess Nelly Weeton, 'there is nobody in the house with whom I can be on equal terms, and I know nobody out of it.'[25] Mary Wollstonecraft frankly hated being a governess: 'above the servants, yet considered by them a spy . . . shut out from equality and confidence'.[26]

Miss Sharp, however, was very much Jane's cup of tea. Good-natured, and 'pretty but not strikingly so', she was not enormously strict.[27] Fanny records one day when formal lessons were cancelled and the whole family 'played at school . . . Aunt Cassandra was Mrs Teachum, the Governess Aunt Jane'. 'We had a most delightful day', Fanny tells us, and 'a Bowl of Syllabub in the evening'.[28] But Miss Sharp's health was not good, and this eventually forced her to leave off governessing. She ended up running a girls' school in Liverpool. When Miss Sharp left Godmersham, her pupil Fanny – who by then called her 'Anny' – wrote that 'we had a sad parting'.[29] And yet this same Miss Sharp was later described, with condescension, by the younger generation of Jane's nieces and nephews, as 'horridly affected but rather amusing'. These fine young ladies and gentlemen would grow out of much that they had loved in their youth.

Jane Fairfax, in *Emma*, speaks feelingly of the 'governess-trade', linking it to the slave trade. In the novel she stands for virtue and dignity and suffering, emerging from the cramped quarters of her aunt and grandmother to grace the drawing rooms of her social superiors. Most tellingly of all, Jane Fairfax is seen 'wandering about the meadows, at some distance from Highbury', for she really has no place in society.[30] Perhaps, ultimately, Jane and Miss Sharp and their like had no real place at Godmersham.

But during Jane's twenties the whole wide world beckoned. There were plenty of other places to go instead.

14

Away from Home

'You are this Evening to enter a World in which
you will meet with many wonderfull Things.'

Jane Austen's *Juvenilia*

IF A YOUNG lady's purpose was to marry and produce children, then
the most exciting moment in her life was her entry into the society of
adults. It was known as a girl's 'coming out' into the world of men. Young
and fresh, the debutante possessed the highest possible value in the marriage
market, a value that could only decline with time. A girl's 'coming out'
therefore needed the most careful management by her parents.

Mr and Mrs Austen of course were anxious that Jane should get about
and meet suitable young men. That's why she was frequently sent away
from home in her late teens and early twenties, to Godmersham, yes,
but also to Southampton, to Gloucestershire, and, of course, to the city
with which she's most associated: Bath. It was all part of this process of
making an entrance into the world.

These visits were far from being Jane's personal choice: she was told
where to go, and how long to stay. It was the start of what would be a
lifetime of being passed around between relatives like a parcel. But it
must nevertheless have been thrilling, at first, to leave Hampshire behind.

To travel by carriage, as Jane did in the 1790s, involved making progress
at a speed of about seven miles an hour, with stops at inns. And seven
miles an hour was good going. You could travel faster if you hired a
post-chaise (a light carriage also used for delivering post, usually painted
canary yellow) rather than using your own vehicle, because you would
also hire a fresh pair of horses every ten to fifteen miles.

To own your own carriage, as Mr Austen did for a short time, was
like owning a car. To hire a chaise was to take a taxi; to travel by the
public stagecoach was to take the bus. Jane's family forbade her from
travelling by stagecoach on the grounds of propriety and safety. But she
still had wild dreams of escape: herself and a friend bowling along irre-
sponsibly in a hired chaise with both its doors open, lying upon its floor
with 'our heads hanging out of one door, and our feet at the opposite'.

She teased her family by threatening to go alone to London to 'walk the Hospitals, Enter at the Temple, or mount Guard at St James'. But in her youth at least she was always obliged to wait until one of her male relatives was ready and willing to take her. 'Till I have a travelling purse of my own,' she sighed, 'I must submit to such things.'

The new turnpike roads were cutting travel times dramatically during Jane's coming-out tour. A 'turnpike' was literally a barrier, originally a row of pikes or spears stuck handle-down into a road, but it now meant a road with pay-points where charges, for road enhancements, were collected. During the Napoleonic Wars, Hampshire had the fastest-improving road network in the country, all the better to get troops to and from the vulnerable south coast.[1] The turnpikes tempted people to go too fast, and a system of penalties was introduced so that coachmen caught 'driving furiously' had to pay a fine of £10.[2] Vehicles might also overturn: such an accident kicks off the action in Jane's novel *Sanditon*. More dangerous still than carriages were the high, light gigs driven by young men: Catherine Morland climbs into one in *Northanger Abbey* only because she is too young and inexperienced to admit that she is frightened.

And travelling, even in Jane's native Hampshire, could even be dangerous. In 1793 the Austens' neighbour Mrs Mary Bramston became the victim of a highwayman on her way home from drinking tea with Madam Lefroy. He said 'he would blow out my Brains if I did not give him my Money', Mrs Bramston recalled, 'I now Start at my own Shadow.'[3] The highwayman must have looked rather like Adam Ant in his 'smock frock, with a handkerchief or crape over his face, and armed with pistols'. He was after his victims' money, watches, and 'ear-rings from their ears'.[4]

It was necessary to break long journeys, like that from Godmersham to Steventon, overnight at an inn. On one trip home from Kent, the Austens stayed at the Bull and George at Dartford, squeezed into 'apartments up two pair of stairs'. Doubtless they checked the bedding before accepting the rooms. 'Nothing is to be more dreaded by travellers', wrote William Buchan, the author of *Domestic Medicine* (1794), 'than damp beds.' Madam Lefroy advised that one should place a glass tumbler between the sheets and check it for signs of condensation. 'If the glass remains perfectly clear, the bed is dry.'[5]

An inn had its own particular bustling character, with the many comings and goings. 'After we had been here a quarter of an hour', Jane wrote from the Bull and George, 'it was discovered that my writing and dressing boxes had been by accident put into a chaise which was just packed off as we came in, and were driven away towards Gravesend on their way to the West Indies.' Horror! They contained all her 'worldly wealth', which must have included not only her meagre jewellery, but also her manuscripts. She wrote another time of 'the Treasures of my Writing-desk drawer'. Taking care of the drafts of her novels, keeping them from damp and fire and neglect, must have been quite a responsibility. One of the villainies of General Tilney, in *Northanger Abbey*, lies in his intention of making more room in a crowded carriage by ejecting Catherine Morland's writing desk: 'she had some difficulty in saving [it] from being thrown out into the street'.

A night at a Georgian coaching inn passed in un-restful mayhem:

> doors opening and shutting, bells ringing, voices calling to the waiter from every quarter . . . The man who cleans the boots is running in one direction, the barber with his powder-bag in another; here goes the barber's boy with his hot water and razors; there comes the clean linen from the washerwoman; and the hall is full of porters and sailors bringing luggage.

Nothing, in fact, is done 'without a noise'.[6] After a five o'clock repast of beefsteaks, though, the Austens spent their evening at the Bull and George 'sitting by the fire' and quietly reading. Mrs Austen, a sufferer from travel-sickness, found herself to be 'refreshed by a comfortable dinner, and now seems quite stout'.

Whether it was Jane who was away from home, or Cassandra, a growing number of letters begin to give us glimpses into their private lives. When they were apart, as they increasingly were, their communication was constant. 'My dear Cassandra', Jane starts. 'Where shall I begin? Which of all my important nothings shall I tell you first?' She expected minute detail in return: 'You know how interesting the purchase of a sponge-cake is to me.'

Jane's biographers often start out by saying how sparse the details of her life are, how it passed 'without incident'. But that's to neglect the enormous stash of her surviving letters, representing hundreds of thousands of words. They have disappointed historians seeking a record of politics, great events and high-flown thoughts. Jane's nephew and early biographer James Edward Austen-Leigh cautions us 'not to expect too much from them'.[7] In more modern times, the letters have disappointed by failing to provide evidence of interior doubts and secret romances, although there is indeed plenty of bitterness, bitchiness and regret. The letters do show Jane happy, sad, and indeed downright depressed. 'I am quite out of heart,' she writes on one occasion, disgusted with herself, 'I am sick of myself, & my bad pens.'

Searching for *something* to praise in his aunt's correspondence, James Edward argued that her handwriting was 'excellent' and that she was good at folding and sealing the paper into a homemade envelope: 'some people's letters looked always loose and untidy – but *her* paper was sure to take the right folds, and *her* sealing wax to drop in the proper place'.[8] In fact, Jane herself was *not* proud of her handwriting, and thought that Cassandra's was so much better that 'it makes me quite ashamed'.

But once you take Jane's letters on their own terms, they are all the richer for their dense detail of domestic life. Georgian ladies' letters, with their family gossip, servant trouble, recipes and dressmaking tips, may sometimes seem trivial. Yet compared to the typical letters of their male relations they are colourful, wide-ranging, profound. 'A man's letters', summarises the historian Amanda Vickery, who has read a lot of them, mainly concerned 'his own illnesses, minor matters of law and local administration, and above all sport – effectively summarised as my gout is still bad; here is the gun dog I promised you; have you finished the will?'[9]

There's a good explanation for why the Georgian age's greatest novelist spends so much time in her letters discussing tea and sugar, and the finer details of the trimmings of clothes. These were the things in their lives over which Jane and Cassandra had control. Where the sisters should live was not their choice. Major purchases like furniture were rare. Independent travel, higher education lay out of reach. What did fall within their grasp was the purchase and the use of household supplies, and the ability to give and accept occasional invitations for visits to friends and relatives. No wonder the letters devote so much attention to these matters.

Consequently, Jane's letters, like her books, spend little time describing a house. A room's prospect or temperature, when she was staying away from home, might be mentioned, but she never describes the wallpaper or the curtains. That's because these too, the permanent fixtures and fittings of life, were beyond her control. 'We're each of us made up of some cluster of appurtenances', says Madame Merle in Henry James's *Portrait of a Lady* (1881). 'One's house, one's furniture, one's garments, the books one reads, the company one keeps – these things are all expressive.' She's right, but she's writing in a later age. Victorian memoirists in general spend more time describing the physical world than Georgian ones: they had much more purchasing power, and more consumer goods from which to build up an impression of themselves to present to the world through their homes. For Jane, a house, its furniture, were given. It was the smaller things, the bonnets, the recipes, that were up for grabs. These represented her personal choice, and were therefore worth describing.

In her letters, Jane often writes about writing itself. 'Here I am, my dearest Cassandra,' Jane wrote, 'seated in the Breakfast, Dining, sitting room' of Henry's London home, and 'beginning with all my might'. It brings her to life as nothing else does. She writes about the very act of writing: 'I must get a softer pen. – This is harder. I am in agonies.' 'I am going to write nothing but short Sentences', she determines, finding it hard to gather her thoughts, 'Oh, dear me, when I shall ever have done?'

She wrote when happy or sad, when alone, when in company. 'Very snug, in my own room, lovely morning, excellent fire, fancy me', begins one letter. 'We are now all four of us young Ladies sitting round the Circular Table in the inner room writing our Letters, while the two Brothers are having a comfortable coze in the room adjoining', she explains in another. There is no sense that writing a letter was an indulgence, or time wasted: it was both a right and a duty for the female members of a family to use letters to knit together its constituent threads. To this end, family news was always included, such as the dates of the arrival of the latest letters from Jane's sailor brothers abroad, so no scrap of news was left unreported.

James Edward Austen-Leigh, who probably did not need or notice the consolation provided by small domestic details well ordered, found no pleasure in the letters' extreme triviality. But *we* can, rejoicing with Jane when she says 'I am happy to hear of the Honey . . . I was thinking of it the other day. – Let me know when you begin the new Tea – & the new white wine. – My present Elegancies [in London] have not yet made me indifferent to such Matters. I am still a Cat if I see a Mouse.'

On top of this, Jane's nephew failed to realise that each letter needs reading with care, for it was in a sort of code. A letter was intended for more eyes than just the addressee's. It would be read aloud – at least in snatches – to the rest of a household, often over breakfast. The bullet-point style of Jane's letters was particularly appropriate for this sharing of nuggets of news. Sometimes the *whole* letter would be read out, usually to an audience of other women. 'Your Letter gave pleasure to all of us,' Jane told Cassandra in 1813, 'we had all the reading of it of course, I *three times*.' She'd read it out to the Godmersham household in general, then to her particular friend the nursemaid, and then to a niece who had missed the earlier reading. On other occasions, a letter's recipient had to take care to reveal only the parts appropriate for public consumption. When Jane and her niece Fanny were corresponding about Fanny's love life, Jane insisted that Fanny include some other, lighter news as well: 'write *something* that may do to be read or told'.

So while the letters were not entirely private, neither were they entirely public, except at the discretion of the sender. And discretion is a very important word for their later history. The Austens would have been horrified to learn how their aunt's letters have been pored over by generations of scholars: 'I can fancy what the indignation of Aunt Cassa. would have been at the mere idea of [their] being read and commented upon by any of us, nephews and nieces, little or great',[10] wrote one family member. Despite Aunt Cassandra's destruction of a great part of Jane's correspondence, some 160 letters did survive, and have been published. In early editions, many disobliging references to other Austen family members, and to bodily functions, were discreetly removed. Why did Cassandra destroy an unknown number of further letters? Quite probably because Jane could be so fantastically rude about her relatives, people whose feelings would be hurt. To that end, Cassandra kept her sister's secrets safe.

The other way that Jane broke the rules when it came to letter writing was in her magnificent ability to subvert and parody the newsy, chatty conventions of female correspondence. Sometimes she created 'a text as bizarre and inconsequential' as those of that minimalist master of black humour, the twentieth-century playwright Samuel Beckett.[11] In her early story *Love and Freindship*, Jane has her heroine Laura go mad after the death of her husband in a carriage accident. Her eyes assuming 'a vacant Stare', Laura loses her reason: 'Look at that Grove of Firs – I see a Leg of Mutton – They told me Edward was not Dead; but they deceived me – they took him for a Cucumber.' One of Jane's real-life letters reveals that she was feeling as mad as Laura: 'I wonder whether the Ink bottle has been filled', runs her letter. 'Does Butcher's meat keep up at the same price? & is not Bread lower than 2/6. – Mary's blue gown! – My Mother must be in agonies.' They couldn't come right out and say it, but this was how Georgian ladies could tell each other that they were going bonkers.

The other marvellous consequence of Jane's letters is that they show us how her early forays into society began to give her real-life fodder for her published novels, which are all set in a more realistic, contemporary world than the rowdy youthful fancies she'd written when she had known nothing other than life at the Rectory.

One such run of early letters tells us about the visit, in November 1797, that Jane was sent to pay to her aunt and uncle Jane and James Leigh Perrot in the great Georgian marriage mart of Bath. The couple had rented no. 1, The Paragon, the first in a curve of thirty-seven terraced houses lining the bendy road out of town towards London. It was just a short walk to St Swithun's Church, where Jane's grandfather had had his funeral before she was born, and where her parents themselves had married.

Jane did not find a husband during her stay, but its significance emerges when Cassandra tells us that 'North-hanger Abby was written about the years 98 & 99.'[12] It was during this time on her coming-out tour that Jane 'acquired the intimate knowledge of the topography and customs of Bath, which enabled her to write "Northanger Abbey" long before she resided there herself'.[13]

Mr and Mrs Leigh Perrot would be figures of importance in Jane's adult life. James Leigh Perrot was Mrs Austen's exceedingly wealthy brother, the one who had inherited a fortune from an aunt. He had been doubly lucky to have done so as a younger son. James's elder brother Thomas had that unexplained illness causing him to live with carers, along with his nephew, Jane's brother George. James Leigh Perrot's wife Jane Cholmley, as she had been born, was the heiress to an estate in Barbados. A prickly, touchy, rather difficult character, Jane Cholmley had married James in 1764. Their riches and childlessness made them into something of a magnet for legacy-hunters. Lesser members of the family were drawn to James Leigh Perrot, with some genuine affection, but also with some genuinely uncertain feelings about entitlement and fairness.

Among the Georgian gentry, the random striking of fortune in terms of a legacy, or its absence, could have a transformative effect upon an individual life. You might be lucky; you might not. No wonder Georgians felt that their fortunes were in the hands of the good Lord, and prayed for resignation. Jane's own particular little branch of the Austen family on the fringes of the lower gentry had aristocrats and fortunes among their forebears. They themselves were downwardly mobile. But just one lucky inheritance – a personal connection made, a timely death – would have sent them on their way back up again.

Having won his own game of Legacy Bingo, Jane's uncle James Leigh Perrot was able to live a charmed life. He was a witty man, 'of considerable natural power'. Like Jane he was good at writing 'clever epigrams and riddles, some of which, though without his name, found their way into print'. But his fortune gave him no need to exercise his talents, and 'he lived a very retired life', split between Bath and his home in Berkshire called Scarlets.[14] At Scarlets, James and Jane enjoyed spending their money, and 'dining with thirty families' in the neighbourhood.[15] Despite his pretensions, Jane was fond of her uncle. Of all the many people technically worthy of the title, it is these two to whom Jane refers as 'my Uncle' and 'my Aunt'. And Uncle James endeared himself to Jane in return by taking a particular interest in her brothers. 'It is pleasant to be among people who know one's connections & care about them', she wrote.

And so, in 1797, the Leigh Perrots invited their twenty-two-year-old niece to go to Bath, there to be introduced by them into good society. The arrival into the city, the pleasure capital of Georgian Britain, was generally a marvellous moment. However bored or tired the traveller might be, a guidebook tells us, 'THE ENTRANCE TO BATH cannot fail in removing this frigid *apathy*'. After all, by the year 1801, some £3 million pounds had been laid out here upon making the city splendid, a sum that equalled the total investment in Britain's cotton industry.[16]

Bath arose before travellers' eyes 'with peculiar grandeur', surrounded as it was 'by the lofty hills'.[17] Its regular rows of stone-built houses, the guidebooks tell us, of 'pale yellow clean appearance, produce an uncommonly interesting effect'.[18] Indeed, 'this town looks as if it had been cast in a mould all at once, so new, so fresh, so regular'.[19] It was a fine sight to those in high spirits. But if one was feeling depressed, the dazzling stone could be oppressive. Jane wrote of the pavements of Bath 'getting very white again' after rain, and has her heroine Anne Elliot complain about 'the white glare' of Bath.

The *New Bath Guide* tells us that in 1799: 'no place in England . . . affords so brilliant a circle of polite company as Bath. The young, the old, the grave, the gay, the infirm, and the healthy, all resort to this place of amusement.' Each day's programme, for visiting gentlefolk, was entirely predictable: a morning rendezvous at the Pump Room, to drink the waters, followed by a walk. 'From the *Pump-Room* to the *Parades*', they trotted, or else took 'a stroll alongside the Avon; – or, a walk in Sydney-Gardens – the inviting level path to the village of Weston – visiting the shops – libraries – exhibitions, &c.'[20] The centre of fashionable life was Milsom Street: 'the peculiar resort of the *beau monde*; and the familiar *nod*, and the "*how do you do?*" are repeated fifty times in the course of the morning'.[21]

Lady visitors might also take a trip out of town to a beauty spot, ideally in the sporty vehicle of a young man. Jane did not miss out during her stay. 'I am just returned from my Airing in the very bewitching Phaeton & four,' she told Cassandra, 'we went to the top of Kingsdown [hill] – & had a very pleasant drive.' Later on, 'after dinner, the Theatre becomes attractive; or to dash off to the [Assembly] Rooms, where dancing and the card-table tend to *finish* and fully occupy . . . the time of a fashionable visitor to Bath'.[22]

The theatre, Jane's great love, must have given her some of her most enjoyable evenings. Bath's was the first outside London to have a royal warrant, and during the time of Jane's stay its reputation was high. Historians of the theatre have noted that her first three novels fall neatly into the contemporary conventions of drama. *Sense and Sensibility* is what was called a 'sentimental comedy', with moments of pathos and the triumph of conventional morality. The sparkling brilliance of *Pride and Prejudice* was more like a 'laughing comedy', full of humour. Then *Susan* (the original title of *Northanger Abbey*) was a 'burlesque', an extended, satirical story in which the world is turned upside down.

On other nights, the party went to balls at either the Lower or Upper Assembly Rooms. The scene is easy to imagine from countless feature films. Sedan chairs crowded the colonnade outside the Rooms in order to drop off their passengers. Bath's hills made carriages impractical, and in a good season 'over a hundred' sedan chair men found plenty of business.[23] Once inside the Rooms, patrons left their cloaks in the cloakroom, before choosing whether to go into the tearoom, card room, or ballroom.

A real-life Catherine Morland named Elizabeth Canning visited Bath in 1792 and wrote home to her mamma to tell her all about it. 'I wore the Lawn, which was much admired', Elizabeth explains.

> At length a little past Seven arrived, we set *Sail*, were soon safe landed, at the upper Rooms, by that time I felt all impatience to be in the Ball Room . . . when we entered it, I was fully gratified, for to be sure I never [saw] so brilliant an assembly. It was amazingly crouded although the minuets had not yet begun, so much so, that we found some difficulty to get seats — I was very much entertained with the bad minuet-dancers.[24]

Elizabeth was satisfied, even if she found the dancing bad, but Jane from a very young age had a clear-eyed view of the potential for ridicule inherent in a ball. In one of her early stories, a mother introduces her daughters to society at their coming-out ball, but the whole thing is a parody:

> poor Augusta could scarcely breathe, while Margaret was all Life and Rapture. 'The long-expected Moment is now arrived (said she) and we shall soon be in the World.' . . . how attentively they observed every object they saw, how disgusted with some Things, how enchanted with others, how astonished at all! On the whole however they returned in raptures with the World, its Inhabitants, and Manners.[25]

One's worth in the world was clearly indicated by the position one was granted in the ranked seating round the edge of the ballroom. The Master of Ceremonies would see to that. In Bath the celebrated reign of Beau Nash as Master of Ceremonies was now over, but his notorious 'eighth rule' of the assembly decreed that the first bench, nearest to the dancing, was to be filled with the cream of the marriage market, displayed as if produce on a stall for the season's richest young men to take their pick of a partner. Meanwhile, it was necessary 'that the elder ladies and children be content with a second bench at the ball, as being past or not yet come to perfection'.[26] Jane, for now, was still 'first bench' material.

The Master of Ceremonies in Bath's Lower Assembly Rooms at the time of Jane's visit was James King, who makes a cameo appearance in *Northanger Abbey*. Henry Tilney flirtatiously tells Catherine Morland that she ought to write in her journal that she had met a 'very agreeable young man introduced by Mr King [himself]; had a great deal of conversation with him'.

And Jane's aunt and uncle must have hoped likewise to introduce their niece to some very agreeable young man. Of course in *Emma* it is to Bath that Jane sends Mr Elton in search of a wife. 'My papa and mamma have been trying for the last three years to match me', complains one young lady named 'Biddy, Willing' in a magazine of 1798. Her parents have taken her backwards and forwards between Brighton and Bath, 'till the family carriage is almost worn out'. But all this effort has sadly resulted in no 'more than a nibble, for I have never yet been able to hook my fish'.[27]

Jane hooked no fish either. Indeed, she demonstrated a regrettable failure to take potential suitors seriously. One Mr Gould 'walked home with me after Tea; – he is a very Young Man, just entered of Oxford, wears Spectacles, & has heard that Evelina was written by Dr Johnson'. In other words, he was immature and ill informed. He wasn't alone in thinking *Evelina* to be the work of Burney's older, clever, well-established admirer, but a husband of Jane Austen could never make such a silly mistake.

Two years later, in May 1799, Jane accompanied her brother Edward and his wife on a second visit to Bath. This time they stayed for six weeks in a house Edward rented in Queen Square. The party were in search of a cure for Edward's incipient gout, that quintessentially Georgian illness. A very painful disease, which often begins in the big toe, it had among its causes a rich diet. As the eighteenth century wore on, and nutrition improved, it was noticed that gout was a disease of rich men. 'Made dishes, rich sauces, puddings, tarts, &c. with glasses of various liquors' were said to cause it, making it almost socially desirable. Gout's leading doctor claimed that 'the generality of men of fashion have the gout before they are fifty'.[28]

The cures Edward was to try included drinking spa water, and even treatment by electricity, although Jane admits to 'expecting no advantage from it'. Bath was certainly the place to come for a quack cure. Guidebooks to the city 'distinctly name thirty-one physicians, thirty-two surgeons, sixteen apothecaries, eight dentists, and eight chemists'.[29] While their treatments could be ineffective, what they were really selling was hope, and that was worth any money:

> Five Times I have purg'd, – yet I'm sorry to tell ye
> I find the same Gnawing and Wind in my Belly;
> But without any Doubt, I shall find myself stronger,
> When I've took the same Physic a Week or two longer.[30]

Jane wrote to Cassandra to describe the process of settling into the house in Queen Square. It's still there, now a law firm's offices, and one can stand outside imagining the Austens opening doors within onto rooms 'quite as large as we expected'. Their landlady, Mrs Bromley, was

> a fat woman in mourning, & a little black kitten runs about the Staircase . . . We have two very nice sized rooms, with dirty Quilts & everything comfortable. I have the outward & larger apartment . . . which is quite as large as our bed room at home, & my Mother's is not materially less . . . I like our situation very much . . . the prospect from the Drawingroom Window at which I now write, is rather picturesque.

Jane would write in *Mansfield Park* that people 'are much to be pitied who have not been given a taste for nature early in life', and it's noticeable that this letter does not praise the fine pavement, or the impressive terraces of houses rising and falling above and below Queen Square. What she singles out for mention instead is the glimpse of greenery in the view from the drawing room: the 'three Lombardy Poplars in the Garden of the last house in Queen's Parade'.

In these grand houses of Bath Jane would now come across the latest domestic technology, such as Count Rumford's new stoves. She makes General Tilney have these fitted into the old open fireplaces of Northanger Abbey, vastly increasing fuel efficiency, but leaving the naïve Catherine Morland disappointed to see a stove instead of the more Gothic 'ample width and ponderous carving of former times'. Rumford himself was a flamboyant American who managed to become both a Count in Bavaria and a Knight in Britain. He worked for a while as a spy, as well as inventing the kitchen range in Munich in 1789. His stoves were only marketed from 1799, so Jane was very up to date if they were indeed mentioned in the first draft of *Northanger Abbey* written 'about the years 98 & 99'.

Another novelty of *Northanger Abbey* lay in the umbrellas Jane placed upon Bath's rainy streets. 'How I hate the sight of an umbrella!' exclaims Catherine Morland. 'They are disagreeable things to carry', agrees Mrs Allen, 'I would much rather take a chair.' Georgian umbrellas of oiled cloth were heavy, and their use invited hostile comment from chairmen or drivers who thought their livings were being undermined. One umbrella-carrier found that 'people would call after me, What, Frenchman, why do you not get a coach? In particular the hackney coachmen and hackney chairmen would call after me.'[31]

Unlike rural Hampshire, many houses in Bath would by now have had Alexander Cummings' new S-trap water closets, where a pool of water trapped in the pipe's bend insulated the bathroom from the smell of the drains beyond. But they were only to be found in the best streets. Mrs Smith's cheap Bath lodgings in *Persuasion* still consist of 'paltry rooms, foul air, disgusting associations', just as in Fanny Price's birth home in Portsmouth (*Mansfield Park*) the 'bad air, bad smells' of chamber-pots emptied into a cess pit behind the house remain.

And in Bath there was much more light. Unlike the villagers of Steventon, the residents of Bath vanquished the dark with plentiful coal firelight, candles and even the oil lamps popularised by Thomas Jefferson. According to him, they produced 'a light equal to six or eight candles'. Jane, with her sensitive eyeballs, preferred the dimmer glow of candles: 'My Eyes are quite tired of Dust & Lamps.'

As she walked out from the house in Queen Square, Jane was both amazed, and slightly horrified, by Bath's shops and fashions. The latest trend was for vegetal headwear: 'flowers are very much worn, & Fruit is still more the thing'. Jane's sister-in-law Elizabeth sported strawberries, and Jane had also seen grapes, cherries, plums and apricots on people's hats. But 'I cannot help thinking', she concluded, 'that it is more natural to have flowers grow out of the head than fruit.'

Jane returned home from all this novelty at the end of June, and it's likely that she then completed the first draft of *Northanger Abbey*. The novel paints a promising, lively, lovely picture of Bath, and it reflects a young person's view of the city. 'Catherine was all eager delight', the narrator tells us, as she arrives. She was come to be happy.

Jane certainly enjoyed visiting Bath, but even the undemanding Catherine Morland ends up a little disappointed. And in Jane's own jolly letter about her arrival at Bath on her second visit there is likewise an undercurrent of small vexations: it was 'too wet and dirty' for them to get out of their carriage, an acquaintance was in mourning so deep that 'either his Mother, his Wife, or himself must be dead', her brother Edward was 'rather fagged', and with a lost trunk, Jane was 'impatient to know the fate of [her] best gown'.

So Bath had a darker side. And in due course Jane would learn more about how it got its name as 'the most dissipated place in the kingdom'.[32]

15

Homeless

'When shall I cease to regret you!'

Marianne on her old home in *Sense and Sensibility*

To be back at home at the Rectory was both a disappointment and a relief. Some things were just more relaxing, such as not having to dress up. 'I have made myself two or three caps to wear of evenings since I came home,' Jane wrote, 'and they save me a world of torment as to hair-dressing.' She describes saving time by having her long hair 'always plaited up out of sight', while her short fringe at the front naturally 'curls well enough to want no papering'. But Jane also brought home some high-flown ideas in the form of a little 'experimental housekeeping . . . I mean to have some little dumplings . . . that I may fancy myself at Godmersham.'

And Mr Austen was perhaps aping his grander relations too as he went on improving the Rectory. In 1792 he ordered what would become a well-loved four-poster bed with white dimity hangings for his wife and himself. Six new painted drawing room chairs, a dozen 'chamber chairs' and eight quires of wallpaper show that the Rectory was becoming a little bit more like the fashionable residences the family had seen in Bath.[1] Later, a 'modern set of circular dining tables' arrived from drunken Mr Bayle, the Winchester cabinet-maker.[2] A new Pembroke table had a lockable drawer, which pleased Mrs Austen, who could now keep her money in it, and 'the little Table' that used to stand in its place 'has most conveniently taken itself off into the best bed-room'. The best bedroom? Presumably Jane means her and Cassandra's own.

But as the 1790s, and Jane's twenties, progressed, the progress slowed. Gradually there set in a diminution of aspirations at the Rectory. This was partly the increasing age of the Austen parents, and partly changes in Hampshire society that saw the falling-off of the balls at Basingstoke that had been such a feature of the girls' youth. 'Our assemblies have very kindly declined ever since we laid down the carriage,' Jane wrote in November 1798, 'so that dis-convenience and dis-inclination to go have kept pace together.' The heavy taxes associated with the wars had caused the carriage to go. The 1790s were hungry years in Hampshire, for even while food production remained high, the demands of the war meant that prices were even higher.

That loss of the carriage represented a constriction of Jane and Cassandra's social life. We hear that Hampshire parties followed an unexciting groove. One unusually lively evening involved fourteen to dinner, plus six more to cards afterwards. After the dinner, Jane tells us, one couple flirted, one gentleman fell asleep, others read aloud 'Dr Jenner's pamphlet on the cow pox, & I bestowed my company by turns on all.'

But the daily grind came to an unexpected end in December 1800, when Mr Austen abruptly decided that at seventy, it was time to retire from parish life. He felt 'incapacitated from age and increasing infirmities to discharge his parochial Duties in a manner satisfactory to himself'.[3]

Vacating the Rectory would also mean that he could give it up to his son James and James's growing family, who'd be much happier there than in their tiny parsonage at Deane. Mr Austen would not give up the income from his livings. He would simply subcontract his son to be his curate for both Steventon and Deane instead of just Deane, as was already the case.

But where were Mr Austen, his wife and daughters to go? He decided on Bath. He and his wife knew the city well from visits to the Leigh Perrots. They could enjoy the city's leisure facilities and good healthcare in their old age. It seemed to Mr Austen to be an obvious decision, and he did not agonise over it. As his family knew, he 'was always rapid both in forming his resolutions and in acting on them'.[4]

However, Mr Austen did not bother to inform his daughters personally, but left it to his wife. After all, these two young ladies in their twenties were still just children to him. This attitude struck his granddaughter Anna, even when she was only nine or ten years of age. 'I thought it so very odd, to hear Grandpapa speak of them as "the Girls".'[5] Everyone else recognised that they were women.

By all accounts, the news of the permanent move to Bath came as quite a horrible surprise. 'Jane was exceedingly unhappy', her nephew records, because 'the loss of their first home is generally a great grief to young persons of strong feeling'.[6] It also came so unexpectedly: Jane had even 'been absent from home when this resolution was taken' and 'had little time to reconcile herself to the change'.[7]

We have a more detailed account of exactly how Jane found out. She and her friend Martha Lloyd 'had been away for a little while' on a visit. Arriving back at the Rectory, they 'were met in the hall' by Mrs Austen 'who told them it was all settled, and they were going to live at Bath'. The conversation was witnessed by James's wife Mary, come over from

Deane to welcome her sister Martha, and Mary recorded that the incident left Jane 'greatly distressed'.[8]

'When shall I cease to regret you!' cries Marianne Dashwood, on being forced to leave her home, Norland Park. 'When [shall I] learn to feel a home elsewhere!' It's tempting to imagine Jane responding in the same way when she too was forced to leave the only home she had known in her twenty-five years. And the family weren't just leaving a home, but also a neighbourhood, 'their dearest friends and connections'.[9] Jane was also deeply attached to the countryside of Hampshire itself: we hear that her delight in its 'natural scenery was such that she would sometimes say she thought it must form one of the joys of heaven'.[10]

By the time Jane's great-niece Fanny came to write a history of the Austen family, tradition had magnified Jane's reaction to the news of the move into 'such a shock that she fainted right away'.[11] The extreme, melodramatic response does sound most unlikely for the creator of a sensible heroine like Elinor Dashwood, who prided herself on taking bad news with 'no danger of a hysterical fit, or a swoon'. Swooning would have been most out of character; indeed, it sounds like a Victorian invention.[12]

Yet there is no doubt that Jane felt pain, not least at the lack of consultation. The decision was taken during a time when, unusually, both Jane and Cassandra were away from home at once. Indeed, the move's proposed timetable would hardly leave Cassandra time to come back to Steventon, and her personal possessions would now be dispersed in her absence. Anguished correspondence flew between them, for which Jane was sorry: 'it appears that I have rather oppressed you of late by the frequency of my letters'.

Perhaps there were factors in their father's decision that were not suitable for discussion with 'the Girls'; perhaps could that explain the lack of consultation. First, they were now twenty-eight and twenty-five. They had met all the young men of Hampshire, and they had been hawked unsuccessfully around the social circles of all their relatives. It seemed imperative to find them husbands.

Disagreeable Aunt Jane Leigh Perrot had a disagreeable explanation for the family's leaving Steventon, a move that in her opinion could not be accounted for upon health grounds alone. Removal was necessary, she thought, because Mr and Mrs Austen 'apprehended a growing attachment between William Digweed and Aunt Jane'. Mr Digweed was one of the brothers from the manor just up the road.[13] It is true that on 23 January, Jane was invited to dinner alongside William Digweed at Deane, and that an unexpected snowfall meant that the carriage was ordered to take her home. Perhaps he made an unwelcome proposal to her in the carriage as they jolted back to Steventon together through the snow, just as Mr Elton does in *Emma*. Jane described herself 'pretty well, I thank you, after it', as if the short journey had been something of an ordeal. But there is no hint as to what was wrong, if anything, with Mr Digweed as a possible suitor for Jane. He himself never married, and years later people still thought that for him 'there was some charm linked with her name'.[14]

And yet, even Bath was no longer quite the same happy hunting ground for husbands that it had been. By the start of the nineteenth century, it was a resort on the decline. As it grew less fashionable, it grew more feminised, a magnet for widows and spinsters. In *Mansfield Park*, for example, her son's marriage causes Mrs Rushworth to 'remove herself, with true dowager propriety, to Bath'. By 1841 there would be 10,767 spinsters to just 4,057 bachelors.[15]

It seems that Jane came right out with it and complained – vigorously – to her parents about having to give up her home to her brother James. One can imagine the conversations in which Jane's parents told her it was only natural that the wishes of the unmarried daughters should give way to those of the eldest son, even more so as he had a family of his own.

We can deduce this because the breaking up of life at the Rectory affected not just the Austens but their servants too. Mr Bond, Mr Austen's old factotum, now lost his job, after a 'most aweful' half-hour shut up with his boss. He chose a new position purely on the grounds that he wouldn't have to move house. 'The comfort of not changing his home', Jane wrote to Cassandra, 'is a very material one. And since such as his unnatural feelings', a new job locally was just what he wanted. These are the words of someone who has recently been told that it is 'unnatural' of her to want to cling to an old home.

Jane's letters continue to be bitter about arrangements for the move. As she records the handing-over of most of the family pictures to James, Jane reassures Cassandra that at least 'Your own Drawings will not cease to be your own.' Even Mr Bond ended up with a piece of Jane's old life, becoming the proud possessor of the family's painting, from the dining parlour, of the Swedish battle.[16]

It gave Jane great regret to see old possessions going over to new hands. The death of Mr Skipsey, an elderly horse of James's, meant that the Rectory brown mare was sent to Deane even before the handover of the house, '& everything else I suppose will be seized by degrees in the same manner'.

Everything else that James didn't want was now sold, including all that new furniture, the sisters' beds, and even Jane's old friends, the family's books. An advert for the auction placed in the *Reading Mercury* reveals that Jane had to leave behind not only her piano but also an extensive collection of music 'by the most celebrated composers'.[17] The other items disposed of, in a second sale of the farming goods on 18 September, were 'five capital cart horses, three sows and 22 pigs', along with equipment such as three market wagons, four ploughs, eight harrows, shovels, prongs, and two 4-inch wheel dung-carts.[18]

James's wife Mary bore the brunt of Jane's resentment. Although they had once been the closest of friends, Jane had turned against Mary since her marriage. She believed Mary to be agitating to get Jane's part of the family out of the Rectory for Mary's own benefit. When Mary and James had a party to celebrate their wedding anniversary, Jane was pointedly absent. 'I was asked, but declined it.'

Leaving the Rectory, under duress like this, was clearly the end of a chapter in Jane's life. But it was something that all unmarried young ladies could expect. Mary herself had been ripped from her childhood home of Deane Parsonage, and in due course she too would have to leave the Rectory to give way for the next generation.

In years to come, James and Mary's daughter Caroline, just like Jane herself, would be forced to leave her birthplace of Steventon Rectory to go and live at Bath. It was a trauma. When Caroline came to write her memoirs as a very old lady, she could get no further than the Rectory. 'The chapter of Steventon is closed', she wrote, and so was her task. 'When I first thought of reviving my own life-long recollections . . . I intended to follow their guidance into the other homes.' But now she found it impossible: 'I could not any longer make out a simple narrative of one family household.'[19] Steventon was her beginning and her end.

And there's a suggestion that not even Jane's mother had wanted to leave Steventon. Years and years later, in 1812, with her husband dead and much else altered, Mrs Austen returned to the Rectory for a final leave-taking. She stayed a fortnight before going back to her home, which she then never left again even for a single night. It was said that as she felt too old to go abroad, Mrs Austen desired that 'her last visit should be to [make] her farewell to the place where [the] most part of her married life had been spent'.[20]

They had to go. But would the Austen ladies ever cease to regret Steventon? The answer seems to be 'no'.

ACT TWO

A Sojourner in a Strange Land[21]

Milson Street, Bath

16

Bath

'. . . the most dissipated place in the kingdom'.[1]

Benjamin Silliman (1805/6)

IN MAY 1801, Mrs Austen and Jane departed for Bath. They were an advance party sent ahead to find the rest of the family a house to rent for their new life. The journey passed in sullen silence. 'We did not speak above once in three miles', Jane reported. Back in Steventon, James and his family lost no time in moving into the Rectory.

Bath, of course, was not a strange place to the Austens. Long ago though it may have seemed, Mr and Mrs Austen had been married there. Mrs Austen's father had also chosen Bath, 'much frequented in those days by clergymen retiring from work', for his own declining years.[2] Looking even further back into the past, Mrs Austen's grandmother had been the sister of the Duke of Chandos, one of the early investors in Bath's eighteenth-century redevelopment, and there was a 'Chandos Buildings' to prove it.

Mrs Austen and Jane were to stay at first with Mr and Mrs Leigh Perrot. They were on their best behaviour. Not only was James Leigh Perrot Mrs Austen's only surviving relative, but he also had the power to make a nice legacy. Although Mrs Leigh Perrot in particular could be a pain, the Austens would take great care, as Jane put it, 'to avoid anything that might seem a slight to them'.

The Leighs were now the main prospect in the deadly serious game of legacy hunting. In 1791 Mr Austen's rich Sevenoaks uncle, 'Old Francis' Austen, had died. Annoyingly, he had left most of his wealth to his own oldest son, who was rich already. 'Old Francis' had bequeathed Jane's father only £500, and had even excluded from his will a niece who had kept house for him for many years.[3] When the crunch came, primogeniture overwhelmed any feelings of fairness or charity.

According to their granddaughter Anna, who visited them there, Mr and Mrs Austen were at first delighted with their residence in Bath. They relished 'the cheerfulness of their Town life, and especially perhaps the rest which their advancing years entitled them to'. Indeed, to the unsentimental Anna, who'd had the good fortune to move into the

Rectory in place of her grandparents, there was nothing to bemoan about the new family arrangements: 'I have always thought that this was the short Holyday of their married life.'[4]

And there are also hints that Jane too grew more positive about the move than pride permitted her to admit to her friends and relatives after her first, extremely negative, reaction. 'I get more & more reconciled to the idea of our removal', she admitted privately to Cassandra before leaving Hampshire. 'We have lived long enough in this Neighbourhood.' And then, Jane wrote, there 'is something interesting in the bustle of going away', and Hampshire life was undeniably boring. But then, just as always when things get too serious, Jane undercuts herself with a joke: 'it must not be generally known however that I am not sacrificing a great deal in quitting the Country – or I can expect to inspire no tenderness, no interest in those we leave behind'.

And really, to be taken to live in Bath wasn't all that bad. Jane complained about 'disordering' her 'stomach with Bath buns', but she was joking. When Fanny Price returns to the home of her hardworking, non-genteel birth family in Portsmouth, Jane convincingly shows just how much Fanny was shocked by the small consideration paid to her own needs and desires, by comparison to the leisurely, luxurious life at Mansfield Park.[5] Fanny *had* to eat buns for dinner at her parents' house in Portsmouth, because she couldn't stomach their rough food. Jane was loved, safe, comfortable. Many, many Georgian women would have envied her.

Perhaps Jane was also encouraged to embrace her new life by the fact that her brother Henry had one too. In January 1801, he resigned his commission in the Oxfordshire Militia to begin a career as an army agent in London, living at 24 Upper Berkeley Street and renting an office in St James's. It was his job to liaise between the Paymaster General, and his own old regiment. He took over the running of his regiment's payroll, and in return convention allowed him to charge one 'warrant man' per company. This meant that he kept for himself the wages of one imaginary soldier in each company, at sixpence a day.

Henry might also act as a private banker for officers of the regiment, forwarding half-pay to soldiers living in retirement in the country, and even – though this was illegal – brokering the buying and selling of commissions.[6] He'd long had an eye for an opportunity. When his regiment was shipwrecked off Ireland, for example, he made the most of it by sucking up to important people in Dublin.[7] While the war lasted, Henry had the hope of making a great deal of money. But there's no denying that merry Henry Austen was in fact a decidedly dodgy fellow.

What would Bath produce for Jane's writing? By tradition, her longest sojourn in the city, undertaken against her wishes, was a barren, sterile, dismal time. People tend to superimpose upon her the feelings of Anne Elliot in *Persuasion*, who 'persisted in a very determined, though very silent disinclination for Bath'.

And it is true that the surviving written results of Jane's residence in Bath were . . . well, meagre. There was her unfinished, rather bitter novel *The Watsons*, written on paper with a watermark for 1803 so probably in progress in 1804. It trails off inconclusively immediately after the heroine muses upon her tricky situation in life: penniless, unmarried, and unwanted by her family, surrounded by 'Hard-hearted prosperity, low-minded Conceit, & wrong-headed folly'. 'She was become of importance to no one', was Emma Watson's gloomy conclusion. Under the circumstances, Jane hadn't the heart to finish Emma's story.

Part of the trouble was that Bath's heyday was over by 1800. The eighteenth-century aristocracy had gathered there for the season, but as the place grew more popular, it became less exclusive. The more Bath society was penetrated by members of the middling sort of people, the more the truly posh withdrew from the great and glittering public gatherings formerly presided over by Beau Nash.

Now Bath social life was increasingly staid, and involved smaller parties at private houses, where one was on constant display and could not hide in a crowd. It did not suit the introverted Jane. This was a city in which status was fluid. It could offer a bold fresh start to those who wished to grasp the opportunity. But to those who did not, Bath was a difficult place in which to create a home. Its society was too diffuse, too unsettled. An evening visit would involve the drinking of tea, and the timid exchanging of confidences among new acquaintances. As soon as friendship developed though, the ending of a six weeks' stay might snatch the other person away.

All this socialising was real work of a kind, for the hours of conversation might result in a contact, a friendship, a legacy. Yet it was work Jane did not relish. 'You were sick of civility', she has one character explain to another, with feeling in *Pride and Prejudice*. 'You were sick of civility, of deference, of officious attention. You were disgusted with the women who were always speaking, and looking, and thinking.'

Someone whom Jane met and did get to know well during these heavy-going evenings was a Mrs Lillingston, a friend of her aunt's, and then there was a Miss Holder. She '& I adjourned after tea into the inner Drawingroom', Jane wrote in 1801, 'to look over Prints & talk pathetically. She is very unreserved & very fond of talking about her deceased brother & Sisters.' Not a very good way of finding a husband, if that was one's purpose, and in no case a good way to have a good time.

But many of Bath's residents had no higher aim than getting through the hours. One visitor found the town as being 'without moral aim or intellectual dignity'. He described Bath's inhabitants as slaving away in pursuit of pleasure, 'till life slides from beneath their feet'.[8] Another described the city as 'a sort of great monastery, inhabited by single people, particularly superannuated females. No trade, no manufactures, no occupations of any sort, except that of killing time, the most laborious of all.'[9]

'Half of the inhabitants do nothing, the other half supply them with nothings',[10] continued the same writer, and Bath's surviving architectural heritage misleads us today by telling only half of the story. In 1800 it was a city of 30,000 permanent inhabitants, swollen each winter with a temporary population of a further 10,000 visitors. The fine big beautiful houses rented by rich invalids have generally been preserved, while the serried, squalid streets of small workers' cottages, once homes to the huge number of people who made a living out of the service industry, have largely been swept away in the name of twentieth-century improvement.

Bath's bustling, commercial centre provided the biggest contrast to life in Hampshire. In *Persuasion*, Lady Russell positively relishes the sounds of the city: 'the dash of other carriages, the heavy rumble of carts and drays, the bawling of the newsmen, muffin-men and milk-men, and the ceaseless clink of pattens'. To her they called to mind 'winter pleasures', a change from the monotony of the countryside, and a welcome 'quiet cheerfulness'. But her younger friend Anne, perhaps like Jane, found Bath depressing, and 'caught the first dim view of the extensive buildings, smoking in rain, without any wish of seeing them better'. She 'looked back, with fond regret' upon the seclusion of her country home.

Among the attractions of Bath was the medical care, and it is true that Mrs Austen's health had been in decline for years. Now she could benefit from the three public warm baths in the city: the Hot Bath at 49 degrees, the King's Bath at 46 degrees, or – the coolest, both literally, and in terms of the most fashionable – the Cross Bath, at 40 degrees.[11] Bath was uniquely placed among its rival British spa towns in having *natural* hot water springs. Patients usually arose early, and the most popular time for bathing was between six and nine. For a shilling, they could travel to the baths, already dressed for immersion, in a special, low kind of sedan chair. The invalid Mrs Smith, in *Persuasion*, in fact 'never quitted the house but to be conveyed to the warm bath'.

To bathe, men generally wore a 'sandy colour' fine canvas waistcoat and drawers and 'a lawn linen cap', while women wore a canvas gown and petticoat, 'with pieces of lead affixed at the bottom, to keep them down under the water'. These outfits were suitably modest for floating around in the warm water in the presence of gentlemen, for bathing was mixed. The ladies brought with them 'japanned bowls or basons, tied to their arms with ribands, which swim upon the surface of the water' to hold their handkerchiefs. While splashing about gently in the warm water, the company 'generally regale themselves with chocolate'.[12]

Although bathing was supposed to be good for your health, it wasn't terribly hygienic. In Tobias Smollett's humorous novel, one bather is shocked by the sight of a sick child with 'scrofulous ulcers' being bathed in the arms of an attendant. 'Suppose the matter of those ulcers, floating on the water, comes in contact with my skin?' he worries. Then, having investigated the plumbing of the baths and the Pump Room, he can't help 'suspecting' that there might be 'some regurgitation from the bath into the cistern of the pump' from which people drank.[13] Whether this was strictly true or not, these rumours persisted. One writer penned a poem about a young bather named Tabitha:

> So while little TABBY was washing her Rump,
> The Ladies kept drinking it out of a Pump.[14]

Jane now accompanied her Uncle James to the Pump Room each morning for his glass of water. But would a healthy young woman really have enjoyed living in this city of invalids, home of the 'Bath chair', a three-wheeled chair with steering, where the talk was 'only of diseases'?[15]

Almost immediately upon her arrival, though, Jane did find herself getting dressed up for a ball in the Upper Assembly Rooms. The fashion now was for closely figure-hugging dresses. Young ladies stalked round Bath, 'showing their shapes to all the men / Up Milsom-street, and down again' in their tight gowns.[16] *The Times* thought that 'if the present fashion of nudity continues its career, the Milliners must give way to the carvers, and the most elegant *fig-leaves* will be all the mode'.[17] This is the period when ladies started wearing drawers, which to us look like highly modest ankle-length trousers. But drawers were rather racy because you'd only need to wear them if you followed the fashion for tight, thin, muslin dresses. Without drawers beneath, a gust of wind against the transparent material would have revealed the wearer's bum. It's unlikely that staid Jane would have followed this new, body-conscious look.

Because the social season was nearly over for the summer, Jane's first Bath ball was 'a rather dull affair' and the attendance at the dancing was 'shockingly & inhumanly thin'. And although she was still only twenty-six, Jane was no longer first-bench material. She was now old enough to run into acquaintances who remembered her and Cassandra when, as she put it, 'we were very charming young Women'.

Social obligations met, Jane and her mother now used the Leigh Perrots' house in the Paragon as a base from which to hunt for a house to rent. Each square, each neighbourhood, had its own characteristics, and Jane carefully observed their nuances. In her Bath novels she would place characters' homes exactly where they ought to belong.

Sir Walter Elliot in *Persuasion*, for example, moves to Bath so that he might 'be important at comparatively little expense'. He rents a suitable house in 'Camden-place, a lofty, dignified situation, such as becomes a man of consequence'. Probably Jane had in mind one of the two houses under the pediment in the middle of the terrace, for Sir Walter's family revel in theirs being the best residence in the street.

However, readers familiar with Bath would have known that in 1788 a landslip had swept away the last five houses in Camden Place, which remains lop-sided and asymmetrical to this day. A Camden Place address implies that your financial situation – like Sir Walter's – is not as sound as it may seem. Sir Walter has a couple of manservants, so he can receive daytime visitors with 'all the state that a butler and footboy could give'. But he hosts 'no dinners' because that would reveal that he can't afford the appropriate manservants to serve the food. In real life an acquaintance of the Austen family, one Reverend Williams, wrote from Camden Place about a terrible dinner party. Miserably under-resourced, it was 'a great drag; invited at five, dinner not announced till six; & only a miserable joskins [country bumpkin] to wait upon 8 people'.[18]

The Austens probably hoped to find a house fairly quickly. The city was almost unrecognisable if you neglected to visit it for a few years, for 'there are so many new Buildings erected'.[19] But many thought Bath's landlords rapacious, and the property bubble bound to burst:

> Ye men of BATH, who stately mansions rear,
> To wait for tenants from the devil knows where.[20]

Despite the apparent over-supply of housing, though, the Austens soon ran into difficulties. Jane reported that Green Park Buildings were too damp, and the houses of New King Street too small. This was a common problem after the spaciousness of the Rectory. One of them was 'quite monstrously little' and 'the best of the sittingrooms not so large as the little parlour at Steventon'. It was a weary business, as the family all had different ideas of what was wanted. Mr Austen was in favour of cheapness, and only with reluctance would he consider what Jane called even 'a comfortable and creditable looking house'. Mrs Austen 'hankers after the Square dreadfully', the location of the house where they'd stayed in 1799. As for Jane herself, she soon became fatigued by the whole negotiation: 'I have nothing more to say on the subject of houses.'

Rent was clearly a difficulty. As the Austens had never paid for their accommodation before, they did not know quite how much they could afford. Jane reported an anxious wait for news of the sale of their effects at Steventon. 'Sixty one Guineas & a half for the three Cows gives one some support under the blow of only Eleven Guineas for the Tables', she wrote. 'Eight for my Pianoforte, is about what I really expected to get; I am more anxious to know the amount of my books.' The books and the piano had been too cumbersome to bring to Bath. Eventually the books were sold, but only for £70. The small sum made Jane very bitter about the privileges that were falling to her brother, now the occupant of her former home. 'The whole World is in a conspiracy to enrich one part of our family at the expense of another', she complained.

Among all the losses, the books were perhaps the worst. Jane would no longer have access to a private library, except during visits to Godmersham Park. She could subscribe to circulating libraries, and did so, but to buy books was beyond her means. At least Bath had nine private lending libraries, generally fitted up like this:

> To the left of the door there's a fireplace and there
> You may lounge, if you please, on a bench or a chair.
> A little way on to the right you'll behold
> The books that are bound up in calf and in gold . . .

These first books to be encountered were the serious works of non-fiction, but what most customers really wanted lay further in:

> In yonder recess you see novels, romances,
> Wise, witty and horrid, made up to all fancies.[21]

Meanwhile, the house hunt continued. On 7 May 1801, an advert tucked away inside *The Bath Chronicle* apparently failed to achieve any response.[22] It was run again on 21 May, this time on the front page, and this time it caught the Austens' eyes. Immediately below a notice to the creditors of a coach-maker who had gone bust was an advert for a house for rent near Sydney Gardens:

> THE LEASE of No. 4, SYDNEY-PLACE, three years and a quarter of which are unexpired at Midsummer. – The situation is desirable, the Rent very low and the Landlord is bound by covenant to paint the two first floors this summer. – A premium will therefore be expected.[23]

The rent, £150 a year, was relatively low because of the relatively short lease. The Austens went to make enquiries.

Perhaps they set out from their headquarters at 1, Paragon, to have a look. Sydney Place was a terrace opposite the green space of Sydney Gardens (which contain what's now the Holbourne Museum). Behind it was a garden, and nearby were meadows, for this was a new development right on the edge of the city. It was in the recently fashionable suburb of Bathwick, across the River Avon from the town centre, and reached via Robert Adam's Pulteney Bridge. Part of the attraction to Mr Austen, who now used a cane, was the level walk into the centre, unlike that from the superior terraces higher up on the slopes of Lansdown Hill.

It was a canny Scottish lawyer named William Pulteney – he'd adopted the surname of his heiress wife, Frances – who had set in train plans to build Pulteney Bridge in the 1760s. 'The pump Room must always be considered the center of Bath', he explained, but a new bridge would bring a good deal of Bathwick within a six-penny sedan chair fare of the centre.[24] He employed Robert Adam to build a bridge lined with shops. In 1801, though, the Austens would have used a temporary bridge because flooding had damaged the main structure, carrying away 'the house of a stay-maker erected on it'.[25]

After the bridge came Great Pulteney Street, and then Sydney Place. The row of houses was typical of the kind of get-rich-quick schemes at which the residents of Bath excelled, but its construction had gone far from smoothly. The property developer William Pulteney had a daughter, Henrietta Laura Pulteney, who became Countess of Bath in 1792 at the age of twenty-six. She was an unusual Georgian heiress in that she took a great deal of interest in her money. A shy woman, her father nevertheless taught her to run the family's property empire, and 'in those affairs which may be called business, she was considered an expert'.[26] In 1788 she drew up a contract with a firm of family builders named Lewis for the construction of numbers one to five Sydney Place.

Unfortunately Mr Lewis then died, which meant the whole deal was off. But the Countess signed a new deal with his two sons and so the work began, the Lewis family taking on a hundred-year lease, and paying a ground rent. This was how most development took place in Bath: the owner of the land entered into a contract with a building firm. The builders would raise the money, construct the houses, and benefit from a grace period before ground rent had to be paid back to the landowner.

No. 4 Sydney Place had cost £700 to build, and the Lewises had to meet various stipulations set by the Countess, such as providing lamps at the front. She, in return, had the responsibility of bringing 'good and wholesome soft water' through 'a sufficient number of principal pipes' to the houses. This was a great advantage of the Bathwick site, which benefited from springs on the hills behind.

One enormous change for the Austens at Sydney Place would be this access to piped water, whereas at the Rectory each bucket had to be carried indoors from the well or pump. Admittedly the water did not flow constantly, as there wasn't enough pressure. Each street had its own 'water day' when the supply was turned on and a house's lead cistern filled for the week. But in Bath it suddenly became a lot easier for Jane, if she wanted, to take a bath.

The agreement for the building of Sydney Place included a drawing for the front of the houses, signed off by the architect Thomas Baldwin. Baldwin was a rather corrupt figure, standing behind much of Bath's building boom, and eventually ousted from his public offices for financial irregularities. No one drew the back of the house, because Georgian Bath was all about making a fine first impression. Nobody cared what the rear looked like.

The deeds of no. 4 show that it was completed in 1792.[27] Sydney Place had been intended to have six sides wrapped round the Gardens, but only two of the six had been completed by 1794 when the war brought an end to the boom years. After the Lewis brothers died, and long after the Austens moved out, the house would end up in the possession of a notorious Bath money-lender. But for now at least, Sydney Place was a fine address, and the Austens' neighbours would include a baronet and a Major-General.[28]

Their new house had the typical plan of Georgian townhouses, two rooms, front and back, on each of four floors. These tall narrow houses, with their necessity of going up and down the stairs all day, struck one foreign visitor as absurd: 'the agility, the ease, the quickness with which the individuals of the family run up and down, and perch on the different storeys, give the idea of a cage with its sticks and birds'.[29]

There was an earth toilet in the small walled garden. In the basement was the kitchen. The entry floor contained the dining room at the front, perhaps with Mr Austen's study behind it. Next came the *piano nobile* with two reception rooms, linked by doors that could be opened to create one larger space.

The Austens also had to get used to burning coal in the fireplace of their elegant drawing room, instead of the wood of Steventon days. Coal was hauled into Bath by collier's ponies. An 'unfortunate *ass*', or coal donkey, was often to be seen, 'staggering under its unconscionable burthen, and labouring up the steep streets', a description which comes from a Bath guidebook that Mr Austen purchased, and which ended up in Jane's possession.[30] Bath's very existence is due to its hot springs, but its location in the hollow between seven hills has the unfortunate effect of trapping mists and damp weather. Add in coal smoke, and you got frequent pea-soup fogs, described by Jane as a mixture of 'vapour, smoke and confusion'.

Up again were three bedrooms, for Mr and Mrs Austen, Jane and Cassandra, and a guest room, while the servants had three rooms in the roof. These three servants, Jane joked, were to consist of 'a steady Cook, and a young giddy Housemaid with a sedate middle-aged Man, who is to undertake the double office of husband to the former and sweetheart to the latter. No children of course to be allowed on either side.'

The original plan had been to furnish the house with Jane and Cassandra's own beds from Steventon, along with Mr and Mrs Austen's bed, 'the best for a spare one, & two for servants'. But it had become clear that the transport would cause too much trouble and expense. When the Dashwoods moved to the West Country in *Sense and Sensibility*, Marianne's piano went with them, but had to be 'sent round by water', a great undertaking.[31] The Austens ended up buying new beds.

Sleeping for a few nights at Sydney Place – it's a holiday house now – reveals a lot about the hierarchies of Georgian society. The house is all about show, and it did make a suitable shop window for Mr Austen to display his unmarried daughters. The entrance hall is elegant, the stairs wide and shallow, easy to glide up or down in a long, narrow dress. The first-floor drawing room is spacious and grand, with the elegant Sydney Hotel, marking the entrance to the pleasure gardens, dominating the view. Next comes the bedroom floor, not quite as high from floor to ceiling, but still very generous compared to modern space standards. Then, as you ascend to the garret storey, everything suddenly changes. You have to squeeze up a tiny bent staircase. You're now in the world of the servants. The stairs are narrow and uneven; the doors are flimsy. This whole top floor under the rafters sighs and settles a little at night. Draughts whistle in through the single glazing and you can hear the noises of the street below. Floorboards shift and groan as you walk. It's like living in a slightly swaying crow's nest, perched on top of the substantial, almost palatial apartments below.

The whole of Bath was built in this gimcrack manner: fine at the front, corners cut where they could not be seen. In *Persuasion*, Admiral Croft actually rather liked his creaky Bath lodgings, because they reminded him of life in his old naval lodgings in Norfolk: 'the wind blows through one of the cupboards in just the same way'. The Austens would have been comfortable in this house; their servants less so.

The house's front façade is very fine, with pretty, light Corinthian columns flanking the staircase window over the front door. But from its back windows you see the raggedy, uneven backsides of another terrace behind. The Austens had that promised painting by the landlord to look forward to, which would smarten up the interiors. The craftsmen of Bath generally did their work from June onwards, after the gentry left town for their country houses, and continued 'till the Return of the Company to Town in Winter'.[32] The novelty colour of 'patent yellow' – 'a new invented colour very bright and durable; dries well' – was extremely popular in Bath.[33] Otherwise known as 'Indian Yellow', it was made out of the concentrated urine of Indian cows given mango leaves to eat, and no water to drink.[34] Perhaps yellow was the colour chosen at no. 4 Sydney Place. It turned out, though, that the painting applied only to the ground and first floors. Jane and Cassandra's bedroom, on the third, was left dingy.

Just across the road from the Austens' new house were Sydney Gardens, sometimes called 'The Vauxhall of Bath'. They offered amusements including swings, bowling greens, and an extensive labyrinth twice as big as Hampton Court's famous maze. No opportunity was lost for merchandising: at the bar, you could buy a plan of the labyrinth to help you find the centre.

'Yesterday was a busy day with me, or at least with my feet', Jane reported to Cassandra after moving in. 'I was walking almost all day long; I went to Sydney Gardens soon after one, & did not return till four.' But like everything in Bath, the gardens did not come cheap. It was sixpence for a single visit, or two shillings and sixpence for a monthly subscription. Here nature was tamed and sanitised, 'being free from dust in summer and dirt in winter'.[35] There could be no sharper contrast with life in Hampshire. Jane, who loved to walk, who considered that the Hampshire countryside must be among the 'joys of heaven', now had to pay sixpence just to see a bit of tawdry greenery.

Did Jane like her new life? We do not really know, because when

Cassandra also came to live at Sydney Place as well Jane had no need to write letters. But the general feeling is that she did not. Jane would not have known what we mean by experiencing depression, but she describes the condition that we'd recognise rather brilliantly in Fanny Price and Marianne Dashwood. Her very occasional letters from this early time in Bath are sad, sharp, lonely. She thought she was going to have to stay there for the rest of her life.

However, having found their new house in May, it was only in October that the Austens planned to move in.[36] In the meantime, they were off on holiday.

17

The Sea

'Nobody could catch cold by the sea;
nobody wanted appetite by the sea;
nobody wanted spirits;
nobody wanted strength.'

Jane Austen, *Sanditon*

Before the Georgian age, you wouldn't have wanted to live by the sea unless you were a fisherman. Why risk being near to something so profoundly untamed and dangerous? Only in the later eighteenth century did people actively seek out the sea for its romantic and its health-giving properties. And some, like Jane Austen, sought it with all their might.

At the end of May 1801, the Austens shot off again from the city to which they had moved so hurriedly. It might seem odd that they purchased an expensive lease only to abandon Sydney Place immediately, but there was that painting to be done, and possibly they had sub-let it in the short term to help cover the cost of the £150 annual rent. After all, now that he had given up the farm, Mr Austen's income was only £600 p.a.

But we also cannot underestimate the attraction of the coast. The hope of holidays was one of the things that helped reconcile Jane to leaving Steventon: 'the prospect of spending future summers by the Sea or in Wales is very delightful'. This meant rented lodgings, and a makeshift life on the shifting sands of the Georgian bathing resort. These 'holidays' lasted weeks, even months. They were, in fact, a way of living cheaply but pleasantly, rather like out-of-season, cut-price package deals to the Canary Islands for pensioners today. In October 1801, one Austen cousin wrote to another 'of our Uncle & Aunt Austen and their daughters having spent the [whole] summer in Devonshire'.[1]

Jane, Cassandra and their parents never travelled abroad, and these were the years when the British were rediscovering their own island. They could not go off on Grand Tours of Europe because, with the exception of the brief Peace of Amiens from March 1802 and into 1803, the Napoleonic Wars meant that 'the Continent was quite shut to the British idler'.[2]

And so the British went instead to the Lakes, or the Peaks like the Gardiners in *Pride and Prejudice*, or to the West Country. As the craze for the 'staycation' grew, it began to be satirised, with characters emerging in popular culture like the poet William Combe's hapless, hilarious 'Dr Syntax', an impoverished parson whose tour of Britain in search of the Picturesque goes disastrously wrong. His journey to the Lake District ends with him falling *into* a lake. He thinks he's found the perfect Picturesque moment in a 'stately wood', until he is set upon and tied up by ruffians. He also gets drunk, and lost:

> The evening low'rd: – a drizzly rain
> Had spread a mist o'er all the plain;
> Besides, the home-brew'd beer began
> To prey upon the inward man:
> And Syntax, muddled, did not know
> Or where he was, or where to go.[3]

Jane was a fan of the comical traveller, and enjoyed looking out in real life for people who had the signature 'long chin' given to Dr Syntax in the story's amusing illustrations by Thomas Rowlandson.

The Austens' movements over a succession of seaside summers are not entirely clear, but they probably visited Sidmouth and Colyton in 1801, choosing the area because they could stay (cheaply) with one of Mr Austen's former pupils. An 1802 tour took them to Dawlish and probably Teignmouth, then right into Wales, possibly to visit Tenby and Barmouth. The evidence for Jane's having been to Dawlish is highly characteristic: twelve years later she complained that 'The Library was particularly pitiful & wretched' there. In 1803 it was the turn of Charmouth and Uplyme in Dorset. They paid two visits to Lyme Regis, in 1803 and again in 1804.

But perhaps the strongest pull towards the sea was the prospect of sea bathing. Doctors were by now recommending bathing as the cure for nearly all ills. Joseph Browne's seminal *Account of the Wonderful Cures Perform'd by the Cold Baths* (1707) suggested that plunging into cold water could cure rickets, scrofula, 'weakness of Erection', and 'a general disorder of the whole Codpiece Economy'. Indeed, his views became reflected in a popular ditty:

> Cold bathing has this Good alone
> It makes Old John to hug Old Joan
> And gives a sort of Resurrection
> To buried Joys, through lost Erection.

Sea bathing was also promoted as the cure for infertility and constipation. As a consequence, a tourist industry grew up to challenge fishing and trade in many maritime settlements. By 1803, the author of *A Guide to All the Watering and Seabathing Places* could claim that it had become 'the rage, to make annual excursions to the coast'.[4] The coastline considered suitable for the genteel visitor expanded as time went on, reaching 'west and south, farther and farther every eight or ten years; from Weymouth to Sidmouth, from Sidmouth to Exmouth, and so on to Dawlish and Teignmouth'.[5]

Sea bathing also had the seal of royal approval. In 1804, Cassandra and Henry Austen visited Weymouth, and were disappointed to miss seeing the Royal Family who had also been on holiday there. Frances Burney noted that Weymouth was a particularly patriotic place. During one visit of George III's, she wrote, 'think but of the surprise of His Majesty when, the first time of his bathing, he had no sooner popped his royal head under water than a band of music, concealed in a neighbouring machine, struck up "God save great George our King"'.[6]

Mrs Austen, with her long-term ill-defined health problems, was an obvious candidate for bathing, but the sea seems to have particularly suited Jane. In 1803 she was in Ramsgate, where she once more met the snooty novelist Sir Egerton Brydges, brother of her friend Madam Lefroy. He found her, in her late twenties, looking extremely well, 'fair and handsome, slight and elegant, but with cheeks a little too full'.[7] But he still never 'suspected that she was an authoress', and never took the trouble to find out.[8]

It was the war that took the Austens to Ramsgate in 1803. The threat of invasion was naturally felt to be greatest along the south coast. Frank Austen had been placed in charge of the 'Sea Fencibles', who had the job of defending Kent. He found his troop's individual members to be quite useless – 'a non-descript half-sailor half-soldier as efficient as neither' – but nonetheless he set industriously about making a detailed survey of all the possible landing places where the French might be expected.[9] There were consolations to the unexciting work. In Ramsgate, as well as receiving visits from his family, he also met his future wife, Mary Gibson.

In some resorts, mobile wooden 'bathing machines' were drawn down from the beach into the waves, while in others, the sea at high tide gushed into a permanent bathing house. A bathing machine was like a garden shed on wheels, and could be pulled by strong men right into the breakers so the bather could jump straight into the water. They were therefore very labour-intensive. As holidaymakers gradually grew more athletic, and more used to swimming, the bathing machines became less necessary, and retreated to their fixed position at the back of the sands as today's beach huts.

A male or female assistant, called the 'bather' or 'dipper', might help the nervous to get up courage, and support the non-swimmer safely among the waves. People generally did not know how to swim until it started to develop as a competitive sport in the 1830s. The Prince of Wales (the future George IV) had his own favourite bather, John 'Old Smoaker' Miles of Brighton, but refused to heed his expert advice. 'Mr Prince, Mr Prince, come back', Old Smoaker would call, if George went out too far, before swimming after him and 'seizing him by the ear' to drag him to shore.[10] Jane, like most of her contemporaries, probably could not swim, as she mentions using a dipper named Molly, who once was 'so pressing with me to enjoy myself' that she stayed in too long, and got too cold.

One Mrs Constantia Orlebar gives us her account of her very first swim, in the tide-filled baths at Southampton. As Jane had likewise visited Southampton in her teenage years, perhaps this is the best guide to how she first experienced immersion in seawater. Constantia wore a 'Green Flannel Gown' and her sister-in-law a leather head-bag 'to preserve her fore Hair in Curl'. The sister-in-law went in first, 'with very tolerable Courage and from farther Practise became most Heroical'. When it was her turn, Constantia owned that 'a Panic struck me, but I gave my hands to Mrs Tring [her dipper] and took the Flounce, which was for a Moment the most wonderful Sensation! I rose above the Water near strangled with the Quantity (by not shutting my mouth) I inadvertently swallowed. How happy did I feel myself when on dry Ground again!'[11]

'The most wonderful Sensation!' The sea in *Emma* stands firmly for sex: it is where Frank meets his love Jane Fairfax; it is where Emma and Mr Knightley go on their honeymoon. For the Georgian gentlewoman, it was clear that to be buffeted about by waves, wonderful and terrible, was a source of physical pleasure.

And for Jane, too, the seaside symbolised passion. According to evidence left to us by Cassandra, the great love of Jane's life was not Tom Lefroy at all, but a mysterious gentleman met during these summer holidays while the family were living in Bath.

It was, according to Cassandra, 'while staying at some seaside place' that 'they became acquainted with a gentleman, whose charm of person, mind, and manners was such that Cassandra thought him worthy to possess and likely to win her sister's love. When they parted, he expressed his intention of soon seeing them again; and Cassandra felt no doubt as to his motives.'[12] So here is the third serious suitor of Jane Austen, notorious spinster!

In the passage above, Cassandra's story was transcribed by her nephew

James Edward Austen-Leigh. But his sister Caroline has a more convincing memory of what Cassandra might have said, worded as if to recall real speech. 'In Devonshire', Caroline recollected, 'an acquaintance was made with some very charming man – I never heard Aunt Cass. speak of anyone else with such admiration – she had no doubt that a mutual attachment was in progress between him and her sister.'[13]

This mysterious gentleman was even given a name by another Austen cousin, Catherine Hubback, who called him 'Dr. Blackall'. Her version of the story has the couple part with the coming of autumn. But the mysterious admirer 'was urgent to know where they would be the next summer, implying or perhaps saying that he should be there also wher- ever it might be . . . he had fallen in love with Aunt Jane'. And there was no 'doubt either that he would have been a successful suitor'.

Here Catherine Hubback is backed up by the evidence of Anna Lefroy, the niece closest to her aunts, and therefore the person most likely to know the truth. 'Even Aunt Cassandra thought him worthy of her sister', Anna told her own daughter. 'They parted on the understanding that he was to come to Steventon.'[14]

Jane's relatives all grow warm in their insistence that something really had happened; that there really was a suitor. 'I have no doubt', wrote her niece Caroline, 'that Aunt Jane was beloved of several in the course of her life and was herself very capable of loveing.'[15]

Unfortunately, the different witnesses are at odds with each other when it comes to what happened next. Some claim that the mysterious suitor was met in 1801, others that it was some six or eight years later. Some recall his name as 'Dr' Blackall, others as 'Mr Edward Blackall'. And then: 'If I do not mistake there were two brothers', one of them a doctor. This latter gentleman, we hear, 'Aunt Cassandra met with again long afterwards', only to find him 'stout, red-faced and middle-aged'.[16]

From all these confused family memories, the only safe facts to emerge are that somewhere early in the nineteenth century, Jane had a holiday romance in a West Country watering-place. Anna Lefroy's daughter Fanny is the most specific about who he really was: 'a young clergyman then was visiting his brother who was one of the doctors of the town'.[17]

Indeed, it has even been suggested that we have already met the mysterious gentleman, back in Hampshire, and that he was none other than Reverend Samuel Blackall, who came courting in the aftermath of Tom Lefroy. The Reverend Samuel did have a brother who was a doctor, Dr John Blackall, physician to the district of Totnes.[18] Perhaps Mrs Austen needed medical advice while in Devon, which would explain the Austens and the Blackalls returning into each other's orbit. Perhaps Reverend

Blackall, who'd lacked the money to 'indulge' himself with a proposal of marriage in 1798, could by now could afford to do so, and sought Jane out for a second time.

But if Reverend Blackall was our mysterious suitor, then why did he never actually make Jane an offer? Several of the Austen family stories agree upon a point that makes it highly unlikely that Blackall was indeed the man in the case. Having parted at the end of the summer, all seemed set for a further meeting between Jane and her love, and probably a proposal. But then there came a horrible letter, some little time after, 'to say that he was dead'.

The story does finally disperse into thin air, like trying to pin down a cloud, when in 1813 we hear that Reverend Blackall, far from dying, got married to another lady instead. And Jane, hearing the news, did not sound at all distressed. She spotted the announcement in the newspaper, and found herself wondering 'what sort of Woman she is'. Lack of knowledge did not prevent Jane from imagining a cold fish: 'of a silent turn & rather ignorant . . . fond of cold veal pieces, green tea in the afternoon, & a green window blind at night'.

As for the talkative, instructive Samuel Blackall himself, Jane remembered him as 'a peice of Perfection, noisy Perfection himself which I always recollect with regard'. This damning with faint praise is what makes people think that the fictional offspring of Jane Austen and Samuel Blackall was the respectable but prosy Mr Collins from *Pride and Prejudice*.

There is just one common factor to all the stories: that the romance took place by the sea. In *Emma*, Emma Woodhouse herself imagines that Jane Fairfax must be in love with the mysterious Mr Dixon because he saves her from the waves, just like Jane's own 'dipper'. Without the strength of his arms, as Miss Bates put it, Miss Fairfax 'would have been dashed into the sea at once'. And just like a Georgian lady plunged into the sea for the first time, Miss Bates too is alarmed and excited at the prospect: 'I can never think of it without trembling!' The sea, then, made ladies tremble.

But for Jane this mysterious, knee-trembling romance of these summers by the sea was to be followed up by a more realistic romance, on the solid dry ground of Hampshire.

18

Manydown Park

'How can you imagine me an advocate
for marriage without love?'

Mansfield Park

THE SUMMER TOUR towards Wales in 1802 finished up with Jane and
Cassandra returning to their old home at Steventon Rectory, to
spend November there with their brother James and Mary.

The next stop after Steventon was to be Manydown Park, home of
their old friends, Catherine and Alethea Bigg. And now, once again,
something happened that the Austens don't want us to know about. 'My
own wish would be, that not any allusion should be made to the
Manydown story', wrote Jane's niece Caroline.[1]

Only four miles from Steventon along the road towards Basingstoke,
the Bigg sisters' house was well known to Cassandra and Jane. They'd
often visited it in Steventon days, sometimes sleeping there after the
Basingstoke balls. Manydown Park is no longer standing today, but it was
described by Nikolaus Pevsner as 'long, plain and flat'.[2] This was no
nobleman's seat. But it was ancient, comfortable, and intriguing.

The house had seventeenth-century origins. William Wither in 1649
purchased a property consisting of 'a faire Hall, a Parlour Wainscotted,
a Kitchen, a Buttery' and 'two Cellars'. Constructed round a courtyard,
a chamber to one side was the old courtroom 'where the lord of the
Manor . . . for nearly 400 years the Withers of Manydown' held a court
to settle the affairs of their tenants.[3] Timber from the Manydown estate
was used to build the roof of the nave of Winchester Cathedral. Another
ancient feature was the well with its ingenious 'raising gear' which lifted
water to first-floor level, thus to power the house's taps.[4]

But it was not a completely old-fashioned mansion. In the 1790s, the
Biggs sisters' father, Lovelace Bigg-Wither, had built a new dining room,
with 'a large drawing room over it'.[5] Lovelace Bigg-Wither was a generous
country squire, a magistrate, and a founder of charities. As a man of
affairs, he was presumably not often to be found reading the 'enormous
great stupid quarto volumes' that Jane spotted in his breakfast parlour. A

widower, with two marriages behind him, he had a large and complicated clutch of children, some with one wife's name, some with the other. These offspring included Catherine and Alethea. Jane and Cassandra must also have looked forward to the company of their friends, and the 'Candour & Comfort & Coffee & Cribbage' they always found at their home.

The Austen sisters arrived on 25 November. Also present at Manydown Park that winter was Catherine and Alethea's rather silent brother, Harris Bigg-Wither. The Wither family had boldly addressed their slightly unfortunate surname by making their family motto a chilling *memento mori*: 'I grow and wither both together'. Harris, who was 'very plain in person', had done a great deal of growing. Despite his lack of conventional good looks, he had 'his size to recommend him – he was a fine big man'.[6]

Jane and Cassandra had been enjoying themselves at Manydown for a week when, on the evening of Thursday 2 December, this quiet young man opened his mouth to say something rather surprising.

He asked Jane to marry him.

And she said 'yes'. It must have been a pleasant evening. The four friends would now become sisters, Jane would end up as mistress of Manydown Park, and there must have been joy and delight.

There were so many advantages to Jane in accepting this offer. There was Harris himself. Although not handsome, 'he had sense in plenty & went through life very respectably, as a country gentleman'. Then, besides his good sense, 'all worldly advantages' would have been due to Jane as his wife, '& she was of an age to know this quite well'.[7]

Indeed, among Jane's feelings there must have been enormous relief. She wasn't on the shelf. She was now almost twenty-seven, approaching what she described, in *Persuasion*, as the 'years of danger'. As Anne Elliot knew, it was very pleasurable 'for a woman to be assured, in her eight-and-twentieth year, that she has not lost one charm of earlier youth'.

The financial wisdom of the decision must also have weighed heavily upon Jane's mind as she accepted Harris's offer. 'Single Women', she wrote, 'have a dreadful propensity for being poor – which is one very strong argument in favour of Matrimony.' Both she and Cassandra were conscious of the fairly grim financial future facing them: 'on their Father's death they & their Mother would be, they were aware, but poorly off'. [8]

And it was no small thing to avoid the social stigma of being a spinster. By the Georgian age, the word had taken its modern meaning of an unmarried woman, as opposed to the operator of a spinning wheel. As the Napoleonic Wars depleted the number of men available for marriage, people developed an even clearer idea of who a spinster was. She had developed a fixed social identity, and it was not a happy one.

William Hayley even wrote a book, his *Essay on Old Maids*, to spell out what would happen to the unmarried daughter of a gentleman. 'It is probable', Hayley wrote, 'that after having passed the sprightly years of youth in the comfortable mansion of an opulent father, she is reduced to the shelter of some contracted lodging in a country town, attended by a single servant.'[9] It's been argued that in any given year two-thirds of eighteenth-century women were single, many as widows, some as spinsters. And they were particularly vulnerable to poverty.[10] Miss Mary Russell Mitford, a spinster herself, painted a miserable picture of the 'old maid and her stunted footboy', her 'affected gentility and real starvation'.[11]

Jane herself knew many single older women in distressed circumstances. Mrs Lloyd, for example, mother of Martha and Mary, had had a companion called Mrs Stent, 'of rather inferior position in life, and reduced from family misfortunes, to very narrow means'.[12] As Jane wrote: 'Poor Mrs Stent! it has been her lot to be always in the way; but we must be merciful, for perhaps in time we may come to be Mrs Stents ourselves, unequal to anything & unwelcome to everybody.'

But almost worse than the physical inconveniences of life as a spinster – at least in William Hayley's opinion – would be the mental ones. Spinsters must be 'considerably embittered', he thought, 'by their disappointment in the great object of female hope'. The 'great object of female hope', was, of course, to get married and have children.[13] Not everyone had the mental strength to tough it out in the face of this enormous social pressure. One unmarried governess, Nelly Weeton, described how 'an old maid is a stock of everyone to laugh at. Boys play tricks upon them, and are applauded. Girls sneer at them, and are unreproved. Upon my word, I think I will write an essay upon the pitiable state of old maids.'[14]

Another advantage of the Manydown match that must have occurred to Jane was that she'd marry not just Harris, but all the Biggs and Bigg-Withers. In an age when one married a family as opposed to just a single spouse, this was an attractive part of the bargain. Jane and Cassandra had been friends for many years with Catherine and Alethea, as well as their older sister Elizabeth. In saying 'yes', we're told by one neglected family source, Jane had been 'swayed by the wishes of some of her own family & by her warm regard for some of his'.[15]

And then, there was the house. The house! Jane would in due course become the mistress of Manydown Park. Perhaps the biggest advantage of all was that the marriage would give her a home. It would 'take her from the Bath she disliked and restore her to the country she loved'.[16] Jane had been writing about this since childhood. As one of her early heroines puts it, 'There are a thousand advantages to be derived from a marriage . . . besides those inferior ones of Rank and Fortune it will procure me a home, which of all other things is what I most desire.' Additionally, Jane would have been able to offer a home to her father and mother, and to Cassandra too. For, as Jane put it in another story, 'luck to one member of a family is luck to all'.

In the circumstances, one of Jane's relations concluded, most young women 'would have taken Mr W. & trusted to love after marriage'.[17]

But the next morning, Jane broke it all off. Ouch. She'd presumably suffered a sleepless night, just as 'headake and fatigue' followed Anne Elliot through the hours after a marriage proposal. We have no information about how Jane actually broke her decision to Harris, but it would seem entirely characteristic if she had written him a letter.

What could she have been thinking? Harris himself was perhaps at the centre of the problem. Although there was nothing terribly wrong with him, he was described as being 'awkward, & even uncouth in manner'. There really was little 'but his size to recommend him'.[18] He may have been big, but he was also rather sickly; indeed only two years previously, Jane had written that 'Harris seems still in a poor way, from his bad habit of body; his hand bled again a little the other day'. This injured hand was a lasting problem. 'I now fear he will never recover the use of it', was the opinion of Madam Lefroy.[19]

Then, there was an age gap of six years between them. And it was very noticeable. Having had an older brother (now dead), and six older sisters, Harris was used to being overlooked. His stammer meant that he did not often speak, and he had failed to complete his degree at Worcester College, Oxford.[20] When he did open his mouth, he could be dreadfully rude. A story is told that he once served a group of guests a horrible punch, made of all kinds of wine mixed up together. 'Gentlemen', he is supposed to have said, 'my punch is like you. In your individual capacity you are all very good fellows, but in your corporate capacity you are very disagreeable.'[21]

One of the Austens was pretty straightforward about the reason for Jane's breaking it off overnight. Harris was so awful, she said, that 'one need not look about for [a] secret reason to account for a young lady's not loving him'.[22] Indeed, she thought that Jane had discovered that 'the place & fortune which would certainly be his, could not alter the man'.[23]

You might also be wondering if Jane's decision was affected by a lingering feeling for Tom Lefroy. But this is highly unlikely. Her encounter with him was now seven years in the past, and as Jane wrote elsewhere, 'seven years I suppose are enough to change every pore of one's skin, & every feeling of one's mind'. And yet, by a cruel coincidence, Manydown Park was the very same house in which Jane had once danced with Tom Lefroy. Perhaps it was the thought of the sensations that Tom had aroused that encouraged Jane to act upon her change of heart: not so much the memory of the man, but the memory of being in love.

After all, Jane did come from this new generation of romantics, who were beginning to believe that, contrary to what their parents had told them, one should never settle for second best. 'You did not love him,' Jane has Edmund say to Fanny in *Manfield Park*, 'nothing could have justified your accepting him'. They sound like words from Jane's own heart. 'Nothing', she later wrote to her niece Fanny, 'can be compared to the misery of being bound *without* Love, bound to one, & preferring another. *That* is a Punishment which you do *not* deserve.'

At the same time, Jane certainly recognised, and to some extent sympathised with, the contrasting belief that money mattered, and to single women more than anyone. She paints a compassionate picture of Charlotte Lucas, who marries a house rather than a man in *Pride and Prejudice*. 'I am not romantic you know,' says Charlotte, 'I never was. I ask only a comfortable home.'

But then Charlotte is not a heroine, and all of Jane's heroines will marry for love and nothing else. Of course their suitors come with material advantages, and no one chooses foolishly, but what it really comes down to, for Catherine Morland, Elinor Dashwood, Lizzy Bennet, Fanny Price, Emma Woodhouse and Anne Elliot, is finding the right man.

Or . . . so you think at first.

Jane's novels are celebrated for the new meanings you pick up each time you reread them. And when Jane approaches the moment when her heroines must marry, it is possible to argue that something a little strange happens to her storytelling. Yes, this is a highly contentious suggestion, but bear with me. If you look at the exact moments where love is brought to a climax, and matches are made, you *may* find them a little abrupt, almost perfunctory. We don't hear Emma Woodhouse accepting Mr Knightley's proposal, we don't see Edmund falling in love with Fanny Price. And in the very final paragraph of *Mansfield Park*, the object of Fanny's affections, like Charlotte Lucas's, is defined as a house. It was Mansfield Parsonage that she now finds 'as dear to her heart' as anything.[24] Perhaps Jane treated these events lightly, almost mechanically, because she didn't really believe that a man, on his own, could bring a happy ending.

So, if there is even a smidgeon of possibility that Jane herself might choose to marry a house, it's important to note that there were problems with Manydown itself. It would not have immediately become her home. Harris Bigg-Wither had a poor relationship with his father, who was ensconced at Manydown, and he would have wanted Jane to live somewhere else until he came into his inheritance.

But looking beyond these immediate, urgent arguments, there were others – more nebulous, less socially acceptable – that Jane must have made to herself as she debated the matter in her mind. Yes, one of the advantages of the match was that it would have enabled her to look after Cassandra, and to bring her to Manydown. Yet they no longer would have been the 'couple' that they had become.

William Hayley thought that women who did not want to marry and reproduce must be 'utterly devoid of tenderness'.[25] And yet Jane and Cassandra did *not* feel those dutiful desires for husband and children. As their mother used to say, the sisters were 'wedded to each other'.[26] Marianne expresses the closeness between sister and sister in Jane's novel *Sense and Sensibility*, a warmer tenderness than that to be found between many a Georgian man and his subservient wife. 'You,' Marianne says to Elinor, 'You, who had known all the murmurings of my heart!' As Jane herself put it, 'there are as many forms of love as there are moments in time'. Why place married love so far above the rest?

What did Cassandra herself think? It's very hard to say, but it may be illuminating that one of the very few recorded disagreements between her and Jane involved the ending of *Mansfield Park*. Cassandra thought that Jane should have married Fanny Price to the rich and worldly Henry Crawford. But despite 'their arguing about the matter', Jane 'stood firmly'.[27] And Mrs Austen too took against *Mansfield Park*, with its celebrated, harrowing scene of a poor woman turning down a rich man because she cannot love him.[28] Cassandra and Mrs Austen's attitude *can* be read as a coded disapproval of Jane's overly nice sensitivities about marrying for money.

Despite Cassandra's possible disapproval of Jane's breaking her engagement, it might have been Cassandra's own example that spurred Jane on. Like Cassandra, Jane could now say that she had the chance of marriage, and had lost it. Like Cassandra, Jane now seemed to become almost like a widow. In the future they even wore the clothes of widows, no longer aiming to attract men. They dressed as a pair, their bonnets 'precisely alike in colour, shape & material'.[29] As their nephew said, his aunts 'were generally thought to have taken to the garb of middle age earlier than their years or their looks required'.[30]

Jane set out exactly how much she valued female companionship in a letter to her niece Fanny. 'You are worth your weight in Gold', she told

Fanny. 'I cannot express to you what I have felt in reading your history of yourself, how full of Pity & Concern & Admiration & Amusement I have been . . . Oh! what a loss it will be when you are married.' As it turned out, Jane was right. Fanny as a married lady would be far less fun. 'I shall hate you', Jane wrote with prescience, 'when your delicious play of Mind is all settled down into conjugal and maternal affections.'

If Jane was close to Fanny, she was even closer to Cassandra, and among the letters that Cassandra destroyed in the name of discretion must have been many more throwing such a light on their relationship. At this stage in Jane's life, the bond between women was not worth breaking except for the very best of marriages. Despite appearances, some old maids were very well aware of the value of their freedom. 'Really', wrote one of them, 'there is so much Care in a Married State & fiddle faddle in most Men's Tempers that I Esteem myself vastly happier in having nothing to do with 'em.'[31]

A fear of friendship diminished, and freedom curtailed, meant that when Jane's friends ceased to be single, her response was often open regret. Catherine Bigg would soon marry herself, an occasion that Jane would mark with a gift of home-hemmed handkerchiefs, and a poem about weeping. Jane wished that the handkerchiefs 'may last for years, Slight be her Colds & few her Tears', before realising that these funereal lines were not quite appropriate for what was *meant* to be a happy occasion. 'Have no Tears to wipe, but Tears of joy!' was her tactful redrafting of her verse.[32]

3 December 1802, the day Jane turned down Manydown Park, is a decisive date in her life because this is the moment she seems to change, from Elinor Dashwood to Anne Elliot, from a person who'd settle for a perfectly reasonable match, to one holding out for the unreasonably perfect. Liberty, and Cassandra, turned out to be more important to Jane than a comfortable home.

After Jane had delivered her refusal to Harris that December morning, she and Cassandra insisted that the Bigg sisters take them at once by carriage back to Steventon Rectory. If Harris had been the one to retract his offer, Jane could have sued him for breach of promise. But ladies were allowed a little more latitude. Indeed, the period of courtship before marriage was the only time in their lives in which they actually held the balance of power in a relationship with a man. Jane had behaved badly, but not terribly.

After the four ladies had escaped to Steventon, though, the circumstances were so upsetting, so extreme, that Jane was forced to reveal something of her private life, for once, to her brother and sister-in-law.

Mary Austen remembered 'a tender scene of embraces and tears and distressing farewells' between Jane and Cassandra and Catherine and Alethea, which 'took place in the hall'.[33]

It all had to come out, and the news of Jane's refusal was 'much to the sorrow' of Mary Austen herself who, always the pragmatist, had 'thought the match a most desirable one'.[34]

Because Mary was there as a witness to the aftermath of Jane's refusal, it became enough of a shared event to enter into Austen family history, and for later generations to embroider into their own versions of their aunt's life story.

Jane's niece Catherine thought that the decision was the right one, even the straightforward one. She claimed to have read letters from Jane, additional letters which haven't survived, which cast more light on the whole affair: 'I gathered from the letters', Catherine wrote, that the acceptance had been made in 'a momentary fit of self-delusion', for 'I am sure she had no attachment to him.'[35] Catherine believed her aunt to have been 'vexed' but 'much relieved'.[36] In this version, Aunt Jane's pain was downplayed; the story made safe for family consumption. It was a simple thing. She would have been mad to marry him.

But Catherine's cousin Caroline, the one whose mother Mary saw Jane that morning at Steventon Rectory, had a more nuanced view. 'To be sure she should not have said yes,' this Caroline concluded, 'but I have always respected her for the courage in cancelling that yes – the next morning.'[37] Courage is the right word to use, for it was courageous to go against so many expectations, in favour of something as tenuous as the freedom to live life as a spinster dependent on others.

The next day after that – a Sunday, most inconveniently for James as a clergyman – Jane and Cassandra insisted on his taking them back to Bath. Jane now wanted to hurry back to Bath, away from Steventon, in a total reversal of the situation of three years earlier.

And in fact there was one further, final explanation that might reveal exactly why Jane so boldly turned down the offer of future financial security, and I like to believe that this was the clincher. An alternative hope of achieving independence, through earning money, seemed likely to be coming to fruition at last.

Jane had reason to believe that she would shortly become a published author.

19

Susan

IN 1803 A curious announcement appeared in a publication called *The Flowers of Literature for 1801 and 1802*. A new novel was in the press. Entitled *Susan*, it was soon to be published by Benjamin Crosby (or Crosbie) and Son.

The announcement did not name the author, but *Susan* was by Jane Austen. This was the book that would eventually end up as *Northanger Abbey*. Of all Jane's novels, it would take the longest and most tortuous route to publication. Cassandra tells us that the novel was substantively written in 1798–9, before the family moved permanently to Bath. But Jane must certainly also have revised it afterwards, for it contains a reference to Maria Edgeworth's *Belinda*, a book that was only published in 1801.

In the spring of 1803, Jane at last managed to sell *Susan*, for £10, to the publisher Benjamin Crosby of London. We don't have a record of her reaction, but she must have been thrilled. These ten pounds were the first Jane had ever earned for herself, and she was twenty-seven. She was the only member of her family, with the exception of George, who had absolutely no personal income. This must have felt vitally important.

And strangely enough, it was probably down to the meanness of Aunt Jane Leigh Perrot.

The Austen family would in later years become assiduous recorders of their recollections of their famous aunt. They have coloured the record so carefully with their own views that it's tempting to take them at their word. But diligent historians have to spy out what's *not* been said, because the untold stories are often the most interesting.[1] You can comb the Austen family memoirs and recollections and find no reference at all to a key event that must have shattered the family. It was an incident of alleged shoplifting, in 1799, in Bath. It also reveals the dangerous, seamy side of the fashionable city.

Jane complained that niggardly Mrs Leigh Perrot was always full of fine words, yet unwilling to pay her debts. 'My Aunt is in a great hurry to pay me for my Cap,' she once wrote, 'but cannot find in her heart to give me good money.' On 14 August 1799, Mrs Leigh Perrot was charged with theft, and committed to Ilchester Gaol.

She'd been accused of stealing some white lace from Miss Elizabeth Gregory's millinery shop in Bath's Bath Street. There were conflicting accounts of exactly what happened. Everyone involved agreed on one thing: that Mrs Leigh Perrot had, quite legitimately, purchased some black lace, and exited the shop.

Then the various testimonies begin to diverge. Apparently, Miss Gregory came out of the shop after Mrs Leigh Perrot, and asked her if she had taken some white lace as well as the black. Mrs Leigh Perrot offered up her paper-wrapped package for inspection, saying 'if I have, your young man must have put it up in mistake'. The parcel was opened up, and there indeed was the white lace. Mrs Leigh Perrot thought it was a shopman's negligence; Miss Gregory thought it was shoplifting.

Although she had got her white lace back, Miss Gregory was not content to let the matter rest. But Mrs Leigh Perrot had a suspicion that the whole thing was a scam. Did Miss Gregory and her accomplices want money in exchange for promising not to report her as a thief? The stakes, after all, were enormous. Even a minor crime against property (the lace was worth 20 shillings) was then punishable by transportation to the colonies. A ring of blackmailers might well have calculated that a rich woman like Mrs Leigh Perrot would simply pay a large sum to avoid this possibility.

But Mrs Leigh Perrot paid out no bribes. She was charged with the theft, and found herself waiting in prison for her trial. Here her faithful husband joined her. Their wealth allowed them to buy accommodation in the warden's house of Ilchester Gaol rather than endure the cells. It was, nevertheless, a cramped and squalid experience. Mrs Austen offered to send Jane or Cassandra to keep them company and to help with domestic duties, but Mrs Leigh Perrot wrote back with a refusal, explaining that she could not have borne to see such 'Elegant young Women' in such grim surroundings.

So that's how a little shopping expedition to Bath Street ended up with an aunt in gaol. And there were many other hazards lurking behind Bath's elegant façade. Mrs Leigh Perrot's experience was extreme, but even the most innocent, law-abiding visitor faced the danger, in Bath, of being rejected by polite society. One might be revealed as lacking either money, or else *savoir-faire*. In Jane's Bath novel, *Northanger Abbey*, the ingénue Catherine Morland treats the city as a kind of obstacle course, full of potential mishaps and humiliations. Schooled by her sensationalist novel reading, Catherine thought that life itself was an adventure, and in Bath she would endure 'dread', 'mortification', 'agony' and 'torment', albeit of a social rather than a physical kind.[2]

It might seem rather trivial to equate social embarrassment with danger. But Catherine Morland's mild adventures in Bath and beyond would give her some vital life experience. Back at home in her father's parsonage, Catherine had devoured many a novel of Gothic adventure and hardship. On the face of it, this was pretty poor preparation for a few weeks spent trying to meet the right people and find a husband.

But, as the critic Thomas Keymer argues, these ridiculous novels have actually taught Catherine something very important. By the end of *Northanger Abbey*, she has discovered that it's easier to survive a visit to a haunted abbey owned by a nasty man than it is to find sincere friendship in the fine houses, ballrooms, shops and streets of the fashionable city. Reading Mrs Radcliffe's Gothic novels prepared Catherine to treat adult life as a perilous adventure, and 'has helped her perceive the General's nature more accurately than anyone else, including his son'.[3]

For Jane, then, it doesn't matter what books you read, even if your choice is 'trashy' Gothic novels. It's what you make of them, how you behave in consequence, that counts. *Northanger Abbey*, at first sight a satire on Gothic fiction, also mounts a subtle defence of the books it appears to mock. Jane is once again teasing us with her 'double-voice'.

Mrs Leigh Perrot's trials were rather more extreme than Catherine Morland's. On 29 March 1800, after some months in prison, she finally appeared in court in Taunton. Plenty of distinguished character witnesses had been drummed up in her support, and finally, much to the relief of her family, she was acquitted.

That looks like the end of the story. But was Mrs Leigh Perrot really quite so innocent of stealing the lace as the verdict suggested? Her own legal counsel thought that she was guilty. Jane too was convinced that her aunt had a mean and covetous personality. Of one unpleasant letter that the Austens received from Mrs Leigh Perrot, Jane wrote that 'the discontentedness of it shocked and surprised . . . *I* see nothing in it out of Nature – tho' a sad nature.'

Even though these events appear nowhere in the family histories produced by various Austens after Aunt Jane's death, they could not be entirely ignored. Jane drops a clue herself in both of her novels *Northanger Abbey* and *Persuasion*. In each case, she places her unprincipled characters in the shopping street called Bath Street.[4] That's because Bath Street was the real-life location of the shop where Aunt Leigh Perrot's misfortune took place.

However, the odd affair had a silver lining. In 1800, the publisher Benjamin Crosby of London embarked upon a joint commercial venture with a Bath printer called Mr Cruttwell, who produced *The Bath Chronicle*. Together they produced a pamphlet for sale called *The Trial of Mrs Leigh Perrot*. It contained a transcript of the trial, 'with Marginal Notes', and presumably appealed to the large numbers of people who had been following this notorious local scandal.

Mr Cruttwell in Bath also acted as a literary agent for Mr Crosby in London. One can imagine a chain of events that now involved Jane, at Sydney Place, being sure at last that *Susan* was ready for publication. She also had *First Impressions* and *Sense and Sensibility* lying complete in the drawer of her writing desk. But it was *Susan*, her Bath novel, which she proposed to publish. After all, *First Impressions* had been rejected once already, and the local connection perhaps gave *Susan* her edge over Elinor and Marianne.

So then we can imagine Mr Austen walking, with his stick, up to Richard Cruttwell's shop in St James's Street, perched on the hill behind the Royal Crescent. He knew exactly where to go because he'd seen the pamphlet about the trial. The bell rang, his hat was removed and Mr Austen spoke. He was the brother-in-law of Mrs Leigh Perrot, whose adventures and vindication Mr Cruttwell had published at some financial gain. Would Mr Cruttwell like to print a new novel? He would not, but he knew a man who might. Here was the address of his associate, Mr Benjamin Crosby, in London. Crosby was the fourth-biggest publisher of novels during the first decade of the 1800s, not least because he had this extensive network of regional scouts.[5]

The deal was not done there and then, but wheels had been set in motion. Now it was Jane's brother Henry's lawyer in London, Mr William Seymour, who would carry out the actual transaction with Mr Crosby on her behalf. And then there was the money! Ten whole, glorious pounds.

In due course, yet another emotional development would arise from all of this. Jane was presumably still smarting from and chagrined by the proposal and break-up at Manydown Park. She had little idea that Mr William Seymour the London lawyer would also begin to think, one day, of asking Miss Jane Austen to become his wife.

But for now, in 1803, with the sale made, there must have been rejoicing at Sydney Place. Mr Austen had shown himself to be an active supporter of his daughter's writing from the start; Cassandra was always on Jane's side. That left just Mrs Austen to be ambivalent.

This fragmentary eggcup was among the archaeological finds from the site of Steventon Rectory, Hampshire. It's not impossible that Jane Austen once used it to eat a boiled egg.

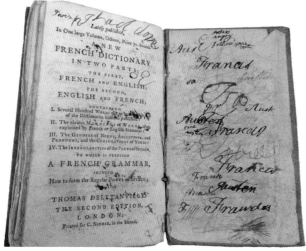

'I wish I had done', scrawled a very young Jane Austen in her French dictionary, at the top of the left page.

The Abbey School in Reading. Perhaps Jane was sent to boarding school to pick up the feminine polish not easily found in a house full of brothers.

Left are Cassandra's illustrations for Jane's spoof history textbook, c. 1790.
Cassandra's later drawing of Jane (top right) suggests that Jane herself sat for
her favourite historical character, Mary Queen of Scots (top left). Echoing their
combative relationship in real life, Cassandra has transformed their mother
(below right) into a character Jane didn't like: Queen Elizabeth I (below left).

Jane's glamorous cousin, Eliza de Feuillide. The illegitimate daughter of the governor of Bengal, Eliza was born in India, grew up in France, and set Hampshire hearts aflutter with her foreign ways.

Reverend George Austen. Jane's father did more than anyone to encourage his literary daughter, and acted as her first literary agent.

Novelist Frances Burney was highly popular at Steventon. The name of an eighteen-year-old 'Miss J. Austen' was printed in the list of the subscribers to one of Burney's books.

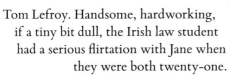

Tom Lefroy. Handsome, hardworking, if a tiny bit dull, the Irish law student had a serious flirtation with Jane when they were both twenty-one.

The first ball where Jane danced with Tom was at Deane House, Hampshire. These balls could be riotous affairs, and Jane once described a hangover from having had 'too much wine'.

Ashe Rectory was the home of Jane's friend and mentor, Mrs Anne Lefroy. Here she danced her last dance with Tom before he broke her heart … or did he?

Jane would have become mistress of Manydown Park had she not broken off her engagement to Harris Bigg-Wither.

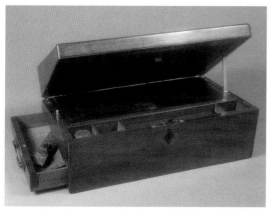

Jane's portable writing desk, a precious 19th birthday present from her father. She'd have kept the manuscripts of her novels in its lockable drawer. Once, by accident at a coaching inn, it was put into the wrong carriage and nearly taken off to the West Indies.

Jane's sailor brother Frank, who impressed Admiral Nelson during his successful naval career, uses his own portable writing desk.

The children's nursery maid, Susannah Sackree, was among the friends Jane made below-stairs at her brother's grand mansion of Godmersham Park in Kent.

At Godmersham Jane was made to feel like the poor relation. Her niece Marianne, shown here with two of her sisters, described how Jane would sit sewing quietly, then suddenly burst out laughing as she thought of a joke for one of her books.

Godmersham Park in Kent, in its beautiful grounds, has much in common with the fictional Palladian mansion in Jane's *Mansfield Park*.

Jane's father, George Austen, here gives away his son Edward to the rich relatives who want to adopt him. It was a sad but shrewd move, which ensured the financial security of his widow.

When Edward Austen came back to Steventon to see his siblings, he had been visibly transformed into a member of the landed gentry, dressed in this very suit of green silk.

Edward Austen took the name Knight after his adoption. Painted here on his Grand Tour, he inherited three estates and two enormous mansions from his adoptive parents.

Dancers get ready for a ball. Georgian Bath had several sets of Assembly Rooms. Jane loved dancing and excelled at it. It brought out the characteristic high colour in her cheeks.

Jane adored the theatre, and indeed any form of entertainment. Her brothers once took her to Astley's Circus in London as a cure for a broken heart. She also used Astley's as the location for a lovers' reunion in her novel *Emma*.

Jane rarely writes kindly of her mother. Perhaps the problem was that they were just too much alike in their sharpness and 'sprack wit'. Jane also found herself dragged down by her mother's constant pessimism. 'She is tolerably well', Jane privately wrote to Cassandra on one occasion, although 'she would tell you herself that she has a very dreadful cold in the head'.

One wonders if Jane was over-reacting, but Mrs Austen's letters *do* make her sound rather annoying. 'You are very good in wishing for such a poor infirm visitor, as myself,' ran one of them, refusing an invitation from a daughter-in-law, 'but indeed I cannot be comfortable from home.' Next comes a scolding: 'you are very bold to buy colour'd shoes', followed by a gloomy fashion report. 'Last week I bought a Bombazeen,' she continued, 'thinking I should get it cheaper than when the poor King was actually dead. If I outlive him it will answer my purpose, if I do not, somebody may mourn for me in it – it will be wanted for one or the other, I daresay, before the moths have eaten it up.'[6]

But the excitement about *Susan's* forthcoming birth was surely over-shadowed early in the new year of 1804, when Mrs Austen for once became seriously ill, in the house at Sydney Place.

Mrs Austen was now fussed over by her anxious family, who called in Dr William Bowen the apothecary. Dr Bowen ran a shop upon Pulteney Bridge with his partner, the suitably named Mr Spry.[7] Whatever treatment Dr Bowen prescribed, it seemed to work. Upon her recovery, just as Jane herself might have done, Mrs Austen wrote a jokey poem about her experience:

> Says Death 'I've been trying these three weeks and more
> To seize on old Madam here at Number Four . . .'

The 'old Madam' is saved, in the poem, and gives thanks:

> To the Prayers of my Husband, whose love I possess
> To the care of my Daughters, whom Heaven will bless,
> To the skill and attention of BOWEN.[8]

This was perhaps a reminder, to the Austens, of what really mattered. It wasn't the sale of novels, and little irritations and differences could be overcome. The most important thing of all was their own strong affection.

And then, curiously, the much-anticipated *Susan* did not appear in print.

This was an incomprehensible delay. First one year passed, then another. Finally, when a novel called *Susan* by someone else completely different appeared in 1809, the game seemed to be over. With a book in the world called *Susan* that was not her own, Jane must have given up hope.

Why did she not ask her publisher what was happening, during those six long years in which *Susan* did not appear? Perhaps she did, and the evidence has not survived. Perhaps, as over the business of Tom Lefroy, she'd been too proud to ask. There were in fact some perfectly good reasons why Mr Crosby might have changed his mind, and decided not to publish *Susan* after all. He was well within his rights to do so. Jane had sold him the copyright of the work, which meant that he had no obligation to publish it. Historians used to argue that he likely had second thoughts about publishing a work that was essentially a spoof upon his core business of lurid, horrid 'Gothic Romances'. *Susan* contained numerous nods to Gothic convention, from the very setting of the spooky Northanger Abbey itself, to tiny moments when the heroine, for example, finds herself 'motionless with horror', or else discovers that 'her blood was chilled'.[9] The books that Catherine Morland gulps down – yes, even *Horrid Mysteries*, which sounds far too good to be true – were real titles of the 1790s.[10] Crosby made good money out of publishing books like this; perhaps he feared biting the hand that fed him.

But more recent research has discovered a much more straightforward explanation. Crosby got into financial difficulties in 1804, the year in which he might have expected to publish *Susan*. Despite his former, and subsequent, success as a publisher, he only succeeded in bringing out one title that whole year.[11] Jane was just terribly unlucky in her timing.

Once the rival *Susan* had appeared, the novel formerly known as *Susan* was renamed in Jane's mind as *Catherine* instead. But she would never see the work published in her lifetime. By the time it eventually appeared in print, after her death, it had become a period piece. The clothes – the muslins, the high hair – were those of the 1790s. Although Jane updated various details, she did keep the overall original period setting, as the story only really worked as a burlesque upon the novels of that decade.[12]

Catherine would eventually end up on people's shelves as *Northanger Abbey*, the title that Cassandra (presumably) chose for it after Jane's death. It was very appropriate. It reflects the real *anger* that animates General Tylney, the Abbey's master, when he discovers that Catherine is not an heiress. It also hints that Catherine might be a *hanger-on*, once her lack of heiress-status is known.[13] And finally, it was the perfect title for a book poking fun at its age: between 1784 and 1818, there were thirty-two other novels published with the word 'Abbey' in their titles.[14]

Jane revised *Susan,* and sold her, during these Bath years, but we don't hear of any other novels specifically being written in Bath apart from her unfinished work *The Watsons*. The city does seem to have cramped her literary style. 'I do not know what is the matter with me to day,' Jane wrote from Bath, 'but I cannot write . . . fortunately I have nothing very particular to say.'

Time then, for escape. Time for the sea.

20

'Wild to see Lyme'

'Just to give you an item of life-a-la-mode /
As it is to be seen in this pleasant abode.'

From *The Lymiad*, a satirical poem about Lyme Regis (1818)

AFTER THE DEBACLE of Manydown Park, the next year's holidays from Bath were to Lyme Regis. It's one of the few real-life places, alongside Bath itself, and London, which Jane put into her novels, so it's worth examining in detail how her daily life there unfolded.

The Austens visited Lyme Regis during the autumn of 1803, witnessing a huge fire that destroyed many of the town's buildings on 5 November. In 1804 they went again for a proper summer holiday. To visit a holiday resort in November was not as surprising as it seems, for Lyme's season really picked up just as Bath's wound down for the winter. People leaving Bath came on to Lyme for its own little three-month mini-season from September to November. There was a direct stagecoach service from Bath to Lyme, whereas for all other destinations you had to change at Axminster.

Tourists were attacted by Lyme's mild winter climate, which earned it the name of 'The Naples of England'. Mimosas bloomed in the shadow of Lyme's very own Vesuvius, the conical hill called Golden Cap. 'It would be very difficult to find a frog in the parish,' was the somewhat implausible boast of Lyme's most distinguished antiquarian, 'such is the absence of all stagnant waters, or unhealthy vapours.'[1]

It may seem odd to find such enthusiasm expressed about the muddy county of Dorset. But to holidaymakers who had never been abroad, the coast at Lyme must have appeared as lush and exotic as the first sight of a Caribbean island. The sun shines pink on the sea, even in winter. The sea foam slides onto golden shingle, and the misty light of warmer climes bathes the heaving hills all around. Lyme is squeezed into a narrow valley between two vast areas of unstable ground, where shale and mud can slip suddenly into the sea, making the land unsuitable for building. It's even dangerous to walk upon because of the possibility of being swallowed by the mud. In Lyme, even nature seems to be letting loose her stays.

For their second stay of 1804, Jane, Cassandra, Mr and Mrs Austen, together with Henry and Eliza, all took lodgings, most probably in Pyne House, no. 10 in Broad Street. Today the building is still split up into holiday flats, with Regency doorways leading hither and thither in a much-altered interior. But common to the entire house is the sound of the beating of the waves on the shingle beach below and, when I stayed there, winter rain on the panes, carried by the southwesterly wind of a storm.

For the Austens, Lyme had an additional attraction beyond its climate. According to *A Guide to All the Watering and Seabathing Places*, its great advantage was its cheapness. 'Magnificence is not essential to enjoyment', the book reassured its readers. Lyme was 'frequented principally by persons in the middle class of life', we're told, hoping 'to heal their wounded fortunes.'[2]

We last met Harriette Wilson, the renowned upmarket courtesan, being bored rigid by Lord Craven and his cocoa trees. She too liked Lyme. 'The society', she wrote, 'was chiefly composed of people of very small independent fortunes . . . or of such who required sea bathing.'[3] People who'd been little fish in Bath could become big fish here: Jane remarked upon the sight, in the local Assembly Rooms, of a party of Irish aristocrats, 'bold, queerlooking people, just fit to be Quality at Lyme'.

At Lyme, lodgings were 'not merely reasonable, they are even cheap'.[4] And therein lay a slight problem. When Frances Burney visited Lyme, she stayed in 'the part by the Sea'. It was cheap indeed, but she does go on to say that 'our abode was so dirty, & *fishy*, that I rejoiced when we left it'.[5]

The economy of late Georgian Lyme Regis gradually began to adapt itself to the growing tourist trade by providing nicer lodgings. 'Housekeepers near the sea', we're told, 'began to fit up two or three front rooms in a homely manner, which is the first indication at Lyme of the lodging-house system, now so generally pursued on the whole line of coast'.[6] This is just the process that Jane describes at the seaside village of Sanditon in her novel of the same name: 'two or three of the best' houses there were 'smartened up with a white curtain and "lodgings to let"'. Harriette Wilson found her own lodgings, in neighbouring Charmouth, simply by knocking on the door of a private house. The naval officer's widow whom she found within was glad to oblige.[7] Harriette liked it all so much that she went on to have two illegitimate babies in Charmouth, paying for her stay by sending tranches of her salacious memoirs up to London for publication.

The guidebook to Lyme recommends both inns, the Three Cups and the Golden Lion, and it warns that the intricate streets of the lower part of the town could be insalubrious.[8] The problem was that the sea often shoved the shingle about so as to block the town's small river, the Lim. As the Lim was also the town's sewer, this caused sanitation nightmares. But it was in this lower, cheaper part of the town that the Austens lodged.

Although Lyme (as Jane always called it, missing out the 'Regis') had not been an important town since the Middle Ages, it was still entitled to send two Members of Parliament up to London.[9] In the seventeenth century it had been Britain's fourteenth-largest port, which is surprising given its poor natural advantages. A man-made harbour exists behind the shelter of The Cobb, a massive, stone-built wall curving out into the sea. Its purpose, as described by Sir Francis Walsingham, was to disperse 'the violence and fretting of the sea, which otherwise would in short time eat out both the town and land thereunto adjoining'.[10]

Even more curiously, the road out of Lyme was so steep that until 1759 it was impassable to vehicles, so everything coming to and from the ships needed to travel by packhorse. Nevertheless it was a significant port with worldwide connections. The churchyard at Uplyme, the adjacent settlement inland, was kept clean by a man named Blackmore, who was really a 'blackamoor', or African galley-slave, who had been rescued from Corsair pirates operating from Morocco.[11] During the Napoleonic Wars, ships departed from Lyme with supplies for the British garrisons in Guernsey, Jersey and Alderney.[12]

Lyme was also chosen as a landing place by the Duke of Monmouth, the illegitimate son of King Charles II, for his rebellion against James II in 1685. Lyme's townspeople were passionate supporters of his doomed cause, and all the children of Lyme knew the song he is said to have written:

> Lyme, although a little place,
> I think it wondrous pretty;
> If 'tis my fate to wear a crown,
> I'll make of it a city.[13]

But the rebellious Royal Duke and his exploits have long been over-shadowed by the simple accident of Jane Austen's holiday in Lyme, and her subsequent description of the place in *Persuasion*. Lord Tennyson even considered moving to Lyme Regis, a place he'd never visited, purely because of the novel. When he arrived to take a look round, he was not tempted by a proffered visit to Monmouth's beach. '"Take me now to the Cobb,"' he demanded, '"that I may see the steps from which Louisa Musgrove fell."' Indeed, Tennyson said that the people Jane Austen had created 'were more real and living to him than Monmouth and his followers'.[14]

Jane and Frances Burney alike fell in love with the countryside round Lyme. 'The Road though which we travelled is the most beautiful', Burney rhapsodised about her own trip. 'The Hills are the highest, I fancy, in the South of this country, the boldest and noblest . . . there was no going on in the carriage through such enchanting scenes; We got out upon the Hills, & walked till we could walk no longer.'[15]

It was during one such similar outing of their own that Cassandra completed her famous sketch of her famous sister. She shows Jane from behind, probably looking out to sea, 'sitting down out of doors, on a hot day, with her bonnet strings untied'.[16] They'd perhaps got as far as one of the lonely beaches around Lyme that were used by smugglers.

This enjoyment of the landscape, implicit in Jane's pose and gaze, was not only good for the physical but also the *mental* health of the Georgians. Burney's journey to Lyme found her 'fairly taken away, not only from the World, but from myself, & completely wrapped up & engrossed by the pleasures – wonders – & charms of animating Nature'.[17] Harriette Wilson also found Lyme to be good for the spirits: 'such a magnificent view of the ocean presented itself, as absolutely fixed us to the spot for nearly ten minutes . . . I cannot describe the scenery like Mrs Radcliffe, I wish I could; but alas! I have not an idea of the kind, and yet I can feel and enjoy it.'[18]

Burney also thought that the journey down into Lyme was an 'approach to the sublime', or the 'sub-Lyme' as the satirical artist George Cruickshank had it. He produced a picture showing the bathers of Lyme wallowing in the waters in a titillating – and probably unrealistic – state of nudity.

But what Cruickshank's *really* doing in his drawing is having a dig at Edmund Burke's contemporary treatise on the aesthetics of landscape. Burke had argued that a beautiful landscape resembled the contours of a woman's body. 'Observe that part of a beautiful woman,' wrote Burke, 'where she is perhaps the most beautiful, about the neck and breasts; the smoothness; the softness; the easy and insensible swell . . . the unsteady eye slides giddily, without knowing where to fix, or whither it is carried.'[19] Cruickshank, by making Burke's vision literal, also made it ridiculous.[20] By including a lascivious male figure with a telescope to the far right, it's as if Cruickshank has shown Burke himself as a pervert, carrying out his philosophical investigations upon Lyme's naked bathers. There again is that deep Georgian connection between the sea and sex.

Squeezed into its narrow valley between the wobbly cliffs each side, Lyme possessed by 1804 the charm and appurtenances of a seaside resort. 'A sort of Brighton in miniature' was how one visitor described it, 'all bustle and confusion, assembly-rooms, donkey-riding, raffling etc. etc.'.[21]

The Austens' lodgings in Pyne House stood at the bottom of Broad Street, very near to the Assembly Rooms. Their landlord, Mr William Pyne, was a subscriber to books of local history. As the Austens came out of their front door, they were immediately in the Shambles, an open-air market. Turning right to go downhill towards the sea, they passed between other cottages, then down a flight of steps. To the right was The Walk, the raised promenade by the sea, 'particularly adapted for invalids', for the enjoyment of the 'soft sea breezes; without encountering any fatiguing acclivities'.[22] Travelling leftwards, the eye next alighted upon the Assembly Rooms, which stood right on the shore. The prospect was closed by the Three Cups Hotel, which is probably where Jane placed her fictional party of friends for their stay in *Persuasion*.[23] The Three Cups took its name from the arms of the Salters' Company, as salt production from seawater had once been big business in Lyme.[24]

The Assembly Rooms down by the sea boasted a ballroom, adjoining 'Card-room' and 'Billiard-table, conveniently arranged under one roof', with a 'charming marine view as far as the Isle of Portland eight miles off'.[25] The ballroom was of 'large dimensions containing three chandeliers and neat orchestra'.[26] The Edwardian historian Constance Hill visited Lyme's Assembly Rooms before they were pulled down to give way to a car park. 'The ball-room is little changed since Miss Austen danced in it that September evening nearly a hundred years ago', she wrote. 'It has lost its three glass chandeliers . . . the orchestra consisted, we are told, of three violins and a violoncello. We visited the room by daylight, and felt almost as if it were afloat, for nothing but blue sea and sky was to be seen from its many windows.'[27]

The author of that Georgian guidebook to Lyme praised its inhabitants for keeping early hours. Mr Austen stayed at the Assembly Rooms until just half-past-nine, and his wife and Jane until ten-thirty, before being walked home by their new manservant James with 'a Lanthorn'. Jane was not short of partners; indeed, was asked to dance at Lyme quite without an introduction by an 'odd-looking Man who had been eyeing me for some time'. She also found fellow female visitors to walk with upon the Cobb. Life at the seaside seems to have relaxed some of her defences, and, of course, it may have been during this visit that the garbled story of Reverend Blackall, or some other lover, unfolded.

The pleasures of the body in Lyme included not only the walking and dancing in a floating ballroom but also the sea bathing. When Jane braved the sea at Lyme she enjoyed it: 'The Bathing was so delightful this morning . . . that I believe I staid in rather too long.'

After Cassandra had gone off with Eliza and Henry to Weymouth,

Jane and her parents moved to smaller lodgings a little further away from the Assembly Rooms. Their new lodgings, nastier than the last, were perhaps in Hiscott's boarding house a little further up the street, which commanded 'very extensive Views of SEA and LAND'.[28] The Austens stayed on there as summer ended, enabling Jane to depict autumn in Lyme so well in *Persuasion*.

With Cassandra absent, some of her usual domestic duties now fell to Jane. The new lodgings had 'inconvenient' offices, and were generally quite dirty. 'I endeavour as far as I can to supply your place,' Jane wrote to her sister with resignation, '& be useful & keep things in order . . . I detect dirt in the Water-decanter as fast as I can, and give the Cook physic.'

The cook may have been sick, but they still had Jenny, who did Jane's hair, and their new servant James was 'the delight of our lives . . . My Mother's shoes were never so well blacked, & our plate never looked so clean.' Jane was also impressed with James's wish to acquire knowledge and to travel. With Cassandra away, it became Jane's responsibility to worry about the servants' happiness. Discovering that James could read, Jane characteristically procured him books and newspapers. The atmosphere of relaxation, even sexual relaxation, spread to the domestic staff: Jane sent James and Jenny together on a walk over the loose ground to Charmouth.

After 1804, Jane may never have returned to Lyme, but she did not forget it. In *Persuasion* she most abnormally includes a few paragraphs which simply praise the town and its setting and its walks and its physical sensations. This peculiar passage doesn't illuminate a character, or move the story forward. Jane simply revels in the pleasures of Lyme, its beach 'animated with bathing machines and company'; its 'green chasms' and 'romantic rocks'; its sands from which one can watch 'the flow of the tide, for sitting in unwearied contemplation'.

In fact, Jane's deep enjoyment of Lyme seems rooted in the fact that it was *not* home. The lodgings were dirty and inconvenient; enjoyment was to be found outside them. Living in lodgings, liberated from domestic duties, Jane revelled in the walking, dancing, or bathing, feeling the physical sensations of the water, light and air. Lyme, as it was in *Persuasion*, was a place to fall in love, to be rejuvenated, to feel sexual desire. However, if the attraction of Lyme really lies in the fact that it was *the opposite* of home, this does have seriously sad implications for the rest of Jane's life.

While Jane did not forget Lyme, the town did not forget her, either. You can still eat at Jane's Cafe, walk in Jane Austen's Garden, and buy souvenirs in the Persuasion gift shop today.

21

Green Park Buildings East

'Surely you may suppose that I have suffered now.'

Sense and Sensibility

IN PERSUASION, THE heroine Anne Elliot's arthritic friend Mrs Smith has fallen on hard times. Mrs Smith lives at a cheap address in Bath, Westgate Buildings, which is too far west to be fashionable. 'Westgate Buildings must have been rather surprised by the appearance of a carriage drawn up near its pavement!' observes Anne's snobbish father when he hears that she has been dropped off there for visits.

The inhabitants of Westgate Buildings could not afford such things. They occupied an area of Bath that had not been desirable since the 1730s, and which had come down heavily since. The Buildings were 'quite in the lower part of the town', as Jane herself put it. One resident in nearby Avon Street complained to the Bath Corporation that 'all kinds of nastiness' were thrown down into the thoroughfare, and that wandering pigs made it 'a perfect dung muckson from one end to the other'.[1]

And yet, in 1804, when the Austens came back from their autumn holiday in Lyme, they did not return to Sydney Place. Their new house was even further west than Westgate Buildings. It was to Green Park Buildings that they went: the very street rejected in 1801 as too damp.

Their precise address was no. 3, Green Park Buildings East. These houses, down by the river, were built upon a platform, for the land flooded often, and they stood rather near to the slums of the city's southern fringe. In 1801, the Austens had rejected a house here because of 'the Dampness of the Offices' and because of 'reports of discontented families & putrid fevers'.

The Austens had probably failed to renew their lease on Sydney Place when it expired because the rent had been rather a strain upon their finances. They regretted the loss of that house. As Jane fumed, their successors the Coles 'have got their infamous plate on their door.'

The cost of living was always on the Austens' minds. Jane wrote with information that she hoped might persuade Mrs Lloyd, mother of her friend Martha, to come to live at Bath. 'Meat is only 8d per pound, butter 12d & cheese 9½d', she explains. But then again, Martha must carefully conceal from her mother 'the exorbitant price of fish'. Indeed, a single cucumber, a highly desirable item, cost the same as a whole pound of butter. The Austens hadn't had to worry about such things when they grew their own cucumbers at Steventon. As Mrs Allen says in *Northanger Abbey*, 'we are sadly off in the country' but in Bath 'one can step out of doors and get a thing in five minutes'. Very true, but such convenience had its cost.

On the other hand, Green Park Buildings – as the name suggests – also had some compensations. There was green space nearby, both between the eastern and western rows of houses, and in the adjacent Kingsmead Fields bordering the river.

The eastern part of Green Park Buildings where Jane lived was destroyed by bombs in the Second World War, but its western twin still stands. The terrace is not entirely uniform, having been built in spurts as capital became available. The houses were, however, generously proportioned. Jane reported, of a house very similar to hers, that 'the dining-room is of a comfortable size' and that 'the apartment over the Drawing-room pleased me particularly, because it is divided into two, the smaller one a very nice sized Dressing-room, which upon occasion might admit a bed'. There was just that one little problem of the damp. Perhaps it was a risk worth taking for a big house at a cheap price.

And so they moved in. Mr Austen, now in his seventies, continued to cut a distinguished figure in Bath society: 'he was still handsome when advanced in age'. His hair had gone white very early in life, but 'it was very beautiful & glossy, with short curls above the ears'. The speed at which hair goes grey is determined by genetics, like eye colour, but Mr Austen's was unusually white (it 'might have belonged to a much older man'[2]) which suggests a deficiency of vitamin B12 in his diet. A snippet of his hair, kept today at the Jane Austen House Museum inside a piece of paper labelled by his famous daughter, is truly white. Mr Austen now had a slow, arthritic walk, shuffling along the pavements of Bath with a stick. Charles Powlett, the Hampshire neighbour who'd once tried to kiss Jane, wrote a poem about an old parson who could almost have been Mr Austen: 'On tithes and obligations no longer intent / The parson came hobbling along.'[3]

Meanwhile, Mrs Austen's face was shrinking back with age to emphasise her witchy nose. On its tip she wore a little pair of spectacles which, with their leather case, were passed down within the Austen family, and which can be seen at Lyme Regis Museum today.

Jane continued to express impatience with her mother's self-perceived ill-health. But according to her more-sympathetic grandson, Mrs Austen's suffering was lifelong, and legendary. 'During the last years of her life,' he wrote, 'she endured continual pain.' Yet he also wrote of her 'characteristic cheerfulness. She once said to me, "Ah, my dear, you find me just where you left me – on the sofa. I sometimes think that God Almighty must have forgotten me; but I dare say He will come for me in His own good time."'

But His own good time had not come yet, for it was Mr Austen who did not seem terribly well in Green Park Buildings. He'd been suffering from occasional fevers and feeblenesses, perhaps not aided by the autumn rains now seeping into the cellars.

The news from elsewhere seemed bad as well. On 16 December 1804, Jane's birthday, a terrible blow fell. It was just one of the frequent accidents of daily life in the Georgian countryside. Madam Lefroy, Jane's much-admired old friend back in Hampshire, had been into town to 'do some errands'. There she bumped into James Austen, and complained about her 'stupid' horse. James left her, she started to ride home, but all of a sudden, the horse bolted. Mrs Lefroy's servant tried to catch hold of the bridle, but 'missed his hold and the animal darted off faster'. The servant was too shocked to be able to explain exactly what happened, but he supposed 'that Mrs Lefroy in her terror, threw herself off, and fell heavily on the hard ground'. A few hours later, she was dead. She was only forty-five.[4]

And so the date of Jane's birth turned out also to be the date of the death of her friend and second mother. In years to come, she fell to brooding over the coincidence. 'The day returns again, my natal day,' she wrote in a poem, 'What mix'd emotions in my mind arise!'[5] ''Tis past and gone', Jane wrote. 'We meet no more.' Experiencing the death of a friend is an important step towards reaching adulthood. But at least Jane had a Christian's hope of meeting Madam Lefroy once again in Heaven, and her poem means that, in a way, her mentor still lives.[6] It's only through Jane that anyone remembers Madam Lefroy's name today.

Among the other tidings from Hampshire was the intelligence that Harris Bigg-Wither had married someone else. It had taken him barely fifteen months since Jane's refusal. Friends reported that he was in 'high spirits',[7] and that he'd taken his bride, Anne Frith, to live at Wymering Manor, a substantial Elizabethan house near Portsmouth. Wymering was a pleasant enough place to wait until the even better mansion at Manydown became theirs, which it did in 1813 when Harris's father died. Anne Frith seems to have had no reason to regret accepting him, as her husband became a respected squire and magistrate.[8] There was just the one downside, but it *was* a significant one. She had to bear his ten children: five sons and five daughters. Perhaps the sight of exactly what this did to Anne explains why none of her five daughters would themselves ever marry.

All this lay in the future, though; Jane for now had no notion of the fate that she'd escaped. We don't know if she found the news of Harris's marriage upsetting or not, but there was definitely much worse to come.

Only a month after Madam Lefroy's death, on 19 January 1805, Mr Austen again fell ill. It started on Saturday morning, in a way that was now becoming familiar: 'an oppression in the head with fever, violent tremulousness, & the greatest degree of Feebleness'. Once again Dr Bowen the apothecary was summoned, the man who'd previously cured Mrs Austen. But this time Bowen thought the case was too much for him. He recommended calling for a qualified physician. Dr Gibbs of Gay Street was brought in.

Today Mr Austen would be given intravenous fluids and antibiotics, but the treatment Dr Gibbs suggested was 'Cupping'. This meant cutting a slit in the skin, and placing a heated cup over it to draw out the blood. When Mr Austen had fallen ill before, cupping seemed to help him, but this time 'he seemed scarcely at all relieved'.

He was probably suffering from an acute bacterial infection, and as Jane does not mention that he had any breathing difficulties, it is likely that it was an infection of the urinary tract. Dr Claire Isaac however, has suggested an intriguing alternative: that he was suffering from malaria. It would not be an obvious conclusion to draw today about a patient who lived in Bath, but in Georgian times mosquitoes carrying malaria (literally: *mal*, or bad, air) were not uncommon in damp, low-lying areas of Britain. If Mr Austen's illness really was malaria, the removal of blood through cupping would have increased his anaemia, and made him worse. It could be that the family's cheap, damp home in Green Park Buildings, down by the river and the mosquitoes, may have had the most unfortunate effect of making Mr Austen gravely ill.

His family believed that the cupping eventually worked, because 'towards the Evening however he got better, had a tolerable night, & yesterday morning was so greatly amended as to get up & join us at breakfast as usual'. He was able to 'walk about with only the help of a stick, & every symptom was so favourable that when Bowen saw him at one, he felt sure of his doing perfectly well'.

However, they were misled. Fevers come in waves, so Mr Austen had probably just crested one of them, and had naturally recovered a bit in the dip before the next wave broke. As Sunday 'advanced, all these comfortable appearances gradually changed; the fever grew stronger than ever, & when Bowen saw him at ten at night, he pronounc'd his situation to be most alarming'. Jane's account continues:

> At nine this morning he came again – & by his desire a Physician was called; – Dr Gibbs – But it was then absolutely a lost case –. Dr Gibbs said that nothing but a Miracle could save him, and about twenty minutes after Ten he drew his last gasp.

Despite the intriguing argument in favour of malaria, the cause of death was most probably septicaemia. In an era before antibiotics, sepsis would almost always be fatal within a couple of days.[9]

And so, on the morning of Monday 21 January, Jane's father died. 'Our dear Father has closed his virtuous & happy life,' she wrote, 'in a death almost as free from suffering as his Children could have wished.'

This was the obligatory description of a nineteenth-century deathbed scene, with the studious mention of the deceased's virtue and peaceful state. And what surprises today about Jane's letters of the following week is just how much she downplays the impact that her father's death would have, upon her own and her family's lives. Here is the stoicism, the resignation displayed by Cassandra at Tom Fowle's death. To modern eyes, Jane's response to the death seems almost hard-hearted. But then, it was the display of a laudable, feminine acceptance of God's will. 'Heavy is the blow', Jane wrote, but 'we can already feel that a thousand comforts remain to us to soften it'. Among these comforts were:

> the remembrance of his having suffered, comparatively speaking, nothing. – Being quite insensible of his own state, he was spared all the pain of separation, & he went off almost in his Sleep. – My Mother bears the Shock as well as possible; she was quite prepared for it, & feels all the blessing of his being spared a long Illness. My Uncle & Aunt have been with us, & shew us every imaginable kindness. And tomorrow we shall I dare say have the comfort of James's presence.

Just as society expected, Mr Austen's daughters had been allocated the task – privilege, even – of being with him in his old age, and witnessing his death, and then mediating all the subsequent business and arrangements for their absent brothers. It was Jane who wrote to Frank to tell him which of his father's personal possessions his mother had set aside for him: his 'Compass & Sun-Dial' in its case and, with bathos, a pair of scissors.

In the first flurry of correspondence after her father's death, Jane used red sealing wax on her letters as usual, but after a week she had managed to acquire black. This was the convention following a death, so that people receiving letters would get preparatory notice before they opened them that the news was bad.[10] Word spread, and so, at Godmersham Park they went into 'mourning for Grandpapa Austen'.[11]

Mr Austen, seventy-three years old, was buried alongside his father-in-law in the crypt of St Swithun's Church where he had married. His memorial was later moved outside, and today by chance it shares the churchyard with that of the novelist he so much admired, Frances Burney. Although Mr Austen's death was reported in the *Bath Chronicle*, his illness was so sudden that many friends were caught by surprise. Charles Powlett called at Green Park Buildings to say goodbye to the family before leaving Bath, only 'to be told by the Servant that his Master had been <u>buried</u> that Morning'.[12]

Obviously Mr Austen's female dependants mourned, but they also now had to think about how they were to live. With him had died any sort of financial security for his wife and daughters. In fact, they were now in a state of crisis, for with Mr Austen's decease his income simply stopped: that is, the tithes from the livings of Steventon and Deane (minus what he had paid his son James to do his work there) plus a small annuity.[13] There were still three months to run on the lease of the house at Green Park Buildings, and the ladies saw these out. But once the lease expired, they could not afford to renew it.

By a will of 1770, Mr Austen had left everything to his wife. She had an income of £122 a year derived from her own family inheritance of £3,350 invested in the South Sea Company (this had been a poor choice, yields were low). Cassandra had the interest on the £1,000 she inherited from Tom Fowle. But Mrs Austen, Cassandra and Jane's combined annual income as a household of three was now only £210.

Pride and Prejudice was already written, in draft form at least, and it would not be the only one of Jane's books in which daughters are left stranded by their parents upon a sandbank of financial insecurity. In *Pride and Prejudice*, Mr Bennet could certainly have saved something substantial for his daughters' dowries had he lived within his income. Anne Elliot, too, belonged to a spendthrift family. As an unmarried woman older than Lizzy Bennet, she is more darkly, bitterly angry that her father has frittered away his estate. Likewise, as the Austen daughters did their sums, they must have wondered how their father, once the possessor of an income of nearly £1,000 a year, could have left them with nothing but the charity of their mother and brothers. 'We are just the kind of people

& party to be treated about among our relations', Jane wrote, regretfully, for 'we cannot be supposed to be very rich'.

For Jane, there was another, additional, loss. Her father had been the only member of the family up to this point, so far as we know, to have taken seriously her ambition to write novels. He was the one who had written to publishers on her behalf; bought her that writing desk. Just as Frank now had Mr Austen's compass, to guide him as he sailed round the globe, her father's legacy to Jane was the desk that she would use for the rest of her life. Of all the surviving remnants of Jane's possessions and physical world, it is this item that has the most powerful resonance, so no wonder it's a prized possession of the British Library today. Perhaps she thought of the man who gave it to her each day as she sat down to write.

Jane's reaction to her father's death was in part literary. She wrote half of *The Watsons*, the story of yet another family of sisters who lack the money upon which to marry. Marry they must, for, as Elizabeth Watson says, 'it is terrible to be poor and old and laughed at'. Despite the story's being left unfinished, we know what Jane had planned: the girls' father 'was soon to die; and Emma to become dependent for a home on her narrow-minded sister-in-law and brother. She was to decline an offer of marriage from Lord Osborne.'[14]

To write a novel in which the penniless heroine turns down the offer of a noble hand and home, to become disgusted with the story, and to give it all up, suggests that Jane, in the wake of the Harris Bigg-Wither affair, in the wake of her father's death, had many regrets. No wonder she did not finish it.

This later time in Bath, bereaved, in a financial panic, was certainly a descent towards the nadir of Jane's life. And yet: was she depressed, completely unable to write, as her most sympathetic biographer of all, Claire Tomalin, has suggested in a work of great perception and subtlety? Was Jane 'screaming inside her head', as she puts it?[15] Yes, surely Tomalin would have been silently screaming in the circumstances; so too would any twenty-first-century woman.

Jane's great gift to us is to have survived these dark days, keeping hold of hope, and staying true to life choices that would expand the very definition of what it means to be a female writer. But we can't simply assign our modern emotional responses straight to her. Indeed, for Jane as a Christian, all was as it should have been. She had honoured her father and done her work well. Jane – genteel Georgian women in general – did not scream. As another historian well attuned to Georgian attitudes has written, movingly: 'to be mistress of oneself was paramount

– genteel ladies aimed to be self-possessed in social encounters, self-controlled in the face of minor provocations, self-sufficient in the midst of ingratitude, and, above all, brave and enduring in the grip of tragedy and misfortune'.[16]

Jane's response was subtler, and more controlled than screaming. 'Let other pens', she wrote, 'dwell on guilt and misery. I quit such odious subjects as soon as I can, impatient to restore everybody not greatly in fault themselves to tolerable comfort, and to have done with all the rest.' She took her regrets and bitterness and turned them into irony and art. She would use these powerful weapons to blow open the lock that kept penniless daughters prisoners inside their family homes. She would learn to show just how unpleasant and how unfair that situation could be.

As was now their duty, Jane and Cassandra's brothers chipped in to pay for their sisters to live at something approximating the standard that everyone expected. Edward promised £100 a year, as he could well afford to, and Jane's brothers Henry, Frank and James each pledged £50. Frank had offered £100, but, realising that this would be a stretch for him, Mrs Austen made him halve it.[17] Where was Charles in all of this? Presumably he argued that as the youngest and least prosperous brother, he had nothing to spare. 'Burn Charles's letter', Henry advised, in a typical piece of Austen cover-up.[18] Destroy the evidence that the family had failed to agree.

On a household income of £460 a year, Jane and Cassandra could afford to live in something approximating the style to which they had been accustomed. But they would now be entirely beholden not to their father, but to their brothers. The trap in which they found themselves was a common one in their social circle. In April 1805, Mary and Martha Lloyd's mother, born a Miss Craven, died. At one low point in her life, this lady had decided to try to live upon the interest of £500. This she did by going to work at a girls' school in Tewkesbury, where she paid 'what she could for her board and made out the rest by helping sometimes in the school, and by doing plain needlework which she took in anonymously'. She had to act furtively, 'for it was not to be known that Miss Craven was earning money as a sempstress'.[19] Not surprisingly, Miss Craven climbed out of her life at the school by going to live with her brother, and then her aunt, and then by getting married, so to become Mary and Martha's mother.

In the Austens' new situation there had to be some changes. No longer could they afford three servants; Mrs Austen must 'reduce her establishment to one female domestic & take furnished lodgings'.[20] This was Henry writing. He and his brothers were now in charge, and could tell their female relatives how to live. On 25 March 1805, the ladies moved to a cheaper, noisier, city-centre house: 25 Gay Street, Bath.

'She will be very comfortable', wrote Henry to Frank. 'A smaller establishment will be as agreeable to them . . . I really think that My Mother & Sisters will be to the full as rich as ever. They will not only suffer no personal deprivation, but will be able to pay occasional visits of health and pleasure to their friends.'[21]

Thoughtless Henry! He sounds very much like the cruel sister-in-law in *Sense and Sensibility*, who packages off her disinherited female relations to live on good wishes but very little else. 'They will live so cheap!' she cries. 'Their house-keeping will be nothing at all. They will have no carriage, no horses, and hardly any servants; they will keep no company, and can have no expenses of any kind! Only conceive how comfortable they will be!' She was really being utterly horrible, condemning her husband's sisters to live on £500 a year (*more* than the £460 a year of the Austen ladies) without any of the trappings of Georgian genteel life. I do wonder if Henry ever suspected where his sister had got the idea for the character of Mrs John Dashwood, one of her most awful creations.

Like Mrs John Dashwood, Jane's brothers seemed relieved to have 'solved' the problem of their female relations. 'I believe [Mrs Austen's] summers will be spent in the country among her Relations & chiefly I trust among her children – the winters she will pass in comfortable lodgings in Bath', wrote James, rather vaguely, to Frank.[22]

He was condemning his sisters to a life of what would sometimes feel like sponging, clinging on as house guests while worrying that their welcome was worn out, or for other reasons connected with not having a home. 'It would be inconvenient to me to stay . . . longer than the beginning of next week', wrote Jane on one such visit, 'on account of my clothes.' She often became anxious about travel arrangements for getting away from a visit, 'for fear of being in the way'. And indeed, life as the poor relations was to begin at once. Edward stepped in with an invitation to Godmersham for the summer.

But single ladies could, and did, band together to face adversity. Martha Lloyd, whose mother had just died, also now lacked a home. After the summer at Godmersham, Martha ('friend and Sister under every circum-stance') joined Jane and Cassandra and Mrs Austen for a stay in Worthing, and then in Bath, and indeed would join them everywhere they lived for the next twenty years. Martha had long been a dear friend of the sisters. 'I love Martha better than ever', Jane wrote. Three against the world were now four.

From this point on, the activities of Jane's brothers would hold a new significance, as their prosperity, or lack of it, would directly affect the female Austens' income. Frank served as a captain under Rear-Admiral Thomas Louis, the 'old Crocodile', as he was called, who'd been a wily member of Nelson's select inner circle of officers. At the Battle of the Nile in 1798, Louis had used his own ship to draw the enemy's fire away from Nelson's. It was also at the Battle of the Nile that the British seized a French ship called *Le Franklin*. Renamed as the *Canopus*, this ship of eighty guns was put under Frank's command. He was doing well. Frank, in the opinion of his commander Nelson, could 'not be better placed than in the Canopus, which was once a French Admiral's ship'. 'Captain Austen', the great leader continued, in words to warm a proud sister's heart, 'is an excellent young man.'[23]

But it had to be admitted that the *Canopus* was rather old and slow. Frank's sisters were in Worthing when, on 21 October 1805, the Battle of Trafalgar unfolded 1,500 miles away. Devastatingly to him, Frank was not present at the great fight, because the *Canopus* had been assigned the duty of protecting the navy's supply route instead. 'I have no other means of keeping my fleet supplied', Nelson explained to Frank, 'the enemy will come out, and we shall fight them.' 'But you will be back first, – so make yourself easy,' he added, in a consolatory aside.[24] In this, though, the great Nelson was wrong. 'Alas! my dearest Mary,' Frank wrote, to the young lady he'd met in Ramsgate and hoped to marry, 'all my fears are but too fully justified. The fleets have met, and, after a very severe contest, a most decisive victory has been gained by the English.'

He deeply regretted having missed the action – 'I shall ever consider the day . . . the most inauspicious one of my life' – and also, of course, like all sailors, he mourned the death of 'our gallant, and ever-to-be-regretted, Commander-in-Chief, Lord Nelson, who was mortally wounded by a musket shot'.[25]

By January, the ladies had left Worthing, and were glumly visiting James and Mary in Steventon before returning to Bath. On 29 January 1806, Mrs Austen took rooms there in Trim Street. The exact address of the Trim Street lodgings remains a mystery, but this was a commercial district of town, a far cry even from Green Park Buildings. When they had been seeking their first Bath home in 1801, Jane had reported that Mrs Austen 'will do everything in her power to avoid Trim St'. But now the time for Trim Street had come.

It's noticeable that their former homes in Sydney Place and Green Park Buildings were right on the edge of town, with green space visible from the windows. Trim Street, though, was entirely urban, quite narrow and dark, and the houses on it were about a hundred years old. Their neighbours in Green Park Buildings had been private individuals (including one Lady Araminta Monck), but in Trim Street the directory lists numerous businesses: a fire office, a couple of attorneys, a milliner and a cabinet-maker as well as Miss Ewing's School for Young Ladies at number one.[26] It doubtless suffered from poor air quality too. The painter Thomas Gainsborough had moved up to Lansdown Hill because he hadn't liked his 'house in the smoake'.[27] Like it or not, Mrs Austen and her daughters, lodging in Trim Street, had become just like the impecunious trio of Mrs Bates, Miss Bates and Jane from *Emma*.

However, there was one unexpected bright spot in all of this. Mrs Leigh Perrot's widowed friend Mrs Lillingston had died, leaving both Jane and Cassandra a legacy. One unattached woman left money to two others in the same position, perhaps in thanks for the long evenings playing cards and being bored. Yes, it was only £50 each, not thousands, but this was money on which they could live for at least a year. Jane would not forget this example of generosity from a lady linked by ties of friendship rather than blood.[28]

'Trim Street Still', Mrs Austen addressed her letters, with melancholy emphasis. It was hard to find anything better. The problem was that the truncated household did not require a whole house. 'We are disappointed of the Lodgings in St James's Square', she wrote, wearily. 'A person is in treaty for the whole House, so of Course he will be prefer'd to us who want only a part – We have look'd at some others since, but don't quite like the situation.'[29]

But the Napoleonic Wars were again working their indirect influence on the female Austens' lives. Despite having missed Trafalgar, Frank would make up for it at the Battle of San Domingo, which was fought on 6 February 1806 just south of the Caribbean island of the same name. And this would lead, in turn, to the Austens leaving Bath.

Although it is much less well known than Trafalgar just a few months before, this engagement was nevertheless vital in sealing the destruction of France's might at sea, and saving Britain from fear of invasion. Sir Thomas Duckworth was the admiral, and when he saw that he had five French ships of-the-line and four frigates at his mercy, he signalled the words 'This is glorious'.[30]

Inglorious blockade duties and frustration at having waited such a long time to bring the French to a tussle spurred on his men. They fought in Nelson's memory. On board the *Superb*, the captain hung a portrait of Nelson upon the mizzen stay, 'where it remained throughout the battle untouched by the enemy's shot though dashed with the blood and brains of a seaman who was killed close beside it'.[31]

Frank wrote joyfully to his wife-to-be of his own success in the two and a half hours of the battle. The first broadside fired 'brought our opponent's three masts down at once, and towards the close of the business we also had the satisfaction of giving the three-decker a tickling which knocked all *his sticks* away'.[32] 'My dearest Mary,' he enthused, 'I am in hopes this action will be the means of our speedy quitting this country, and perhaps to return to Old England. Oh, how my heart throbs at the idea!'[33] Jane, too, was delighted, and begged Frank by letter to come home and 'reap the reward which your principles & exertions deserve in the enjoyment of domestic comforts'. Feeling flush with prize money, Frank Austen decided that he could now afford a wedding. Indeed, he found himself 'in a great hurry to be married'.

San Domingo was the action that also saw Captain Wentworth in *Persuasion* – Jane's attractive, decisive, sailor character inspired by Frank – promoted to the rank of commander. After San Domingo, many sailors came home to enjoy the peace. In Captain Wentworth's case, it explains why, 'not immediately employed', he was able to come to Somerset to woo Anne Elliot. With the ending of the war came weddings.

And now the four ladies were to become five. Frank decided that his new bride Mary would be best off, during his expected future absences at sea, living with his mother, sisters and Martha Lloyd. He decided to rent them a house in Southampton, handy for the dockyard at Portsmouth. He himself was at the mercy of what Jane's niece Fanny called the 'horrible abominable beastly Admiralty'.[34] They still had the power to send him anywhere in the world.

And so, on 2 July 1806, Mrs Austen and her daughters finally left Bath, ultimately heading towards a new life with this new sister-in-law in Southampton. As Jane wrote later, their leaving of Bath took place with 'happy feelings of Escape!' Horace Walpole before her had been equally glad to leave this city supposedly specialising in health. 'It does one ten times more good to leave Bath than to go to it', he claimed.[35]

That chapter, thankfully, was closed. And although the female Austens did not quite know it yet, a tantalising new prospect of wealth was about to open up before them.

22

A House Fit for a Heroine

'Here was another strange revolution of mind!'

Mansfield Park

THE FEMALE AUSTENS left Bath for good on 2 July 1806. On the very same day, a very old lady reached the end of her life, at her house in Kensington, London. It was a death with powerful potential to solve all Jane's problems, and to change her life dramatically for the good. The lady's name was the Honourable Mary Leigh.

But the female Austens knew nothing of this as they vacated their house in Trim Street. They planned to spend a cheap summer paying family visits before going to live at Southampton. This anxious season provided real-life examples of some of the central concerns of Jane's heroines: wealth, legacy and family duty.

Jane must have been under a good deal of pressure. She was thirty years old; her father was dead; she was dependent on the charity of her brothers. She, her mother and Cassandra, were *en route* to her cousin Edward Cooper's house, for another spell of living at someone else's expense. And Jane was still unpublished. Annoyingly, Edward had the previous year got into print himself, as a writer of sermons, and his book was doing very well.[1] Jane really needed a break.

But before they went to Edward Cooper's home in Staffordshire, the Austens broke their journey with some of Mrs Austen's Leigh relations, at Adlestrop, near Stow-on-the-Wold in Gloucestershire. Reverend Thomas Leigh, their host, was caught up in a great deal of business regarding the estate of the Honourable Mary Leigh, the old lady who had just died. Perhaps it was not the best time for a family visit. Or then again, perhaps it was the perfect time to remind the Reverend Leigh, who seemed likely to inherit great wealth, that his cousin Mrs Austen was now an unprotected widow, and that her two daughters were unmarried and un-dowried. 'I do not know where we are to get our Legacy', Jane wrote, 'but we will keep a sharp look-out.'

Adlestrop was an enclave of Mrs Austen's family, the Leighs. There was the Reverend Thomas Leigh and his sister, Miss Elizabeth, in the Rectory (now Adlestrop House), and the Reverend Thomas's nephew James Leigh at Adlestrop House (now Adlestrop Park) nearby. Most people who have heard of this Cotswolds village will remember Edward Thomas's 1914 poem about its railway station, and the blackbird he heard there during the unexpected stopping of his train. It's a short, poignant poem, made even more moving by the fact that he would shortly die in battle:

> And for that minute a blackbird sang
> Close by, and round him, mistier,
> Farther and farther, all the birds
> Of Oxfordshire and Gloucestershire.

The other reason for Adlestrop's fame is that it was the location of a scheme by the landscape gardener Humphry Repton, he of the 'Red Books' showing drawings of his clients' parks both 'before' and 'after' his improvements. His work generally included undulations, water and clumps of trees. Reverend Thomas Leigh – 'respectable, worthy, clever, agreeable', as Jane described him – had brought Repton in to improve the estate, although the new picturesque garden he created came at the cost of enclosing the village green. Reverend Leigh had the bug for 'improvements' on a far grander scale than the shrubbery achieved at Steventon.

Repton prided himself on making his improvements look utterly natural, imitating nature 'so judiciously, that the interference of art shall never be detected'.[2] For his invisible hand, his clients had to pay the princely sum of five guineas a day, and Jane's discovering this would lead to the comedy of Mr Rushworth's 'improvements' at Sotherton in *Mansfield Park*. 'I think I had better have him at once', Mr Rushworth says of the latest landscape gardener. 'His terms are five guineas a day.' 'Well, and if they were *ten*,' cried Mrs Norris, 'I am sure you need not regard it.' Mr Rushworth's fortune and estate could survive some self-indulgent landscape gardening, and so could Reverend Leigh's. Especially as it now appeared that he would benefit enormously from the will of the Honourable Mary.

And in fact this whole summer would be full of echoes of the story of *Mansfield Park*. Jane had been to the comfortable Rectory of Adlestrop before, and it's likely that she read there her relative Mary Leigh's history of the Leigh family. Mary includes among her ancestors the story of three sisters. One of them married a wealthy man, the second, unspectacularly, a merchant, while the third 'elop'd at night' with a man of no profession, had numerous children with him, and lived in 'low circumstances'.[3] Rather like the Ward sisters in *Mansfield Park*; Lady Bertram, with her baronet; Mrs Norris, with her clergyman; and Mrs Price, with her drunken sailor.

But the Austen ladies weren't to spend long at Adlestrop. The Reverend Leigh whisked them away with him, on 5 August, to pay an unexpected visit to a much grander house, the deceased Honourable Mary Leigh's Stoneleigh Abbey.

Stoneleigh Abbey was by far the grandest mansion in Jane Austen's life. The newspapers had reported the commonly held belief that Reverend Leigh was to inherit it, and that after him it would then pass to Mrs Austen's brother, James Leigh Perrot.[4] But the Leigh family's legal arrangements were just unclear enough to fan the flames of what would turn out to be a long and vicious dispute. Other heartbeats besides Jane's were rising at the thought of a legacy. There was to be what one family member called 'a palpable scramble for Stoneleigh'.[5]

Jane Austen's novels, like Henry Fielding's before her, often examine the issue of who gets possession of a home. In previous centuries, inheritance had always been the prerogative of the oldest not the youngest, the male not the female. In the early nineteenth century, though, Jane would use fiction to question – and ultimately, to undermine – this established order. In her stories, homes are given to the virtuous rather than the well-born: a magnificent mansion to Lizzy Bennet of the improvident father, and a snug parsonage to poor relation Fanny Price.

A happy home, bought with Captain Wentworth's fortune, would also come to Anne Elliot, who was at the start of her story a displaced person living as a guest in other people's houses. Anne Elliot, in the last of Jane's novels, makes it clear that one deserved a home compatible with one's virtues, not one's rank. Members of the Navy, she says, 'who have done so much for us', have the greatest claim of all to 'the comforts and all the privileges which any home can give'.

Now, in the uncertain fog over the Stoneleigh inheritance, virtue instead of blood would be tentatively, but radically, put forward as an argument for inheritance. It would be specifically suggested that Jane and her relatives needed the money most; they, therefore, deserved to get it.

The Abbey itself had fallen upon dark times. It had all begun to go wrong with Edward, the fifth Lord Leigh, the so-called 'Lunatick Lord'.

Originally Stoneleigh had been a Cistercian house, founded on the banks of the River Avon by Henry II in 1154. Its ruddy-red stone gatehouse isn't quite that ancient, but is still seven hundred years years old. Following the Dissolution of the Monasteries, the Abbey fell into the hands of Thomas Leigh, a successful businessman and Lord Mayor of

London. At thirty-eight he married the seventeen-year-old Alice, who dutifully gave him nine children. Stoneley Abbey became 'Stoneleigh' to reflect their surname.

Thomas and Alice Leigh's descendants prospered, at least for a while. Their grandson, another Thomas, was a zealous Royalist who gave money and hospitality to Charles I. This family background helps explain Jane's own ardent love of the Stuarts. When Stoneleigh was captured by the Parliamentarians, this Thomas Leigh, now a baron, was 'sent to Coventry', the nearby Parliamentarian stronghold, for punishment, an action which gave rise to the phrase.

In the 1720s, the third Lord Leigh went on the Grand Tour of Europe and came back determined to rebuild the old abbey. He made a start, adding on his hulking great new west front, but money and inclination ran out before he could finish the other ranges that he'd had in mind.

So far, so good for Stoneleigh Abbey: it had been handed smoothly from father to son seven times, and most of those involved were called Thomas. On 11 May 1767, the fifth Lord Leigh made his will. He was about to set out on a Grand Tour, and he wanted to leave everything in order. Lacking wife or children, he left his estate to his sister, the Honourable Mary.

He had no notion that he would come back a deeply changed man. On 2 October, an ominous payment appears in the family accounts, to one Dr Monro. Dr Monro was physician to the Bethlehem, or Bedlam, Hospital in London. During the course of the next year, he would attend upon the fifth Lord Leigh for twenty-three further treatments. Lord Leigh had, in eighteenth-century parlance, gone mad.[6]

He died in 1786, aged only forty-four, having been for many years 'a Lunatick of unsound Mind'.[7] He'd undergone treatment by the same 'mad-doctors' who looked after King George III. When he died, the will he'd made as a healthy young man was still valid. In it, he bequeathed his estate to his sister for her lifetime, and then – and this was the wording that was crucially vague – 'unto the first and nearest of his kindred, being male and of his blood and name, that should be alive at the time'.[8]

The 'Lunatick Lord's' sister, the Honourable Mary, is an intriguing figure: rich, reclusive, and living in solitary splendour at Stoneleigh Abbey. One of her descendants recorded the family tradition that she was 'of a very short stature and rather plain of feature' and that 'she lived a somewhat retired life and never married. It used to be said that she disliked being looked at and that the village people had orders not to look at her as she passed.' The myths are pervasive: to this day visitors taking the tour of Stoneleigh Abbey are shown a chair with cut-down legs, said to be the diminutive Mary's.

Despite her shyness, the Honourable Mary had been something of a fairy godmother to the Austen family. She'd given Jane's brother James his first living, at Cubbington, close to Stoneleigh Abbey. James was merely an absentee curate, treating it as a sinecure, and he happily accepted a second curacy from her as well. She also gave £200 for the care of Mrs Austen's disabled brother.

In her own will, the Honourable Mary expressly wanted to avoid any Dashwood-style expulsions and family ructions. She insisted that her heirs were to reach agreement within six months after her death, 'it being my wish . . . to prevent any Contests concerning the property'.[9] But it was almost inevitable that 'Contests' would follow, because her brother's will had been imprecise enough to allow several members of the family to muscle in.

There were the two main branches of the Leigh family with a claim to be 'the first and nearest of his kindred' to the fifth Earl.[10] Some more distant claimants, like Mr Hanbury Leigh and Colonel Smith Leigh, had even added 'Leigh' to their names in the hope of fulfilling the clause that the heir should be of the Earl's name. And now James Leigh Perrot realised that he, almost as much as Reverend Leigh, could claim to be 'first and nearest'. It was given out among the family's lawyers that it was in fact *Mrs* Leigh Perrot whose 'influence has great weight with his determination'. He (or his mean wife) wanted a down payment in return for giving up their claim to the whole estate. It was a kind of genteel blackmail.

It was an anxious time for the elderly Reverend Thomas Leigh of Adlestrop (Jane's cousin once removed), and James Leigh Perrot (Jane's uncle), both of them in the frame as possible heirs. After the Honourable Mary's death, her lawyer Joseph Hill and the apothecary who came to embalm her body at once sealed up the drawers of her desk with wax. They were to be opened only at Child's Bank in London, so that the will could be read with everybody present. Reverend Leigh caused offence by not rushing to London for this. But then, he had taken the time to go to Stoneleigh to attend his aunt's funeral.

As the negotiations commenced, James Leigh Perrot now suggested that he might give up his claim to the estate if offered £20,000 plus an annuity of £2,000 a year. These were astronomical sums to his impoverished sister and nieces. Reverend Thomas Leigh proposed that within any such settlement James Leigh Perrot should also make provision for Jane, her siblings and her cousins, motivated by his regard for the 'Cooper and Austen families, & to ensure to Mr L.P. the means of better providing for them who are so very numerous'.[11] Indeed, the family lawyer was himself urging James Leigh Perrot that £8,000 of his share 'should be settled on Mrs Austens Family & Mr Coopers'.[12] But this Mr Leigh Perrot 'resisted' – perhaps at the behest of his wife – and nothing was agreed.[13]

And so it was all still up in the air when, on 5 August, Reverend Thomas, his sister Miss Elizabeth, the lawyer Joseph Hill and the three Austen ladies travelled to Stoneleigh in two carriages. They arrived at five o'clock, and Reverend Leigh had written ahead to ask the Stoneleigh servants 'to have beds & every thing ready'.[14]

In the late afternoon, then, the coaches must have drawn up along the carriage sweep at the external staircase on the main west front. This house was almost monstrous in its size and splendour. The Abbey's ranks of staring windows glowered down upon the Austens as they climbed the steps. Jane's mother counted these windows of the west front (in-accurately making it forty-five instead of forty-four) in order to tell her daughter-in-law exactly how grand it was. There is in Mrs Austen something of Mr Collins, who cannot refrain from telling Lizzy Bennet how many windows the house has, as they approach Rosings in *Pride and Prejudice*, and who fails to keep to himself 'what the glazing altogether had originally cost'.

The mis-counting of the windows was not the only mistake Mrs Austen made. Like *Northanger Abbey*, Stoneleigh Abbey was disappoint-ingly un-Gothic. As Mrs Austen wrote, 'I had figured to myself long Avenues, dark rookeries, & dismal Yew Trees, but here are no such melancholy things.'[15] The Abbey boasted some utterly Georgian interiors. The party entered through the bright and airy saloon with its pillars of yellow scagliola (timber, coated with crushed-up coloured marble) and turned right into the oak-panelled eating room. 'And here we found ourselves on Tuesday', ran Mrs Austen's account of the visit, 'Eating Fish, venison, and all manner of good things, at a late hour, in a Noble large parlour hung around with family Pictures – every thing is very Grand & very fine & very Large.'[16]

The house was essentially a royal palace of the 1720s, with a suite of rooms leading one after another to a rich bedchamber at its northern end. Mrs Austen liked the pleasant eating room looking out over the river, but admitted that most of the state apartments were 'rather gloomy, Brown wainscot & dark Crimson furniture, so we never use them.'[17] The lugubrious dimness of these rooms had likewise oppressed earlier Leighs, hence the 'Lunatick Lord's' re-plastering of the Saloon and staircase to inject a little light.

But the Reverend Thomas found it hard to show the Austens around the house, because it was simply too big and complicated. He 'almost dispairs of ever finding his way about', Mrs Austen reported, 'I have proposed his setting up <u>directing Posts</u> at the Angles' of the passages.[18]

The Reverend Leigh's sister Miss Elizabeth was likewise at a loss. When Jane's young niece, Caroline, visited a couple of years later, she noticed 'that Miss Elizabeth never felt quite at home in Stoneleigh Abbey'. 'The evening of our arrival', for example, Miss Elizabeth 'wandered about the house trying in vain to discover <u>what</u> room had been prepared for me and my maid. She <u>knew</u> she had ordered it to be near my mother's, but she could not find either apartment. I remember seeing her turn down the bedclothes in several rooms, to see if there were sheets on the bed.'[19] Eventually one of the housemaids was found, and she explained that Miss Elizabeth had gone up the wrong staircase.

Imagine the Austens exploring all these rooms for the first time, amazed by the riches within. The mansion also had no fewer than eighteen manservants, headed by the steward ('a fine large respectable looking man') and Reverend Leigh had to buy them all black mourning outfits.[20] The party were presumably shown round by the housekeeper. It seems likely that Jane transformed her remarks into those of Mrs Reynolds, who gives the guided tour of Pemberley. Housekeepers of a great mansion would have regularly given tours to visitors. When a group of tourists turned up to Holkham Hall, Norfolk, in 1772, in the hope of seeing inside, they were told they'd have to wait 'an hour at least, as there was a party going round'. And when they got to the waiting room, they discovered yet another party there already, ahead of them in the queue.[21] But now the Austens got their own private tour.

Despite the formality and size of the rooms, young Caroline Austen on her own visit found Stoneleigh much more relaxed than socially ambitious Godmersham. 'I think I was very happy at Stoneleigh', she wrote. 'Nobody teized me, or wanted me much in the parlour, and I had the range of the house.' She entertained herself by playing an old spinet in the picture gallery.[22] At the end of each day she would go with her nursemaid 'along a vaulted passage' to the housekeeper's room to have her dinner there.[23] You can imagine Jane revelling in some of the same freedom.

Mrs Austen nevertheless enjoyed embroidering the Abbey as richly as she could in the remainder of her letter to her daughter-in-law, describing the best bedchamber with its 'high dark crimson velvet bed' as 'an alarming apartment just fit for a Heroine.' 'There are 26 bed chambers in the new part of the house,' she continued, '& a great many (some very good ones) in the old.'[24]

As they settled into their visit, Mrs Austen and Jane got into the habit of going every morning to 'prayers in a handsome Chapel', its pulpit hung with black for the Honourable Mary's death. Jane, who had probably never seen a private chapel before, made use of this room to help conjure up the chapel at Sotherton, which was similarly austere: 'A mere, spacious oblong room . . . with nothing more striking or more solemn than the profusion of mahogany, and the crimson velvet cushions appearing over the ledge of the family gallery above.'

Daily prayers in the chapel were an essential part of life in a grand household. The worshippers were there to witness the spiritual overlordship of God, but also the temporal lordship of the Leighs, in their elevated gallery, literally looking down on their servants ranged below.

To this day a set of crimson velvet cushions still peeks over the edge of the chapel gallery at Stoneleigh, just as Jane described at Sotherton. But Stoneleigh's chapel was in one essential quite different to Sotherton's: it was still in use, whereas Sotherton's was not. Despite the excellent condition of the rest of the estate of the idiotic Mr Ruthworth's Sotherton, its heart – its chapel – was dead.

After chapel, and breakfast, Mrs Austen went prowling about. She was now sixty-seven years old, but had lost none of her old interest in estate management. It had just lain dormant for a while in her Bath lodging house. 'The garden contains five acres and a half', she noted. 'The ponds supply excellent fish the park excellent venison; there is also great plenty of pigeons, rabbits & all sort of poultry, a delightful dairy where is made butter good Warwickshire cheese & cream ditto'.[25] She sounds like nobody so much as the thrifty Mrs Norris, who returned home from Sotherton having wormed gifts of cream cheese and pheasants' eggs out of the housekeeper.

But everything at Stoneleigh existed on a slightly grotesque scale. Things went to waste. In the kitchen garden there was an excess of fruit. Even with all the servants, and all the visitors, and the 'assistance of a great many blackbirds and thrushes' to help eat it up, the surplus 'was rotting on the trees'.[26] The provision of food and drink in general was on an epic scale. One manservant, Mrs Austen was stunned to note, 'does nothing but brew & bake. The quantity of the casks in the strong beer cellar is beyond imagination.' The beer was almost too strong to drink.[27]

The breakfast given to the Austen ladies was completely over the top, consisting of 'Chocolate, Coffee, and Tea, plum cake pound cake, hot rolls cold rolls, bread and butter'.[28] All Mrs Austen found herself equal to was some dry toast. There was so much money being thrown away here that it turned the stomach.

The Austen ladies were not the only impoverished females who had turned up at Stoneleigh Abbey to eat their fill and to see what else might be had. Also present was the elderly dowager Lady Saye-and-Sele, whose husband had killed himself. Frances Burney once described her as 'a lady all alive', her head 'full of feathers, flowers, jewels and gew-gaws' and her face 'thin and fiery'.[29] The old lady unwittingly provided Jane with much amusement: 'Poor Lady Saye & Sele, to be sure, is rather tormenting,' Mrs Austen wrote, 'tho' some times amusing, and affords Jane many a good laugh.'[30]

But while Mrs Austen was looking after the poor distressed dowager ('she fatigues me sadly on the whole'[31]), Jane was also amusing herself with yet another member of the house party. Robert Holt-Leigh was a Member of Parliament, described by Mrs Austen as 'a single man the wrong side of forty; chatty and well bred, and has a large estate'.[32] Of course, like Mrs Bennet, she noticed these things. Robert was struck by Jane, became 'a great admirer' of 'her pretty face', and gave her some 'tributes of admiration'.[33] After all, Jane and Cassandra were still 'very sensible elegant Young Women & of the very best dispositions', as Mr Hill the lawyer described them.[34] At Stoneleigh, flirtations flourished as thickly as the fruit in the garden. Jane's young cousin, George, pursued his own wooing, consisting of 'animated fooleries', with another visitor, a Miss Bendish, 'who is very young & rather handsome'.

But on 14 August 1806, Mrs Austen and her daughters left Stoneleigh to go to the Coopers at Hamstall Ridware, Staffordshire. The visit was over, and the flirting was over too. Jane and the Honourable Robert Holt-Leigh went their separate ways, '& never met again'.[35] She probably did well to cast him off, for despite his admirable qualifications on paper, he had at least one illegitimate child.

Hamstall Ridware was a bit of a comedown after Stoneleigh: a modest parsonage, on the fringes of the Peak District, where Jane's cousin Edward was living and working. She probably gnashed her teeth at the galloping success of his book of sermons. Gallingly, it was published by the very same publisher who had turned down *First Impressions* in 1797.[36] She certainly did not enjoy the sermons themselves, describing them as getting 'fuller of Regeneration & Conversion than ever' as later volumes appeared. Edward's son was an irritating mini-version of the author himself, a second 'pompous Sermon-Writer'.

Jane certainly turned against her brimstone-y cousin on this visit, hoping on a future occasion that he would leave the bereaved alone and 'not send one of his Letters of cruel comfort' to a widower. To add injury to insult, Edward Cooper's eight children all got the whooping cough, and passed it on to Jane too.

As they left Staffordshire, though, Jane and Cassandra and their mother still kept alive a desire that they might benefit from the will of the Honourable Mary.

On 3 September, Mr Hill wrote at last with firm news. The old lady had left 'Miss Austen' and 'Miss Jane Austen' each 'a single brilliant centre' ring worth five guineas.[37] A diamond ring was not to be sniffed at, but they had not given up hope of getting more when a final settlement was reached.

Both the Reverend Thomas Leigh and James Leigh Perrot were in their seventies, and both were already well off. The extended family certainly thought that the two old gentlemen would spread the Honourable Mary's wealth around a little. 'Mrs Knight is kindly anxious for our Good,' Jane wrote, '& thinks Mr L.P. *must* be desirous for his *Family's* sake to have everything settled.' Naturally, the matter was much on her mind. 'A Legacy might make it very feasible', she wrote, of a 'very sweet' but very expensive project to spend a Christmas in Kent. 'A Legacy is our sovereign good.'

Back at Stoneleigh, Reverend Leigh started splashing money about, and once again called in Repton to make improvements. But he never moved into the Abbey properly, and eventually sloped off back to a more peaceful life in Adlestrop.[38] He left his nephew James Henry to take day-to-day charge, and under their combined careful stewardship, Stoneleigh became even more prosperous. In the middle of the nineteenth century, the estate was producing £30,000 a year – that's more than a million pounds a year today – and the Leigh family remained the largest landholders in Victorian Warwickshire.[39]

Meanwhile, as the Austens left Staffordshire, a new life on a much smaller scale awaited them, once again in urban rented lodgings. On 24 July 1806, Frank had finally married his Mary Gibson, at Ramsgate. Jane was to go to meet her new sister-in-law, who was also her new housemate.

23

Castle Square

'Want for nothing but patience – or give it
a more fascinating name: Call it hope.'

Sense and Sensibility

JANE'S EARLIEST MEMORY of Southampton must have been the 'putrid fever' she suffered there when a pupil at Mrs Cawley's school. And here, as in Bath, she would survive rather than thrive.

When she arrived in October 1806, though, Jane must have been glad to be back near the sea she loved. She must also have had clearer, happier memories of Southampton from a visit to her cousins there in December 1793, made as part of her coming-out tour. The Dolphin Inn (now Hotel) provided the venue for high times and parties; it was there that Jane danced the night of her eighteenth birthday.

Frank had escorted his sisters on that 1793 trip, and his career was the reason they now came back to Southampton again. Close to the dockyard at Portsmouth, Southampton had long been a town full of troops. Some thirty years earlier, under the patronage of the king's brothers the royal Dukes of Cumberland and Gloucester, Southampton had also become something of a successful spa, with waters to be drunk, a soft climate, fine views across the river, and drives in the nearby New Forest. But Southampton was losing ground to other, more fashionable destinations, such as the up-and-coming Brighton. In 1806, Southampton was still trying to present itself as a spa, but its glory days were nearly over. Its future lay not in tourism, but as a commercial port.

The road into town ran between aisles of trees admired by Jane's favourite landscape writer William Gilpin.[1] Then it passed through the ancient gates in the city walls. Many travellers ended up at either the Star or the Dolphin Inns on the wide High Street beyond; the Star still has its Georgian sign proudly announcing that the daily stagecoach to London 'PERFORMS 10 HOURS'. Today the money has been sucked out of the High Street and into the West Quay shopping centre, so the Dolphin where Jane danced now overlooks a lap-dancing club, an Army recruiting centre, and two Chinese takeaways.

In Southampton there were plenty of places for Jane to swim. The West Quay in 1806 was the location of Mr Chilton's 'range of convenient and permanent baths', where the 'water is changed every tide'. Further on were Mr Goodman's 'baths and machines, commodious and well frequented', and Mr Cole's 'lately constructed bathing-machines'.[2] There was also a chalybeate spring 'at the bottom of Orchard-street', of which 'a middle-sized tumbler is a sufficient dose'.[3] On the other hand, Southampton's detractors advised that you *shouldn't* drink the water, because it produced disorders 'ascribable in most instances to the presence of carbonate of lead'.[4] In other words, what was supposed to cure you might well kill you.

As well as having potentially poisonous spa water, the town – unlike Brighton – lacked a beach. In marked contrast to the British guidebook writers, one French visitor painted a warts-and-all picture. He counted only 'one street of any consequence, and a walk planted with stunted trees along the bay'.[5] He did notice 'a very singular edifice', the castle, with 'hovels' crowding up against its walls. The view from the castle extended 'over a field of red-tile roofs and chimneys, to the slimy banks of Southampton bay'.[6] Jane would end up living in the shadow of this gimcrack castle's walls.

Southampton's most notable Georgian addition was the Polygon, a twelve-house residential development to the north that was supposed to rival the Royal Crescent in Bath. Its developer, though, went bankrupt after only four were completed. Nearby, a 'most magnificent hotel' with stabling for five hundred horses was intended to steal trade from the town centre, but it too closed down in 1774.[7] Jane would take walks along the 'fine gravel road' that surrounded this incomplete modern-day ruin, 'to which company frequently resort for an airing'.[8] Nature was trying to reclaim its own: 'the Hornbeam grows to great size and richness in the Polygon', while 'the Nightingale is heard not only in the woods, but even within the town'.[9] It's a perfect emblem of late Georgian leisure: a failed lady novelist taking an airing round a failed hotel, perhaps being moved by the melancholy remains of commercial ambition.

The Dolphin, where Jane had danced in her teens, was just a couple of steps away from Castle Square, where the Austens ending up living for two years from February 1807. Another dancing venue was the Assembly Rooms, where the patrons were an unruly lot. These Rooms had a published regulation decreeing that you had to take the dancing position assigned to you by the Master of Ceremonies, like it or not, because pushing-in had 'been the origin of much dispute'.[10]

Southampton did have a good number of libraries: Fletcher's Reading

Society, Mrs Sheet's Library, and Skelton's Circulating Library with its 'Newspaper for the benefit of the ladies'.[11] And Jane also enjoyed boat trips; a 'pleasure-vessel' was easily engaged for a 'cheap and agreeable aquatic excursion'.[12] But Southampton's most fashionable visitors simply passed straight on through it. They continued towards the Isle of Wight, there to indulge in the modish pastime of yachting at Cowes.[13]

While the Austens were still in temporary lodgings before moving to Castle Square, Jane once again found herself buffeted by the concerns of housekeeping, visitors and infuriating brothers. 'When you receive this,' she wrote to Cassandra, 'our guests will be all gone or going; and I shall be left to the comfortable disposal of my time, to ease of mind from the torments of rice puddings and apple dumplings, and probably to regret that I did not take more pains to please them all.'

One of these unwelcome visitors was James, and Jane still just failed to get on with her eldest brother. To her, 'his Chat seems all forced, his Opinions on many points too much copied from his Wife's, & his time here is spent I think in walking about the House & banging the Doors', or wasting the servants' time by 'ringing the Bell for a glass of Water'.

By contrast, easygoing, craft-loving Frank, who was used to making do with the cramped accommodation on board a ship, was happy to entertain himself in the ladies' lodgings in Southampton by 'making very nice fringe for the Drawingroom-Curtains'. James had no such resources. If he wasn't hunting, giving sermons or reading his books, he didn't know quite what to do. Jane also found her brothers' wives hard work: James's wife Mary not interested at all in books; Frank's wife Mary pregnant, and subject to faints. When Frank had to go away, 'Mary was very low all day.'[14] Jane felt that another brother, Charles, was also too much in thrall to his new wife, the golden-haired, teenaged Fanny Palmer, whom he had met in Bermuda.

And Jane's letters written from Southampton are just as snappish as those from Bath. She felt alienated from the busy social life generated by Frank's naval friends, and had grown no closer to her mother. When both Cassandra and Martha were away from home, Jane wrote that their delayed return would not bother her, 'for I am now got into such a way of being alone'. All 'alone', except for the presence of a mother and a myriad of acquaintances. Jane was becoming an observer of the world, embittered, lonely and yet at the same time not lonely, because she had got used to it.

And she was, as always, beholden. Frank was good and kind, but Jane could never forget that he was also paying the bills. She kept up the tone of a supplicant, even when it came to her writing. 'And by the bye,' she once asked Frank by letter, 'shall you object to my mentioning the Elephant in [*Mansfield Park*], & two or three other of your old Ships? I have done it, but it shall not stay, to make you angry.' Jane could not afford to make her brother angry. Indeed, a woman 'may take liberties with her husband,' she wrote in *Pride and Prejudice*, 'which a brother will not always allow.'

The Austen party – Jane, Cassandra, their mother, Frank's wife Mary and Martha Lloyd – must have been relieved when they moved from temporary lodgings into something more permanent. Castle Square, their chosen address, was advertised as 'a retired spot, bounded on the West by the River, commanding truly Picturesque Views'.[15] The ladies' house at no. 3 is no longer standing, and has been replaced by a road inauspiciously named 'Cement Terrace'. Then, though, it was 'a commodious old-fashioned house in a corner', with views across the sea. Its garden was enclosed by the old city wall, which was lapped on its other side by high tide.[16] The Austens would have had superb views to the west across Southampton Water. Here, sometimes, porpoises could be seen; occasionally even whales, 'rolling and springing on the surface of the water, then disappearing, and rising again at another point to renew their awkward gambols'.[17] Today, that whole swathe of sea has disappeared: it was reclaimed as dry land, and built upon, and many of the town's historic houses have been destroyed. It takes some effort to imagine just how pleasant it must have been.

But pleasant it certainly was, at least in summer. You could walk along the top of the venerable city walls which extended 'a mile and a quarter' right around the town.[18] They accidentally formed 'a most beautiful terrace to the gardens which belong to the houses in the High-street and Castle-square . . . commanding an enchanting view of the bay'.[19] The walls, the Austens' substantial, three-storey house, and the greenery of its garden, are visible in old prints. Southampton's houses were packed in tightly, but the Austens had, as always, been drawn to a glimpse of green. 'We hear that we are envied our House by many people,' Jane wrote, '& that the Garden is the best in the Town.'

The garden must have been the main attraction, for the 'commodious old house' itself was in poor condition, and a good deal of work was necessary to make it ready for occupation. For the ladies who had lived in a new and elegant house in Bath, this was a case of making the best of it. A dressing table for the room Jane was to share with Cassandra was constructed out of an old kitchen table. There were beds to be made, and 'Window-Curtains, sofa-cover, & a carpet to be altered'. Green baize was to be laid on the floors in the bedrooms.

But even after all their efforts, the house remained rather uncomfortable. 'We are cold here', wrote Jane. 'Castle Square weather' was their name for Southampton's north-west wind, and Jane expected 'a severe March, a wet April, & a sharp May'. 'Beware of damp beds at Southampton', had been Madam Lefroy's advice. The wind brought down the chimney, which the masons 'found in such a state as to make it wonderful that it shd have stood so long'. The family were lucky to have escaped being 'thumped with old bricks'.

Then a blocked gutter caused water to run into the store cupboard. 'We have been in two or three dreadful states within the last week', Jane wrote, 'from the melting of the snow &c. – & the contest between us & the Closet has now ended in our defeat'. In this store room, the ladies were advised by household management books to keep their soap ('cakes should be cut with a wire or string, into oblong squares, and laid up, on a dry shelf'), candles, starch, loaf sugars ('kept tied up in paper'), preserves, tea, coffee, chocolate, dried fruits, seeds, rice, bread ('best kept in an earthen pan with a cover'), writing paper, and citrus fruit, which 'may be preserved a long time, packed in fine, dried sand, with their stems upwards, and kept from the influence of the air'.[20] The Austens certainly kept apple butter and preserved ginger in their closet. Despite the size of the house, space was generally short. A gift of two hampers of apples meant that 'the floor of our little garret is almost covered', and sometimes beds for guests were lacking.

The compensatory garden – a gardener was engaged to improve it – was to contain sweetbriar, roses, syringa, currants, gooseberries and raspberries. The Ordnance Survey map of 1846, albeit a couple of decades later, shows the garden with a complex layout of shrubberies, walks, and what might even be a little garden mound. Jane requested Cassandra bring back 'some flower-seeds from Godmersham, particularly Mignonette' after a visit to Kent, and their tender plants would be taken inside on a 'very cold blustering day & placed in the Dining room'.

Life in Castle Square was given interest by the proximity of the Austens' eccentric landlord, the Marquis of Lansdowne. He'd built the curious building known as Lansdowne Castle just opposite, a 'fantastic edifice', as Jane called it. He himself was long and lean, and rode about 'on a long lean horse' generally followed by 'a very little page, called his dwarf, mounted on a diminutive pony. The knight, the dwarf, and the castle, seemed made for each other.' And yet, he was a 'good sort of man'. The people of Southampton, 'although they laugh at the castle and the castle-builder, all speak well of him, and are hardly willing to admit that he was mad'. These were the words of a visiting Frenchman, who further added that 'the qualifications required for acknowledged insanity, are by no means easily attained in England, where a greater latitude is granted for whims, fancies and eccentricities, than in other countries'.[21]

Southampton's really was an ancient castle, but Lord Lansdowne had in 1804 remodelled it into a Gothic fortification with modern conveniences. Incorporating the motte of the medieval castle, the new one seemed to 'overlook the world . . . the view was magnificent, both by land and water'.[22] Appropriately for the inhabitant of a Gothic castle, he was the patron of the local Archery Society. The eccentric lord aroused hostile comment by hanging the walls of his castle with portraits of the revolutionaries Robespierre, Bonaparte and Marat, and was followed about by government spies as a result. In 1808 he managed to capsize his sailing boat on the River Test right outside the Austens' garden.[23]

Lord Lansdowne lived in his castle with his mistress, who later became his wife. A 'vulgar Irish woman near fifty', Jane thought that she wore too much make-up. 'The old sow', Lord Lansdowne's affectionate term for his lady, had been born Maria Maddock. Like Jane, she was the daughter of a clergyman. Before she hooked her Marquis, she had already managed to marry and outlive a baronet.[24] One acquaintance even thought Lady Lansdowne capable of becoming 'a dangerous rival' to Lady Hertford, the celebrated mistress, mature in years, of the Prince Regent. She was certainly even plumper and 'larger than Mrs Fitzherbert', the Prince's famously buxom, illicit spouse.[25]

This odd couple became one of the sights of Southampton, and people came to see 'the strange house' that Lord Lansdowne had built, and 'its stranger Mistress' who braved the 'muddy streets' in her 'blue silk shoes'.[26] Jane's visiting nephew James Edward loved the sight of her carriage drawn by eight ponies, 'each pair decreasing in size, and becoming lighter in colour, through all the grades of dark brown, light brown, bay and chestnut'. He delighted in looking down from his aunts' window to 'see this fairy equipage put together; for the premises of this castle were so contracted that the whole process went on in the little space that remained of the open square'.[27]

Of course, money remained a concern in Castle Square. A connection of Frank's 'offered to introduce us to some acquaintance', Jane wrote, 'which we gratefully declined . . . she seemed to like to be rich, and we gave her to understand that we were far from being so'. For 1807, unusually, we have an account of Jane's year's expenditure, recorded just as her father recommended in the back of a diary.[28]

At the start of the year, she had £50.15s.6d in hand, and ended it with £6.4s.6d. She had laid out money on 'waterparties and plays' during her brother Edward's visit in September, and made a journey to Chawton at a cost of £1.2s.10d. The cost of clothes ('Cloathes & Pocket') came in at £13.19s.3d and 'washing' at £9.5s.11½d. There were 'Presents' at £6.4s.4d. and 'Charity' at '£3.10s.3½d', while 'Letters & Parcels' cost £3.17s.6½d. A special expense – Jane was feeling flush because of Mrs Lillingston's legacy – was £2.13s.6d. for 'Hire Piano Forte'. 'I will practice country dances,' she planned, 'that we may have some amusement for our nephews and neices, when we have the pleasure of their company.' Now she was foreshadowing Anne in *Persuasion*, who, as an old maid, would play for the rest of the company to dance, and whose 'eyes would sometimes fill with tears as she sat at the instrument', desiring 'nothing in return but to be unobserved'.

Jane's accounts show that a quarter of her money went on charity and presents. Her food and lodging were not included her account, as her brothers paid for them, but even so this was a high proportion of her discretionary expenditure to go on other people. A contemporary gentleman was advised to spend one-third of his income on household expenses, one-quarter on servants and transport, and one-quarter for clothes, the education of his children and personal expenses. Presents or charity do not feature, as these were a female preserve.[29] Perhaps Jane felt, having been gifted all the money she had, that she was under an obligation to 'pay it forward' to other people with even less than her.

Another new feature of life in Southampton was that Jane was now living with no fewer than seven other women. There was her mother and sister, also Martha Lloyd, and Frank's wife, Mary. With Jenny, the cook, Molly, the maid, and Phoebe, the under-maid, that made eight. And when Mary engaged a nurse, eight became nine.[30] As Jane specifically mentions that there were five beds in the house, some of them must have shared. Indeed, Jane's letter to Cassandra saying that 'The Garret-beds are made, & ours finished to day', implies as much. It's important because the question of whether Jane and Cassandra regularly shared a bed has been much disputed. 'Cassandra was indeed the person she slept with', wrote Terry Castle in a provocative essay of 1995, which was pounced upon by other historians who pointed out that no, the sisters had their own separate beds in Steventon, and during their later long residence at Chawton.[31] But in temporary lodgings, it was different. One more drawback to lacking a permanent home was even less personal space.

Soon there was a tenth female in the house. Frank's Mary, although she was 'so ill as to alarm them all extremely', gave birth to a healthy girl.[32] The opinion of Jane's many-babied sister-in-law Elizabeth at Godmersham was sought. 'Take notice of how often Elizabeth nurses her Baby in the course of 24 hours, how often it is fed & with what', Jane commanded Cassandra. And yet Jane is not really interested: 'you need not trouble yourself to *write* with the result of your observations, your return will be early enough for the communication of them'.

So Frank was now a father. He was also doing well in his career. His family followed Frank's upward progress with extreme enthusiasm, and with the constant badgering of relatives and contacts on his behalf. 'Frank is made', began one exuberant letter from Jane to Cassandra bringing news of a promotion. 'He was yesterday raised to the Rank of Commander.' 'If you don't buy a muslin Gown' on the strength of it, this letter concludes, 'I shall never forgive You'.

According to his nephew, Frank was 'a strict disciplinarian' but 'maintained this discipline without ever uttering an oath'. These high moral standards certainly appealed to his Victorian descendants. We're told, with approval, that he was known as '*the* officer who kneeled at church'.[33] His family never quite knew when to anticipate their paragon's return home from the sea. 'I give you all Joy of Frank's return,' wrote Jane in 1808, 'which happens in the true Sailor way, just after our being told not to expect him for some weeks.'

Charles, Jane's younger naval brother, was also doing well. He'd had the honour of sailing with the Duke of Sussex, one of the sons of George III, and found him 'fat, jolly & affable'. Then, in 1801, he'd received £30 as his share of the prize for taking an enemy ship. 'But of what avail is it to take prizes,' Jane asked, 'if he lays out the produce in presents to his Sisters?' 'He has been buying Gold chains and Topaze Crosses for us,' she explained to Cassandra, 'we shall be unbearably fine.'

In her novels, wrote her great-nephew, Jane 'never touched upon politics, law, or medicine . . . but with ships and sailors she felt herself at home'. Well, she did touch upon politics indirectly, but it is certainly true that Jane wrote plainly and confidently of the ships and postings of her naval characters. Her letters don't on the whole make much reference to the kind of news that filled the papers, but they do include any Navy news. In 1809, for example, she describes all of its officers rushing off 'to help bring home what may remain by this time of our poor Army, whose state seems dreadfully critical'. This was the heroic, epic and tragic retreat of the British army to Corunna in the face of Marshal Soult of Napoleon's empire. Despite his trouncing at Trafalgar, Napoleon had escaped from imprisonment, and was back on his imperial prowl.

In *Persuasion*, Jane would appoint the officers of the Navy as heirs to the old landed gentry, of whom a typical specimen was the wastrel Sir Walter Elliot. The most sympathetic characters are Admiral and Mrs

Croft, happily married, straightforward, energetic. It was the tendency, even the duty, of naval officers to wish for war, with its opportunity of promotion, prize money and glory. But their female appendages were less enthusiastic. Jane and the little household in Southampton must surely have shared the dreams of peace put into writing by their contemporary Sarah Spencer: 'no expeditions, no fleets to be stationed God knows where; poor sea captains *obliged* to live at home'.[34]

If there was a high price to be paid in terms of anxiety for having brothers at sea, it was perhaps even worse to be married to a sailor. We have seen that Frank's idea of what to do with his wife Mary was to park her with his sisters. But Charles took a different tack. Like Mrs Croft in *Persuasion*, his young Bermudan wife Fanny lived with him on board, rather than waiting for him on dry land. Fanny would not even meet her Austen in-laws for four years because Charles's ship did not return to England in all that time. Charles and Fanny's oldest girl, Cassy, was prone to sea-sickness, and in 1813 Jane was party to painful discussions about whether to send her to live on the land, or keep her with her parents on the ship but in a state of perpetual illness. 'She has been suffering so much lately from Sea sickness, that her Mama cannot bear to have her much on board', Jane explained. But Cassy herself, understandably, did not wish to be left behind. Pitiful Fanny! Living on board, burdened with children, she at least had the compassion of her sensible sister-in-law Cassandra: 'I am afraid they will find themselves very very poor.'[35]

And yet the experimental household of ladies in Southampton was not entirely successful either. It was clearly begun with the best of intentions. 'Pray can you tell me of any little thing that wd be probably acceptable to [Mary]?' wrote Jane to Cassandra. 'I wish to bring her something; – has she a silver knife, – or wd you commend a Broche?' But as soon as Mary had the chance, she moved across to the Isle of Wight, out from underneath the nose of her mother-in-law, and diminished the Castle Square *ménage*.

One welcome pair of visitors to Southampton in 1808 were Catherine and Alethea Bigg. Jane had been staying at Godmersham, and was forced to reveal to her brother Edward the real reason why she needed to rush back to Southampton in time to meet them. 'My honour, as well as my affection will be concerned in it,' she told Cassandra, if she missed the Biggs. To be absent from home when they came would indicate that she was still sore about the business of Harris Bigg-Wither, which she wasn't. But having to reveal to Edward her 'private reason for my wishing to be at home' was hurtful to Jane's pride. There again was that damnable dependence on her brothers.

An equally appreciated visit of the summer of 1807 was paid by Jane's niece Fanny Austen of Godmersham, seventeen years younger, but much beloved. Jane 'could not have supposed that a neice would ever have been so much to me . . . I always think of her with pleasure'. They had many shared secrets, including a nonsense language featuring the letter 'P', in which the phrase 'strike the harp', for example, became 'Prike pe Parp'. Jane took Fanny to the theatre in Southampton, which held an 'uncommonly crowded' benefit night in June in aid of British prisoners-of-war in France.[36] Aunt and niece walked up and down Southampton High Street 'till late' in the evening.[37]

But poor Fanny was soon to receive a horrible shock. When, back at Godmersham, her mother Elizabeth Austen was brought to bed for her eleventh child in seventeen years, she did not get up again. She'd been thirty-five. 'Oh! the miserable events of this day!' Fanny wrote. 'My mother, my beloved mother torn from us! After eating a hearty dinner, she was taken *violently* ill and *expired* (may God have mercy upon us) in ½ an hour!!!!'[38]

Cassandra had been staying at Godmersham when the tragedy happened. In Southampton Jane, after suitable expressions of shock and grief, could not help questioning her about the experience. 'I suppose you see the Corpse,' she wrote, 'how does it appear?' Jane imagined what was happening at Godmersham Park as if it were a scene in a novel, the 'sad gloom – the efforts to talk – the frequent summons to melancholy orders & cares – & poor Edward restless in misery going from one room to another – & perhaps not seldom upstairs to see all that remains of his Elizabeth'. Almost as upset was Sackree, the children's maid, who would sadly sit and reflect upon Elizabeth's 'Person and actions and her happiness in Nureseing her babys'. 'What tears I have shed', Sackree wrote.[39]

After such a disaster, Cassandra simply could not leave Godmersham. She was needed both as substitute mother and as that vital female figure who could keep the household ticking over. Six months after Elizabeth's death, Fanny wrote that Aunt Cassandra had 'been with us, ever since the day poor little John was born' and 'has been the greatest comfort to us all in this time of affliction'.[40]

The aunts and uncles of the bereaved Godmersham children clamoured to take them in and look after them while Edward tried to recover from the loss of his wife. Two of his boys had been at school in Winchester when she died, and were at once sent to Steventon. 'I own myself disappointed,' Jane admitted, 'I should have loved to have them with me at such a time.' And indeed, it was soon decided that the boys should come on to their grandmother's in Southampton.

Aunt Jane did her best for the bereaved children. 'We do not want amusement', she wrote. They played cup and ball, 'spillikins, paper ships, riddles, conundrums, and cards', and walked out to watch 'the flow and ebb of the river'. Jane was anxious that the boys should have all the mourning clothes they wanted: 'I find that black pantaloons are considered by them as necessary; and of course one would not have them made uncomfortable by the want of what is usual on such occasions.'

Jane paints a harrowing picture of the boys, fourteen and thirteen, struggling to comprehend their loss. One minute George is 'very happy' on the quayside, 'flying about from one side to the other', enjoying a boating trip up, then intently reading a book while 'twisting himself about in one of our great chairs'. Meanwhile Edward is 'most industriously making and naming paper ships, at which he afterwards shoots with horse-chestnuts, brought from Steventon on purpose'. But then, the next minute, there are 'many tears', George sobbing aloud over a letter from his father, and Edward 'much affected by the sermon' at church, which happened to be on the too-pertinent subject of 'all that are in danger'.

Another depressing event that took place in Southampton was the final falling-through of the great hopes that had sprung up at the time of the visit to Stoneleigh Abbey. By 1807 there was still no sign of any legacy or gift from the Honourable Mary Leigh's estate, and that was despite a settlement having eventually been reached. 'Yes, The Stoneleigh Business is concluded', Jane wrote. But it was concluded in secrecy. James Leigh Perrot went away happily with his £24,000, plus £2,000 a year, in return for giving up his claim to Stoneleigh Abbey, the annuity to be paid to his wife for life should he (as likely) predecease her. Eventually, upon Mrs Leigh Perrot's death, all this money would go to Jane's brother James. Also at that point a legacy of a thousand pounds each would be paid to all James's siblings except George.

This amount, £1,000 (or ideally, £1,500), if paid over immediately, would have set Jane up for life. One and a half thousand pounds is about the sum she gives to five of the six heroines of her main novels, with the exception of the rich Emma Woodhouse. Even Fanny Price, the poorest among them, has 'the provision of a gentlewoman'. Cassandra already had this, possessing £35 a year of her own from the £1,000 she'd inherited from Tom Fowle. If she and Jane had now received a further £35 a year each, their income would have been just over £100 a year, or just enough to support a limited but genteel and independent lifestyle. But Mrs Leigh was as fit as a fiddle, and for Jane and her siblings the prospect of getting their hands on their £1,000-a-piece lay far into the future. What the Austen ladies had really wanted was money now, upon account. But nicety prevented them from asking, and logic prevented them from expecting.

Nor did they really know exactly what had been going on. Mrs Leigh Perrot's letters said 'as little as may be on the subject by way of information & nothing at all by way of satisfaction'. She kept the details of her own good fortune to herself. Instead, the letters the Austens received from her searched about, as Jane put it, 'with great diligence and success for Inconvenience and Evil'. As a consequence of the striking of the deal, arrears were owed to the Leigh Perrots by Reverend Thomas Leigh. But none of the parties involved revealed to the Austen branch of the family exactly how much they were. 'The amount of them is a matter of conjecture,' Jane wrote, '& to my Mother a most interesting one; she cannot fix any time for their beginning, with any satisfaction to herself, but Mrs Leigh's death.'

Although James Leigh Perrot and his wife kept nearly all the money for themselves, they did allow James, as head of the family, an extra £100 a year, thereby increasing his annual income to £1,100. 'My expectations for my mother, do not rise with this event', was Jane's grim comment. It must have seemed that the spoils were being given to those who already had plenty. Even as Mrs Leigh Perrot did her best in her letters to complain – about the weather in Bath, and her cough – her satisfaction inevitably shone through. As Jane put it, with 'the negociation . . . so happily over indeed, what can have power to vex her materially?'

The answer was that Mrs Leigh Perrot was one of those rich people who can simply never have enough money. There's even some evidence that her family thought her a mild kleptomaniac. When she was tried for the business of the stolen lace, back in Bath, her own counsel had privately believed her guilty, even though he got her off. And later events bore out his opinion. A few years afterwards, she was spotted stealing a plant from a nurseryman. He challenged her. One account has her positively deny 'the charge, but he insisted on searching her pockets where it was found; she burst into tears, and intreated that it might not be put into the papers'.[41] It later made its way into family tradition that Mrs Leigh Perrot just had 'an invincible propensity to stealing'.[42] It would have been a minor, embarrassing matter, except that she also seems to have stolen a comfortable financial future from Jane.

By the autumn of 1808, it became clear to Jane that the 'termination of the family treaty' would not result in any cash. In Southampton, the rising rents in their street 'made a great impression', and they had to give up their beloved garden. From 1807, the Austens no longer paid rates upon it, and the occupier in the local rate book was now listed as their neighbour the Marquis.[43] What with Frank's Mary spending as little time as she could at Castle Square, the ladies decided there wasn't much to keep them there. The experiment had failed. Once again they needed somewhere cheaper to live, casting about, like the feckless Lydia Wickham in *Pride and Prejudice,* 'from place to place in quest of a cheap situation'. It took some time for her daughters to convince Mrs Austen to move, but eventually she came round: 'to the purchase of furniture . . . she is quite reconciled, & talks of *Trouble* as the only evil' of the plan.

It would be a great advantage to have a landlord who was also a brother, and Edward offered them the use of a cottage in Kent. It was not ideal. But Edward's wife's death seems to have convinced him that he and his motherless family should spend more time in his native Hampshire, and that he should live more often at Chawton House, the secondary property he owned there. He also offered his mother and sisters a rent-free cottage in the village nearby. They took it. The decision brought them full circle, to return to the life they had formerly enjoyed in a Hampshire hamlet.

The prospect seemed to please Jane, and to give her the courage to take an important action. We don't have any evidence of writing that she might have done in Southampton, not even the sort of unfinished work that survives from Bath. But perhaps it was the brutal Stoneleigh disappointment that encouraged Jane to think once again of earning money by her pen. It was so miserable being poor. Southampton social life included mild gambling at evening parties, but Jane sat out the games: 'the stake was three shillings, & I cannot afford to lose that'.

Perhaps at one of these parties she and Cassandra had met the four Southampton sisters named Purbeck, spinsters all, who lived together 'in not very affluent circumstances but above the reach of want'.[44] Two of them, Elizabeth and Jane Purbeck, lived by their pens as the authors of no fewer than six novels, published anonymously. One of these was *The Political Quixote,* a follow-up to Charlotte Lennox's *The Female Quixote.* Jane reread Lennox's book in Southampton, perhaps because she had met the Purbecks and they'd been talking about it. Maybe the town gave an unexpected gift to Jane in the form of this pair of role models, hard-working, professional, anonymous, female novelists, who lived 'happily and much respected'.[45]

Whatever the precise motivation, it was on 5 April 1809, just before leaving Southampton, that Jane made her latest, and most vigorous, effort to get into print. Having sold the copyright of *Susan* back in the spring of 1803, she decided to try to get it back.

Although Bath had been bad, Southampton was the lowest point of Jane's life. But it was also the turning point. 'Want for nothing but patience', Jane says in *Sense and Sensibility*. Yet give patience 'a more fascinating name: Call it hope'. Now, at the age of thirty-three, well into the 'years of danger', Jane realised that good fortune was not going to come knocking on her door, either in the form of a husband or a legacy. But she could go out looking for good fortune herself.

There is a briskness, indeed an urgency, in the letter that she now wrote to Crosby and Co., the publishers who had purchased *Susan*. 'Gentlemen', she writes, with respect to *Susan*, 'this work of which I avow myself the Authoress.' She wants to know why it has never been brought into print and whether the manuscript has been lost 'by some carelessness', in which case she offers to supply another copy. She wants an answer, quickly, as she is about to leave Southampton. And if they do not want to publish her work, why, then she will take it elsewhere.

She wrote care of the Post Office in Southampton, under the pseudonym of Mrs Ashton Dennis. This enabled her, devilishly, brilliantly, to sign off her letter with those initials. The last line reads 'I am Gentlemen &c &c MAD'.[46] Yes, she was getting impatient.

There would be fewer balls in the country village of Chawton, so Jane indulged in a last burst of Southampton gaiety. She enjoyed being asked to dance at the Dolphin by a handsome foreigner, and was 'pleased with his black eyes'. It had been half a lifetime since she had danced at the Dolphin as a young lady on the brink of life, and now she was dancing again in 'the same room in which we danced 15 years ago!' Up the same creaking stairs was the long narrow ballroom with its two deep curved bay windows overlooking the High Street. Jane thought them over, those last fifteen years, and despite 'the shame of being so much older', she 'felt with thankfulness that [she] was quite as happy now as then'.

The stage was set for a new beginning.

ACT THREE

A Real Home

24

Chawton Cottage

'They saw her ready still to share
The labours of domestic care.'[1]

James Austen

'CHAWTON MAY BE called the *second*, as well as the *last* home of Jane Austen', wrote her nephew, for during her time in Bath and Southampton 'she was only a sojourner in a strange land, but here she found a real home amongst her own people'.[2]

It makes for a lovely story. But is it true? This is definitely the official viewpoint of the Hampshire Austens, who wanted to root their famous aunt in their own soil and claim her for their own. It does seem correct, though, that the return to Hampshire and the home she found at Chawton Cottage gave Jane the stability and the freedom from domestic care that led at last to the published phase of her relatively late-blooming career as a novelist. The books she either wrote or rewrote in this, the best known of her homes, are the books we know today.

The building is now the Jane Austen House Museum. Even in Jane's time it was never actually called Chawton Cottage, but the name is still a useful shorthand. It's a pretty place on a spring day, on a quiet village street with tulips in its garden and a tearoom opposite. But while the Hampshire Austens might not have been willing to admit it, in Jane's day it was noisier and less picture-perfect. In fact, it was a very long way from perfect at all.

That Mrs Austen had a home in her old age was due to the decision she made years before, to bargain away a son in return for a fortune. Edward did not entirely leave Godmersham Park after his wife's death. But he did spend more time at the Great House in Chawton, in the times between renting it out to tenants. Sometimes he also lent the house to his brother Frank.

The cottage he gave to his mother and sisters was previously occupied by Mr Seward, steward of Edward's Chawton estate. There's no explanation as to what took Edward so long to offer his relatives a home; surely he could have done so immediately after Mr Austen's death. Perhaps the ladies had wanted to make a go of Frank's plan of living in Southampton, and had only gradually admitted defeat. With Edward at the Great House in Chawton and his female relatives in the cottage nearby, the village now became Austen Central. It had its satellites, for Frank Austen soon settled his Mary and their children in the small town of Alton just up the road. And Steventon, only fifteen miles away, was still the home of James Austen and his own Mary.

Before moving in, Jane and Cassandra in Southampton sought information about their new home. 'There are six Bedchambers', they discovered, lapping up details from their brother Henry, who'd visited on their behalf. He reported also upon the garrets, one of which could be used for the manservant the ladies had determined upon employing. They'd had enough of being an all-female household in Southampton, and wanted a man about the house. They'd be able to afford it, too, now that they weren't going to be paying rent.

The house had been built in the late seventeenth century, or perhaps the early eighteenth, when its name was Petty John. It belonged to a yeoman, the farmer of a small piece of freehold land. Eventually Petty John, being 'situate on the North Side of the King's High-Way', was sold to Thomas Knight, of Chawton, in 1769 for £126.[3]

This was the point at which the house became an inn, as is often mentioned in family tradition. When in 1787 the contents of the building came to be sold they included 'a brewing copper with a cock and iron work' and 'about 10 hogsheads of good old beer'. It was something of a rowdy house, and two murders were committed either in it or in the street outside. By 1791, the innkeeper had been ejected, and the house occupied instead by Bridger Seward, who'd been bailiff to Edward's foster-father. Seward died, and in 1809 it was his widow who quit the house in favour of Jane.[4]

The house was conveniently situated for its short life as an inn, being right at the roadside at a forking of the ways to London, Portsmouth and Winchester. Anna Austen painted a watercolour view of the cottage which shows the fingerpost naming the roads, as well as white geese on the water on the pond in the green outside. That pond, however, was a little too close to the house for comfort. 'Our Pond is brimfull & our roads are dirty & our walls are damp,' Jane would write during one miserable March, '& we sit wishing every bad day may be the last.'

L-shaped in plan, Chawton Cottage was higgledy-piggledy but nevertheless packed in plenty of accommodation. It was 'quite as good as the generality of Parsonage houses then', thought Jane's nephew, 'the ceilings low and roughly finished – some bedrooms very small – none very large but in number sufficient to accommodate the inmates, and several guests'.[5] Anna's watercolour shows the cottage with a cream rendering, rather than the rosy red brick that creates such a lasting impression today.

Visitors entered through a door from the road that's no longer used today. To the right and left, the Austens' visitors would have found the 'two parlours, called dining and drawing room'.[6] The drawing room had once had a window looking out onto the road, but the ladies had it blocked up. A new one was cut through to overlook the garden, to give them a view of 'turf and trees' instead of the highway. The old farmer's cottage was being made into a cut-price, pocket-sized version of a country house.

Edward's estate account book shows that the building works 'at Mrs Austen's' cost him £45 in 1809, with £35 to follow on plumbing.[7] He also laid out money on 'trenching', on gardening, and even spent £3 on hay, presumably for the ladies' donkey, which pulled their donkey-cart.[8] Edward was 'experienced and adroit in such arrangements', wrote his nephew, 'and this was a labour of love to him'.[9]

Unlike the drawing room, the dining room had to face onto the road. But it transpired that Mrs Austen enjoyed sitting here 'for an hour or two in the morning, with her work or writing – cheered by its sunny aspect, and by the stirring scene it afforded her'.[10]

The Austen grandchildren, like their grandmother, liked being able to watch the life of the road. From the window they could spot vehicles travelling to or from Winchester. At the end of Winchester College's term they'd see 'a countless number of Postchaises full of Boys', packed with 'future Heroes, Legislators, Fools, & Vilains'. This was a turnpike road, for which tolls must be paid. The Austens lived just by a tollgate or payment point for the use of the stretch of road extending 'from GOSPORT, in the County of Southampton, to CHAWTON POND'.[11]

Every day the cottage was shaken by the heavy passage of the stage-coach. 'Collyer's Flying Machine', as it was called, went by daily except Sunday. It left Southampton at half-past-six in the morning for its habitual run to the Belle Sauvage Inn, Ludgate Hill, London, where it arrived ten or twelve hours later. The coach carried an armed guard for the protection of its passengers against highwaymen, and it cost £1 to travel inside and 17 shillings outside.[12]

'Collyer's daily coach with six horses was a sight to see!' remembered one young Austen. From the cottage's bedroom windows you must have been able to look out on a level with the passengers travelling on the stagecoach's roof. This was one of the rousing sights of Georgian England. 'A stage coach', writes one early nineteenth-century traveller, 'carries animation always with it, and puts the world in motion as it whirls along.'

'As the coach rattles through the village,' he adds, 'every one runs to the window', and from inside the vehicle you could see plenty of 'fresh country faces and blooming giggling girls.'[13] 'Collyer's Flying Machine' boasted a famous postilion, the person who rode one of the front horses to keep the team working well together. 'Dickey Dung Prong', as he was nicknamed, was a 'daring youth', such a good rider that he could 'stand on the back of a horse while at full speed'.[14] Sometimes the Flying Machine was driven by Mr Falkner of Alton, which is why Jane also in her letters calls it Falkner's Car, or even – when joking around with her niece Anna in a Gothic mood – the 'Car of Falkenstein'.

Sometimes the coach flew *too* fast. In 1792, the ironwork fastening one of the front wheels gave way, causing the vehicle to be 'instantly overturned' and 'entirely beat to pieces'.[15] Once there was an even more torrid drama. On a Monday evening in June 1793, the Flying Machine was chosen by a lady escaping to London from the consequences of her affair with a soldier. Her jealous husband hired a post-chaise that charged through Chawton in pursuit. He overtook the stagecoach just past Alton, and the lady 'was compelled to return, with all her boxes and booty, to the no small entertainment of the rest of the passengers'.[16] 'Most delightful', it seemed to a child who normally lived in the country quiet, 'to have the awful stillness of night so frequently broken by the noise of passing carriages, which seemed sometimes, even to shake the bed'.[17]

But perhaps only the very young and very old could appreciate the noise and movement. Jane and Cassandra might have regretfully contrasted the tranquillity of Steventon Rectory, with its carriage sweep and terraces and walks, with Chawton Cottage, shaken as it was by heavy traffic. The house was 'so close to the road that the front door opened upon it', while a very narrow fenced strip of garden 'protected the building from the danger of collision with any runaway vehicle'.[18] Chawton today seems rural and remote, but during the Napoleonic Wars, with traffic thundering up and down to the docks, living there must have been rather like living next to a dual carriageway.

However, the cottage still made claim to being a respectable residence, which meant that its grounds had the inevitable shrubbery. Beside and behind the house a high wooden fence protected the garden, and within it trees were planted 'to form a shrubbery walk – which carried round the enclosure, gave a very sufficient space for exercise – you did not feel cramped for room'.

The next generation of Austens again and again stress that the cottage was not 'cramped' and that its rooms, though 'low', were 'sufficient'. They really do protest too much, leaving the impression that the house to their young minds was inadequate, even embarrassing. It was 'altogether a comfortable and ladylike establishment', concluded Caroline, 'tho' I believe the means which supported it, were but small'.[19]

Her cousin Anna was more abrupt, believing that her rich uncle Edward could have done more. After all, his account book shows that he was getting more than £5,000 a year – Mr Bingley's income – from his Hampshire estates *alone* in 1810, not even counting his larger Kentish property.[20] But Chawton Cottage was quite simply 'small & not very good'; it was 'not all that their home might & should have been'. According to Anna, Jane put up with it because 'what was decreed by those she loved must be wisest'.[21] Of course Chawton Cottage was an enormously spacious dwelling by the standards of agricultural workers. But for someone who'd had the chance of being the mistress of Manydown Park, and whose brother was the owner of two grand mansions, it was something of a second best. Yet perhaps Jane preferred it that way, placing liberty in a cottage above captivity at Godmersham Park.

Jane's novel *Sense and Sensibility* contains something of a commentary on cottage life. 'I advise every body who is going to build, to build a cottage', says the ignorant Robert Ferrars. 'Some people imagine that there can be no accommodations, no space in a cottage; but this is all a mistake.' His speech proves his insensitive misunderstanding of the four-bedroom cottage where the four female Dashwoods have to live. They cannot afford anything bigger, and indeed their cottage has 'dark, narrow stairs and a kitchen that smokes'. He, on the other hand, believed that any cottage *must* contain a dining room with space for eighteen couples to dance, a drawing room, a library and a saloon. The spacious and delightful *cottage ornée* was a fashionable force in architecture. But the Marie-Antoinette-ish game of playing at living in a 'cottage' was offensive to those who, through necessity, really did.

Mrs Austen, Jane, Cassandra and Martha Lloyd moved into their cottage on 7 July 1809. With its six beds it could quickly get full up when the four of them were joined by relatives. 'It was a cheerful house,' wrote a niece, 'my Uncles, one or another, frequently coming for a few days.'[22] Jane shows us her young nieces and nephews joyfully 'romping' in 'the Back Court'. The rebarbative James was a dutiful visitor, often riding over with his daughter Anna from Steventon to Chawton, 'through the pretty cross roads & rough lanes inaccessible to wheels which lay between the two places'.[23] But these visiting relatives could cause angst, as the little household ran on a shoestring. When Charles came to stay with his family, they noticed 'he does not include a Maid in the list to be accommodated, but if they bring one, as I suppose they will, we shall have no bed in the house even then for Charles himself – let alone Henry – But what can we do?'

The answer was to use the Great House, which Edward often placed at their disposal as overflow accommodation when it was not full of tenants or other family members. And, in fact, few people 'lived' anywhere for very long in the Austen family. They were constantly staying with each other. This includes Jane and Cassandra, who were still often away from home on visits. It was Mrs Austen who would become the odd one out in settling down so fixedly in one spot for many years. The cottage was generally known as 'Mrs Austen's', partly because she was the senior member of the household, partly because she was the only one who was pretty much always there.

Frank was soon off to China once again after he had got his family established at Rose Cottage in Alton. In 1811, he won a substantial bonus, £1,500, for transporting gold and treasure from China to Britain as the agent of the East India Company.[24] Royal Navy captains often did some commercial business on the side like this, for example bringing home payment for goods received from the Company. The irony was that God-fearing Frank, 'the officer who kneeled at church', made his fortune out of the opium trade.

At Chawton Cottage his sisters still shared a room, probably the one looking out over the back of the house from the left-hand side at the top of the stairs. As family history put it, the attachment between the sisters 'was never interrupted or weakened. They lived in the same home, and shared the same bed-room, till separated by death.'[25]

Their two single beds must have almost entirely filled their room, but here they treasured their private time. When Anna wrote a novel of her own, Jane told her how she'd read it aloud to Cassandra, with 'a great deal of pleasure', in the privacy of their 'own room at night'. In this small space, they somehow must have managed to wash in a basin placed in the tiny corner cupboard, to stir up the fire in the little grate when it was cold, and to store their clothes. The bedroom must also have contained their limited jewellery: their topaz crosses, gifts from their brother Charles; Jane's bracelet of blue beads, and her gold ring with a turquoise stone. These items have survived; perhaps also they had the 'brilliant' rings they'd inherited from the Honourable Mary Leigh. Thus their small store of treasures, gifts, reminders of departed female relatives, was mounting up. As any jeweller will tell you, inexpensive jewels are valuable not for their financial worth, but for their sentiment.

Of all Jane's homes, it's Chawton Cottage that provides us with the best information about her daily habits. 'Aunt Jane began her day with music', explains her niece, 'she chose her practising time before breakfast – when she could have the room to herself – She practised regularly every morning.'[26]

After that, 'at 9 o'clock she made breakfast – *that* was *her* part of the household work – The tea and sugar stores were under *her* charge – *and* the wine – Aunt Cassandra did the rest'. 'Aunt Cassandra did the rest' because, at long last, Mrs Austen 'had suffered herself to be superseded by her daughters' in household management.[27]

I like the fact that although Jane's household duties were limited, she was placed in charge of the intoxicants, tea and sugar being considered to be powerful and dangerous. The tea was valuable enough to be kept in a locked caddy. By this period servants were as addicted to caffeine as their mistresses, and often requested a tea allowance as part of their wages.[28] Jane had to order supplies from Twinings of London. 'I am sorry to hear that there has been a rise in tea,' she wrote in 1814, 'I do not mean to pay.' Another country clerical household made use of a less orthodox means of supply: 'Andrews the Smuggler brought me this night about 11 o'clock a bagg [of tea]. He frightened us a little by whistling under the Parlour Window just as we were going to bed.'[29]

The ladies had their breakfast in that dining parlour right next to the road: indeed, a friend reported that she'd once 'heard of the Chawton Party looking very comfortable at Breakfast, from a gentleman who was travelling by their door in a Post-chaise'.[30] Afterwards began the never-ending duty of needlework, that busy-work symbolising gentility and obligation. Among the cottage furnishings was a footstool worked by Jane's nephew William, a gift received as a welcome 'proof of his affection & Industry'. Jane wrote that it was far too precious for everyday use: 'we shall never have the heart to put our feet upon it'. The gift, handmade itself, inspired further labour, for as Jane wrote: 'I must work a muslin cover in sattin stitch, to keep it from the dirt.' They also made patchwork coverlets. 'Have you remembered to collect peices for the Patchwork?' Jane asks. 'We are now at a stand still.' The surviving example at Chawton Cottage today contains three thousand diamonds from both dress and furnishing fabric, all cut out and sewn by hand. It does not sound like the life of a novelist, but the mysterious thing about Jane's writing was that no one ever saw her at it – or at least never admitted it. And she carefully kept it that way.

In the afternoon Jane and Cassandra 'generally walked out – sometimes they went to Alton for shopping'.[31] The town was only a mile away, the road was good, and after social events they occasionally made 'a beautiful walk home by moonlight'. And sometimes, but rarely, they went 'to call on a neighbour – They had no carriage, and their visitings did not extend far'. Nevertheless Jane was an enthusiastic collector of gossip about the locals: 'She liked immensely to hear all about them. They sometimes served for her amusement.'[32]

Mrs Austen may have abdicated her domestic responsibilities, but she still exerted a powerful hold over her daughters. 'It had been ruled in the family that Mrs Austen was never to be left alone,' her granddaughter noticed, 'why, I do not know, for I am sure she was at that time, and long afterwards, perfectly well able to take care of herself.'[33] Jane continued cool towards her mother, sighing, when away from home, that Mrs Austen 'will like to have me write to her. I shall try at least.'

Mrs Austen at nearly seventy still enjoyed working in the cottage's 'good kitchen garden'.[34] She did not content herself with the ladylike 'cutting of roses & tying up of flowers' but went hard at it with – still – the potatoes. 'She dug up her own potatoes,' we hear, '& I have no doubt she planted them, for the kitchen garden was as much her delight as the flower borders.' For this work, she 'wore a green round frock like a day labourer'.[35] I wonder what the gentlemanly Edward, or his haughty daughter Fanny, made of a grandmother who dressed like a worker?

Mrs Austen's efforts made a border 'very gay with Pinks and Sweet Williams, in addition to the Columbines' and then there were also Jane's favourite syringas. Fruit-wise, Jane reported excitement when 'an Apricot has been detected on one of the Trees', and the ladies once enjoyed 'a great crop of Orleans plumbs – but not many greengages' (dessert plums). Plans to diversify the orchard behind the house failed. 'I will not say that your Mulberry trees are dead,' Jane warned Cassandra, 'but I am afraid they are not alive.' As in the old Steventon days, they kept poultry. 'The Chickens', Jane wrote, are 'fit for the Table – but we save them for something grand'.

The ladies dined unfashionably early, in mid- or late afternoon depending on the time of year. They ate before the setting of the sun so that the cook could work without candles. In 1801, at the great sale of the contents of Steventon Rectory, 'a table set of Wedgwood' had been one of the items to go.[36] Now, with pleasing circularity, the Austen ladies acquired its replacement. A new Wedgwood service was chosen by Jane in London, and delivered to Chawton a month or so later. 'I had the pleasure of receiving, unpacking & approving our Wedgwood', Jane reported. 'It all came very safely . . . tho' I think they might have allowed us rather larger leaves, especially in such a Year of fine foliage as this. One is apt to suppose that the Woods about Birmingham must be blighted.' Jane confuses Birmingham with the Five Towns of the

Potteries, where Wedgwood had his works. But then she had never been quite that far north.

Despite her lack of interest in housework, Jane didn't mind collecting recipes (also called 'receipts'), which her housemate Martha Lloyd carefully copied into a book. 'The real object of this Letter is to ask you for a Receipt', Jane joked to Alethea Bigg in one postscript, 'but I thought it genteel not to let it appear early. We remember some excellent orange Wine . . . made from Seville oranges, entirely or chiefly.' The Austens made wine from all sorts of fruits. Jane had a well-recorded enjoyment of alcohol, perhaps believing, like Elinor Dashwood, that a glass has 'healing powers, on a disappointed heart'.

Otherwise, to judge by Martha's recipes, the food at Chawton Cottage was unfashionably plain. 'Hogs Puddings', 'Cabbage Pudding' and 'Vegetable Pie' were about as exciting as it gets, along with 'Sausages' and 'Toasted Cheese'. The reopening of the continent after the Napoleonic Wars reintroduced the English to the wonders of French cooking, with its rich sauces. But there was something disreputable about a 'made dish', as it was called, by contrast to straightforward English food. The objectionable Mr Hurst in *Pride and Prejudice* dismisses Lizzy Bennet when he discovers her to prefer 'a plain dish to a ragout', the French word for a rich, sophisticated, slow-cooked stew.

Jane's six novels beautifully illustrate the gradual changing fashions in food, starting from the partridges from the local woods 'remarkably well done' by Mrs Bennet's cook in *Pride and Prejudice*, and ending with *Persuasion*, where the characters don't eat much at all. In their urban lives, it is a trip into Molland's, the real-life pastry cook of Bath, which finally brings Anne and Captain Wentworth together, rather than a home-cooked family meal. The history of a society shifting from country to city is captured here.

The ladies would spend the evenings together, not least to save money by the pooling of candles. You needed the light of several candles together to sew or embroider. 'Will you ring the bell for some working candles?' asks Lady Middleton in *Sense and Sensibility*, when she wants her guests to make a toy for her daughter. Mrs Austen describes one similarly placid Sunday evening when 'I was on the Sopha with the head-ache' and Anna, Jane and Cassandra 'were sitting round the Table', presumably all of them working by candlelight. Mrs Austen used the evening, despite her headache, to compose a poem.[37]

All in all, the ladies were well pleased with this new home. Jane wrote a half-serious doggerel verse praising the cottage and its small delights. Even while her topic was tiny and domestic, she still used the grandiose metre of Byron's *Marmion*. The years had gone by, much had changed, but Jane was *still joking*.

> Our Chawton home – how much we find
> Already in it to our mind,
> And how convinced that when complete
> It will all other Houses beat,
> That ever have been made or mended,
> With rooms concise or rooms distended.[38]

The significance of Chawton and its modest comforts comes through in the three novels conceived there. Each of them contains strong emotions about home. Jane's earlier heroines, Lizzy and Jane Bennet, and Catherine Morland, expect to leave their homes upon marriage, and are quite reconciled to the fact. But Fanny Price and Anne Elliot, characters Jane created at Chawton, have more complex feelings. To them, the loss of a home is something like the loss of a limb. It is deeply damaging.[39] But both of them will learn – even the materially blessed Emma Woodhouse will learn – that home isn't a building, it's a state of mind. I think we can read from this that despite Chawton's physical disadvantages, Jane felt as happy here as anywhere, with Cassandra to look after her and her routine assured. Like Jane, the governess Nelly Weeton had to content herself with a box-like room '7 feet by 9, with a bed, a chest of drawers, two chairs, and a wash-stand in it, (don't peep under the bed now!) with just spare room for myself and the fire, and a tea-tray put over the wash-stand to serve for a table'. But in this tiny, cramped space, she had 'many a snug sit', and 'a fire in my room on a cold winter's evening, was one of the greatest comforts I had'.[40] The Georgian lady who could accustom herself to what she had could be content.

What did Jane look like in her thirties? '*We* do not grow older of course', she joked, about herself and Cassandra, but of course they knew that they did. Being declared 'a pleasing young woman' by a gentleman left Jane delighted. 'That must do,' she wrote, 'one cannot pretend to anything better now – thankful to have it continued a few years longer!'

Never one to have suffered fools gladly, to those who did not know her well she was actually growing rather terrifying. Jane referred to herself and Cassandra collectively as 'we, the formidables'. She admired an acquaintance who left a party with 'a great deal of decision & promptness, not waiting to compliment & dawdle & fuss'. There were, of course, compensatory advantages to growing older. 'As I must leave off being young,' Jane admitted, 'I find many Douceurs . . . I am put on the Sofa near the Fire & can drink as much wine as I like.'

Yet acquaintances did not see this softer, self-indulgent side. 'She has stiffened', wrote one, rather hostile, country neighbour, 'into the most perpendicular, precise taciturn piece of "single blessedness" that ever existed.' Jane had called herself formidable, and this lady agreed: 'it must be confessed that this silent observation from such an observer is rather formidable'.[41] Another lady described how Jane 'used to sit at Table at Dinner parties without uttering much probably collecting matter for her charming novels'. But this was the impression given to strangers. The same witness reported Jane as 'a most kind & enjoyable person to Children'.[42]

Jane's niece Anna, who spent a good deal of time with her in these Chawton days, describes her minutely: 'tall & slight, but not drooping . . . Her complexion of that rather rare sort which seems the peculiar property of *light brunettes*. A mottled skin, not fair, but perfectly clear & healthy in hue; the fine naturally curling hair, neither light nor dark; the bright hazel eyes to match, & the rather small but well-shaped nose.' Anna was slightly mystified by her aunt's appearance. 'One hardly understands how with all these advantages she could yet fail of being a decidedly handsome woman', but so it was.[43]

Then again, Anna's half-sister Caroline thought Jane decidedly 'pretty': her face 'rather *round* than long – she had a *bright*, but not a *pink* colour – a clear brown complexion and very good hazle eyes . . . She always wore a cap – Such was the custom with ladies who were not quite young . . . I never saw her without one, to the best of my remembrance, either morning or evening.'[44] At Chawton, it was easy to keep her young nieces out of the private space of Jane's bedroom. But at Godmersham, her spoiled nieces came running into her bedchamber whether she liked it or not. These Godmersham girls remembered Jane without that matronly cap: 'long, long black hair down to her knees'.[45]

The most attractive description of Jane as an adult comes from yet another niece, and it pleases because it fuses her appearance and her character together: 'a tall thin spare person, with very high cheek bones great colour – sparkling Eyes not large but joyous & intelligent . . . her keen sense of humour I quite remember, it oozed out very much in Mr Bennet's Style'.[46] I love the idea of wit 'oozing' out of Jane, as if she could not help it.

The only certain portrait of this elusive face of Jane's is that sketch in pencil and watercolour by her sister Cassandra in the National Portrait Gallery. Unsmiling, even grumpy, it did not serve the Austen family's later idea of Aunt Jane.

As demand grew in later years to know what the famous authoress looked like, an artist was commissioned by the family to fashion Cassandra's sketch into a prettier, smilier, more submissive Jane, in a more decorative, decorous dress, who sits on an unmistakeably and anachronistically Victorian chair. One of the Austen nieces, Cassy, admitted that although this image was a 'very pleasing, sweet face', it did not look '*much* like the original; – but *that*, the public will not be able to detect'.[47]

But for now no one wanted to know what Jane Austen looked like. Why should they?

25

Published!

'Please to pay to Jane Austen spinster
the sum of one hundred guineas.'

Jane as a girl writes herself an imaginary cheque

JANE'S 'MAD' LETTER of 1809, complaining to Crosby and Co. about the non-publication of *Susan*, did not have the desired effect.

Mr Richard Crosby wrote back immediately saying that if she tried to publish it elsewhere he would 'take proceedings'. The copyright was his. She could have it back, but only in exchange for the £10 he had paid for it. This ended the matter for Jane, as she didn't have the money.

But unlike previous setbacks, this one spurred her on, for she now sought other means to get published. Even her earliest stories show that she wanted to be paid for her work. At the start of one of them, *Lesley Castle*, she wrote out a spoof cheque from her brother Henry promising her one hundred guineas. And now she once again sought Henry's help.

In August 1809, just after the move to Chawton Cottage, we find evidence that Jane was back at work as a writer. She revisited some of her early Steventon Rectory stories, adding the date 'August 18th 1809' into *Evelyn*, for example, while in *Catherine* she updated the books mentioned in the plot. Jane had also been revising *Sense and Sensibility*, the book once known as *Elinor and Marianne*. The cost of the London post had doubled to two pence in 1801, so Jane corrected this in her text. She decided that Marianne would certainly be fond of the coming man of poetry, Sir Walter Scott, and included his name. She was bringing the book up to date in the hope of sending it out into the world.

Jane agreed with her brother Henry that he should act as her literary agent, and he was now successful. In the winter of 1810, *Sense and Sensibility* was accepted for publication. It was to be brought out by Thomas Egerton, a publisher of military books.

Egerton was not an obvious publisher for a new novel, but he was friendly with Henry Austen. They'd known each other's names, at the very least, from the days when Egerton had distributed James Austen's student magazine, *The Loiterer*, from his office in London. Henry's role as an army agent probably brought the two of them back in touch. Egerton's 'Military Library' in Whitehall produced books for officers with titles such as *Hints to the Gentlemen of the Corps of Mounted Yeomanry*, or the *Elucidation of Several Parts of His Majesty's Regulations for the Formations and Movements of Cavalry*. These were odd stablemates for *Sense and Sensibility*, but this was a proper publisher with an extensive list willing to take on Jane's work at last. The wars had kept Egerton's market for his military books buoyant, so – in a roundabout way – it was Napoleon himself who helped to bring Jane into print.

Jane must have been delighted to be in business, even though it was at some considerable financial risk. *Sense and Sensibility* was to be published 'on commission', which means that Jane herself was liable for any losses it might make, even though she was also due a share of any profits. Today this might be called 'self-publishing', something a little aside from the mainstream, but it was in fact a pretty standard way of proceeding in 1810.

Henry tells us, in his memoir of his sister's life, that Jane was convinced that *Sense and Sensibility* would fail commercially. She was so sure, he claims, that sales of her book 'would not repay the expense of publication, that she actually made a reserve from her very moderate income to meet the expected loss'.[1] The sum in question was about £180, which was the cost of printing the 750 copies agreed as the first print run.[2]

In truth, Henry is painting a pretty but misleading picture here of a shrinking violet lady-authoress. Jane would not have published at all if she had *expected* to make a loss. And she could not afford £180: she had no income to save up to meet this supposed loss. If there were losses, it was Henry who would have to pay. Indeed, Egerton probably only took Jane on as an author because he trusted Henry, her banker brother, to underwrite the project. He was correct. Henry *could* have afforded it, although his optimistic nature probably encouraged him to think it unlikely that he'd be called upon to cough up.

For Jane, the wait had been long. She admitted her anxieties about the passage of time, about the competition from other writers, and of being 'always half afraid of finding a clever novel *too clever* – & of finding my own story & my own people all forestalled'. She joked about discovering rivals in the unlikeliest of places. Even her bosom friend Martha Lloyd must not be allowed to reread *First Impressions*, Jane claimed, for 'she is very cunning, but I see through her design; – she means to publish it from Memory, & one more perusal must enable her to do it'.

But the wait had also been beneficial. Jane had simply never given up. Rather than sinking into disillusionment after rejection, she had just gone on rewriting, getting better and more experimental.[3] If her father's first offer had been accepted, and *First Impressions* published as it stood in her twenties, surely she would not have been the great writer she was. And we would not have had *Pride and Prejudice.*

Jane's joy, though, must gradually have faded, as the printing process seemed to take forever. She went to stay in London with Henry for the period when she was needed to correct the galleys. Although life at Henry's house was packed full of pleasures, Jane told Cassandra that work came first. 'No indeed,' she wrote, 'I am never too busy to think of S&S. I can no more forget it, than a mother can forget her sucking child.' And Henry did not forget his duties either: 'he *has* hurried the Printer, & says he will see him again today'.

In fact, the economics of the publishing industry meant that Thomas Egerton had no strong motivation for speed. Even if he were to sell all 750 copies of *Sense and Sensibility*, he would make a profit of just £35 as he was only publishing 'on commission'.[4] It was Jane (or more accurately Henry) who was running the risk, and winning the potential reward. The highest possible amount they could have hoped to make was £140.

What did the dilatory printer actually do as he got to work? First of all, he had to 'cast off' the book. This meant deciding how many pieces of duodecimo paper – big sheets each capable of producing twenty-four pages, or twelve leaves – would be used. This paper was the greatest expense of all in the printing process, and was also subject to tax. It made publishers conservative in their print runs, as Jane would find out. It was better to make a small profit on 750 copies, than to print 2,000 and have to remainder some of them for waste paper.[5]

Next the printer would split up the novel so that he could ask several compositors at once to start putting the type together to produce their own particular designated sheets. This required enormous dexterity. The compositor had to whip out individual metal letters from their places in wooden trays and pop them into place, separating each line of text by a thin piece of metal called a 'slug'.

Then, plump printer's balls with wooden handles, their leather faces smeared with sticky black oily ink, were smacked down onto the metal type. Once it was good and inky, the paper, in a wooden frame, was lowered down upon the type by the wooden arms of the printing press, and firm pressure was applied. The words were on the paper at last. London's first steam-powered press would be acquired by *The Times* newspaper in 1814. But for now, all the work was done by the power of human muscle.

The first sheet to be printed would then be checked and copy-edited, either by the author or the publisher, before the required number of copies of that particular sheet were run off. Then, the metal type would be broken up, and the compositors would all start work on their second designated sheets.[6] The finished printed sheets also needed to be cut up, folded, and sewn together, a job often done by women. Finally, the printed pages were sent to the bookbinder, which was a totally separate business from the printer. If you wanted, your bookbinder would match the binding of your particular copy to that of the rest of your library.[7]

All this took a long time. *Sense and Sensibility* went to the press in January 1811, but it was not available to the reading public until October. Three days before publication, the strain of waiting and wondering how it would be received was beginning to tell upon Jane. She tried to forget about it. 'When stretch'd upon one' s bed,' she wrote, 'with a fierce throbbing head . . . How little one cares / For the grandest affairs!'[8]

But finally on 30 October 1811 a newspaper called *The Star* drew readers' attention to the new publication with an advert, and the next day the *Morning Chronicle* did the same. Contained in three volumes, and priced at fifteen shillings, sales of this intriguing new novel called *Sense and Sensibility* were boosted by a positive review that appeared in the *Critical Review* in February of 1812. It praised Jane's characters for being 'naturally drawn, and judiciously supported. The incidents are probable, and highly pleasing, and interesting . . . it reflects honour on the writer, who displays much knowledge of character, and very happily blends a great deal of common sense with the lighter matter of the piece.'[9] Another review appeared in May in *The British Critic*. A friend remembered Jane taking enormous pleasure in her reviews, saying 'Well! that *is* pleasant! Those are the very characters I took most pains with, and the writer has found me out.'[10]

The first print run of *Sense and Sensibility* did sell out entirely, and made Jane a nice stash of money. But it did not make Jane Austen's a household name. This was not least because her name never appeared on it. 'By a Lady', the title page declared. In one printed advert for the book, 'By a Lady' was mistakenly turned into 'By Lady A', which gave the author an interestingly aristocratic air of mystery.[11]

It was conventional for a novel to be published anonymously, but one imagines that it also gave Jane – the most private of people – a certain pleasure to have a secret. She was tickled, during a visit to the circulating library at Alton, when her niece Anna actually picked up a copy of *Sense and Sensibility*, saying, 'Oh that must be rubbish I am sure from the title.'[12]

Why did so many authors publish anonymously? Well, the whole business of publishing at all was considered by genteel people to be just a little bit vulgar. You could protect yourself from such accusations by publishing your work anonymously. It was also a little classier to sell your copyright outright to a publisher, placing yourself at a greater distance from the marketplace, than to publish at your own risk as Jane had done.

One important eighteenth-century trend had been for an author to crowd-source his or her book by raising subscriptions in advance from people who wanted to read it. But this was embarrassing, and it was hard to get people to pay up upon their promises. Publishing by subscription was thought to be a particularly vulgar thing for women to do. Often, female authors claimed they had been forced into print by one of the 'acceptable' reasons: the need to support an invalid husband, or destitute children.[13] The novelist Charlotte Smith even had to get her husband to sign her publishing deals – as a married woman, the law forbade her from signing a contract herself. 'Literature', wrote the poet and Jane's near contemporary Robert Southey, 'cannot be the business of a woman's life; & it ought not to be.'[14] (His letter was addressed to an aspiring young author named Charlotte Brontë, so you'll be pleased to learn that he wasn't taken too seriously.)

While that first run of about 750 copies of *Sense and Sensibility* did sell out, a second run, advertised from October 1813, did not. By comparison with modern publishing, the print run was low. But then again, those two adverts in the newspapers were the only means of selling it, apart from word of mouth, until those two reviews came along several months later. The second edition was again to be at Jane's financial risk. 'I suppose . . . I shall owe dear Henry a great deal of Money for Printing', she wrote. (She was in fact wrong about this; the printers would subtract what she owed from what they owed her.)

Jane was also clearly anxious about her novel's reception by her relatives. Generous old Mrs Knight was in on the secret, and a great supporter: 'I think she will like her Elinor', Jane hoped. But with its theme of impecunious female relatives being forced out of a family home, *Sense and Sensibility* strayed onto dangerous ground. Her brother James might have looked with new eyes upon his displacement of his sisters from Steventon Rectory. Or the Leigh Perrots might have been prompted to think again about their treatment of their impoverished relatives. Jane simply couldn't afford to alienate these people.

Yet her success as a writer meant that Jane's secret could not stay safe forever. Slowly but surely, her relatives gradually came to realise that Aunt Jane was a published novelist. Few of them, though, would ever understand within her lifetime just how startlingly good she was. Jane's nephew James considered that his aunt took neither pleasure nor pride in her work. 'I do not think that she was herself much mortified by the want of early success', he said. 'Money, although acceptable, was not necessary for the moderate expenses of her quiet home. Above all, she was blessed with a cheerful contented disposition, and an humble mind.' When she did get some cash, he claimed, she was so far from expecting it that she thought it 'a prodigious recompense for that which had cost her nothing'.[15]

Well, that might have been her nephew's view of things, but it's long been agreed among historians that Jane's own views were very different. As she grew in confidence, and learned more about the publishing business, she became bolder, more professional and more mercenary in her decisions. And she was very, very fond of the money she earned.

Part of the difficulty that Aunt Jane's relatives had in seeing what lay before them in plain sight was that she wasn't the only author in the family. She did not stand out. There was her cousin Edward, with his sermons. And then, until the very end of his life, their mother regarded James, not Jane, as the real writer of the family. Her eldest son was no man-of-business, Mrs Austen admitted that much, but 'Literary Taste and the power of Elegant Composition he possessed in the highest degree'.[16]

Indeed, her family were at pains to domesticate Jane's talent, to put it into a context they understood, which had the effect of belittling it. 'Every country has had its great men,' wrote her niece Caroline, 'whose lives have been and are still read . . . Such a one was my Aunt'.[17] Caroline was actually doing her best to talk up Jane Austen's achievements, but clearly lacked the language with which to do so. 'Great' writers were so obviously supposed to be male, and not anyone's aunt.

Considering that Jane had at least three different novels locked up in that writing desk of hers, why did she start by publishing the novel that is the least favourite of most modern readers? The answer is simple. It was the most conventional, the one most like other contemporary novels. Elinor was a respectable character, expressing praiseworthy thoughts that actually make her a bit dull. Lizzy Bennet, charming as we find her today, was strikingly bold, almost brash, for her time. When she eventually appeared in print, many Georgian readers would consider her to be offensively uppity.

And Jane even toned down the very mild humour of *Sense and Sensibility* for the second edition.[18] In the first, Mrs Jennings reveals that she thinks Colonel Brandon has an illegitimate daughter. The vapid Lady Middleton's 'delicacy was shocked; and in order to banish so improper a subject as the mention of a natural daughter, she actually took the trouble of saying something about the weather'. In the second edition, this joke disappeared. Perhaps someone said something that made Jane feel it was too coarse, too intimate, too much something for Cassandra's ears.

One of the most common complaints about *Sense and Sensibility* is its ending. Many modern readers are not convinced by Marianne's marriage to the good, kind Colonel Brandon, whom she does not love. Let's return for a moment to the controversial suggestion that, for a writer of stories about marriage, Jane is surprisingly unromantic at the crucial moment. People who see some merit in this argument perhaps don't believe in love and marriage and happy endings more generally, for in Jane Austen's work you find, above all, what you seek. It holds as many different meanings as there are readers.

So what is it that these sceptical readers might spot? Lizzy Bennet only marries Mr Darcy with 'uncomfortable feelings' about their differing rank, which 'took from the season of courtship much of its pleasure'. In *Mansfield Park,* we don't actually see Edmund falling in love with Fanny because he does so off-stage, after an interval that Jane almost can't be bothered to specify: it happened 'exactly at the time when it was quite natural that it should be so'. Indeed, there is nothing special about Emma Woodhouse's marriage to Mr Knightley either, as it was just a 'wedding very much like other weddings'.

But if you follow me this far in the idea that Jane was undermining the very moment where you'd expect marriage to be most praised, there could be an explanation. Remember that 'double-voiced' nature of Jane's letters? The same applies to her novels. At first reading, these are stories about love and marriage and the conventional heterosexual happily-ever-after. Only at the second does a sneaky doubt perhaps creep in to suggest that maybe marriage is not the best thing that could ever happen to these women.[19]

It *has* been suggested that with these clever layers of meaning, Jane was perhaps even more subversive than we give her credit for. Yes, she was writing for the commercial market. But she was also writing for her female cronies, for Martha Lloyd, Cassandra and Miss Sharp. She glibly provided the happy endings that society expected, but in an off-hand, almost perfunctory fashion.[20] You don't have to believe in Jane's happy endings if you don't want to.

I like to think that this is the band of spinsters' last laugh.

26

Pride and Prejudice

'. . . much too clever to have been written by a woman'.

The verdict of a 'gentleman, celebrated for
his literary attainments' on *Pride and Prejudice*

ONE DEBATE THAT divides historians of Jane's life is exactly 'when' she wrote her novels. Her own family split her life into two productive periods, one at Steventon, the other at Chawton, with dead time in between. 'As soon as she was fixed in her second home', claimed her nephew, 'she resumed the habits of composition which had been formed in her first.'[1] Scholars have since disputed this suggestion of a two-phase career, pointing out that her nephew had no way of knowing that Jane hadn't been writing and rewriting all along. But I'd like to try to answer a different question. When *on any given day* did she write her novels? How did she 'find the time'?

Jane's niece Marianne paints a delicious picture of her aunt doing two things at once: 'working' on one task with her needle, and on another with her brain. When she was staying at Godmersham Park, we're told, Jane would:

> sit quietly working [sewing] beside the fire in the library, saying nothing for a good while, and then would suddenly burst out laughing, jump up and run across the room to a table where pens and paper were lying, write something down, and then come back to the fire and go on quietly working as before.[2]

So perhaps Jane was creating her plots and characters without other people being aware of it. Jane did not in general tell people what she was up to, except for Cassandra. It was said in the family that 'with this dear sister – though, I believe, with no one else – Jane seems to have talked freely of any work that she might have in hand'.[3]

Life in Chawton fell into an established routine that allowed Jane to be extremely creative. It seems that Cassandra and Martha shouldered the burden of the business of running the house, recognising that Jane had other contributions to make. But this arrangement was not discussed with outsiders. According to the most celebrated account of Jane's writing habits:

> She was careful that her occupation should not be suspected by servants, or visitors, or any persons beyond her own family party. She wrote upon small sheets of paper which could easily be put away, or covered with a piece of blotting paper. There was, between the front door and the offices, a swing door which creaked when it was opened: but she objected to having this little inconvenience remedied, because it gave her notice when anyone was coming.[4]

So it was, her nephew thought, that he and his cousins must have often unknowingly disturbed their aunt 'at the little mahogany writing desk' exactly at the moment that 'Fanny Price, or Emma Woodhouse, or Anne Elliot was growing into beauty and interest'.[5] His sister Caroline confirmed that far from tucking herself away to write, Jane's 'desk lived in the drawing room. I often saw her writing letters on it, and I beleive she wrote much of her Novels in the same way – sitting with her family.'[6] In other words, Jane was a writer who was *pretending that she wasn't*.

But there are hints that feeling forced to hide her profession like this irked her. The one time she gives us an account of her preferred way of living and working comes in a letter written during a visit to her brother Henry's home, which was then in Hans Place, London. He was out each day at his bank, leaving Jane by herself. 'I find more space & comfort in the rooms than I had supposed,' she wrote, '& the Garden is quite a Love . . . I live in [Henry's] room downstairs, it is particularly pleasant, from opening upon the garden. I go & refresh myself every now & then, and then come back to Solitary Coolness.' As Jane was hard at work on *Emma* at the time, this is a unique glimpse of the conditions in which she was most happy: an empty house, Henry's shady study, just his one single maid to bother her; a garden where she could take a break whenever she wanted. It's tempting to think that this, not the opulence of Godmersham, was real luxury to Jane. But it's also upsetting to think that for most of her life she didn't have it. Even Chawton Cottage was full of interruptions and company and domestic duties. Although in public Jane could not admit that she was irritated by the encroachments of other people upon her time, she did so in private. 'I really am impatient myself to be writing', she railed. 'I can command very little quiet time at present, but yet I must begin.'

This apparent effortlessness where her writing was concerned pleased Jane's family. She may have been a brilliant novelist, they thought, but more importantly, she was a good, Christian, domesticated, family-orientated aunt. Jane's nephew James admired her work as much as, if not more than, any other Austen. But the critic Kathryn Sutherland points out that even he places her abilities as an author in the same category of other, less significant skills: '*she* could throw the spilikens for us, better than anyone else, and she was wonderfully successful at cup and ball'.[7]

The Austens are also curiously concerned with Jane's *handwriting* as much as with her writing: its neatness, its legibility. Her brother Henry records her words as coming 'finished from her pen', while her niece Caroline records the 'excellence' of her calligraphy. Yet, as Sutherland points out, the surviving samples of Jane creative work reveal scratchings-out, reworkings and experiments. Sutherland finds here evidence not of a neat writer, but 'of a restless and sardonic spirit'.[8]

The British Library contains the only surviving part of a manuscript from any of Jane Austen's completed novels. It's a draft of the last two chapters of *Persuasion*, and it reveals that Jane rewrote the whole of the end of the story.[9] Its original conclusion had Wentworth offer Anne his hand in person, while in the rewritten – and far more dramatic – ending, he did so by letter; a letter composed while he and Anne were in a room with other people. Jane must have changed her mind because she realised that the hiding of feelings, the pressure to keep up the social façade, made the moment even more exquisitely exciting. Jane herself understood very well that one might have to write something important, even life changing, in the presence of other people.

The cancelled chapters of *Persuasion* also reveal that it is indisputable – just as her family claimed – that Jane wrote on small pieces of paper. At least, they were large pieces folded up by hand to make little books. Sometimes, if Jane wanted to rewrite a passage, she would pin a new piece of paper on top of the old. Perhaps the same pins made their way from dresses to novels and back again. Although we see no possible comparison between Jane's skill at dressmaking and at writing, her family did. As her nephew put it, 'the same hand which painted so exquisitely with the pen could work as delicately with the needle'.[10] And it is also true that Georgian paper was made out of rags, and that books had to be sewn together by hand. Jane's written work and her needlework did have more in common than we might at first assume.

It was probably in the winter of 1811, after *Sense and Sensibility* had been published but before it was known to be a success, that Jane started to revise the book originally called *First Impressions*. She now turned it into the *Pride and Prejudice* we'd recognise. The story of Jane and Lizzy Bennet had remained a firm Austen family favourite. 'I do not wonder', Jane wrote to Cassandra, 'at your wanting to read *first impressions* again.' But when Jane came to revise it for publication, it had to have a new title. Another novel called *First Impressions* by a different author had appeared in 1801.

Just how much was changed between *First Impressions* and *Pride and Prejudice*? The conventional narrative is that Jane had a white-hot period of creativity at Steventon Rectory, essentially creating the book when she was Lizzy Bennet's own age. But certainly extensive revisions were also made at Chawton Cottage. 'I have lopt & cropt', Jane explains, and the dates and days given in *Pride and Prejudice* fit precisely with the calendar for the years 1811 and 1812.[11] (It is also true, though, that it fits the calendar of 1805–6 as well.[12])

But Kathryn Sutherland argues that there is another possible version of events: that all six completed novels were substantially the work of Jane's thirties, in her temporary homes as well as Chawton, and that their publication was the 'culmination of some twenty years of uninterrupted fictional experimentation'.[13] Sutherland asks an important question about the importance of home and family to Jane. If she really could be productive *only* when she felt 'at home', as her nephew claims, why are her books so intensely critical of her characters' homes? 'Given the hard critical gaze Austen turns upon homes and families in her fictions,' Sutherland asks, 'can it be that they are exclusively the products of home and rootedness?'[14]

Perhaps not, and we've seen that even Chawton Cottage was in some ways unsatisfactory: cramped, noisy, full of visitors, full of anxieties about wine, sugar and tea. But at least here we have some evidence, lacking from earlier years, that it had become agreed that Jane would be excused household duties. It sounds like a tiny thing – and indeed it was – but a tiny trickle of water gradually hollows out a stone. Jane's ducking out of the housework in order to write would lead inexorably onwards, upwards, towards women working, to women winning power in a world of men. This is the significance of trying to reconstruct the detail of Jane Austen's daily life.

Pride and Prejudice, whether the product of Jane's twenties, or thirties, or even of both, is firmly set in Austen-land, that carefully realised country neighbourhood with the occasional big house and plentiful parsonages. Here people very familiar from Jane's real life lived, quarrelled and loved. 'You are now collecting your People delightfully,' Jane advised her niece Anna, when the latter came to write a novel of her own, '3 or 4 Families in a Country Village is the very thing to work on.' Not for her the extravagant adventures of a novel like Mary Brunton's *Self-Control* (1811), with its heroine who was 'wafted down an American river in a boat by herself'. Why stop there, Jane asked? Why not have her waft right across the Atlantic and end up at Gravesend?

Indeed, Jane would eventually draw up a satirical 'Plan of a novel according to hints from various quarters' – a compilation of implausible suggestions made to her by various well-meaning but hopeless helpers.[15] The heroine of this imaginary spoof novel was of course to be 'faultless in character, beautiful in person, and possessing every possible accomplishment'. She is to travel around Europe in order to provide a constant change of scene, and 'wherever she goes, somebody falls in love with her'. Dramatic tension is introduced by the heroine's being short of money. She has to 'work for her bread,' becoming 'worn down to a skeleton, and now and then starved to death'. Only at the end, in 'the very nick of time', does the heroine accidentally run 'into the arms of the hero'.[16]

Unlike this implausibly 'perfect' woman, Jane's most memorable heroines are defiantly flawed. Jane described Lizzy Bennet as the most 'delightful a creature as ever appeared in print', and was proud of her creation. 'How I shall be able to tolerate those who do not like *her* at least, I do not know', she wrote. But there would indeed be those who disliked Lizzy, those who thought that she had far more to say than a proper heroine should. Only an 'entire want of taste', thought Jane's fellow author Mary Russell Mitford, 'could produce so pert, so worldly a heroine'.[17]

Jane's most discerning readers, such as William Gifford, the editor of the *Quarterly Review*, understood exactly what she was up to. Gifford thought that *Pride and Prejudice* was 'really a very pretty thing. No dark passages; no secret chambers; no wind-howlings in long galleries; no drops of blood upon a rusty dagger – things that should now be left to lady's maids, and sentimental washerwomen.'[18]

And so Jane stuck to describing the sort of people she knew in real life. Equally well known alongside her novels is a neat little passage she penned about her creative process. She describes 'the little bit (two Inches wide) of Ivory on which I work with so fine a Brush, as produces little effect after much labour'. Some people even thought that her work was so 'realistic' that it lacked creativity. *The British Critic*, for example, in 1818 described how 'in imagination, of all kinds, she appears to have been extremely deficient'. Indeed, she 'seems to be describing such people as meet together every night, in every respectable house . . . and to relate such incidents as have probably happened, at one time or other, to half the families in the United Kingdom'.[19] Indeed, Jane did have photographic accuracy in recording the world around her. She has only ever been caught out in two errors. First, in *Emma*, she makes apple trees blossom, incorrectly, in June. And then, in *Mansfield Park* Lady Bertram's pug, called 'Pug', appears to be of different sexes at different times, although perhaps even this was deliberate. Jane could have been intentionally making Lady Bertram too dim to realise the gender of her pet (as well as being too lazy to give him – or her – a proper name).

Jane's fictional world was so perfectly, minutely and solidly constructed that it took another brilliant and unusual writer, Charlotte Brontë, a generation later, to pull it down. Brontë memorably described *Pride and Prejudice* as 'a carefully-fenced, highly cultivated garden with neat borders and delicate flowers – but no glance of a bright vivid physiognomy – no open country – no fresh air – no blue hill – no bonny beck. I should hardly like to live with her ladies and gentlemen in their elegant but confined houses.' She concludes her demolition job with 'these observations will probably irritate'.[20] Yes, Charlotte Brontë, they do irritate, as you could hardly have written *Jane Eyre* unless Jane Austen had previously constructed something worthy of demolition.

And the last word may go to Virginia Woolf:

Jane Austen was born before those bonds which (we are told) protected woman from truth, were burst by the Brontës or elaborately untied by George Eliot. Yet the fact remains that Jane Austen knew much more about men than either of them. Jane Austen may have been protected from truth: but it was precious little of truth that was protected from her.[21]

In the autumn of 1812, Jane reached an agreement with Thomas Egerton for the publication of *Pride and Prejudice*. The sales of *Sense and Sensibility* must have impressed him, for he now offered to give Jane what seemed like better terms. He proposed a deal based not on commission, but upon an outright purchase of the copyright. He offered not the £150 that Jane wanted, but a reasonably flattering £110. 'We could not both be pleased,' she wrote, modestly, '& I am not at all surprised that he should not chuse to hazard so much.'

Jane was also pleased that the transaction had been concluded because of the 'great saving of Trouble to Henry', who'd once again been acting as her agent. Henry had other things on his mind, for the fascinating Eliza was ill. Just like her mother, she had found a 'swelling' in her breast. In her high-spirited manner, she did not let on that she was gravely sick: 'from my Looks no one would suppose any thing ailed me'.[22] Jane had decided to hand over the copyright partly to avoid Henry's having to run around chasing up the printers as he had done before.

But this would turn out to have been a terrible business decision, as Egerton would now make a great deal of money out of Jane. This time, knowing that the balance of the risk and the reward lay with him, Egerton

was much less dilatory in bringing Jane's new novel to the public's attention. Both he and she knew that it was brilliant. It was on 27 January
1813 that Jane at Chawton took delivery of her 'own darling Child from
London', holding a finished copy of *Pride and Prejudice* in her hand at last.

That evening, a neighbour named Mary Benn, the impoverished sister
of a clergyman, came for dinner with the Austen ladies. Jane reports that
afterwards 'we set fairly at it & read half the 1st vol. to her', but without
revealing who the author really was. 'I beleive it passed with her unsus-
pected', Jane reported. 'She was amused, poor soul! . . . she really does
seem to admire Elizabeth.' Jane's account of the evening with Miss Benn
suggests that she and her mother read the book aloud, presumably taking
on the parts of the different characters like a play.

To judge from the numerous scenes within Jane's own novels where
one character reads aloud to another, it was acceptable for men to
'perform' as readers before women, but not women before men. Women
could, however, read aloud to one another, and that of course was how
Jane entertained Cassandra in their room, 'while we undressed'.

And yet Jane's brother Henry records that Jane herself had an 'extremely
sweet' voice, and 'read aloud with very great taste and effect'.[23] So the
Austen family certainly had heard her in action. 'I knew her take up a
volume of Evelina and read a few pages', recalled a niece. 'I thought it
was like a play. She had a very good *speaking* voice.'[24] Even friends were
sometimes allowed to hear these 'performances'. One of them recalled
that an unexpected visitor's disrupting a reading by Jane from Sir Walter
Scott was 'like the interruption of some pleasing dream'.[25]

Indeed, the critic Patricia Howell Michaelson argues that the way Jane
lays out her paragraphs, and the frequent use of *italics* to indicate which
words should be stressed, were all intended to aid someone 'performing'
the novels aloud.[26] It looks like Jane's books encouraged women's voices
to be heard: not only as words on the page, but also out loud, in real
life, in the drawing rooms of late Georgian England.

Pride and Prejudice had terrific sales, helped by more reviews. *The
Critical Review* in March 1813 praised the novel for the 'delineation of
domestic scenes. Nor is there one character which appears flat, or obtrudes
itself upon the notice of the reader with troublesome impertinence.' It
sounds like damning with faint praise, but this reviewer was feeling his
way towards what Virginia Woolf would eventually say, more pithily:
that 'of all great writers she is the most difficult to catch in the act of
greatness'.

Jane was to enjoy with *Pride and Prejudice* a wild, noteworthy, enviable
success. Egerton's £110 for the copyright seemed less generous when

demand allowed him to print a second edition in 1813, and then a third in 1817. Jane received nothing from these but acclaim.

But the sensational sales of *Pride and Prejudice* also helped the sales of its predecessor, *Sense and Sensibility*. 'You will be glad to hear that every Copy of S.& S. is sold,' Jane told Frank, '& that it has brought me £140.' 'I have now', she claimed with justifiable pride, 'written myself into £250.' It gave Jane great pleasure to buy Cassandra presents: 'do not refuse me. I am very rich.' Henry, to Jane's 'great amusement', now opened an account for her at his own bank.

Thomas Egerton was now talking about publishing Jane's next *three* novels. She was already at work on *Mansfield Park*. 'I have something in hand', she wrote, 'which I hope on the credit of P. & P. will sell well, tho' not half so entertaining.' We know she also already had thoughts of *Emma* to follow, and another one after that.

How did the Austen family react to all this success? When *Pride and Prejudice* first came out in 1813, Jane was grateful that Cassandra was away from home. As Jane put it, 'it might be unpleasant' for her 'to be in the Neighbourhood at the first burst of the business'. Initially, Jane was pleasantly surprised by just how well her relatives managed to keep the secret of her anonymity. It was inevitably the proud and loquacious Henry, however, who let it out. Meeting a lady who was 'delighted' with *Pride and Prejudice*, Henry grandly told her that his sister had written it, 'with as much satisfaction' as if it had been Jane's own wish. Henry did not even tell Jane that he had blabbed: she discovered the fact from her niece Fanny.

Once a few people knew, the news inevitably travelled, and Jane became aware that 'the Secret has spread so far as to be scarcely the Shadow of a secret now'. Eventually she gave up worrying about it. 'I beleive whenever the 3d appears, I shall not even attempt to tell Lies about it', she wrote. Instead, she resolved to 'rather try to make all the Money than all the Mystery I can of it'.

Word-of-mouth publicity about this unknown author of the book of the season was spreading in circles far beyond Hampshire and Kent. The highly intelligent Annabella Milbanke, who would end up marrying Lord Byron, praised *Pride and Prejudice* for avoiding all 'the common resources of novel writers, no drownings, no conflagrations, nor runaway horses, nor lap-dogs and parrots, nor chambermaids and milliners, nor recontres and disguises. I really think it is the <u>most probable</u> fiction I have ever read.'[27]

Jane's own neighbours gradually began to see her with new eyes. 'Till "Pride and Prejudice" showed what a precious gem was hidden in that unbending case,' wrote Mary Russell Mitford, 'she was no more regarded in society than a poker or a fire screen or any other thin, upright piece of wood or iron that fills its corner in peace and quiet. The case is very different now; she is still a poker but a poker of whom every one is afraid.'[28]

'Poker' Jane was still as jittery as any novice novelist, eager to hear that people had read and enjoyed her work. She was grateful for a letter of praise from Cassandra that arrived just 'at a right time' to cheer her up. The printers had made some errors with *Pride and Prejudice*, the worst being where 'two speeches are made into one'. The perfectionist in Jane could never quite relax and enjoy her success. But on the whole she was 'quite vain enough & well satisfied'.

She was also glad for the generous comments of friends. 'Oh! I have had more of such sweet flattery from Miss Sharp!' she wrote, using two of her infrequent exclamation marks. 'She is an excellent kind friend. I am read & admired in Ireland too', she added, as news filtered through to her about people who had read her work, even without knowing her name. 'I do not despair', she wrote, 'of having my picture in the Exhibition at last − all white & red, with my Head on one Side'. She meant to be portrayed just as Joshua Reynolds painted society beauties.

But even while Jane dreamed of fame, she did her best to seem just the same at home. 'I am trying to harden myself,' she told Frank. 'After all, what a trifle it is in all its Bearings, to the really important points of one's existence even in this World!' He and her family agreed: it was more important that she went on being their familiar sister, aunt and daughter.

'"Aunt Jane" was the delight of all her nephews and nieces', wrote one of them. 'We did not think of her as being clever, still less as being famous; but we valued her as one always kind, sympathising, and amusing.'[29] The frequent influxes of nieces and nephews to Chawton Cottage could nevertheless exasperate their aunt. Jane's niece Caroline remembers how 'I was always creeping up to her, and following her whenever I *could*, *in* the house and out of it.' She recalled 'my Mother's telling me privately, I must not be troublesome'.[30] 'One does not care for girls till they are grown up', Jane admitted. But adolescents genuinely delighted and inspired her. Another niece remembered lifelong how one morning Aunt Jane had entertained three girls 'in giving a conversation as between myself and my two cousins, supposed to be grown up, the day after a Ball'.[31]

What a treat. And just up the road from the cottage, at Chawton Great House, lived one of Jane's favourite girls in the whole family, Fanny Austen.

27

The Great House

'I hope Edward's family-visit to Chawton will be yearly'

Jane writes in 1813

Of all Jane Austen's homes, Chawton is the most accessible to those who wish to walk in Austen-land. There is Chawton Cottage to visit, but also Chawton Great House, home of Jane's rich brother Edward, and now a library devoted to female writers. As members of the Jane Austen Society say, 'we are here on enchanted ground'.[1]

While Edward's adoptive mother Mrs Knight had lived, he'd spent a good deal of time at Godmersham in order to be close to her home in Canterbury. But everything changed in 1812 when she died. By the terms of her will, he now owned it all: Godmersham, Steventon, Chawton and the rest of the property in Hampshire. Like Jane, Edward was now drawn back to the county of his birth.

He might have come home, but Edward was no longer an Austen. The will decreed that he had to change his name to honour his bene-factors. 'We are therefore all *Knights*', squealed Edward's daughter Fanny, 'instead of dear old *Austens*. How I hate it!!!!!!'[2] Jane was rather less excited. 'I suppose,' she wrote drily, 'I must learn to make a better K.' She could not really excite herself about the Godmersham family, with the exception of Fanny herself.

Fanny was now living only ten minutes' walk away from her aunt. She described Chawton Great House as a 'fine large old_house, built long before Queen Elizabeth I believe'.[3] She was not quite right. The Knights had bought the land upon which the house stood in April 1551, and from about 1583 one John Knight replaced a medieval manor house with the structure that's still largely Elizabethan today.[4] An iron fireback found in the house with the initials 'JK' and the date 1588 must have been made to celebrate John Knight's financial contribution towards the campaign against the Spanish Armada.[5] Construction work continued in fits and starts until the 1660s, with the addition of two wings in red brick. Both the Hall and Gallery were said to be haunted. In the early eighteenth century Elizabeth Knight made further improvements, and when she died childless the estate passed to her cousin, Thomas Brodnax Knight of Godmersham Park.

To Edward's children, the Great House was a wonderful, Gothic playground. There 'are such a number of old irregular passages', wrote Fanny, 'it is very entertaining to explore them, & often when I think myself miles away from one part of the house I find a passage or entrance close to it, & I don't know when I shall be quite mistress of all the intricate, & different ways'. 'It is very curious', she continued, 'to trace the genealogy of the Knights & all the old families that have possessed the estate, from the pictures . . . we are not at a loss for amusement.'[6]

The house was packed full of fascinating old knick-knacks, and Fanny recorded one wet day spent looking 'at all Papas curiosities'.[7] It may have been a more romantic residence than Godmersham, but the Great House was also less comfortable. 'We are half frozen at the cold uninhabited appearance of the old house', wrote Fanny in her diary one April.[8]

When Edward and his children were in residence, there was constant interaction between the Great House and the Cottage. 'I went up to the G House between 3 & 4, & dawdled away an hour very comfortably', Jane writes in 1814. 'We all five walked together into the Kitchen Garden & along the Gosport Road, & they drank tea with us.' Then again: 'we go on in the most comfortable way, very frequently dining together, & always meeting in some part of every day'. Even when Edward and his family were away, Jane 'liked to stroll about the grounds – sometimes to Chawton Park – a noble beech wood, just within a walk'.[9]

Edward's female relations were always glad when their benefactor came to Chawton. He 'enjoys himself as thoroughly as any Hampshire born Austen can desire', Jane approved. The Great House 'is not thrown away on him . . . he talks of making a new Garden . . . we like to have him proving & strengthening his attachment to the place by making it better'.

Near the house stood the church, and Edward Austen Knight's nearest neighbour was Mr Papillon, the rector, just across the road. The family never tired of pretending that one day he was going to marry Jane. 'I am happy to tell you that Mr Papillon will soon make his offer,' Jane was still writing, even in the very last year of her life, 'probably next Monday.' 'His *intention* can be no longer doubtful in the smallest degree', she adds, because he had been detected in the act of looking for a new house.

In such a substantial household as Edward's there were constant comings and goings among the servants, which provided good gossip to amuse the neighbourhood in general and Jane in particular. One maid, despite being 'very active & cleanly', had to leave her place because 'she cannot agree with her fellow servants. She is in love with the Man – & her head seems rather turned.' The servants' love lives were considered to be the property of their employers. Mrs Digweed of Steventon, for example, 'parts with both Hannah & old Cook, the former will not give up her Lover, who is a Man of bad Character, the Latter is guilty only of being unequal to anything'. Poor Hannah, to lose her job because her employer did not approve of her boyfriend!

For a couple of years from August 1814 onwards, Edward lent the Great House to his brother Frank. Villagers later remembered how 'a nice dog' named Link each morning 'went with William Littleworth the manservant from the cottage up to Chawton House to fetch the milk', Link carrying the pail home in his mouth.[10]

This William Littleworth came to Chawton Cottage aged twenty-one as the Austen ladies' long-desired manservant, and Jane thought him 'a good-looking lad, civil and quiet, and seeming likely to do'. He was a cousin of the Littleworths of Steventon, Jane's foster-family from when she was a baby. Jane was indeed once again, as her nephew had it, 'amongst her own people'. William Littleworth had other business besides the milk up at the big house: he was courting Frank Austen's under-cookmaid, Mary Goodchild, and ended up marrying her.[11]

Fanny and Jane often spent the day together up at the Great House. 'Aunt Jane spent the morning with me . . . Aunt Jane and I had a delicious morning together . . . aunt Jane spent the morning with me and read Pride and Prejudice', Fanny's diary tells us repeatedly.[12] It makes it all the more surprising, years letter, that Fanny was so decidedly cool about Jane, writing that horrible, snobbish letter about the aunt to whom she had once been so close. Given the warmth of Jane's surviving letters to Fanny, this seems strange and nasty. But there are suggestions of what was to come even in the 1810s. Jane was proud of the commercial success of her books, but to Fanny she mentioned it only lightly: 'as you are much above caring about money, I shall not plague you with any particulars'.

'Yes my love,' runs Fanny's notorious letter, 'it is very true that Aunt Jane from various circumstances was not so *refined* as she ought to have been from her *talent*.' The Austens, claims Fanny, 'were not rich & the people around with whom they chiefly mixed, were not at all high bred, or in short anything more than *mediocre & they* . . . were on the same level as far as *refinement* goes'.[13]

What we are seeing here is not just pure regrettable snobbery, but also a clash between generations. Jane Austen belongs to the more rowdy Georgian age, while her niece, who lived long enough to become a prim Victorian, disparages the manners of a whole generation along with her formerly beloved aunt. In addition, it shows the chasm between two branches of the family that was bridged only at the moment when Edward was plucked from his siblings and planted in the richer soil of Kent. Fanny describes her mother's mother in Kent as 'dearest Grand Mama'. But her birth grandmother, Mrs Austen in Chawton, never gets the same affectionate accolade.[14] After Jane's death, the two branches of the family, Hampshire and Kent, Austen and Knight, would embark upon a struggle for the control of and credit for Jane's life and legacy. The divisions were already present in her lifetime.

Down the road at the cottage, life settled into the dull and domestic. 'It was a very quiet life, according to our ideas', wrote a niece, 'but they were great readers.'[15] Enough said. Perhaps, in cutting back upon their social lives, Jane and Cassandra had simply grown tired of the effort involved in maintaining appearances. The author Mary Berry, sixty in 1823, remembered how differently she had felt when she'd been twenty-one: 'what regrets I had then at having been born a woman, and deprived of the life and position which, as a man, I might have had in this world! But I am calm and resigned now. I shall say no more about it.'[16]

Jane's letters even began to develop an elegiac tone. 'How many alterations you must perceive in Bath!' she wrote to Martha, gone there on a visit, '& how many People & Things gone by, must be recurring to you!' Her letters as she grew older are more frequently peppered with pity for spinsters, widows and other clingers-on to other people's charity. 'Perhaps', one day, she wrote, 'one may be as friendless oneself, & in similar circumstances.'

'I hate tiny parties', Jane also admitted, 'they force one into constant exertion'. She had always been too introverted to make friends easily, and this grew more pronounced as she grew older. Her manner, Frank admitted, was 'rather reserved to strangers so as to have been by some accused of haughtiness'. Jane described one heavy evening of socialising, which began at seven, as a 'Labour' from which the home team of female Austens were eventually 'delivered' at 'past eleven'. Even a poorly chosen guest at a dinner could cause grave annoyance to ladies getting a little set in their ways: 'it will be an Eveng spoilt . . . Another little Disappointment.' And it was true that Jane could seem 'somewhat stiff & cold to strangers'.[17]

The talk at the dinner parties of Hampshire was of the death of old Mr Harwood of Deane, in whose house Jane had danced with Tom Lefroy. His son expected to inherit an estate worth £1,200 a year, just as six generations had done before him. But unknown to his family, old Mr Harwood had 'borrowed and mortgaged so freely' that he was able to leave his widow and sister nothing. The son now found himself 'a ruined man . . . blighted in all his hopes and prospects'. Such an example, so close to home, must have made the Austen ladies bless the Lord who had given them more solvent relations.[18]

The disaster affected Jane because it affected one of her friends. It was the wreck of the hopes of one of the Bigg sisters, Elizabeth, the widowed Mrs Heathcote, who had planned to marry the younger Harwood and become mistress of Deane. She went on living quietly at Manydown Park, but then, in the very next month, her own father died. Young Harris Bigg-Wither and the wife he'd married instead of Jane turfed Elizabeth out of Manydown, and in 1814 she had to go to live in Winchester.

Jane was also a cheerleader for the matrimonial prospects of the former Godmersham governess, Miss Anne Sharp. Each time she took a new situation, Jane hoped that her employer would fall in love with Miss Sharp. 'She writes highly of Sir Wm – I do so want him to marry her! . . . Oh! Sir Wm – Sir Wm – how I will love you, if you will love Miss Sharp!'

Closer to home, Thomas was gone away from Chawton Cottage to be married, to be replaced by Browning, who is 'quite a new Broom & at present has no fault . . . rather slow; but he is not noisy & not at all above being taught'. He possessed two great advantages: 'The Dogs seem just as happy with him as with Thomas – Cook and Betsey I imagine a good deal happier.' Dogs were essential for security in this country household.

The Austens' successive cooks were paid only £8 a year, nothing near the £25 that the same post in a big house could command. There were high hopes of each 'new Cook', and one of them made an auspicious beginning with a splendid apple pie: 'good apple pies are a considerable part of our domestic happiness'. With their slightly unsteady set-up, the female Austens never seemed quite to manage the long-term, rock-solid relationships with their domestics that the authors of *The Complete Servant* found desirable: 'nothing is so comfortable and *creditable* to all parties, as when a servant lives *many years* in the same family'.[19]

Elsewhere in the wider family, the Reverend Thomas Leigh and his sister were not made particularly merry by the possession of Stoneleigh Abbey. 'The change came too late in their lives to be pleasant to them', wrote Caroline Austen.[20] Another visitor to Stoneleigh thought Reverend Thomas and Miss Elizabeth were 'perfectly encumbered with the wealth, to which they succeeded in a late period of life'.

This latter visitor, Mary Berry, was certain that Stoneleigh Abbey had been wasted on the pair. 'What a magnificent possession of real wealth!' she exclaimed. 'It has been long thrown away on people who have done no good, encouraged no improvements, employed no fine arts, collected nothing.'[21] A house like Stoneleigh was intended to have life and fire breathed into it by its owner and a considerable establishment. It was like a huge piece of performance art. If the inhabitants of a great house like Stoneleigh lacked the means or the inclination to live in a grand manner, the whole world considered it to be an opportunity lost.

When the Reverend Thomas finally died, Mrs Leigh Perrot was presented with yet another opportunity to be dissatisfied. Had she and her husband not accepted the settlement money, they would now have won the prize of the Abbey itself. 'Poor Mrs L.P.', mocked Jane, 'who would now have been Mistress of Stoneleigh had there been none of that vile compromise which in good truth has never been allowed to be of much use to them – It will be a hard trial.'

It's been pointed out that the compromise was not at all 'vile' for the Leigh Perrots, and that they greatly enjoyed having the money. But Jane here was mimicking the plaintive tones of her aunt, just the sort of character to use the words 'vile compromise' and 'hard trial' about being given a huge unexpected legacy.[22] So the death of the Reverend Thomas Leigh left 'more worthless nephews & nieces than any other private man in the united kingdoms', as Jane put it. She was referring to herself and her siblings who had, with the exception of James, still not received a penny. The business had become something of a scandal in the close-knit community of friends and relatives. Jane was pleased that one lady would 'be not at all satisfied unless a very *handsome* present be made us immediately' from the Leigh Perrots. But the handsome present never arrived.

All this meant that Jane had more reason than ever to write, and to write for money. Her next book would capture that all-too-familiar feeling of being the poor relation in a great house. In February 1811 she started planning *Mansfield Park*.[23] She could no longer go on mocking the novels of sensibility of the 1790s, as she had done in *Susan*, *Sense and Sensibility* and to some extent in *Pride and Prejudice*. She had to find new subject matter. What we now call the Romantic Movement was well underway. Jane read Lord Byron, but put him firmly into his place: 'I have read the Corsair, mended my petticoat, & have nothing else to do', she wrote. She pretended to be chagrined when Sir Walter Scott started writing novels as well as poetry. 'Walter Scott has no business to write novels, especially good ones', she complained. 'It is not fair. – He has Fame & Profit enough as a Poet, and should not be taking the bread out of other people's mouths.' She did admire his work enormously, but *Mansfield Park* would be about as far removed from it as possible.

It was the first of her novels conceived in the new century, and it shows. *Mansfield Park* is not set in the conservative countryside of Jane's youth, where life had revolved around a parish's manorhouse and church, and girls went to balls. The French Revolution and Napoleonic Wars had changed all this. *Mansfield Park* takes place 'in the unstable world of the nineteenth century' and looks on the established order with an 'element of censure, a disapproval and sense of guilt', as the critic Warren Roberts put it. The estate of the Bertrams, owners of Mansfield Park itself, was both good and rotten at the same time, and Jane's characters respond to the great questions of the age: slavery, religion, wealth, right, wrong. 'This novel could have had "reform or ruin" as its motto,' Roberts argues, 'one of its subjects is the improvement of society.'[24]

But it's still firmly rooted in Jane's life and youthful experience. The famous theatricals at Mansfield Park, 'the Mansfield theatricals' as Julia Bertram calls them 'in a sarcastic manner', take us right back to the little company in the barn at Steventon Rectory. Georgian debates about whether amateur acting was virtuous, or its opposite, were very lively, and Jane uses this to create the drama. Jane, the enthusiastic theatre-goer, displays accurate knowledge of how acting companies really worked in her description of the Mansfield theatricals. Tom Bertram is both actor and company manager, as was the case on the professional stage, and Fanny finds herself in the role of the prompter, which has a low official status, but is the vital glue that holds the production together.[25] The play Jane's characters perform in the book, *Lover's Vows*, was shown no fewer than seventeen times in Bath while Jane was living there, so presumably her choice is one of the fruits of her residence in the city of sin.[26]

Mansfield Park also, notoriously, addresses the issue of slavery. The house's very name echoes that of Justice Mansfield, whose various rulings against the owners of slaves – that slaves could not be made the subject of insurance claims, that their owners could not be financially compensated for their deaths – were important steps towards the beginning of slavery's end. In Jane's story the family's wealth comes from the Antigua estates to which Sir Thomas repairs to sort out various business hiccups, and the nasty Mrs Norris even takes her name from an infamous slave trader operating in West Africa.[27] 'Did not you hear me asking him about the slave trade last night?' Fanny queries her cousin Edmund, revealing that she alone, timid Fanny, is the only one among the whole family brave enough to address Sir Thomas on the issue of where the money really comes from.

But above everything else, *Mansfield Park*'s central theme is finding a home. As the critic Paula Byrne points out, the word appears more than 140 times in the text.[28] Our heroine, Fanny, gradually makes herself 'at home' at Mansfield Park, working her way into the place, gradually cramming her own room full of her carefully chosen pictures and treasures. When she refuses the highly eligible Henry Crawford, she is sent 'home' to Portsmouth, in order to gain a corrective perspective. Once there, lonely, out of place, she begins to see Mansfield, her adopted home, as the place where she really lives.

Here Jane is ripping up an idea that was centuries old: the idea that one is rooted to one's birthplace, and that place and blood are more important than life experience or talent. Her own life had taught her that people can survive – even thrive – after transplantation. Fanny, travelling back to Portsmouth, experiences the very modern condition of nostalgia: she misses not so much a real place, but her memory of a place.[29] And eventually, by returning to Mansfield Park and making herself indispensable there, she manages through her own efforts to create a new and better home for herself. It's a very meritocratic story.

As far as we know, this novel was both begun and completed at Chawton Cottage, and Jane refers to it in her letters as being in progress between January and September 1813. Jane always pays scrupulous attention to the dates in her stories, and those in *Mansfield Park* follow the calendar of 1808–9.[30] By January 1813, the character of Mrs Grant certainly existed, and was well known to Cassandra, for Jane mentioned her in a letter just as if she were a real person: she described a real-life whist party as having 'just as many for <u>their</u> round Table, as there were at Mrs Grants'. Cassandra was so well up on the development of the plot that she disagreed with Jane about what ought to happen. She wanted Jane to let 'Mr Crawford marry Fanny Price'. But despite a debate, Jane 'would not allow the change'.[31] Jane still deferred to her sister in everything, except novel-writing.

Jane's brothers are in the story, too. William Price came back from the sea to his sister, just as Frank did, giving great joy through the 'unchecked, equal, fearless intercourse with the brother and friend'. And Fanny herself has something in common with Edward, taken from his own blood family and brought up in the splendour of Godmersham Park.

Jane completed the book 'soon after' June 1813, and by March 1814 *Mansfield Park* was available in its proof form. Jane and Henry read it together in the carriage as they travelled up to London. 'He took to Lady B. and Mrs N. most kindly,' Jane reported, '& gives great praise to the drawing of the Characters.'

She was understandably concerned about what Henry might think of *Mansfield Park*, for she had put him 'in' it too, and in a less than flattering light. Jane borrowed many essential features from Henry and Eliza, for Henry Crawford and his sister, the scintillating, entertaining but morally dubious Mary. Both pairs formed a private alliance against society, and were keen to suck the pips of pleasure from it. But all we know of Henry's overall opinion is that he found the whole work '*extremely interesting*', which could mean almost anything. Jane waited, as tense as a new mother, for its birth: 'Before the end of April', she wrote, anxiously, it will 'be in the world'.

Yet even before its reception was known, Jane had already started work on *Emma*. And once again her family would be involved.

28

The Diversions of Young Ladies

'The young niece who brought her troubles to
Aunt Jane for advice and sympathy knew she
could depend absolutely on her silence.'[1]

Fanny Lefroy

A S JANE BEGAN her new novel, *Emma*, her thoughts turned to two
young ladies. Jane's favourite nieces, Fanny Austen Knight and Anna
Austen – both of them, like Catherine Morland 'in training for a heroine'
– were now old enough to have romances of their own. Their stories
are worth following for what they can tell us about Jane's attitudes to
life and love. Her letters to her nieces as they reach maturity are things
of beauty: sympathetic; bracing; interested. Jane liked babies, can seem
ambivalent about children, but definitely adored young adults. 'The fun
must be imperfect', she wrote, 'till the heroine grows up.'

Both girls appealed to Jane because of, not despite, their flaws. Both
were motherless, and slightly unhappy at home. Anna's problem was her
stepmother, with her 'tartness of temper'. This was the former Mary
Lloyd, who, according to one family report, did not love Anna, and
'made her of no estimation, & the last & least in her father's house'.[2]

Fanny was less histrionic and self-indulgent than Anna. But she too
had lost her own mother, at fifteen, and was forced in consequence to
look after her ten young siblings. The family could never get governesses
to stay after Miss Sharp. Once, when the governess was ill, Fanny writes
that she'd 'had the chiln',[3] just as if she were their mother not their sister.

Jane closely observed her two nieces, but ultimately they left her
mystified. 'Who can understand a young Lady?' she asked. But certainly
she loved them. 'My dear Anna,' Jane wrote, 'there is nobody I think of
oftener, very few I love better', while she found Fanny to be almost
'another Sister'.

Jane, in fact, mothered these girls, and her fiction reveals her belief that
motherhood could be a social, not a biological function.[4] Blood mothers
may be ridiculous or ill-advised, like Mrs Bennet or Mrs Dashwood, but
mothers in the form of mentors are often wise, generous, caring. Mrs

Gardiner, her aunt, gives Lizzy Bennet better advice than Mrs Bennet does, while Emma Woodhouse has a fine surrogate in the shape of Mrs Weston. In this sense, Fanny and Anna were Jane's own children.

And Jane's nieces both turned out, under her influence, to be writers. Fanny was an assiduous diary-keeper. Anna had more serious literary pretensions. She and her aunt laughed together over the works of inferior authors, such as the silly and prosy *Lady Maclairn, The Victim of Villainy* published under the name of Rachel Hunter in 1806. Anna and Jane maliciously enjoyed the ridiculous way in which Hunter's characters burst into tears on no fewer than forty-four occasions in the story.

Anna would get novels from the circulating library at Alton in order to 'relate the stories to Aunt Jane . . . as she sat busily stitching away at a work of charity'. They'd ridicule most of the novels, and greatly they 'both enjoyed it, one piece of absurdity leading to another'. Eventually the two bright sparks annoyed Aunt Cassandra, who 'fatigued with her own share of laughter wd. exclaim 'How *can* you both be so foolish? & beg [them] to leave off'.[5]

The two cousins Anna and Fanny knew each other from Anna's visits to Godmersham Park. Fanny's diary tells us that they spent their time together outdoors. 'Anna and I read romances in the Gothic seat', she writes, or else 'went gy[p]seying in the Park. We took a basket of Bread & Cheese & a bottle of Water, some books & work & Paper & Pencil. We enjoyed ourselves very much.'[6] She had an odd idea of what gypsies did with their time if she thought it included sketches and needlework, but doubtless the girls spent much of the day chatting.

Jane gave well-informed and charming encouragement to Anna as she embarked upon the semi-serious project of a novel of her own. 'The Spirit does not droop at all', she wrote, and of her niece's dilatory plotting: 'Nature & Spirit cover many sins of a wandering story'. Jane also gave Anna some celebrated comments on the importance of accuracy. 'When Mr Portman is first brought in, he wd not be introduced as *the Hon*ble', she noticed, '*That* distinction is never mentioned at such times.' She advised Anna to stick to what she knew: 'Let the Portmans go to Ireland, but as you know nothing of the Manners there, you had better not go with them.' At the same time, though, Jane praised Anna's eye for the absurd and the pretentious: a passage about 'the madness of sensible Women, on the subject of their Daughters coming out, is worth its weight in gold'.

In the autumn of 1809, a real-life family drama began to unfold. Against the wishes of her family, Anna had become engaged. Rather predictably, given the circles she moved in, her beloved was yet another

Hampshire clergyman. Mr Michael Terry had studied at St John's College, Cambridge, and was to become the rector of his family village of Dummer. He was at first sight a reasonable catch: 'tall & good looking & well connected with the certainty of a comfortable family living'. Inevitably, Anna also felt the attraction of 'the warmth of the love & its sweet flatteries in contrast to the slighting & depreciation of home'.[7]

But her parents were angry and failed to approve of the match. Anna was only sixteen; he was double her age. He was also slightly awkward; neighbours described the man as 'poor blundering Michael Terry'.[8] James and Mary Austen sent Anna to Kent. A stay at Godmersham Park might help her to get over him.

There, however, Fanny fanned Anna's feelings, and did her best to play matchmaker. The suitor's sister got involved in the business, and letters started to fly between Hampshire and Kent. 'Anna heard from Charlotte Terry', Fanny reported at Godmersham, fascinated, 'explaining her brother's conduct more satisfactorily.'[9] Fanny herself wrote to Aunt Cassandra 'explaining *Anna's* conduct in the late affair'.[10] Then at last Fanny's diary transforms into 'Joy! Joy!' The occasion was that 'Papa' had 'heard from Uncle James!' and Uncle James had agreed to the engagement.[11] Fanny's diary often fizzes with enthusiasm, and she adores the word 'amazingly'. 'We shall miss her amazingly', Fanny says, for example, and she uses 'amazingly' almost as frequently as Jane's ebullient Miss Isabella Thorpe ('I am amazingly agitated') in *Northanger Abbey*.[12]

Now Mr Michael Terry was allowed to write directly to Anna, who opened his letters with glee. A typical Austen, she produced a poem about her feelings:

> With what delight I view each line
> Trac'd by the hand I love
> Where warm esteem & Grace combine
> A feeling heart to move[13]

But when Mr Michael Terry actually turned up at Godmersham to see Anna, the longed-for lover in the flesh was a little disappointing. 'The meeting was awkward', Fanny reported. Mr Terry was 'much younger looking and more shy than I had an idea of. I should not like him, but if Anna does, that does not signify.' Fanny was so much on the couple's side against the parents that she persuaded herself to allow Mr Terry a second chance. 'He improves amazingly upon acquaintance,' she wrote, 'and I like him *very* much. We left the *Lovers* as much together as possible.'

At the end of March, Edward Austen took his niece Anna, now a happily engaged young lady, back to Steventon. Fanny reported on it all with ardent attention in letters to her former governess. 'It must interest *any*body to hear of such a *very* young person as *Anna* going to take so important a step', she exclaimed, for Anna 'is not more than 17. The Gentleman is turned of 30, & is a Clergyman in Hampshire, a Mr. Terry a very respectable Man.'[14]

But perhaps Mr Michael Terry was a bit too 'respectable' for his own good. Perhaps it was the parental opposition that had made the shy and blundering clergyman seem more attractive than he really was. For, having finally overcome all the many obstacles in the way of her match, Anna went to stay with her new family, and then, returning, decided that she could not go through with it.

'Heard from Anna,' wrote Fanny, 'she is actually wishing to break off her engagement!!! What a girl!!!'[15] How exciting it all was. 'Heard from Anna,' Fanny wrote, 'and *all is over*, she has no longer anything to do with Mr. Michael Terry. Heavens! What will she do next?'[16] Presumably there were sighs of relief at Steventon, and presumably Anna discovered that there is nothing so disappointing as getting one's own way.

Jane was glad that the match was off, for she was worried about Anna's slightly flighty character. Jane does not spare her niece in letters intended for Cassandra only, describing how even in good times it was a 'miscellaneous, unsettled happiness which seems to suit her best'. The occasional severity of Jane's remarks in her surviving letters helps to explain why Cassandra might have destroyed so many of the rest of them. Few aunts would want a niece to read such sharp conclusions upon her character, or upon the injury that Jane thought Anna had done to her looks by cutting her hair short: 'that sad cropt head'.

But Anna was still pretty desperate to leave Steventon Rectory. She was soon in love again, and again with a Hampshire clergyman. He was the youngest member of the Lefroy family: Ben, son of Jane's friend the deceased Madam Lefroy. Mr Ben Lefroy had the great attraction of proximity, as he was living back at Ashe Rectory, just a short walk away from Steventon. Yet Jane did not really approve of this second suitor either. The announcement of the engagement 'came upon us without much preparation', she complained, yet 'there was that about [Anna] which kept us in constant preparation for something'. Jane was apprehensive about the match for 'he hates company & she is very fond of it'. There was 'some queerness of Temper on his side & much unsteadiness on hers'.

Anna and Ben Lefroy had spent much of their engagement – 'nearly every afternoon' – in 'the shrubbery walk' at Steventon Rectory. It annoyed Anna's stepmother Mary intensely, who'd never 'seen any couple so foolishly devoted'.[17] But when it came to actually getting married, Mr Ben Lefroy proved himself to be rather lackadaisical. He was offered a curacy that would have provided an income for the couple, but he failed to accept it. 'He must be maddish', was Jane's conclusion. But then again, 'there often appears to be something of Madness in Anna too'.

Under the circumstances, the family was sadly rent apart. Anna was reluctant to stay with her grandmother and aunts at Chawton while they held this low opinion of her fiancé. Despite their differences, though, Anna would for the rest of her life remember how she and Jane had lived in the greatest intimacy just before and after her marriage, when 'the original 17 years between us seemed to shrink to 7 – or to nothing'. For Anna, it became 'a habit with me to put by things in my mind with a reference to her and to say to myself, "I shall keep this for Aunt Jane."'[18]

Anna Austen was self-willed, handsome, full of life, and often quite mistaken about things. Another family member remembered that when *Emma* 'came out many of the neighbours found in the description of her person no less than in her character a strong likeness to Anna Austen. Certainly such a likeness existed.'[19] 'I am going to take a heroine whom no one but myself will much like', Jane had proclaimed, in creating Emma Woodhouse.[20] Jane was right: her earliest readers did not much like Emma, and Fanny Knight 'could not bear' her.[21]

But many of Jane's readers today love Emma, and would probably have found much to admire in the independent, creative, moody and modern-sounding Anna Austen. Jane's idea of a heroine lay ahead of its time. She appreciated that many people would disagree with her down-to-earth, realistic assessment of what young ladies were really like. 'He & I should not in the least agree . . . in our ideas of Novels & Heroines', she wrote of one naïve young gentleman she'd encountered. 'I particularly respect him for wishing to think well of all young Ladies', Jane continued, 'it shews an amiable & a delicate Mind.' But then she sticks in the knife. The thought of 'perfect' young ladies, as we've heard before, made Jane personally feel nauseous and naughty.

Meanwhile Fanny, having observed her cousin's romance with such lascivious interest, was also embarking upon adventures of her own. Along with her friends, two Marys and an Emma, she'd become one of the belles of Kentish society. They were all of them slightly in love with a gentleman called Mr George Hatton. They gave him the codename of 'Jupiter', or else 'the Planet', or sometimes the 'brilliant object'.[22] Cassandra, visiting Godmersham, disapproved of all this flighty behaviour, and Fanny was on the receiving end of 'A lecture from Aunt Cassandra on *Astronomy*'.[23]

Less disapproving, and more *interested* than Cassandra, Jane delighted in Fanny's letters and conversations about the progress of her love affairs, even if she too counselled caution. 'Your mistake has been one that thousands of women fall into', she warned. 'He was the *first* young Man who attached himself to you. That was the charm, & most powerful it is.'

Aunt Jane '& I had a very <u>interesting</u> conversation', Fanny wrote in her diary. 'Alas! Alas! Why have I so little resolution?'[24] Aunt Jane asked the very same thing. 'Who can keep pace with the fluctuations of your Fancy, the Capprizios of your Taste, the Contradictions of your Feelings?' she wondered. 'It is very, very gratifying to me to know you so intimately.' 'Oh!' Jane finished, 'what a loss it will be, when you are married.'

Jane also had another powerful argument for Fanny's not rushing quickly into marriage. 'By not beginning the business of Mothering', she wrote, 'quite so early in life, you will be young in Constitution, spirits, figure & countenance.' Fanny's former friend Mrs Hammond, meanwhile, was 'growing old by confinements & nursing'. Jane's reading of Fanny's competitive character must have made her confident that her niece would be receptive to such a point.

Jane revelled in every detail of the progress of Fanny's romance with her unimpressive young man. Fanny had searched out something, anything, to worship as a physical relic. 'Your trying to excite your own feelings by a visit to his room amused me excessively', Jane wrote. 'The dirty Shaving Rag was exquisite! – Such a circumstance ought to be in print. Much too good to be lost.' And now Jane very nearly came clean about the fact that she was using Fanny for copy. 'I really am impatient myself to be writing something on so very interesting a subject', she admitted. Very soon Fanny would be able to read in *Emma* that Harriet Smith likewise worships 'the end of an old pencil, – the part without any lead', simply because her beloved Mr Elton had tossed it aside.

Jane was successful in her campaign to deter Fanny from marriage. Her Godmersham niece would remain single until she had reached the rather grand old age of twenty-seven. And even if Jane failed to deter Anna, her wedding to Ben Lefroy was decidedly low-key. Mrs Austen wrote her granddaughter a rather doleful poem of congratulation:

> You must not look for perfect bliss,
> That's for a better life than this.[25]

No one seemed wild with joy at the ceremony, held at Steventon Church on 8 November 1814. 'The season of the year . . . the grey light within of a November morning making its way through the narrow windows' gave 'a gloomy air to our wedding', wrote one attendee.[26] Anna and Ben went to live in Hendon, north of London, where Jane would visit and poke around in Anna's room to see what new clothes she had bought. In August 1815 the couple moved back to a farmhouse much nearer to Chawton. But, just as Jane feared, she'd never again be quite so close to Anna. The novel-writing was given up; Anna soon had her children to think about.

Both Anna and Fanny had perhaps served their purpose, though, in helping Jane decide how to depict a prosperous, confident young lady like Emma Woodhouse. To claim Anna or Fanny as 'models' for *Emma* is too strong a word to use, but like Anna, Jane's new heroine would be a little headstrong. Like Fanny, she would exude entitlement, with her 'comfortable home and happy disposition'. After just over a year's work, Jane completed the creation of her most brilliant heroine ('handsome, clever and rich') on 29 March 1815. Jane was scrupulous in saying that she never 'worked from life', never inserted 'real' people wholesale into her fiction. But some people and events from real life do nonetheless have echoes in her books.

As well as creating Emma Woodhouse in 1814, Jane also brought out *Mansfield Park*. Henry was helping to correct the proofs in March, and Jane had hoped that the book would be on sale in April. But as usual there were delays, and Thomas Egerton ended up publishing it in May. An advertisement in *The Star* on the 9th stated that it was published 'this day'. Priced at 18 shillings, all of the approximately 1,250 copies were sold within six months.

For a woman used to a personal allowance of just £20 a year, the profits of the first edition of *Mansfield Park* were riches indeed. Jane made more than £300.[27] But it's heart-breaking to realise that although she published three further novels in her lifetime, she'd never have such a financial success again. Jane could not have afforded to live entirely by her pen in anything like the style to which she was accustomed. She was never to even approach becoming wealthy from her work, earning a lifetime total of only around £668.[28] To put this into perspective, an agricultural labourer in 1814 could hope to earn £40 annually. A solicitor, whose income was probably around £1,500 a year, would have matched Jane's total lifetime earnings in six months.

But she could not have known this in 1814. 'The first Edit: of M.P. is all sold', she wrote in November, 'Henry is rather wanting me to come to Town' to discuss a second. To bring out this second edition, or not, was a difficult decision. 'I am very greedy & want to make the most of it', Jane wrote, but 'it is not settled yet whether I *do* hazard' it. The problem was that 'people are more ready to borrow & praise, than to buy'.

This was a little exasperating, for though Jane admitted that she liked 'praise as well as anybody', she loved '*Pewter* too'. But despite Henry wanting Jane to be in town to discuss her career, despite the ever-pressing requirement for 'pewter', there were as always those pesky domestic duties keeping her in Chawton. She 'could not very conveniently leave home now', she explained; she could not go to London to look after her business.

So everything was uncertain: a trip to London, the second edition, even her future with Thomas Egerton. Other publishers, perhaps not realising the difficulties Jane had encountered in getting into print at all, felt that she'd simply chosen the wrong firm. 'We are particularly interested for the success of Austen', wrote a rival publisher at Longman, 'and we sincerely regret that her works have not met with the encouragement we could wish.'[29] The implication is that the staff of Longman felt that they could have done a much better job of bringing them out.

And Jane herself had thoughts of a new publisher for *Emma*. She had rather fallen into the hands of Thomas Egerton, that specialist in military publishing, and she was not entirely satisfied with him. By March 1814, she did manage to get away from Chawton for long enough to take the fair, finished handwritten copy of *Emma* to London to offer it to Mr Egerton. He liked it, and again wanted to buy the copyright. But he did not offer her quite enough money.

So now Jane made the bold decision to change publisher. She also had an offer for her new book from John Murray, a much more distinguished publisher than Thomas Egerton. He'd been tracking Jane Austen's progress as an author for a couple of years, and decided the time had come to make his move. John Murray had asked his trusted reader, William Gifford, to look at *Emma*, and he reported extremely positively. 'It will certainly sell well', Gifford concluded. 'Of *Emma* I have nothing but <u>good</u> to say. I was sure of the writer before you mentioned her.'[30] Gifford suggested that Murray should also try to obtain the copyright to *Pride and Prejudice*, for Egerton had made a bit of a hash of producing it. There was probably a market for a new and better edition. 'I have lately read it again – tis very good', Gifford noted, but 'wretchedly printed in some places, & so pointed [punctuated] as to be unintelligible'.[31]

John Murray made a bold offer to Jane of £450 for *Emma*. But to Jane it looked far less attractive when it became clear that he also wanted the copyrights of *Mansfield Park* and *Sense and Sensibility* thrown in as well. 'He is a Rogue', of course,' Jane wrote, 'but a civil one . . . He sends more praise however than I expected. It is an amusing Letter.'

She had Henry write back on her behalf to complain. 'The Terms you offer', he wrote to Murray in a lordly manner, 'are so very inferior to what we had expected, that I am apprehensive of having made some great Error in my Arithmetical Calculation.' Henry claimed that John Murray himself had 'expressed astonishment' at Egerton's having printed such small runs of both *Mansfield Park* and *Sense and Sensibility*.[32] Why was he not showing more confidence in this new author whom he professed to admire so much?

Jane was older and wiser than she had been. It had been a mistake to sell the copyright of *Pride and Prejudice* to Thomas Egerton for a fixed sum. So now she rejected John Murray's offer of an outright sale, and decided instead to publish *Emma* with him, but 'for herself', i.e. at her own risk. She had confidence in her readers' reception of her work. She was willing to play for higher stakes.

So, on 3 November, Jane asked to see Murray face to face, as 'a short conversation may perhaps do more than much Writing'. She'd broken free from Chawton, had even broken free from Henry as her agent. She was in London, and ready to do the deal herself.

29

Parading about London

'[I] was ready to laugh all the time, at my being where I was. –
I could not but feel that I had naturally small right
to be parading about London in a Barouche.'

Jane, 1813

A s Jane went to London in the autumn of 1814 to negotiate a new
publishing contract, her confidence was high. Now that she was in
her thirties, she moved around the country and the capital much more
freely than when she'd been a 'nice' young lady in her teens, or entirely
dependent on her family in her twenties. Publishers were clamouring
for her work. She had her own money. She had the sheen of success.

Also, it was becoming easier and quicker to travel. In the Chawton
years, Jane quite often stayed in London with her brother Henry. To get
there, she used the stagecoach system and the turnpike roads that made
travel in Britain faster and easier than elsewhere in Europe. The French
visitor Louis Simond, for example, was amazed how in England 'to go
up to town from 100 or 200 miles distance, is a thing done on a sudden,
and without any previous deliberation. In France the people of the prov-
inces used to make their will before they undertook such an expedition.'[1]

A new current of creativity and excitement flowed through Jane's
letters home during these trips, which combined business with pleasure
and shopping. 'I have so many little matters to tell you of,' she wrote,
'that I cannot wait any longer before I begin to put them down.'

She visited London in 1811, 1813, 1814, and then throughout the autumn
of the victorious year of 1815 in which Napoleon was finally defeated at
Waterloo. She often used Henry as her agent, in return looking after him
when he fell ill. She got to know London well, and the addresses of her
characters reveal precisely calibrated details about their station in life and
character. Admiral Crawford, for example, lives near Berkeley Square, just
by the real-life Admiral Byng. The rich Mrs Palmer lives in Hanover
Square, close to the real-life Duchess of Brunswick. Mrs Jennings has
managed to elevate herself to Berkeley Street, although her late husband
'had traded with success in a less elegant part of the town'. The ridiculous

but rich Mr Rushworth of course has 'one of the best houses' in Wimpole Street. Those who are poorer, or who care less about fashion, live further east: the vulgar Miss Steeles in Bartlett's Buildings near Holborn and Elizabeth Bennet's relations the Gardiners in Gracechurch Street in the City: the arrogant 'Mr Darcy may perhaps have *heard* of such a place as Gracechurch Street, but he would hardly think a month's ablutions enough to cleanse him from its impurities.'[2]

Jane was now considered by her brothers to be worldly-wise enough to travel to London by stagecoach alone rather than having to wait about until a male relative was ready to accompany her. 'I have explained my views,' she wrote, when her escort was in doubt, 'I can take care of myself.'

In 1814, she went up in Collyer's Flying Machine, with four people alongside her inside the vehicle, and a further fifteen clinging onto the roof. One crossed one's fingers for small, quiet co-passengers, and this time Jane was lucky: 'I had a very good Journey, not crouded', because two of her companions were 'Children, the others of a reasonable size; & they were all very quiet and civil'. She was luckier than the traveller who once found his personal space invaded by an 'overgrown female', 'puffing and panting as if she had not half an hour to live'. He and his companion 'screw'd ourselves up in each corner and allowed her to take the middle when she sat or rather fell down with the grunt of a rhinoceros and remained a fixture for the whole journey'.[3]

The coaches from Hampshire disgorged their passengers in Ludgate Hill, while those serving the west of England terminated at the White Horse Cellar in Piccadilly. Such coaching yards were full of whooping as vehicles arrived or moved off, the 'the *coachy's* "all right – ya-hip!" and the sounding of the bugle by the guard . . . the journey to most minds commences with pleasure and delight'.[4] Upon arrival came the challenge of rooting out your own luggage 'from all the other Trunks & Baskets in the World', while the bouncing of the coach – a 'long Jumble' – left you extremely tired.

It really was more comfortable to travel in a private carriage, if you could, and sometimes Henry gave Jane a lift. In 1813, he carried her from Chawton to his home in Sloane Street, Knightsbridge, a distance of about fifty miles. It took all day, much longer than the stagecoach. As they weren't swapping horses every few miles, they had to allow Henry's hard-working animals to take rests. 'A 12 hours Business', Jane wrote. 'I was very tired too, & very glad to get to bed early.'

Once in London, Jane travelled about by foot or in a hackney carriage for sightseeing, or else borrowed Henry and Eliza's own carriage. One day Jane found herself riding in the carriage all by herself: 'I liked my solitary elegance very much, & was ready to laugh all the time, at my being where I was.' She was a long way from being the shy young country mouse who'd dreamed of running wild in London. But then, as always, Jane employs that strategy of self-deprecation that was so much appreciated by her family. 'I could not but feel', she adds, 'that I had naturally small right to be parading about London in a Barouche.'

The streets of London along which she passed were garish to the eye, lined by shops screaming out their purpose in 'large golden letters'. Along commercial streets, like the Strand, the passer-by might read 'Children educated here', 'Shoes mended here', 'Foreign spirituous liquors sold here', and 'Funerals furnished here'.[5] One of Jane's sightseeing destinations was William Bullock's collection of natural history specimens in Piccadilly, which included a stuffed great boa snake and more than sixty different kinds of monkeys. She also visited The Gallery of the British Institution in Pall Mall. Here, regular exhibitions of paintings were staged for members of the public who climbed up to the three big first-floor exhibition rooms. Jane concedes that she 'had some amusement at each, tho' my preference for Men & Women, always inclines me to attend more to the company than the sight'.

She did, however, greatly enjoy an art exhibition at Vauxhall Gardens, where she hunted through the portraits looking for likenesses of her characters, and indeed thought she had found Jane Bennet. Jane hunted for Lizzy Bennet too, but found her not, whimsically explaining her absence: 'I can only imagine that Mr D. prizes any Picture of her too much to like it should be exposed to the public eye. – I can imagine he wd have that sort of feeling – that mixture of Love, Pride & Delicacy.'

Shopping was just as much an attraction as sight-seeing, and Jane was a determined, if thrifty, consumer. While she now had a bit more money, she still faced the same challenge of finding appropriate, moderately stylish, but affordable things to wear. One morning she and Eliza's maid Manon walked out from home in Knightbridge to Grafton House off New Bond Street, to visit the haberdasher's Wilding & Kent. The obvious route for the pair to take from Sloane Street was to Hyde Park Corner, then along Piccadilly, a round trip on foot of nearly five miles.[6] Round the corner from the haberdasher's was Sackville Street, where one Mr Gray sold real jewels to real people, just as he would also sell an over-decorated tooth-pick case to the vapid Robert Ferrars in *Sense and Sensibility*.[7]

Upon Jane and Manon's arrival at Wilding & Kent, 'the whole Counter was thronged' so that they had to wait '*full* half an hour'. Such a shop would be 'filled with goods, unrolled and displayed in the most advantageous manner.' Cards pinned to each article made claims such as 'this beautiful piece of muslin at so much, two shillings in a yard cheaper than any other shop in London'.[8] One of the heroines of Jane's youth, Burney's Evelina, was almost daunted by the persistence of London's shop assistants. 'There seem to be six or seven men belonging to each shop,' she explained, 'I fancy they thought I only wanted persuasion to buy every thing they showed me. And, indeed, they took so much trouble, that I was almost ashamed I could not.'

But Jane could be delighted with even just the meagre purchase of some trimming and three pairs of silk stockings. 'I am getting very extravagant & spending all my Money', she told Cassandra; '& what is worse for *you*, I have been spending yours too', on 'pretty coloured muslin'. She quietly mocked her niece Fanny's lack of shopping success on another trip: 'She is rather out of luck, to like neither her gown nor her Cap . . . I consider it as a thing of course at her time of Life – one of the sweet taxes of Youth to chuse in a hurry & make bad bargains.'

In London the wheel of fashion seemed to be spinning faster and faster, and Jane and Cassandra were beginning to lose interest in keeping up. Stays usually lasted six years before they fell apart, but long before the end of that time the body-shape they were intended to create would have fallen out of fashion. 'I learnt,' Jane wrote, 'to my high amusement, that the stays now are not made to force the Bosom up at all; – *that* was a very unbecoming, unnatural fashion.' She was also 'amused by the present style of . . . enormous Bonnets', and welcomed a general move towards covered chests and long sleeves.

Jane's female relatives nevertheless bullied her into a certain amount of London-style dressing up: 'Mr Hall was very punctual yesterday & curled me at a great rate. I thought it looked hideous, and longed for a snug cap instead, but my companions silenced me by their admiration. I had only a bit of velvet round my head.' She was delighted that the latest mode allowed her to swathe her arms. 'Mrs Tilson had long sleeves too, & she assured me that they are worn in the evening by many. I was glad to hear this.'

Once Jane was dressed to go out, the theatres beckoned. These were not places for sitting quietly in the darkness, imbibing deep cultural experiences. Both audience and actors shared the same level of lighting, and the spectators were not afraid to make a noise. One theatre-goer complained that 'there is no end to their calling out, and knocking with their sticks, till the curtain is drawn up', and even after the play began, often 'did a rotten orange, or the peel of an orange, fly past me . . . one of them actually hit my hat'.[9] There were only two legitimate or 'patent' theatres in London, licensed to put on serious plays. At the other 'illegitimate' theatres, drama had to be delivered by stealth, mixed up with burlesque and various 'Sing-song & trumpery' entertainments which disappointed Jane. She liked to follow the careers of the stars, and once, when Sarah Siddons failed to appear, Jane admitted that she 'could swear at [Siddons] with little effort for disappointing me'. But she did not always want to be running about town being entertained: 'I am very glad to be quiet now', she admits on one occasion.

There was nevertheless a good deal of social life at Henry's London house, for as always he was capable of 'putting Life & Wit into the party'. Unlike the sullen days in Southampton when Jane had been unwilling to make new acquaintances, we now hear that she found 'all these little parties very pleasant'. They weren't always little, either. No fewer than eighty people were invited by Eliza to one party in 1811, which got reported in the papers the next day. She also hired professional musicians, including a harpist, to entertain her guests. The harp was rather a sexy instrument, which required expensive lessons from a master. Eliza herself was a harp-player, and it was a skill that Jane gave likewise to the entitled and entrancing Mary Crawford, and to her fellow lightweight characters the Musgrove sisters, and Georgiana Darcy.[10]

For their party, Henry and Eliza's house was dressed up with 'flowers &c. & looked very pretty'. A special mirror was lent for the mantelpiece by the craftsman who was engaged in making a new one that was not yet finished. Jane positioned herself in the connecting passage outside the drawing room in order to check out all the arriving guests. It 'was comparatively cool, & gave us all the advantage of the Music at a pleasant distance, as well as that of the first veiw of every new comer'.

Whatever Jane may have decided privately, other people thought that she was still on the marriage market. Henry's lawyer, William Seymour, of 19 Cavendish Square, London, had been transacting publishing business for Jane ever since her days in Bath. He was one of the many who took a fancy to her, and yet again a proposal was on the cards.[11] He once spoke of how he had 'escorted' Jane 'from London to Chawton in a postchaise, considering all the way whether he should ask her to become his wife!'[12] But, perhaps confronted with a distinct lack of encouragement, he never actually came out and proposed to her.

Jane was once asked for her favourite among her own characters, and she answered 'Edmund Bertram and Mr Knightley; but they are very far from being what I know English gentlemen often are'.[13] And thank goodness Jane did not meet in real life an Edmund Bertram, or a Mr Knightley, because if she had married she would doubtless, like her niece Anna, have produced human rather then paper progeny. So – for their failures of courage or determination – we can, must, give thanks to Charles Powlett, who wanted to kiss Jane when she was twenty; to Tom Lefroy, seen off by Madam Lefroy; to the talkative Reverend Samuel Blackall; to the silent Harris Bigg-Wither; to the Reverend Edward Bridges; to Robert Holt-Leigh, the dodgy MP who flirted with Jane in 1806; and to William Seymour, her brother Henry's lawyer, who failed to ask Jane to marry him as they travelled in that carriage.[14]

Jane did not fully embrace the opportunities that her London social circle presented. She wasn't keen to meet a Miss Frances Burdett, the daughter of the rich, radical MP: 'I am rather frightened by hearing that she wishes to be introduced to *me*. If I *am* a wild Beast, I cannot help it.' Likewise, she refused to join a literary circle on the night that 'the celebrated Madame de Stael would be at the party'.[15] She was unwilling to become a literary lioness herself, or to hunt other lions. 'I have made up my mind', she wrote to her niece Anna, 'to like no Novels really, but Miss Edgeworth's, Yours & my own.'

But the sparkling social life at Henry's house was soon to come to a sad end. Eliza's breast cancer finally killed her on 25 April 1813. It was generally Cassandra who got landed with the duties of nursing and sitting up and watching through the night. But perhaps that old special bond between Jane and Eliza meant that it was Jane who went up to town once more with the sad mission of witnessing her gay cousin's death.

Eliza's demise left her old French servants stranded in England, and Jane brought Mrs Perigord down to Chawton Cottage for a break, again showing how long-serving domestic staff could become members of the family.[16] Later, back in London again, Jane heard all about the diminished household's new plans. Henry was to move to a smaller house, and the French ladies were still to attend him daily, or at least 'as often as he likes or as they like'. Mrs Perigord and her mother were full of talk of 'servants & Linen'. The elder lady, Madame Bigeon, was not too upset to prepare Jane and other of Henry's relatives 'a most comfortable dinner of Soup, Fish, Bouillee, Partridges & an apple Tart'. Jane considered that Henry, too, had not 'a Mind for affliction. He is too Busy, too active, too sanguine. Sincerely as he was attached to poor Eliza . . . her Loss is not felt as that of many a beloved Wife might be.' Certainly he had not shared a bed with her towards the end, for after her death Jane and other female relatives used it.

So Henry now became a merry widower. He went to a ball at White's Club, at which his sisters could only imagine his sociable behaviour: 'Oh! what a Henry.' They even thought he might be able snag the rich heiress Miss Burdett.

But in the autumn of 1815, still single, Henry fell gravely ill, and Jane came to town to nurse him. This explains why she was able to ask to meet her new publisher John Murray face to face in November to tell him that his terms were not good enough. Jane invited Murray to call, and they reached a deal for the publication of both *Mansfield Park* and *Emma*. It was not a copyright sale; Jane would both bear the risk and receive the reward.

Jane now shared a publisher with Lord Byron and Sir Walter Scott. And something was about to happen to give hopes that *Emma* would be her most successful book yet.

30

Carlton House

'And indeed if the Princess should lose her dear life
You might have a good chance of becoming his wife.'[1]

Jane's nephew thinks she could end up married to George IV

In 1815 Jane ended up staying much longer than expected in London, even after her business with John Murray was concluded, in order to stay with Henry until he was better.

His symptoms were miscellaneous: 'a fever . . . something bilious . . . there is a little pain in the Chest'. It was, however, a serious business, for 'a severe Relapse' threw him back into danger. Indeed, his siblings were summoned to his bedside, where 'they hourly expected his death'. He did get better, but 'Aunt Jane remained some weeks longer to nurse the Convalescent.'[2]

Henry's illness left him so weak that he could not 'hold a pen', and Jane had to go on being her own literary agent. On 23 November she wrote again to John Murray to complain, this time about the loss of time in bringing out *Emma*. 'I am so very much disappointed & vexed by the delays of the Printers', she wrote, 'that I cannot help begging to know whether there is no hope of their being quickened . . . I expect to leave London early in Decr, it is of consequence that no more time should be lost.' This time she was 'soothed & complimented into tolerable comfort', as she put it. It was explained that the printers had been waiting for the stationers to provide paper, and Mr Murray himself was 'so very polite indeed, that it is quite overcoming'.

Jane had good reason to think that the printers might well hurry up, because *Emma* was to be dedicated to royalty. This had happened because one of the un-looked-for consequences of Henry's illness was that Jane found herself being introduced into the circle of the Prince of Wales.

Henry had been receiving medical treatment from Dr Matthew Baillie of Lower Grosvenor Street, among whose other patients was the Prince of Wales. Henry, as usual, could not resist telling his doctor exactly who his sister really was, and Dr Baillie in return passed on the exciting news that the Prince was 'a great admirer of her novels', that 'he read them often, and kept a set in every one of his residences'.[3]

What's more, Dr Baillie informed 'his Royal Highness that Miss Austen was staying in London', and the Prince then asked Dr Clarke, the librarian of his residence at Carlton House, to call upon Jane. Dr Clarke did so, personally passing on to Jane the Prince's hope that she would visit Carlton House herself to see the library.[4]

That is how Jane received her invitation to visit the home of the Prince Regent. He was not completely unknown to the Austen family, but they rather disapproved of him. Back in Hampshire, Jane's brother James had hunted in his youth with the hounds based at Kempshott Park, a property rented by the Prince of Wales, and the master of the hunt's diary shows that sometimes James and the Prince were out on the same day.[5]

Indeed, Jane's father and 'His Royal Highness Prince of Wales' also rubbed shoulders within the pages of the account book of Ring's furniture depot in Basingstoke.[6] Mr Ring's clerk listed the blubbery, overweight prince as the 'Prince of Whales' in the company's account book; a subversive joke about the prince's obesity that was also made in contemporary caricature. The Hampshire Austens had no fawning attitude towards royalty, and the Prince had widely sacrificed respect through his lax morals and loose living. He also became a figure of fun because of his buxom mistress, Lady Conyngham, who was said to have 'not an idea in her head; not a word to say for herself; nothing but a hand to accept pearls and diamonds with, and an enormous balcony to wear them on'. Jane once joked that alterations to a new outfit made her look bosomy, 'more like Lady Conyngham', which, of course, 'is all that one lives for now'.

The Prince Regent lived in a palace appropriate for a libertine. Designed in the 1780s and 90s by Henry Holland in the grand style of the French *ancien régime*, Carlton House is often used to sum up the new 'Regency' style which would flood England in Jane Austen's adult years.

Jane probably borrowed Henry's carriage again for her visit, arriving along Pall Mall and passing through a screen of tall pillars protecting Carlton House's courtyard from the road. There were sentries at the gate to bar access to the Prince's many angry creditors. The carriage would have crossed the courtyard and deposited her under the vast Corinthian portico. There she would have found the prince's pompous librarian, Dr Clarke, ready to lead her into the granite green hall.

The rooms Jane was about to see no longer reflected Holland's restrained and exquisite taste. With the dawn of the nineteenth century, the Prince had fallen out with his architect, sweeping away most of the beautiful interiors Holland had designed, and replacing them with gaudier, even golder ones. Holland's work had radiated a cool classicism. While some features remained – such as his theatrical staircase, which Jane now climbed – the rest were jazzed up. Holland was replaced by a picture dealer named Walsh Porter, then by the architect James Wyatt, and then by his rival John Nash, in a merry-go-round of architectural advisors that revolved faster and faster as time went on.

The Prince also constantly changed his mind about soft furnishings, furniture, and even architectural fittings: in the Rose Satin Drawing Room, for example, the fireplace was changed four times between 1784 and 1819. Meanwhile the silken seat upholstery was changed from lemon yellow to green to crimson, and was blue at the time of Jane's visit. During the course of the next decade, the Prince bought gold taffeta and then green silk intended for use in this room. But he changed his mind before they could even be installed, and the green silk ended up at Brighton Pavilion instead.[7] Another visitor to Carlton House was left overwhelmed by the 'beauties of old china vases, gold fringes, damask draperies, cut-glass lustres, and all the other fine things'.[8]

The hospitality of Carlton House was as legendary as its opulence. The most infamous of all its parties was the celebration held in 1811 to mark the start of the Prince's reign as 'Prince Regent', or official stand-in as king. The crush was so great that some ladies fainted and others lost their shoes or even had their clothes 'torn off'. The Prince Regent's parties were notorious not only for their nudity but also for their splendid repasts: goldfish swam along a miniature river channelled across his banqueting table.

Jane's brother may have hunted with the Prince Regent, her cousin Eliza may have appeared at court herself, but Jane had never got closer than going to watch the ladies in court dress arriving at St James's Palace. This was her first visit inside one of the royal residences. Jane remains tactfully silent about what she saw, but afterwards wrote to Dr Clarke for advice on a matter of etiquette. He had given the impression that the Prince Regent would be glad to have *Emma* dedicated to him. 'Equally concerned to appear either presumptuous or Ungrateful ', Jane requested guidance on exactly how to proceed.

As she did not hold a high opinion of the Prince Regent, Jane was distinctly cool about dedicating her work to him. In fact, she'd harboured no intention of doing so, until 'advised by some of her friends that she must consider the permission as a command'.[9]

And so it really was. Clarke wrote back that it was certainly 'not *incumbent*' upon Jane to dedicate her work to the Prince Regent, but that she was perfectly free to do so if she liked. It was almost impossible for her to refuse. He also thought that she might like a few hints about what to write next. He wished to be allowed to suggest 'the Habits of Life and Character and enthusiasm of a Clergyman . . . Fond of, & entirely engaged in Literature – no man's Enemy but his own'.

In other words, he meant that Jane should write a book about himself. Generations of readers have had a laugh at Dr Clarke's expense, just as Jane now did. 'The comic part of the Character I might be equal to,' she replied, deadpan, 'but not the Good, the Enthusiastic, the Literary.' She concludes, magnificently, that she had no taste anyway: 'I think I may boast myself to be, with all possible Vanity, the most unlearned, & uninformed Female who ever dared to be an Authoress.'

Jane's contempt for the Prince's librarian overflowed into everything to do with royal ways. She disapproved of the morals as well as the low necklines of Regency high society, describing an over-fine lady as 'at once expensively & nakedly dress'd'. She always mentioned elopements or adultery with censure. The Prince Regent himself was as adulterous as any of his subjects, and a great public battle was being played out between him and his wife in the court of public opinion. It had, of course, been an arranged marriage. 'One damned German frau is as good as another', he is supposed to have said, on being told that his bride was Caroline of Brunswick. In this very public split between the Prince Regent and his wife, the Austens were disposed to be on the 'side' of the princess. Frank Austen had been among the sailors of her escort, who had all loved her, when she first arrived in Britain from Brunswick in 1795. Poor Caroline! When she arrived in London on 5 April 1795, there to marry her prince just three days later, she was horrified. 'My God!' she said, 'I found him very fat, and nothing like as handsome as his portrait.'[10]

'Poor Woman, I shall support her as long as I can,' Jane wrote, as the marriage inevitably broke down, 'because she *is* a Woman, & because I hate her Husband.' She was not alone. Tens of thousands of women signed addresses in support of Caroline, including 14,000 women from Bristol and more than 9,000 from Edinburgh.[11] Feelings ran so high in London that *The Times* was forced in 1820 to print a retraction of its statement that 'The Address of the Married Ladies of London' had been signed by 8,500: 'The fact is, Sir, that there were 17,652 respectable names.'[12]

Despite all this support, the Princess's behaviour had not been perfect, and she was accused of having taken lovers of her own. The allegations were probed by a so-called 'Delicate Investigation'. Jane was disconcerted by the news coming out about Princess Caroline's own bad behaviour, but gave her the benefit of the doubt: 'if I must give up the Princess,' she wrote, 'I am resolved at least to think that she would have been respectable, if the Prince had behaved only tolerably by her at first'.

In the light of all of this, Jane's reluctant dedication to poor Caroline's horrid husband was short and sharp. She wanted the title page to say simply: 'Emma, Dedicated by Permission to H.R.H. The Prince Regent'. In the event, though, publisher John Murray suggested something more tactful. *Emma* ended up being dedicated 'TO HIS ROYAL HIGHNESS THE PRINCE REGENT, THIS WORK IS, BY HIS ROYAL HIGHNESS'S DUTIFUL AND OBEDIENT HUMBLE SERVANT, THE AUTHOR.' Jane is so unctuous that she veers dangerously close to parody.

It's notable that in the later Victorian editions of *Emma*, the dedication to the Prince Regent was quietly dropped from the title page. As Jane's own views suggested, his stock had fallen, and would fall further, in a more strait-laced age, while Jane Austen's would rise. By the middle of the nineteenth century, her name was better able to sell books than his.[13]

On 16 December 1815, her fortieth birthday, Jane returned from London to Chawton, having avoided the fate predicted for her by her nephew. 'You might have a good chance of becoming his wife',[14] he had written of her new Royal acquaintance.

And at the end of the month, *Emma* was published by John Murray. Presumably Jane sent a special advance copy, as requested by his librarian, to the Prince Regent. She thought this was a bore. She was entitled to twelve author's copies, which she usually gave as gifts to her relations. Now she felt under obligation to dish the free copies out to influential readers instead.

And there's an amusing coda to the business of the Prince's librarian. He did not leave well alone, but went on 'encouraging' his pet authoress. 'Pray continue to write,' he begged, '& make all your friends send Sketches to help you . . . do let us have an English Clergyman after *your* fancy.' The proposed 'English Clergyman' continued to bear a remarkable resemblance to Dr Clarke himself. 'Describe him burying his own mother − as I did − because the High Priest of the Parish in which she died − did not pay her remains the respect he ought to do. I have never recovered from the Shock.'[15] As well as showering her with impertinent literary advice, he also invited Jane to use his own London library. Perhaps he too had thoughts of making her his wife.

On Christmas Day 1815, an advert appeared on the front page of the *Morning Chronicle*. The 'books published this day', it read, include 'EMMA: a Novel. − By the Author of Pride and Prejudice'. Despite the wretched, thankless business of the royal dedication, Jane must have been filled with pride and pleasure.[16]

ACT FOUR
The End, and After

No. 8 College Street, Winchester

31

Disasters

'This was a bad year for our family'.

Caroline Austen (1816)

PERHAPS ENCOURAGED BY the expected sales boost of the Prince's name, John Murray published a generous two thousand copies of *Emma*. But this proved to be too large a number. Now, for the first time since the breakthrough of getting published in the first place, Jane ran into professional difficulties.

It was also a mistake to have decided in favour of that second edition of *Mansfield Park*, which John Murray brought out in February 1816. Both it, and *Emma,* were accidentally placed in competition with each other, and it seems to have hurt them both. In fact, the losses on *Mansfield Park* pretty much cancelled out Jane's profits on *Emma*. Amazingly, this meant that her most sophisticated and perfect book only made her £38 and 13 shillings. John Murray sent her a royalty cheque, welcome indeed, but it must have been disappointing to find that it was only for so small a sum. Events had proved Murray to be less of a 'rogue' than Jane had thought. If she'd accepted his initial offer of £450 for the copyright of three books, she would have made more money than in fact she did.[1]

And all this was despite *Emma* winning an impressive eight reviews between March and September 1816. One of them was from no less a personage than Sir Walter Scott, although his piece in *The Quarterly Review* was unsigned. Jane was on the whole pleased with the review, except for its omission of *Mansfield Park* entirely from the discussion of her works. She was disappointed that 'so clever a Man as the Reveiwer of *Emma*, should consider it as unworthy of being noticed'. The exclusion of *Mansfield Park* denied her the opportunity to shift a few more copies of that pesky second edition.

Scott rightly praised *Emma* as an entirely new form of novel, presenting not 'the splendid scenes of an imaginary world' (of the kind he himself specialised in), but 'a correct and striking representation of that which is daily taking place around him'.

But perhaps herein lay the difficulty for Jane's commercial success.

Emma was just too experimental; too daring; too different. Other, less clever reviewers than Scott certainly missed the point. *Emma* 'is amusing', wrote one of them, 'if not instructive; and has no tendency to deteriorate the heart'.[2] And then again, 'The fair reader may also glean by the way some useful hints against forming romantic schemes.'[3]

Four years after *Emma* was published, 539 copies were remaindered.[4] After *Pride and Prejudice*, Jane must have been a little shaken by this. She was grateful for any hint that people had enjoyed *Emma*, being eager for praise 'in my present State of Doubt as to her reception in the World'. She was desperate, as she put it, 'to beleive that I had not yet – as almost every Writer of Fancy does sooner or later – overwritten myself'.

Even in Hampshire, even in Austen circles, some people didn't like *Emma*. Jane, perhaps hurt, perhaps amused, collected their opinions and wrote them down. Her neighbour Mrs Digweed 'did not like it . . . in fact if she had not known the Author, [she] could hardly have got through it', while Mrs Dickson 'did not much like it', but 'liked it the less', from the very silly reason of 'there being a Mr. and Mrs Dixon in it'.[5]

Did the Prince Regent read his copy of *Emma*? Did he enjoy it? There's a loud silence there. Jane had shelled out twenty-four shillings for a special morocco binding for the Prince's presentation set.[6] But the fact that *Emma* made her way very quickly into the Royal Library suggests that she did not spend much time upon the royal bedside table.

Jane did hear from the indefatigable Dr Clarke, who returned to her 'the Thanks of His Royal Highness the Prince Regent', and told her that 'many of the Nobility' who had been staying at the Brighton Pavilion with the Prince had paid Jane 'the just tribute of their Praise'. It's funny to think of Jane's stories of rectitude in rectories being read in the Prince's Oriental pad in Brighton, the most notorious, luxurious and licentious palace in England.

Clarke had some news of his own, too: that he had just been appointed Chaplain to the Prince of Coburg. He could not resist suggesting that Jane should write a 'historical Romance illustrative of the History of the august house of Cobourg', or, as Sir Walter Scott might have put it, a historical romance in 'the big bow-wow strain'.

Jane replied that she was 'unequal to the task'. 'I could not sit seriously down to write a serious Romance under any other motive than to save my life,' she said, '& if it were indispensable for me to keep it up & never relax into laughing at myself or other people, I am sure I should be hung before I had finished the first Chapter.' 'No,' she concluded, 'I must keep to my own style & go on in my own Way; And though I may never succeed again in that, I am convinced that I should totally fail in any other.' Her sales figures were telling a different story. If her goal was financial, then she was failing as a novelist. But here is Jane nonetheless determined, successful, sure of herself. She may be laughing at Dr Clarke, but she truly was at the very height of her creative powers.

In fact, the greatest danger to her producing further books was not the commercial success, or otherwise, of her publishing. Nor would it be a loss of confidence or lack of direction. The threat came from the fact that she was once again in danger of losing her home.

The Austens had suffered a quite astonishing series of losses as the decade of the Regency opened. In 1814, Charles Austen's wife Fanny died. Their home had been on board his ship, to save money, and it was here that post-natal complications killed her. 'She ought sooner to have removed', wrote a Leigh cousin.[7] This was Jane's second sister-in-law lost to childbirth.

That same autumn of 1814, Edward came under legal attack. A 'clever and rather scampish brewer of Alton', James Baverstock, formed a consortium with the aim of challenging the legality of Edward's inheritance of his Hampshire estates from the Knights.

Just like the Stoneleigh Abbey business, it all stemmed from an ambiguously worded legal document. The loophole lay years in the past, from the time of the giving of the estates, including Chawton Great House and Cottage, to Thomas Brodnax-May-Knight of Godmersham. Mrs Knight's will had named the Hinton family as the next heirs should Thomas Brodnax-May-Knight's line fail. The Knight line clearly *had* failed, James Baverstock and the Hintons now argued, as Edward Austen was not a blood relative. And, in addition, the entail that cut out the Hinton claim in favour of Edward had been executed out of the legal profession's term-time.[8] Did this make it invalid? The Baverstock–Hinton party certainly thought so. If the claim was successful, then Edward stood to lose the majority of his property, and his female relatives their Chawton home.[9] Insecurity, that vanquished foe of old, was back in their lives.

The business dragged on for four unsettling years, from the autumn of 1814 to April 1818. Finally Edward bought his way out of trouble by cutting down and selling a great deal of timber in Chawton Park, where Jane had loved to walk. By this means he raised £15,000 to pay off the claimants.[10] Most of the money ended up being swallowed up in lawyers' fees.

Meanwhile, there was no good news coming in from Jane's friends either. Miss Sharpe was still in employment, but not doing well. Jane was accustomed to letters describing her 'distressing' and 'harassed' condition. Henry's housekeeper Mrs Perigord went in 1816 to France, to see what was to be had there now that peace had returned, but discovered only 'a scene of general Poverty & Misery, – no Money, no Trade'. 'This', wrote Caroline Austen of the year 1816, 'was a bad year for our family.'

Meanwhile, Caroline's own father, Jane's brother James, was growing old and weird. 'I notice that gradually less and less did my father make any visits,' Caroline tells us, 'he had long ceased to dine out.'[11] James himself appreciated that he was growing increasingly unsociable, describing himself as:

> scarcely able to maintain my share
> Of conversation, in the circle small
> Of long known neighbours, & long valued friends;
> How lost were I midst strangers![12]

And then, as Caroline Austen puts it, 'the second and most serious misfortune was my Uncle Henry's bankruptcy, announced on 16th March, an entire surprise at our house, and as little foreseen I believe by the rest of the family'.[13] Henry's bankruptcy was like a thunderclap that echoed through the whole Austen clan. If, as Jane wrote, 'the luck of one member of the family is luck to all', the same holds true of misfortune.

Despite his success on the surface, Henry's affairs were in poor order. He lacked diligence and follow-through. This is revealed by a trail of failed enterprises such as his Old English Ale Brewery, which, he proposed, would supply the West End with a 'wholesome and nutritious Beverage',[14] or his doomed attempt to go to France to lay claim to that estate of Eliza's guillotined first husband. 'The result would have been different,' his relations thought, 'if instead of trusting to his own sharpness, he had put the case into the hands of a French lawyer.'[15]

A younger Henry had been fortunate enough to be in the right place at the right time to make a good deal of money. Back in 1813, Jane had been delighted by his receiving another promotion, to the position of Receiver-General of the county of Oxfordshire. This was the representative of the government to whom its residents had to pay their Land Tax. In return for their trouble, Receivers-General usually held on to the money for six weeks, investing, and earning interest upon it, before handing it to the Treasury.

Even before that, from 1806, Henry had also become involved as a partner in no fewer than three country banks in Alton, Petersfield and Hythe. Banks were sprouting up all over late Georgian Britain, as the Bank of England had only really served London. In the economic crisis following the Napoleonic Wars, though, the habits of the Receivers-General of Taxes were coming under public scrutiny, and public criticism, for the money they squeezed out of the process. The coming of peace also saw a significant fall in the sums that Henry was handling for the army: the payrolls administered by his bank dropped from £112,000 in 1813 to £34,000 in 1815.

On top of that, he had taken some poor lending decisions. Seduced as always by the thrill of belonging to high society, he had lent £6,000 to Lord Moira, who was known to be £100,000 in debt. It was foolish to lend money to a man of whom the spendthrift Prince of Wales had said: 'Moira and I are like two brothers, when one wants money he puts his hand in the other's pocket.'[16]

On 15 March 1816 Henry Austen's bank failed, one of thirty-five that would collapse in that difficult year following the war. He was declared bankrupt and left London.[17] Henry was somewhat ungracious about it, claiming that it was caused 'by the egregious folly' of his partners, not himself.[18]

Despite his charm, despite his being 'so highly gifted by Nature', those who knew him best concluded that Henry had an essential lack of character.[19] Poor Henry, so lively, and with such 'great conversational powers', did not have his brothers' knack for making a home and family. He might have been entertaining company, but he had 'less steadiness of purpose, certainly less success in life, than his brothers'.[20]

And his brothers were drawn into the aftershock of the failure of Henry's bank. Indeed, the whole family was affected. Mr James Leigh Perrot lost £10,000 he had put up as Henry's backer. One can see James Leigh Perrot's loss as making up for his failure to give the Austens any share in the Stoneleigh settlement. His wife, of course, was particularly angry. What a vast sum Henry 'has occasioned us to lose by his imprudence', she wrote, and 'what might have been the consequence if the Stoneleigh settlement had not occasion'd such an encrease of Property as to enable us to bear up against our losses'.[21]

Henry's brother Edward lost £20,000 with the failure of the bank, and this was particularly disturbing. Coming on top of his legal difficulties, Edward's financial difficulties might result in the female Austens losing Chawton Cottage. And Henry and Frank, unable to afford it, now stopped the £50 annual payments that they had been making to their mother and sisters since 1805.

At least Jane at least was safe, or safe-ish, for she had invested the profits of her books in Navy 5 per cent stock. But she did lose, from her account with Henry's bank, £13 of profit from *Mansfield Park*, and

£12 from the second edition of *Sense and Sensibility.*[22] £25 was nowhere near £10,000, but it was nonetheless a significant loss for her.

This period of setbacks and doubts would colour Jane's most elegiac novel, *Persuasion*, which she began on 8 August 1815. As well as opening with loss and regret, it also tackled another subject that must have been on her mind as she entered her forties: the ageing of the body.

32

A Poor Honey

'I have still a tendency to Rheumatism'.

Jane writes in 1817

JANE THROUGHOUT HER life had given short shrift to the sick. A 'Poor Honey' was her name for a woman who revelled in weak health, relishing 'spasms & nervousness & the consequences'. In *Emma,* Jane writes in moral terms of 'the fancifulness, and all the selfishness of imaginary complaints'. She had always scoffed at people who claimed to be ill. So when her own health began to fail, she met the issue head-on: with denial.

Denial actually mattered more than you might think when medicine still involved a good deal of belief rather than science. Prayer and positive thinking could make you feel better. And you had to trust your own instincts. 'How are you, as to Health, strength, Looks, stomach &c?' asked Jane in a letter to Cassandra in 1811. To live in an age when the doctor was expensive, several miles away, and not that well equipped to diagnose you anyway was to understand that folk medicine and self-treatment were terribly important.

Jane's friends had always swapped recipes for medicine just as they had for food. Mrs Lefroy recommended a gargle of 'port wine Vinegar Honey & sage tea' for a sore throat, while Martha Lloyd's cookbook, partly compiled at Chawton Cottage, includes cures for 'Mad Dog Bite', 'Pain in the Side', and 'Swelled Neck', as well as veterinary concoctions such as treatments for 'Wounds in Cattle' and 'Mange'.[1] Furthermore, the Georgians did not have our distinction between a mild and a life-threatening illness. Jane often talks of nursing a cold by staying entirely indoors, and of other health precautions that sound a bit over the top. But then, a cold in Georgian times was not necessarily 'just' a cold. You had no way of knowing if it would lead to something very serious, like consumption. Or not. The Georgian Parson Woodforde, for example, was deeply concerned that he had 'got the Piles coming', but eventually decided that it was just the result of 'eating a good deal of Pease Pudding two or three days ago'.[2]

Jane and her family simply had to put up with the small aches and ailments of life before paracetamol. When she took her young Godmersham nieces to the dentist in London, for example, it was 'a sad Business' which 'cost us many tears'. Poor Lizzy 'is not finished yet', we hear, for despite being filed once already, her teeth 'are to be filed again'. Then, on another visit, 'poor Marianne had two taken out . . . when her doom was fixed, Fanny Lizzy & I walked into the next room, where we heard each of the two sharp hasty screams'. The dentist also insisted upon messing around with Fanny's perfectly good snappers, leading Jane to 'think he must be a Lover of Teeth & Money & Mischeif'.

At home in Chawton, Jane had a frequent reminder of the callous randomness of disease in the form of her sister-in-law Mary's face. The Lloyd family had had smallpox in their house in 1771, 'of the confluent sort, and those who recovered bore the marks of its virulence all through their lives'. 'Confluent' smallpox saw the individual smallpox sores spread until the entire surface of the skin was covered. It arrived via 'the coachman, who concealed the fact, till too late, that it was in his own cottage'. Mary's father, a clergyman, left his family to their fate, and moved into lodgings, so that he himself would not carry the infection with him 'into church on Sundays'. The disease took his only son, and left his daughter horribly scarred.[3]

While she had never been as ill as Mary, Jane shows in her letters that neither had her life been free from physical complaints. In her thirties she continued to have minor trouble with her eyes, complaining of strain and pain. 'I cannot wear my spectacles, and therefore can do hardly any work but knitting *white* yarn', she wrote in 1814. Jane's round spectacles, complete with green silk hanging cord, were kept in a black, embroidered case, and both items are stored inside her writing desk at the British Library today.

But there were signs from 1813 onwards that there was something more serious amiss with Jane's health. Fanny Knight's diary mentions that Aunt Jane in July was suffering from 'a bad face ache', and in August she stayed inside the Great House rather than walk with the rest of the family in the cool evening air.[4] The next week, Jane again 'caught fresh cold in her face'.[5] A facial neuralgia like this can be extremely painful. Lizzy of the teeth, Fanny's sister, remembered Jane sometimes walking along the path to the Great House with 'head a little to one side, and sometimes a very small cushion pressed against her cheek, if she were suffering from face-ache, as she not unfrequently did in later life'.[6] To walk about with a cushion suggests a rather dreadful degree of discomfort.

It's painful to read the letters from the last couple of years of Jane's life with the knowledge that she was beginning to experience the symptoms of what would prove to be a fatal illness, even though she was not yet forty. From the spring of 1816 Jane's letters start to mention that she'd been feeling distinctly poorly, with back pain, 'pain in my knee now & then', and 'a good deal of fever'. There is no consensus about what Jane's condition was. In 1964, Sir Zachary Cope retrospectively diagnosed her illness as Addison's disease, a disorder of the two small adrenal glands that sit on top of the kidneys. People with Addison's disease – which is very rare – fail to produce enough cortisol and aldosterone, and experience weakness, fainting and cramps. But other physicians almost immediately disagreed with Cope's diagnosis.

At first, Jane's illness did not affect her work. Early in 1816, 'when four novels of steadily increasingly success had given the writer some confidence in herself',[7] Jane bought back the copyright of *Susan* from Crosby & Co. She purchased it, as she had sold it, anonymously. Then came the pleasure of revealing the truth: 'When the bargain was concluded and the money paid, but not till then, the negotiator had the satisfaction' of revealing 'that the work, which had been so lightly esteemed, was by the author of "Pride and Prejudice"'.[8] It's quite pleasing to imagine Mr Crosby's mortification. He was doomed to be remembered as the man who missed one of the greatest opportunities in the history of publishing.

But the signs of Jane's increasing weakness were there for those who took the trouble to see them. One niece remembered how, after dinner at Chawton Cottage, Aunt Jane would often lie down, but not upon a sofa. Instead, she would line up '3 chairs' as a makeshift piece of furniture, which 'never looked comfortable'. Jane called it '*her* sofa', and preferred it to the real one. Her reason was that she wanted to leave the actual sofa free for her mother. She wanted Mrs Austen to be able to lie down 'whenever she felt inclined.'[9]

Her daughters had spent years dancing around Mrs Austen's strange requirements, and Jane had learned that it was easiest to avoid the sources of conflict. She put a rare comment in her own voice into a draft version of *Persuasion*: 'I confess myself almost in despair after understanding myself to have already given a Mother offence.' No wonder she removed it from the final text. It was too personal.

Mrs Austen's requirements also included not having to think about unpleasant things. Mary Austen, James's wife, had understandable reservations about her stepdaughter Anna's engagement to Ben Lefroy. With her habitual plain speaking, Mary made what Jane thought was the mistake of mentioning her concerns to Mrs Austen. 'How can Mrs J.

Austen be so provokingly ill-judging?' Jane asked. 'Now my Mother will be unwell again.'

In May 1816, Jane and Cassandra visited Cheltenham together, there to seek a cure in its celebrated spa for Jane's mysterious pains. Their affection for each other had not lessened, but neither had the pecking order between them. Despite Jane's professional success, 'the habit of looking up' to her sister, 'begun in childhood, seemed always to continue'. Jane would always say that Cassandra 'could teach everything much better than *she* could – Aunt Cassa. *knew* more'.[10] As time went on, though, it became ever more true that the two of them 'were everything to each other. They seemed to lead a life to themselves, within the general family life, which was shared only by each other.'[11]

Cheltenham, however, seemed to do no good. On their way home they visited the Fowle family at Kintbury, of which Cassandra had once seemed destined to be a member. By now they were very old friends indeed. The visit had a melancholy air, and the Fowles 'received an impression that Jane's health was failing – altho' they did <u>not</u> know of any particular malady'.[12] Her friends thought (perhaps with the benefit of hindsight) that she 'visited each familiar spot as if she were taking leave of it'.[13]

In September, Jane made the link between her mysterious medical condition and what we would call 'stress', although it's a term that's only been used since the early twentieth century. 'My Back', she wrote to Cassandra, who was away in Cheltenham again, 'has given me scarcely any pain for many days. – I have an idea that agitation does it as much harm as fatigue, & that I was ill at the time of your going, from the very circumstance of your going.' If Jane's condition really was Addison's disease, then it is true that distress at being parted from her sister could have brought it on. But the medical historian Annette Upfal has recently argued that Jane was not suffering from Addison's, but from Hodgkin's disease, a type of cancer of the white blood cells. Hodgkin's has a cruel cycle of illness and improvement, and it could be that it had simply happened to strike at this particular moment. The disorder builds over a few weeks to a high fever and night sweats, which then fade away, leaving the victim feeling better but extremely weak because of the number of red blood cells the fever has destroyed.[14]

In Cassandra's absence, Jane was forced to step up and do the house-hold work at Chawton Cottage, a source of much regret. 'I was not sorry when Friday came', she wrote, the day that saw the departure of her brother Edward. 'I wanted a few days quiet, & exemption from the Thought & contrivances which any sort of company gives.' 'I often wonder', Jane went on to Cassandra, 'how *you* can find the time for what you do, in addition to the care of the House.' The greater burden of family duties in general did fall upon Cassandra, such as buying bedding and sorting things out up at Chawton Great House when Edward was not there.[15] When Cassandra was away from Chawton and unable to see to the housekeeping, Jane's writing time suffered. 'Composition seems to me Impossible,' she wrote, 'with a head full of Joints of Mutton & doses of rhubarb.'

Jane was so anxious not to think of herself as an invalid that her letters talk constantly about her supposedly returning health. '*I* have certainly gained strength through the Winter & am not far from being well', she wrote at the start of 1817. 'I think I understand my own case now so much better than I did . . . I am more & more convinced that *Bile* is at the bottom of all I have suffered.' She was referring here to the idea that the human body consisted of four different liquids, or humours. According to this way of understanding biology, disease was the result of the humours falling out of balance. In Jane's case, she believed that black bile, one of the four, had grown too strong in relation to the others: yellow bile, blood and phlegm. According to this belief system, the consequences of having 'too much' bile were physical – hence Jane's pain – but also mental. An excess of bile would produce melancholy. Melancholy had been a physical condition in the seventeenth century, but now the Georgians were starting to think of it as an emotional state.[16]

This is a foretaste of the modern belief that creativity and depression are linked, although even the ancients thought that melancholy was a particular affliction of great men. Jane's reference to 'bile' having caused her illness could be a hint that if she were alive today she might be diagnosed with what we would call depression, a condition that seems to lurk, for those who look for it, behind her letters over many years. We can spot its signals of helplessness – 'I must submit' – and joylessness – 'I am sick of myself, & my bad pens' – and irritability: 'I was as civil to them [some acquaintances] as their bad breath would allow me.'

Jane's letters have been carefully combed by medical historians looking for evidence of what was really wrong, and on Sunday 23 March we come to what may be a vital clue. She writes that after having 'not been well for many weeks', with 'a good deal of fever at times', she is 'considerably better now'. She has even been recovering her 'looks a little, which have been bad enough, black & white & every wrong colour'. This discolouration of the skin is a symptom of both Addison's and Hodgkin's diseases, although in Addison's the marks would not have promptly disappeared again, as Jane's did. She was once again 'very pale' in April.[17] One point to the Hodgkin's theory; Addison's nil.

But then the disease, whatever it was, made another of its cyclical turns. 'I am almost entirely cured', she writes, 'Aunt Cassandra nursed me so beautifully!' It's heart-breaking to read these hopeful words in the light of our knowledge that Jane wasn't really getting better, however hard she might try to convince herself.

In the good intervals, Jane once again revised the manuscript formerly known as *Susan*, now *Catherine*, and which would end up as *Northanger Abbey*. She got it ready to be sent to her publisher. But she did not actually let it go. As she writes in 1817, 'Miss Catherine is put upon the Shelve for the present, and I do not know that she will ever come out.'

A bit of good news was much needed. After the failure of his bank, Henry went back to the first plan he'd had for life, before Eliza had come along with her tempting wicked ways, and became a curate. This at least returned him to Hampshire and his family. 'London is become a hateful place to him,' Jane wrote, '& he is always depressed by the idea of it.' Her world too was closing in. No more would she lark about in London. She would never again leave the county of her birth.

Mrs Austen meanwhile also limped on in poor health, defying all the expectations that her weaknesses, complaints and illnesses should have finished her off years ago. She was still in hopes of getting something, anything, from the Leigh Perrots. When her brother James Leigh Perrot fell ill at his home in Berkshire, Jane described how her mother in Hampshire would sit 'brooding over Evils which cannot be remedied & Conduct impossible to be understood'. Indeed, it was so generally distressing to the family to have Uncle James in limbo, neither alive nor dead, that Jane wrote: 'I shall be very glad when the Event at Scarlets is over', as 'the expectation of it keeps us in a worry.'

Jane's niece Anna too, was in poor health, suffering difficult pregnancies and miscarriages. She could not come to see her aunt, Anna's husband reported, being 'not *equal to so long* a walk; she *must come in* her *Donkey Carriage*'. Jane, too, had taken to travelling by donkey carriage, as it was the only way that she was able 'to go about with At Cassandra in her walks'. Defunct shoes from the Austen ladies' donkey are often dug up in the garden at Chawton Cottage to this day.[18]

Anna, seventeen years younger than her sick aunt, was reduced to the same condition of immobility by childbearing. 'Poor Animal,' wrote Jane, 'she will be worn out before she is thirty. – I am very sorry for her.' Jane usually signed off her letters with just 'Your affectionate aunt', or 'yours affectionately', but when Anna was pregnant, her tone changed.

Ever conscious of the dangers soon to come, Jane ended her letter with 'Yours very affectionately My dear Anna.'[19]

Surely Jane would get better, Anna would survive, James Leigh Perrot would die, leaving the ladies some money at last? Surely, after all their suffering, the Austens deserved a lucky break? After all, life is full of second chances, and none more beautiful than those in the novel Jane was now writing: *Persuasion*.

33

Unfinished Business

'Anne Elliot had been a very pretty girl,
but her bloom had vanished early.'

Persuasion

WHILE JANE HAD been hobnobbing with princes and discussing *Emma* with John Murray, the year 1815 had also seen her beginning *Persuasion*. It's often described as 'autumnal', belonging as it does to this last season of Jane's life, and with its frequent references to change and decay. And yet autumn is several times praised in *Persuasion* for its beauty: 'that season of peculiar and inexhaustible influence on the mind of taste'. *Persuasion* is the novel to which many of Jane's readers 'graduate'. Once they have enjoyed the sparkling romance of *Pride and Prejudice*, and weathered the trauma of *Mansfield Park* and the trials of *Emma*, they mature to this story of regret and redemption. The circumstances of its writing, once known, make *Persuasion* all the more poignant.

Started on 8 August 1815, *Persuasion* was completed almost exactly twelve months later.[1] It was set very precisely in the period of peace between the months June 1814 and February 1815, when Britain's naval officers were on shore leave. Just after the novel ended, its early readers would have been aware, Napoleon was going to escape from Elba, and war would be resumed once again.[2] This story of sailors and the sea was set in the calm before the storm.

Circling back to her oldest theme of all, Jane begins *Persuasion* once again with the loss of a home. Anne Elliot is expelled from Kellynch Hall by her vain father's fecklessness. She then begins a rootless period, living with her sister, with her friend, and in rented accommodation in Bath. Unlike Jane's own stay in Bath, it all ends happily with Anne's finding a home, a permanent home, with her husband.

But in this case, we don't get to see this longed-for home. The house that Anne and her husband will purchase with his fortune is not visited or described like Lizzy's Pemberley or Fanny's parsonage. By now, more than ever, 'home' had for Jane become a state of mind. She no longer needed bricks and mortar. Like her sympathetic invalid character, Mrs

Smith in *Persuasion*, Jane found that as her body began to fail her, her brain and spirit endured. Endurance, the Georgian single woman's most valuable quality, would see her through. Mrs Smith's home was:

> limited to a noisy parlour, and a dark bed-room behind . . . but here was something more; here was that elasticity of mind, that disposition to be comforted, that power of turning readily from evil to good, and of finding employment which carried her out of herself, which was from Nature alone. It was the choicest gift of Heaven.

Persuasion, the last of Jane's completed novels, takes us back to earlier romances, but in a minor key. Anne Elliot has learned the lessons that Marianne Dashwood had not. She's kept her sensibility in check, not indulged her feelings, refused to feel the force of love. But now, approaching middle age, the story tells of Anne's tentative, reluctant re-embrace of sensibility. As John Mullan notes, '*Persuasion* seems a work designed to redeem "feeling" and "feelings". The words appear on almost every page.'[3]

Persuasion seems the deepest, most romantic, of Jane's novels. Her friend Ann Barrett thought that Jane had put her whole self into it. 'Anne Elliot was herself; her enthusiasm for the navy, and her perfect unselfishness, reflect her completely.'[4] And Anne's final reconciliation with Captain Wentworth is a wonderful treat after a life favouring sense rather than sensibility, cautious pragmatism rather than romantic optimism.

It's all too tempting to see Anne as Jane, a temptation that Jane's sister only increased. Cassandra, normally so buttoned-up and silent, gives us a rare insight into her own feelings about Jane's life, perhaps indicating regret that prudent advice had been followed, and loves perhaps lost. In her personal copy of *Persuasion*, Cassandra marked out this line of Jane's writing: 'she had been forced into prudence in her youth, she learned romance as she grew older – the natural sequel of an unnatural beginning'.

'Dear dear Jane!' was Cassandra's comment, 'this deserves to be written in letters of gold.'[5]

Persuasion may give every reader hope of finding love against the odds, but in other ways it had a gloomy outlook that must have reflected Jane's own concerns in this last decade of her life. As she looked about her and saw society settling down after the Napoleonic Wars, Jane spotted a growing conservatism and new restrictions being placed upon women's lives. In some ways, the 1810s are reminiscent of the 1950s, a more censorious decade following the adventurous years of the Second World War.

In *Persuasion* we are presented with the most feminine of Jane's heroines. Some people may find Anne Elliot, although deeply sympathetic, to be at core a little too self-mortifying. It's a fact drawn into sharper focus by Captain Wentworth's being Jane's most masculine hero. And troubling questions remain as to what Anne was to *do* after marriage. Lizzy Bennet was to become mistress of Pemberley, with significant responsibility over the lives and prosperity of many people. Anne Elliot was going to follow Wentworth to sea like a devoted dog, and surely, when children came, she'd just have to wait around for him at home. As post-war prosperity returned, nineteenth-century expectations grew that a husband would support his wife. This was at the expense of them becoming partners in a mutual enterprise such as Mr and Mrs Austen's establishment at Steventon Rectory. To some women, this perhaps felt like being shut up in a box. It's a trend that appears in Jane's other late novels too. Emma Woodhouse's sister, for example, living in town, married to a rich lawyer, has no real work to do except to grow overly anxious about the health of her children.[6] The Victorians were going to invent, and to worship, the stay-at-home mum. Jane could see this coming, and did not like it.

In August 1816, *Persuasion* was complete. Short, sweet and perfect, it is half the length of *Mansfield Park*, and the words seem to have flowed with ease. Despite Jane's problems with her health, she began to tell people about her new book. In March 1817 she indicated that she had 'something ready for Publication, which may perhaps appear about a twelvemonth hence. It is short, about the length of Catherine.'

Jane, as always, was self-effacing about her efforts. 'You will not like it, so you need not be impatient', she told her niece Fanny. But then, she remembered that Fanny had turned against the assertive Emma Woodhouse, so maybe she *would* enjoy the proto-Victorian, self-effacing Anne. Yes, Fanny 'may *perhaps* like the Heroine', Jane reconsidered, 'as she is almost too good for me'.

And Jane seemed in no rush to publish *Persuasion*. Jan Fergus, a historian who has closely studied Jane's publishing decisions, thinks that she might have been deliberately hoarding it, along with *Catherine/Northanger Abbey*, keeping the novels back from any publisher until she could save up enough income to pay for the printing herself. This would mean that she'd win that much bigger financial prize if they were successful. So, poignantly, Jane was playing a long game, even when the days left to her were short.

Jane must have been consoled after the financial disappointment of *Emma* by having received 'nearly twenty pounds' from the second edition of *Sense and Sensibility*. The money gave her a 'fine flow of Literary Ardour'. And so, encouraged, in January 1817, Jane began yet another novel, *Sanditon*, the one that she would never finish. She was constantly casting about for material. Now that so many of Jane's nieces and nephews were emulating their aunt by writing 'novels' of their own, she made a joke when one of their efforts went missing. Perhaps she herself had purloined it, as its stolen plot would give her 'two strong twigs & a half towards a Nest of my own'.

Her aim this time was to take a pot shot – ironically – at the whole business of health spas and seaside resorts. It was to be from her own point of view of the resolutely healthy: 'I have not much compassion for colds in the head.' In terms of her health, she claimed to be 'tolerably well again, quite equal to walking about & enjoying the Air; & by sitting down & resting a good while between my Walks, I get exercise enough'. It was a good deal of trouble to get out and harness up the donkey to pull its little cart, so Jane mentions her plan to 'take to riding the Donkey . . . it will be more independent & less troublesome than the use of the Carriage'. I can't quite tell if she is joking.

When Anna recovered far enough from one of her numerous childbirths to come over to Chawton in her own donkey carriage, she discussed the story of *Sanditon* with her aunt. She claimed afterwards that members of the Parker family were 'suggested by conversations which passed between Aunt Jane & me during the time that she was writing this story'.[7]

The manuscript of *Sanditon*, which tells the story of the Parkers, the Heywoods and the Denhams, was in progress in February and March when Jane was sick and 'kept a good deal in her own room'. Even so, 'when equal to anything she could always find pleasure in composition'. A couple of the pages are written in pencil rather than Jane's usual ink pen, easier to manipulate for a lying or lolling invalid.[8] Jane's world had shrunk down to her home, indeed to a single room, but here was a way of getting out of it.

As well as spoofing seaside resorts, *Sanditon* takes off in a new direction for Jane, and shows her, even under these conditions, to have remained inventive to the end. Unlike her previous novels, it has a much firmer sense of solid detail to it: the houses; the sea; the blue shoes for sale in the shops. It seems that Jane in her bedroom was travelling in her mind on a seaside holiday, for *Sanditon* was inspired by the memory of a real place.

Way back in 1805, after Mr Austen's death, the bereaved Austen ladies had gone to Worthing for a spell of cheap living, from September until at least early November. They were joined there by quite a party from

Godmersham Park including Miss Sharpe and Fanny Knight. The presence of the Godmersham set explains the choice of fashionable Worthing rather than a super-cheap resort like Lyme.

Worthing was 'much frequented . . . by people of fashion, on account of the fine sands, which are esteemed the best in the kingdom'. Its rise to prominence as a smart resort had been fast, and helped by a stay in 1798 by Princess Amelia. 'In a short space of time', we hear, 'a few miserable huts and smuggler's dens have been exchanged for buildings, sufficiently extensive and elegant to accommodate the first families in the kingdom.'⁹ In 1803 proper drains were installed, from 1804 you could reach Worthing by a new turnpike road, and by 1805 there were 'no less than six streets built here'. This means six terraces of four-storey houses, generally with bay windows on the Brighton model, so you could look out down the street to get views of the sea.¹⁰

Jane's temporary home in Worthing was to be Stanford, or Mr Stanford's, Cottage, with three floors' worth of rooms, and a fine position near the centre of the resort. The English Channel could be seen from the semi-circular bay windows of the house's southern side, which looked directly across a field and then the waves. This view from Mr Stanford's Cottage, standing in the middle of the half-completed resort, must have been just like that from Mr Parker's house in *Sanditon*: 'a miscellanous foreground of unfinished buildings, waving linen, and tops of houses, to the sea, dancing and sparkling in sunshine and freshness'. The real-life Mr Stanford was a tailor who found it lucrative to rent out his house to the seasonal visitors whose names would be listed among the town's new arrivals published in the *Brighton Gazette*.¹¹

A narrow pathway ran down the eastern side of the Austens' rented cottage to the lending library on the seafront. Stafford's Marine Library was one of two such 'very respectable' institutions in Worthing.¹² Formerly a four-storey building, its surviving remnant is now the office of a bus company. Probably, just as in Jane's fictional *Sanditon*, people would read the library's subscription book with interest to see who'd arrived in town.¹³ A 'library' wasn't just about the books; it was also a social centre. Jane's library in *Sanditon* also sells various knick-knacks, and in the circulating library at Ryde on the Isle of Wight you could even rent bedrooms and sleep.¹⁴

It was Sir Walter Scott who contrasted Jane's novels to 'the ephemeral productions which supply the regular demand of watering-places and circulating libraries'.¹⁵ Her books are nevertheless in dialogue with the pulp fiction that crowded the shelves of the libraries of Worthing or Sanditon. They spoof its wild and romantic settings and plots, as in

Northanger Abbey, or turn its heroines upside down, from feminine wimps to fighters, as in *Pride and Prejudice*. Jane took library rules and broke them.

As an inveterate visitor to seaside resort towns, Jane was also familiar with the activities of their 'promoters' like Thomas Parker, the hero, or anti-hero, of *Sanditon*. Worthing had its own real-life resort promoter for Jane to observe: Mr Edward Ogle. He became a friend – Jane called him 'sweet Mr Ogle' – and he probably gives certain aspects of his character to *Sanditon*'s energetic and indefatigable Mr Parker.[16] There is something admirable about Mr Parker's relentless, misguided optimism that Sanditon would become a fashionable resort, even in the face of an unenthusiastic public, and in his insistence on the healthiness of the place: 'nobody could catch cold by the sea; nobody wanted appetite by the sea; nobody wanted spirits; nobody wanted strength'.

But Jane really was too ill to finish the story. On 18 March 1817, work stopped, never to be resumed. It would eventually be published, unfinished, in 1925 under the title of *Fragments of a Novel by Jane Austen*. 'I have really been too unwell the last fortnight to write anything', she wrote in April. 'I have been suffering from a Bilious attack, attended with a good deal of fever.'

Once again a stressful event might have brought on a reoccurrence of Jane's illness. Uncle James Leigh Perrot had finally died, his will had been read, and any lingering Austen hopes had been finally dashed. Despite Mrs Austen's wish that 'her younger Childn had more, & all her Childn something immediately', it was now confirmed that he'd left everything to his wife. All his wealth would go to James Austen in due course, except for £1,000 for each of James's siblings (except George). But none of the Austens would see any money until after Mrs Leigh Perrot's own death. For Jane it was all 'too late, too late in the day', and besides, she thought that Mrs Leigh Perrot might well live another ten years. Indeed, as if to spite all her hungry relatives, Mrs Leigh Perrot did indeed cling on to life until she was ninety-two.

At least Mrs Leigh Perrot remained consistently unhappy as well. 'When the Stoneleigh settlement increased our Income,' she wrote in later years, 'Horses & a new Chariot were purchased – but Alas! ill-health was then making the considerable addition of Fortune of less & less use to us.'[17] It was lucky that her sister-in-law and nieces did not hear her complaining that all her money was of no use to her.

Mrs Austen could console herself only with the thought that her brother had expected to outlive her, and that he would have arranged things differently had he known that he would go first. Jane did not take the news well, and she once again made that link between emotional stress and illness. She felt so awful that she actually summoned Cassandra to come home at once from Berkshire, where she'd gone for their uncle's funeral. This, of course, Cassandra did, and then, equally of course, 'either her return, or my having seen Mr Curtis [the doctor], or my Disorder's chusing to go away, have made me better this morning', Jane wrote.

Her uncle's death caused Jane to think about making a will of her own. She wrote one out on 27 April 1817, not troubling to get it witnessed properly. She planned to leave £50 to the feckless Henry and £50 too for Madame Bigeon, the French nurse and housekeeper who had served Henry and before him Eliza for such a long time. I imagine that after the business of the Leigh Perrots' will she thought first of the people who needed the money the most. But after Henry and Madame Bigeon, Jane left everything else she possessed 'to my dearest Sister Cassandra Elizth'.[18] The next month her brother James likewise made a will, leaving money to Henry, Frank, Cassandra and Charles. He neglected his disabled brother George, but also his sister Jane. It indicates that her family now believed that Jane would not live long.

By May, Jane was clearly an invalid. 'I have kept my bed since 13. of April,' she admitted in a letter to her friend Anne Sharpe, 'with only removals to a Sopha.' But her spirit was indomitable: '*Now*, I am getting well again . . . & *really* am equal to being out of bed, but that the posture is thought good for me.'

Her niece Caroline was shocked to discover, on a visit to Chawton, how sick Jane really was, as one wouldn't have detected it from her letters.

> 'She was in her dressing gown,' Caroline wrote, 'sitting quite like an invalide in an arm chair – but she got up, and kindly greeted us – and then pointing to seats which had been arranged for us by the fire, she said, "There's . . . a little stool for *you*, Caroline." It is strange, but those trifling words are the last of her's that I can remember.'[19]

Jane in decline became very conscious of the love of her family all around her. 'Every dear Brother so affectionate & so anxious!' she wrote, 'and as for my Sister! – Words must fail me in any attempt to describe what a Nurse she has been to me . . . I have so many alleviations & comforts to bless the Almighty for!' Like Mrs Smith, Jane looked for good in evil.

The centre of Lyme, seen from Jane's lodgings. The Assembly Rooms, the beach and the walks allowed her to dance, swim, enjoy nature, and loosen up.

Bathers at Lyme Regis. The picture's a spoof on Edmund Burke's idea that the sublime landscape is a like a beautiful woman. The artist undermines the whole idea by showing Burke as a pervert with a telescope (far right).

Jane and her family enjoyed a holiday in Mr Pyne's lodging house in Lyme Regis. There are hints that the mysterious great romance of her life took place here by the sea.

Great Pulteney Street, Bath, as seen from the pleasure gardens where Jane would go in search of greenery during her family's time in Sydney Place.

Jane used to stay with her aunt and uncle in The Paragon, the terrace to the right. Some were sickened by Bath's competitive social scene, and Jane once wrote of the 'white glare' of the city's characteristic stone.

The Austens took their time in choosing this fine townhouse, 4 Sydney Place, as their home in Bath. Jane and Cassandra shared the upstairs back bedroom. But eventually the family realised they couldn't quite afford the rent.

Jane, drawn by her sister Cassandra during these years of living in Bath. It's characteristic that Jane hides her face as she – probably – looks out to sea.

Jane would go with her rich and self-indulgent uncle to drink the waters at Bath's Pump Room. He kept the whole Austen family on tenterhooks about what he'd do with his money.

In 1806 a 'palpable scramble' broke out among Jane's relatives for the inheritance of the magnificent Stoneleigh Abbey estate in Warwickshire.

What Jane actually took away from her stay at sumptuous Stoneleigh was literary inspiration. The chapel is almost identical to the one she invented at Sotherton in *Mansfield Park*.

The Dolphin Hotel in Southampton, where Jane danced at a ball on her eighteenth birthday, and then again when she lived in the town as an unhappy spinster in her thirties.

This prettified image of Jane was an author publicity portrait produced after her death. Her niece described it as a 'pleasing, sweet face', but really not 'much like the original.'

This page, from a part of the manuscript of *Persuasion* that Jane rejected, shows how she worked: confidently, vigorously, and relentlessly seeking perfection.

Jane got enormous pleasure, in her thirties, from her role as confidante to her favourite nieces Fanny (shown here) and Anna. In her letters she gave them bracing advice on love, life and literature.

Fanny ended up living near Jane at the Great House in Chawton, Edward Austen's property just up the road from the cottage that he gave to his widowed mother and sisters.

The cottage at Chawton looks charming in this image painted by Jane's niece Anna, but its proximity to a pond and a busy road made it less than perfect as a home.

A packed Georgian stage-coach. The cottage at Chawton was shaken by the passage of 'Collyer's Flying Machine', the coach that thundered daily between London and Southampton.

The cottage at Chawton was Jane's home for the published phase of her career. Her mother and sister let her off the house-work, allowing her instead to write her novels.

Cassandra Austen, Jane's sister, was the most important person in Jane's life. Dignified in the face of the unexpected death of her young fiancé, Cassandra taught Jane emotional restraint.

The cramped rented flat in the upper part of this house was the sisters' home for the last weeks of Jane's life, chosen because it was near the hospital in Winchester.

34

College Street

'There began to be a <u>hope</u> of,
at least, a <u>respite</u> from death.'

Mrs Austen on her daughter Jane

I T BECAME CLEAR that Jane, 'quite like an invalide', was in need of more specialised medical attention than Chawton could provide.

The local apothecary from Alton 'did not pretend to be able to cope', Jane wrote; 'better advice was called in'. It came from Winchester, 'where there is a Hospital & capital Surgeons', and whither Jane was to go 'for some weeks to see what Mr Lyford can do farther towards re-establishing me in tolerable health'.

The hospital in Winchester, founded in 1736, had moved in 1758 into a fine new building designed by John Wood of Bath. The first such institution outside London, Winchester Hospital had a high reputation, and even attracted medical students from the capital. It was paid for by subscriptions raised from the wealthy. The hospital's wards were for paupers, and admission was also refused to the terminally ill. On both counts, then, Jane could not be admitted to the hospital, but would be nursed privately instead in rented lodgings. Here Giles King Lyford, the hospital's chief surgeon, would pay her visits. This Mr Lyford was also the young nephew of old Mr Lyford of Basingstoke, who had been importunate with Jane at the ball at Manydown Park where she had danced with Tom Lefroy. Certainly Jane's life had come full circle.

James and Mary Austen sent their carriage to take Jane and Cassandra from Chawton to Winchester, and Jane prided herself upon being 'really a very genteel, portable sort of Invalid'. The lending of the carriage was exactly the 'sort of thing which Mrs J. Austen does in the kindest manner!' Jane admitted. One thinks, however, that it was the least that James and Mary Austen could do for their sister, as they were to get the estate of Mrs Leigh Perrot, and she was not.

The journey went smoothly, although Jane in the carriage was distressed by the sight of her brother Henry riding alongside as an escort and getting completely soaked. He 'attended us on horseback', she wrote, 'riding in rain almost all the way', almost as if it were already a funeral cortège.

Jane and Cassandra's lodgings were on the first floor of a house in College Street, now no. 8, a property belonging to a Mrs David. She was among the hospital's patrons, and owned several houses on the street.[1] The lodgings had been discovered and arranged for the sisters by their friend Mrs Heathcote. This was the former Elizabeth Bigg, now living with her own sister Alethea in the Cathedral Close just round the corner.

Jane's very first surviving letter mentions being with both Elizabeth and Alethea at a ball. Friends since their early teens, now all four single women were together once more. Jane and Cassandra had visited Elizabeth and Alethea in Winchester in the Christmas period of 1814, staying in their spacious, gracious red-brick house at no. 12 (modern no. 11) Cathedral Close.[2] And now Elizabeth and Alethea 'made all the arrangements for them, and did all they could to promote their comfort during that melancholy sojourn'.[3]

Like Jane and Cassandra, Alethea had remained unmarried, but Jane must have thought over Elizabeth's different fate with mixed feelings. Alone of the four, Elizabeth had, at thirty-three, made the opposite choice to Jane's, and taken a husband. He was not a dashing young lover, but a man more than twice her age, a cathedral prebendary who had a house in the Close. But Mr Heathcote had promptly and conveniently died, leaving Elizabeth with a son, a name, and a measure of the social consideration that was always lacking to spinsters. It allowed her to sail through middle age enjoying the most powerful status available to Georgian women: that of being a widow, with control over her own life and resources. Did Jane, looking at her friend's pleasant life and her nice big house in the very shadow of the Cathedral, regret having said 'no' so often? Did she ruefully consider that she could now have been offering Cassandra a comfortable home, just as Elizabeth did to Alethea, if she had said 'yes' to the Bigg sisters' brother? By way of compensation, though, these final days would reveal that Jane's friends were *more* than friends. They, and Cassandra, were the family that Jane had chosen for herself.

Life in College Street was very quiet. Jane hardly went out, and had, like Fanny Price, to 'live upon letters' for her knowledge of what was happening among her relatives. She was well pleased with the rooms, although this town-centre rental was a far cry from the spacious country rectory where she had been born. The house reminds one of Fanny Price's birth home in Portsmouth, where the parlour was so tiny that 'her first conviction was of its being only a passage-room to something better', and where 'the smallness of the house and the thinness of the walls brought everything so close to her, that . . . she hardly knew how to bear it'.

Jane's sense of resignation, though, turned 'small' into 'neat'. 'We have a neat little Drawg-room', she wrote of the first-floor chamber with a patched-on bow window overlooking the garden of Dr Gabell. Dr Gabell was the headmaster of Winchester College, to whom James Austen paid school fees for his son James Edward. Constance Hill in 1902 visited the ladies' drawing room, where 'white muslin curtains and pots of gay flowers on the window' lent a 'cheerful' air. 'We almost fancied we could see Miss Austen seated in the window writing', she continued, glancing 'across the high-walled garden, with its waving trees, to the old red roofs of the Close, with the great grey Cathedral towering above them'.[4] Leaving the house and turning right, Cassandra within moments could reach the water meadows, whose autumn mists would inspire Keats to write about the season of 'mellow fruitfulness' when he visited in 1819. Turning left, it was just a couple of steps to John Burden's bookshop, still a bookshop today, which had been patronised long ago by Mr Austen.[5]

Cassandra recorded Jane's opinion of the Cathedral: it was 'a Building she admired so much'. But it was also a building that had fallen asleep. Regency Winchester's population was rising, though the place would never again regain the importance it had held in Saxon times as one of the first towns in Britain. The Cathedral's crypt was now used as a vault for wine, and the medieval castle just a few steps away from Jane and Cassandra's house in College Street had become an informal quarry.[6] In line with a more general stagnation of Anglican worship, the Cathedral's congregation was shrinking. The radical William Cobbett attended a Sunday service in 1830 in this building that can seat more than a thousand people, yet found himself part of a congregation of a mere 'fifteen women and four men! Gracious God!'[7]

To the sisters, the Cathedral was part of the attraction of College Street, but there was no denying that the cramped rooms of their lodgings were the steepest comedown yet. The building after Jane's time would become a well-known pastry-cook's shop. Jane was in fact living the life predicted for her by the author of that miserable book on *Old Maids*: 'having passed the sprightly years of youth in the comfortable mansion of an opulent father, she is reduced to the shelter of some contracted lodging in a country town, attended by a single servant'.[8]

The sisters' lifestyle in these weeks brings to mind nothing so vividly as that of Miss Bates in *Emma*, whose concerns are so small and domestic. At random moments during any conversation, the jabber-mouth Miss Bates is likely to 'fly off, through half a sentence, to her mother's old petticoat. "Not that it was such a very old petticoat either − for still it would last a great while − and, indeed, she must thankfully say that their petticoats were all very strong."'

At some point during these days in Winchester, Jane would write the very last letter of hers that survives. It has been ingeniously pointed out by the critic Carol Houlihan Flynn that in this letter, Jane herself almost *becomes* Miss Bates.[9] She writes of some acquaintances, 'all good humour and obligingness', but mentions their inadequate dress sense, and hopes that they will follow the coming fashion of 'rather longer petticoats than last year'. Those are literally the last words of her last letter − petticoats! It is utterly consistent with the rest of her whole correspondence: tiny, domestic, disparaging. But it also stakes a claim for the importance of these trivial details. They are not beneath her attention, or ours.

Meanwhile Jane and her sister were as close as ever they had been, and 'their sisterly affection for each other could scarcely be exceeded'.[10] 'What I owe to her,' Jane exclaimed, 'and to the anxious affection of all my beloved family.' She confessed that she could 'only cry over it, and pray to God to bless them more and more'. Back in the days when she had been in fine fettle, Jane had written that 'it is a Vile World, we are all for Self & I expected no better from any of us'. But as the end drew near, like many people, she experienced an unexpected state of grace.

On 6 June, Mary Austen came over to Winchester to stay in College Street and to help out. This was the Mary about whom Jane had been so acerbic over the years. But everyone knew that she provided practical, reliable help in a crisis, and she now came 'to make it more cheerful for them, and also to take a share in the necessary attendance'.[11]

And so, at last, Mary and Jane were reconciled. On 9 June, Jane became much worse: 'Mr Lyford thought the end was near at hand, and she beleived <u>herself</u> to be dying'. Under this conviction, we hear, Jane 'said all that she <u>wished</u> to say to those around her', including the words: 'You have always been a kind sister to me, Mary.'[12] Indeed, *in extremis*, Jane's 'sweetness of temper never failed her; she was considerate and grateful to those who attended on her'.[13]

The rest of the family were now getting ready for the end. James Austen wrote to his son at Oxford that he should prepare himself 'for what the next letter <u>may</u> announce', while James's daughter Caroline added, 'I now feel as if I never loved and valued her enough.'[14] Jane was visited by her brothers, even Charles, who came despite the severe illness of his own daughter. On Thursday 19 June, he wrote that he 'Saw her twice & in the evening for the last time in this world as I greatly fear, the Doctor having no hope of her final recovery.'[15]

But then, with one of her illness's cruel upswings, Jane again seemed to get a little better. Mary Austen went home, and Mrs Austen reported that her younger daughter 'continued very cheerful and comfortable, and there began to be a <u>hope</u> of, at least, a <u>respite</u> from death'.[16]

35

A Final Home

'Oh Pray for me.'

Jane Austen's last recorded words

THE CLOSEST PLACE of worship to the sisters' lodgings in College Street was not in fact the Cathedral, but St Swithun's Church, which is situated within the old flint gatehouse protecting the entrance through the ancient city walls. Jane could still enjoy the occasional period of lucidity and creativity, and St Swithun now inspired her.

Jane had encountered St Swithun before. Her parents were married in his church in Bath and her father was buried there too. St Swithun himself died in Winchester, and his remains were moved and reburied in what was then the new Winchester Cathedral on 15 July in the year 971. The story goes that the saint was so angry about the disturbance of his corpse that he caused it to be a day of heavy rain. And so the rainfall of St Swithun's Day became significant: if it were wet that day, tradition decreed that forty days of rain would follow.

On 15 July 1817, St Swithun's Day, Jane wrote a poem expressing the hope that the rain would keep away for the sake of the Winchester Races. Her family were not proud of this last work of her pen, describing it as a 'joke about a dead Saint, & Winchester races, all jumbled up together'.[1]

But by some strange chance, this last known piece of creative writing also contains a bold statement of Jane's power and permanence. She writes in the character of the ancient St Swithun, wielding his control over the weather, yet her words also contain the odd trick of speaking prophetically to us in the future: 'I'll triumph in shewing my powers', Jane says.[2] 'When once we are buried you think we are dead,' she continues, 'But behold me immortal.' Someone – presumably Cassandra – later underlined those words in Jane's manuscript.[3]

She was entirely right. We do indeed behold her immortal. But two days later, on 17 July, Jane's pain returned.

She nevertheless in the last months of her life considered herself blessed. 'If I live to be an old Woman', Jane had written to Anne Sharp before this final decline, 'I must expect to wish I had died now, blessed in the tenderness of such a Family, & before I had survived either them or their affection.'

Jane writes so fondly of her family, but looking at her situation in College Street, it's very striking that her family . . . weren't there. Following Jane's death the Austens claimed her as the daughter of the Rectory, a member of a closed, happy band. But now, despite occasional visits, Jane had no sibling close to hand except for Cassandra. She would never see her mother again. James returned from business in London to Steventon at the start of July, but does not seem to have travelled the sixteen easy miles to say goodbye to his sister. Neither did Frank from Chawton. It was Henry and Charles, Jane's 'particular' little brothers, who did pay farewell visits, but even they did not stay.

Into this void stepped Jane's alternative family, the women celebrated in this book: the single women. There were the Biggses round the corner; there was Cassandra. And the only other member of the whole Austen clan actually to come to live at Winchester and share in the nursing was Mary.

Mary had gone home to Steventon, thinking Jane improved, but now Cassandra asked her to come back again, 'because the Nurse could not be trusted for <u>her</u> share of the night attendance, having been more than once found asleep'.[4] On the face of it, it seems odd that Mary, so often and so snidely criticised by Jane, was the family member who provided the most help. But Mary Austen had been Mary Lloyd, and Mary and Martha Lloyd were second sisters to Jane and Cassandra. So while the men made flying visits, said how sorry they were, and left, the women stuck together and stayed.

James, absent in Steventon, nevertheless kept up with the news, writing to his son that Jane's 'symptoms which returned after the first four or five days in Winchester, have never subsided, and Mr Lyford has candidly told us that her case is desperate . . . with such a pulse it was impossible for any person to last long'.[5]

In College Street, Jane was out of bed between 9am and 10pm, 'Upon the Sopha t'is true'. But she ate her meals with Cassandra 'in a rational way, & can employ myself, & walk from one room to another'. She was still hopeful, telling a friend that 'I have been out once in a sedan-chair, and am to repeat it, and be promoted to a wheel-chair as the weather serves'.

But soon Jane could no longer even write. Now she could only receive love and letters. Fanny Knight was a committed correspondent. 'Never shall I forget', Cassandra later told her, 'the proofs of love you gave her during her illness in writing those kind, amusing letters.' She described how Jane would take each one and 'read it herself, afterwards she gave it me to read & then talked to me a little & not unchearfully of its contents'. But at the same time, 'there was then a languor about her which prevents her taking the same interest in any thing, she had been used to'. One day Cassandra asked Jane if she wanted anything. 'Nothing but death', Jane replied, characteristically quoting the words of Christian from *The Pilgrim's Progress* as her answer.[6] Cassandra surely responded – as the quotation continues – by beginning 'to cry out lamentably'.

On 17 July, Cassandra went out on some small piece of business in the town, and returned to find Jane sinking. Jane herself had sent Cassandra out – 'to do an errand' which she 'was anxious about' – perhaps in the hope that this would spare her sister a deathbed scene. But when Cassandra got home again, Jane was still alive, if only just. Mr Lyford had been called, and had 'applied something to give her ease'. This strong drug, probably morphine, kept Jane in a 'state of quiet insensibility' throughout the night. It was at half-past-four the next morning, 18 July, the very lowest point of the twenty-four-hour cycle, when Jane's crisis came.

Mr Lyford would later say that that he 'supposed a large blood vessel had given way . . . after a four months illness she may be said to have died suddenly'.[7] He would have often said such things, so that his patients' families would have believed their loved ones died unexpectedly, without pain.

The truth was a little different. Jane's death lasted the whole of the short summer night. Throughout it Cassandra 'sat close to her with a pillow in my lap to assist in supporting her head, which was almost off the bed, for six hours'. Fatigue forced Cassandra to let Mary Austen take over until three o'clock, but then she returned to her station. Jane was still alive: 'a slight motion of the head with every breath remaind till almost the last'. Mary Austen's own diary, as practical as her character, records that 'Jane breathed her last ½ past 4 in the Morn. only Cass & I were with her.'[8]

Cassandra would dwell in detail on her sister's death in the accounts of it that she wrote in the following days. Jane 'felt herself to be dying about half an hour before she became tranquil & aparently unconscious', we hear. 'During that half hour . . . she could not tell us what she sufferd . . . some of her words were "God grant me patience, Pray for me Oh Pray for me." Her voice was affected but as long as she spoke she was intelligible.'

Jane's corpse now looked full of peace as it lay on the College Street bed. 'She gave me the idea of a beautiful statue', Cassandra said, with 'such a sweet serene air over her countenance as is quite pleasant to contemplate'. But Cassandra was painting one of those 'pictures of perfection' that the Austen family demanded, and which would perhaps have made Jane herself feel 'sick & wicked'. Who knows what her corpse really looked like? There is no doubting, though, that Cassandra's loving eyes saw a thing of beauty. Cassandra now performed the few final tasks: 'I was able to close her eyes myself & it was a great gratification to me to render her these last services.'

'The most perfect affection and confidence ever subsisted between them', wrote their niece, 'and great and lasting was the sorrow of the survivor when the final separation was made.'[9] Throughout this book Jane's voice has dominated, growling, laughing, teasing, praising. Despite her lower position in the hierarchy between the two of them, Jane has overpowered Cassandra and almost erased her from our story. Cassandra has her slightly unfair reputation for emotional coldness, too. Indeed, after her sister's death, in words that are often quoted against her, she almost boasted of her stoicism: 'I am not at all overpowered & very little indisposed.'

But don't forget that Georgian convention, that belief in the rectitude of resignation, which explains so much about these two women's lives. To me, Cassandra's cold words ring false. It is only with Jane's death that Cassandra now picks up her pen to stab us in the heart with words as moving as any written by her late sister: 'I *have* lost a treasure, such a Sister, such a friend as never can have been surpassed, – She was the sun of my life, the gilder of every pleasure, the soother of every sorrow, I had not a thought concealed from her, & it is as if I had lost a part of myself.'[10]

That should have been Jane's epitaph, not the mealy-mouthed, family-approved statement of her virtues and piety that would end up on her gravestone.

24 July saw Jane moved to her final home in Winchester Cathedral. The funeral was to take place in the morning, because it had to be over before ten o'clock when the Cathedral's service was to begin. As was customary, female relations stayed at home, while Jane's brothers Edward, Henry and Frank did their duty and attended the internment. Curmudgeonly James was represented by his son, because he felt 'that in the sad state of his *own* health and nerves, the trial would be too much for him'.[11] It was therefore a quiet occasion. The Cathedral's Precentor even managed to get the date wrong in the register, reporting it as having taken place on 16 July, when Jane had still been alive.[12]

So, as had been the case lifelong, the brothers went forth, while Cassandra remained at home. She watched from the lodging-house

window as the 'little mournful procession' travelled 'the length of the
Street'. At the end, it turned right, under Kingsgate and into the Cathedral
Close. Then, Cassandra recorded, 'it turned from my sight . . . I had
lost her for ever'.

Jane's memorial stone in the Cathedral, as is well known, made no
mention of her novels. It praised instead 'the benevolence of her heart,
the sweetness of her temper', then – and only then – 'the extraordinary
endowments of her mind'. The cover-up of how extraordinary Aunt
Jane really was had already begun.

Besides commissioning a memorial, the Austen family now had admin-
istrative duties to fulfil. The *Hampshire Chronicle* recorded Jane's death,
sandwiched between reports of a wedding and a robbery.[13] There was
tax to pay. The Stamp Office form, dated 10 September, records that
she had died with £25 'Cash in the House' and £45 'Cash at the
Bankers'.[14] It really wasn't much to show for six world-changing novels.
Cassandra withdrew the £45 from Hoare's bank, and closed Jane's account
there. In her lifetime Jane had earned just over £650 from her writing.
It was obviously an achievement of which she was proud, but it was
meagre compared with other novelists she'd admired such as Frances
Burney (£4,000) and Maria Edgeworth (£11,000).[15] If Jane had lived to
see the fruits of what she'd invested in 'Navy Fives', she'd have enjoyed
just £30 a year. Ironically, that was hardly more than the dressing allowance issued to her by her father in her youth.

Cassandra kept busy with these tasks, but also occupied herself with
keeping Jane alive in memory. 'I know the time must come when my
mind will be less engrossed by her,' she admitted, 'but I do not like to
think of it.' Mrs Austen is curiously absent in all of this, staying put in
Chawton. As Terry Castle has argued, it was Cassandra, all along, who
had been Jane's 'real mother. And to the degree that Austen's fictions
are works of depth and beauty and passionate feeling – among the supreme
humane inventions of the English language – one suspects in turn it is
because she loved and was loved by Cassandra.'[16]

On 28 July 1817, Cassandra sent Anne Sharp a few reminders of her
friend: 'a pair of clasps which she sometimes wore & a small bodkin
which she had had in constant use for more than twenty years'. Such
tiny memory tokens were important in the world of these women with
their limited personal space. Anne had also asked for, and been given, a
lock of Jane's hair, and Cassandra sent one to Fanny too. Martha Lloyd,
Jane's friend and housemate for decades, got her topaz cross, and kept it
to the end of her life.

This giving of the locks of hair gives rise to another twist in the tale of what Jane's fatal illness might have been. In the twentieth century, one such lock of hair made its way into the possession of a pair of Austen enthusiasts, Alberta and Henry Burke. In Austen circles, it is said that they had the hair tested, and discovered that it contained a significant quantity of arsenic.

Poisonous arsenic was an ingredient in all sorts of Georgian medicine, such as Fowler's Solution, a popular tonic invented in 1786. It certainly has powerful properties, and modern medical researchers are once again turning to arsenic as a possible cure for leukaemia. But it still must be handled with great care. Taking a tonic or medicine containing arsenic could bring on bilious attacks, just as Jane had experienced.

Perhaps Jane, suffering from something much milder, was unintentionally poisoned by her doctors.[17]

36

'Was there anything particular about that lady?'

'The most perfect artist among women,
the writer whose books are immortal.'

Virginia Woolf

IN JANE'S LIFETIME, the world had seemed to be opening up for female
novelists to explore. 'British women will rise to immortal celebrity',
predicted Mary Robinson in her *Letter to the Women of England on the
Injustice of Mental Subordination* (1799). Eventually, she claimed, their works
will 'challenge an equal portion of fame, with the labours of their classical *male* contemporaries'.[1] In this she was right. But it would take an
awfully long time, perhaps longer than she could ever have imagined.

On 22 July, an announcement of Jane Austen's death in the *Courier*
newspaper, probably drafted by Cassandra, named her publicly for the
first time as the author of all four novels then published. As well as briefly
stating the bald facts of her authorship, it also stressed with care that Jane
wasn't 'just' a writer, she was also a lady, with manners 'most gentle; her
affections ardent; her candor was not to be surpassed, and she lived and
died as became a humble Christian'.

Jane's brother James claimed her as the family's own in a poetic obituary.
He also – somewhat unconvincingly in the light of the evidence of her
letters complaining about it all – praised her as a housekeeper:

> But to her family alone
> Her real & genuine worth was known:
> Yes! They whose lot it was to prove
> Her Sisterly, her Filial love,
> They saw her ready still to share
> The labours of domestic care.[2]

James continued that the Austen family, of course, were not 'jealous of
fair female fame', even when it sprang up so unexpectedly in their midst.
I believe that any jealousy was defused precisely *because* Jane conscien-
tiously performed 'the labours of domestic care' as best as she could. She

worked hard to ensure that she could not be criticised, as a lady-writer, for shirking her more important lady-duties.[3] And she was successful. James's poem is really saying, yes, she may well have been a great writer. But more importantly, she was still able to rustle up something for dinner.

Still reeling from their year of disasters, the Austen family in general were pretty short of money, and now they saw Aunt Jane's unpublished novels as a resource to be exploited. There is no evidence that Jane herself tried to get them published in the last year of her life, or even fully considered them as finished.[4] But in December *Northanger Abbey* and *Persuasion* were published by John Murray, together, as one bumper edition. He'd paid £500 for the copyright. The joint edition also included a 'Biographical Notice' written by Henry Austen. For the first time, the world could read the story of the life of the author it would come to love a little too late.

But even though people could now discover Jane Austen's name, it was far from well known. Her fame grew only gradually. Some decades after her death, the verger of Winchester Cathedral wondered 'whether there was anything particular about that lady; so many people want to know where she was buried?'[5]

What was to come next? Well, the revival of chivalry epitomised in Sir Walter Scott's work had already started to take root in Jane's lifetime. If you believed that men, even ordinary men, were like chivalric knights, then ladies must be delicate flowers whose honour had to be defended. The idea that women should get back into their homes and stay there, retreating from their Georgian freedoms, was growing dangerously dominant.

But it was Austen's novels, and particularly the combative Lizzy Bennet and Emma Woodhouse, which would open up a rich seam of nineteenth-century female characters who were not afraid to speak their minds. A few years after Charlotte Brontë's *Jane Eyre* came out, another novelist, Mrs Oliphant, described it as a 'declaration of the Rights of Woman'. Charlotte Brontë may not have admired Jane Austen; Jane Austen may not have declared the rights of women quite as loudly or clearly as Brontë would do. But she cleared the way for it to happen.

Jane was right to predict that her literary niece Anna would give up the habit of composition when she took up her new role as a mother. But Anna in old age did write down her memories of her favourite aunt, and her words are read today perhaps more often than any novels of hers would have been.

Meanwhile Fanny Knight, too, eventually did marry, choosing a much older man, and becoming a stepmother. She faced a difficult situation when her eldest stepdaughter eloped to Gretna Green with her own younger brother, and she was annoyed when her aunt Cassandra and cousin Anna sympathised with the young lovers.[6] Fanny had certainly become a prim and proper Victorian ma'am, but this scandal also provides some of the background to her catty remarks about her formerly beloved aunts. Fanny's eldest son became Lord Brabourne, and, having inherited his mother's letters from Jane Austen, published them, and became an authority on Austen family history.[7]

Mrs Austen lived on at Chawton with Cassandra and Martha for another ten years, dividing at her death what was left of her money between all her children except George. Her lucky son, Edward, gave his share to George, who would live to the age of seventy-two. One of his carers attended George Austen's funeral, and certified him in the parish record as a 'gentleman'. As far as we know, none of the Austens were there, and George was buried without a stone in Monk Sherborne churchyard. Cassandra also lived to the age of seventy-two, continuing at Chawton Cottage until 1845, where she was remembered as 'a pale, dark-eyed old lady, with a high arched nose and a kind smile, dressed in a long cloak', who took a 'great interest' in the young girls of the village.

Charles at seventy-four was still on board his ship when he died of cholera. He might not have been as well respected as his brother Frank, but he was sincerely mourned: 'his death was a great grief to the whole fleet. I know that I cried bitterly when I found he was dead.'[8] Frank beat the lot of them to live till ninety-two, having 'lived to attain the very summit of his profession' as Senior Admiral of the Fleet.[9] He still had in his possession that loving letter of advice from his father, George Austen.

James's three, Edward's eleven, Frank's eleven and Charles's eight children meant that there were plenty of people to keep the family name – and the family's cherished image of Aunt Jane – alive and well. Jane was dead, but her novels were beginning to live lives of their own. Novels of romance had existed before Jane wrote, indeed, she lapped up Samuel Richardson and Frances Burney herself. But what she did was to bring romance – the possibility of finding an overwhelming, personal, one-of-a-kind, unique love – into the grasp of ordinary people.

The birth of the novel gets a lot of attention as an artistic creation, and rightly so, for no other form of art has so utterly transformed the way that people thought and felt. For until you had seen such a relationship described by Jane Austen, you did not know that you wanted it. You had other expectations from marriage: security, wealth, children, respect and the comfortable feeling of having satisfied God's requirements of your time on earth. Only with Austen did women begin to think that they wanted – no, needed – to find Mr Darcy. Only with Austen were women's thoughts and feelings beautifully, accurately and amazingly brought to life. Only with Austen did women begin to live as they still live today.

Tom Lefroy lived to old age, and to great success in his career as Chief Justice of Ireland. He certainly survived long enough to begin to realise what extraordinary power must have lurked within the rather ordinary-looking young woman with whom he had danced in Hampshire. Fifty years after Jane's death he would remember, and sometimes speak, 'of his former companion, as one to be much admired, and not easily forgotten by those who had ever known her'.[10]

And in the twentieth century Jane Austen became more famous than ever. Dorothy Darnell was the founder of the Jane Austen Society, now a formidable global network of Janeites. She describes how in 1942 she searched out the 'last living person, I think, who had known someone who had heard people speak of having seen Jane Austen'. Mrs Luff of Alton was over eighty years old in 1942 when Dorothy Darnell spoke to her, but her grandmother as a little girl had 'heard the grown-ups' talking about Jane Austen and her life in Chawton.

What Mrs Luff's grandmother clearly remembered was their description of Jane Austen in the act of 'running across the field to call on her friends'. I like to think that this last, insubstantial image of Jane running through the Hampshire grass in fact shows her running away from all the eager hungry biographers keen to get their teeth into her.

But let her run away from us. Let our final image of Jane be one of speed and power, not lying immoveable upon her unfamiliar bed in the cramped rented upper room in Winchester, but instead running, running across the field to see her friends once again.[11]

Epilogue

What happened to Jane's homes?

IN 1820, HISTORY repeated itself when a new generation of single female Austens were forced out of Steventon Rectory. At the death of James Austen, the living was given to Jane's brother Henry, whose finances dictated that he should have pupils in the house just as his own father had done. Jane's sister-in-law Mary, who'd so joyfully occupied the Rectory at Jane's departure, felt that even nature wept: 'a deluge seemed to come to drive us away . . . one night we were roused by a rush of water pouring into the cellars, with the noise of a cataract . . . the men punted themselves out in a tub'. A week later, having eaten all their meals upstairs, Mary and her daughter Caroline Austen, like Mrs Austen and Jane before them, set off 'about 9 o'clock to make the day's journey to Bath'.[1]

But when the Steventon living came to be held by one of Edward Austen Knight's sons, the old house in the wet valley was no longer good enough, and it was knocked down. Indeed, the whole village was rebuilt on high ground. In 1883, a Steventon resident reported that the Rectory's garden had until only recently still been in feral flower: 'garden flowers used to bloom every season in the meadow where it formerly stood'.[2]

Cassandra never moved away from Chawton. 'The small house and pretty garden', wrote her niece, 'must have been full of memories . . . she read the same books and kept in the little dining-room the same old piano on which her dear sister had played.' This niece, Fanny Caroline, Anna's daughter, remembered, 'when my mother and I were staying with her when I was about seventeen, being greatly struck and impressed by the way in which she spoke of her sister, there was such an accent of *living* love in her voice'.[3]

Chawton itself grew tranquil when the main road was diverted elsewhere. When Cassandra died, her cottage 'was divided into habitations for the poor, and made to accommodate several families'. It reverted to its pre-genteel state: 'trees have been cut down, and all that could be termed pleasure ground has reverted again to more ordinary purposes'.[4] Cassandra and Jane's old manservant, William Littleworth, lived in the village for many decades more, working as a gardener. He eventually gained possession of the little round table at which Jane is said to have done some of her writing. It was from his descendants that it was purchased and returned to Chawton Cottage where it remains today.[5]

In Bath, Green Park Buildings East were bombed, and the Austen house in Trim Street remains unidentifiable, but the house in Sydney Place still stands opposite the elegant Holburne Museum, split into four rentable holiday flats. You can also stay in Pyne House, Lyme Regis, on a similar arrangement. Castle Square, Southampton, was demolished by the time the Ordnance Survey map of 1870 was made, and on its site stands a noisy pub. The cottage in Worthing is a pizza restaurant; Godmersham Park is a college for opticians. But Stoneleigh Abbey still stands serene on the banks of the Avon, rescued from dereliction by the remarkable work of a Trust set up for the purpose. Most of it consists of private flats, but the beautiful state apartments are open and anyone can take a tour, just as Jane did, and peep into the 'chamber fit for a heroine'.

Many of these buildings were visited by the writer Constance Hill and her sister on a pilgrimage to Austen-land in the early years of the twentieth century, and from then on the houses would be more highly valued. In the 1940s, the cottage in Chawton began its extraordinary second life as a shrine to Jane Austen, and Chawton House its life as a library dedicated to women's literature. Both of them are well worth visiting today, and I urge you to go.

Acknowledgements

My thanks go to Rachel Jardine, Pam McIntyre, John Das and Sebastian Barfield and everyone else at BBC Bristol for all our adventures together. I owe a special thank you to my brilliant colleague and collaborator Sally Holloway, and to Lucy Felmingham-Cockburn for excellent research assistance. I'm most grateful to Debbie Charlton and her team for valuable new information about their investigation of Steventon Rectory site, and to Richard Tanner of the North Waltham, Steventon, Ashe and Deane Local History Society. I'd also like to thank Michael Davis and Diana White of the Jane Austen Society of Bath, for showing me the deeds to 4 Sydney Place, as well as Jeanice Brooks, Judith Hawley, Jennie Batchelor, Elaine Chalus and Claire Isaac, the last for her intriguing suggestion about the cause of Mr Austen's death. Claire Harman inspired me to learn more about Frances Burney, while Rebecca Lilley at Godmersham Park, David Eaves, Dorothy Ingle and the Trustees of the Stoneleigh Abbey Charitable Trust, and the staff of the Jane Austen House Museum and Chawton House Library gave all sorts of help. My text has been read and improved by the brilliant and entertaining John Mullan as well as Sally Holloway, and they have both my sincere thanks, and no responsibility for its deficiencies. This book would not exist without the ingenuity of the delightful Maddy Price, and many thanks to Rupert Lancaster, Nick Fawcett and their colleagues at Hodder. I'll always be grateful to Felicity Bryan and her agency. Finally, I dedicate my work, with love, to my very own Mr Knightley, Mark Hines.

Sources

Manuscript sources were consulted at the British Library, Hampshire Archives, Kent History and Library Centre and The Shakespeare Birthplace Trust Record Office.

Books that deserve special mention are, of course, the collected works of Deirdre Le Faye, who has published on many aspects of Jane Austen. Her *Jane Austen: A Family Record* (2004 edition) and her *Chronology of Jane Austen and her Family, 1600–2000* (2013) edition have been vital. All unreferenced quotations in the text come from Deirdre Le Faye's edition of *Jane Austen's Letters* (1995), retaining Jane's own spelling. I have not cluttered the text with date references to the letters as it is such a simple matter to find them. In addition, Kathryn Sutherland's scholarly and rigorous Oxford World Classics edition of *J.E. Austen-Leigh, A Memoir of Jane Austen and Other Family Recollections* (2002) has been absolutely indispensible.

As an introduction to the houses where Jane Austen lived, you can't beat Kim Wilson, *At Home with Jane Austen* (2014). Two essay collections on Jane Austen have stood out for me: Edward Copeland and Juliet McMaster's *Cambridge Companion to Jane Austen* (2011 edition) and Janet Todd's *Jane Austen in Context* (2005). For the wider context, I'm particularly indebted to Malcolm Day, *Voices from the World of Jane Austen*, Cincinnati (2006), Amanda Vickery, *Behind Closed Doors: At Home in Georgian England* (2009) and Roy and Lesley Adkins, *Eavesdropping on Austen's England* (2013). Paula Byrne's unusual biography, *The Real Jane Austen, A Life in Small Things* (2013) is outstanding in a crowded field.

The wonderful project http://www.janeausten.ac.uk/index.html, a joint project of King's College London and the University of Oxford, funded by the Arts and Humanities Research Council, brings high-quality photographs of all Jane's surviving fictional works to your own computer.

I also recommend the writings of the enthusiastic and knowledgeable contributors to the websites of the Jane Austen Society of North America (JASNA), the Jane Austen Centre in Bath's website www.janeausten. co.uk, and the websites 'austenonly', 'Jane Austen's World', 'The Republic of Pemberley', 'Molland's' and Kathryn Kane's 'regencyredingote'.

Bibliography

Abell, Francis, *Prisoners of War in Britain, 1756 to 1815*, London (1914).

Adams, Oscar Faye, *The Story of Jane Austen's Life*, Madison (1891).

Adams, Samuel and Sarah, *The Complete Servant*, London (1825).

Adkins, Roy and Lesley, *Eavesdropping on Jane Austen's England*, London (2013).

Allen, Louise, *Walking Jane Austen's London*, Oxford (2013).

Andrew, Donna, *Aristocratic Vice: The Attack on Duelling, Suicide, Gambling, and Adultery in Eighteenth-Century England*, Yale (2013).

Anon., 'By a Society of Ladies', *The Lady's Monthly Museum*, London (1798).

Anon., *Hampshire Notes and Queries*, vol. 1, Winchester (1883).

Anon., *The New Bath Guide*, Bath (1799 edition); *The Improved Bath Guide*, Bath (1809 edition); *The Original Bath Guide*, Bath (1811 edition).

Ard, Patricia M., 'George Austen's Absence from Family Life: The Shifting Biographical Response', *Persuasions Online*, vol. 34, no. 1 (winter 2013).

Aspinall, A., *Letters of the Princess Charlotte, 1811–1817*, London (1949).

Austen-Leigh, James Edward, *A Memoir of Jane Austen* – see Kathryn Sutherland, ed.

Austen, Caroline, *Reminiscences of Caroline Austen* – see Deirdre Le Faye, ed.

Austen-Leigh, Joan, 'Jane Austen: The French Connection', in *Persuasions*, vol. 20 (1998), pp. 106–18.

Austen-Leigh, Richard Arthur, *Austen Papers, 1704–1856*, Colchester (1942).

Austen-Leigh, William, *Jane Austen, Her Life and Letters: A Family Record*, New York (1914 edition).

Axelrad, Arthur M., *Jane Austen's Sanditon: A Village by the Sea*, Bloomington (2010).

Ayres, James, *Building the Georgian City*, London and New Haven (1998).

Bailey, Joanne, *Parenting in England, 1760–1830*, Oxford (2012).

Bamford, Frances, ed., *Dear Miss Heber*, London (1936).

Barker-Benfield, G.J., *The Culture of Sensibility*, Chicago (1992).

Bearman, Robert, ed., *Stoneleigh Abbey: The House, Its Owners, Its Lands*, Stoneleigh, Warwickshire (2004).

Bence-Jones, Mark, *Clive of India*, London (1974).

Black, Maggie and Deirdre Le Faye, *The Jane Austen Cookbook*, London (1995).

Borowitz, Albert, 'The Trial of Jane's Aunt', in *A Gallery of Sinister Perspectives*, Kent, Ohio (1982), pp. 89–110.

Boyle, Laura, 'The Harp as a Status Symbol' (20 June 2011); https://www.janeausten.co.uk/the-harp-as-a-status-symbol/

Brabourne, Lord Edward, *Letters of Jane Austen* (London, 1884), 2 vols.

Brade-Birks, S. Graham, *Jane Austen and Godmersham*, Ashford Local History Series no. 1, Kent County Council (n.d.).

Brannon, Philip, *The Picture of Southampton, or Strangers Handbook* (Southampton, n.d., early 1840s).

Bree, Linda, Peter Sabor and Janet Todd, eds, *Jane Austen's Manuscript Works*, Toronto (2013).

Breihan, John and Clive Caplan, 'Jane Austen and the Militia', *Persuasions*, no. 14 (1992), pp. 16–26.

Brown, A.J., *Georgian and Victorian Southampton* (Southampton, n.d.).

Brown, H. Rowland, *The Beauties of Lyme Regis*, Lyme Regis (1857).

Brown, Julia Prewitt, *Jane Austen's Novels: Social Change and Literary Form*, London (1979).

Brydges, Sir Egerton, *The Autobiography, Times, Opinions and Contemporaries of Sir Egerton Brydges*, London (1834)

Buchan, William, *Domestic Medicine*, Edinburgh (1794).

Burke, Edmund, *Substance of the Speech . . . In the Debate on the Army Estimates*, London (1790).

Bussby, Frederick, *Jane Austen in Winchester*, Winchester (1973).

Butler, Marilyn, 'Austen, Jane (1775–1817)', *Oxford Dictionary of National Biography*, Oxford University Press, 2004; online edition, Jan. 2010.

Byrne, Paula, *Jane Austen and the Theatre*, London (2002).

——, *The Real Jane Austen*, London (2013).

Campbell, R., *The London Tradesman*, London (1747).

Caplan, Clive, 'Jane Austen's Soldier Brother', *Persuasions*, vol. 18 (1996), pp. 122–43.

——, 'Jane Austen's Banker Brother: Henry Thomas Austen of Austen & co., 1801–1806', *Persuasions* (1998), vol. 20, pp. 69–90.

——, 'The Brewery Scheme is Quite at an End', *Report of the Jane Austen Society* (2010), pp. 92–6.

Castle, Terry, 'Sister-Sister', a review of Le Faye, ed., *Jane Austen's Letters*, Oxford (1995), in *The London Review of Books*, vol. 17, no. 15 (3 August 1995), pp. 3–6.

Chapman, R.W., ed., *The Works of Jane Austen*, vol. VI, *Minor Works*, Oxford (1954).

Clery, E.J., 'Gender', in Edward Copeland and Juliet McMaster, eds, *The Cambridge Guide to Jane Austen*, Cambridge (1997), pp. 159–75.

Colley, Linda, *Britons*, New Haven and London (1992).

Collins, Irene, *Jane Austen and the Clergy*, London (1993).

Copeland, Edward, '*Persuasion*, The Jane Austen Consumer's Guide', *Persuasions*, no. 15 (1993), pp. 111–23.

——, *Women Writing about Money: Women's Fiction in England, 1790–1820*, Cambridge Studies in Romanticism (2008).

——, and Juliet McMaster, eds, *The Cambridge Companion to Jane Austen*, Cambridge (2011 edition).

Dames, Nicholas, *Amnesiac Selves: Nostalgia, Forgetting, and British Fiction, 1810–1870*, Oxford (2001).

Davidson, Hilary, 'Reconstructing Jane Austen's Silk Pelisse, 1812–1814', *Costume*, vol. 49, no. 2 (2015), pp. 198–223. DOI: 10.1179/0590887615Z.00000000076.

Davies, Rev. J. Silvester, *A History of Southampton*, Southampton and London (1883).

Davis, Michael, 'Jane Austen in Bath: 4 Sydney Place', *The Jane Austen Society Report* (1997), pp. 28–34.

Day, Malcolm, *Voices from the World of Jane Austen*, Cincinnati (2006).

Doran, John, *A Lady of the Last Century*, London (1873).

Douch, Robert, ed., *Visitors' Descriptions of Southampton*, Southampton Papers, no. 2 (Southampton, 1961).

Dow, Gillian and Katie Halsey, 'Jane Austen's Reading: The Chawton Years', *Persuasions Online*, vol. 30, no. 2 (spring, 2010).

Downing, Sarah Jane, *Fashion in the Time of Jane Austen*, Oxford (2010).

Edmonds, Anthony, *Jane Austen's Worthing*, Stroud (2013).

Egan, Pierce, *Walks Through Bath*, Bath (1819).

Elwin, Malcolm, *Lord Byron's Wife*, New York (1963).

Emily J. Climenson, ed., *Passages from the Diary of Mrs Philip Lybbe Powys*, London (1899), p. 157.

Englefield, Sir Henry, *A Walk through Southampton*, Southampton (1805).

Feltham, John, *A Guide to All the Watering and Sea-Bathing Places*, London (1813).

Fergus, Jan, *Jane Austen: A Literary Life*, Basingstoke and London (1991).

——, 'The Professional Woman Writer', in Edward Copeland and Juliet McMaster, eds, *The Cambridge Companion to Jane Austen*, Cambridge (2011 edition), pp. 1–20.

Flynn, Carol Houlihan, 'The Letters', in Edward Copeland and Juliet McMaster, eds, *The Cambridge Companion to Jane Austen*, Cambridge (2011 edition), pp. 97–110.

Fowles, John, *A Short History of Lyme Regis*, Lyme Regis Museum (1991).

Freeman, Jean, *Jane Austen in Bath*, Alton (1969).

Fremantle, Anne, ed., *The Wynne Diaries*, Oxford (1935–40).

Galperin, William, *The Historical Austen* (Philadelphia, 2003).

Gay, Penny, '*Emma* and *Persuasion*', in Edward Copeland and Juliet McMaster, eds, *The Cambridge Companion to Jane Austen*, Cambridge (2011 edition), pp. 53–71.

Gillett, Eric, ed., *Elizabeth Ham by Herself 1783–1820*, London (1945), p. 19.

Gillies, John, *Memoirs of Rev. George Whitefield*, Middletown (1839).

Gilpin, William, *Observations on the Western Parts of England*, London (1798; 1808 edition).

Gore, Ann and George Carter, eds, *Humphry Repton's Memoirs*, Norwich (2005).

Granville, Augustus B., *The Spas of England and Principal Sea-Bathing Places*, London (1841).

Gregory, John, *A Father's Legacy to his Daughters*, Boston (1832).

Grover, Christine, 'Edward Knight's Inheritance: The Chawton, Godmersham, and Winchester Estates', *Persuasions Online*, vol. 34, no. 1 (winter 2013).

Hall, Edward, ed., *Miss Weeton: Journal of a Governess*, Oxford (1939).

Halperin, John, 'Jane Austen's Lovers', in *Studies in English Literature, 1500–1900*, vol. 25, no. 4 (autumn, 1985), pp. 719–36.

Hamilton, Alexander, *A Treatise on the Management of Female Complaints*, Edinburgh (1813).

Harman, Claire, *Jane's Fame*, Edinburgh (2009).

Harris, Jocelyn, *A Revolution Almost Beyond Expression*, Newark (1997).

——, 'Pride and Prejudice and Mansfield Park' in Edward Copeland and Juliet McMaster, eds, *The Cambridge Guide to Jane Austen*, Cambridge (1997), pp. 159–75.

Hemlow, Joyce, et al., eds, *The Journals and Letters of Fanny Burney (Madame d'Arblay)*, Oxford (1972–2014).

Herzog, Don, *Poisoning the Minds of the Lower Orders* (Princeton, 1998).

Hett, Francis Paget, ed., *The Memoirs of Susan Sibbald, 1783–1812*, London (1926).

Hill, Constance, *Jane Austen: Her Homes and Her Friends*, London (1902).

Hobhouse, John Cam, *The Wonders of a Week at Bath*, London (1811).

Honan, Park, *Jane Austen: Her Life*, London (1987; 1997 edition).

Hore, Peter, *The Habit of Victory,* National Maritime Museum (2005).

Hubback, John Henry and Edith Charlotte, *Jane Austen's Sailor Brothers,* London (1906).

Hunt, Margaret, *The Middling Sort,* Berkeley (1996).

Huxley, Victoria, *Jane Austen and Adlestrop,* Adlestrop (2013).

Jarvis, Robin, 'Hydromania: Perspectives on Romantic Swimming', *Romanticism,* vol. 21, issue 3, pp. 250–64.

Jeffery, Arthur, *Jane Austen in Southampton,* City of Southampton Society, Southampton (n.d.).

Jenkins, Elizabeth, 'Some Notes on Background', in *Reports,* vol. 3 (1976–85), pp. 152–68.

Jones, Hazel, *Jane Austen's Journeys,* London (2014).

Jones, Tom Beaumont, *The English Heritage Book of Winchester,* London (1997).

Kaplan, Deborah, 'Domesticity at Sea', *Persuasions,* no. 14 (1992), pp. 113–21.

Kaplan, Deborah, *Jane Austen Among Women,* Baltimore and London (1994).

Kelly, Helena, 'Austen and Enclosure', *Persuasions Online,* vol. 3, no. 2 (spring 2010).

Kelly, Sophia, ed., *The Life and Times of Mrs Sherwood,* London (1854).

Keymer, Thomas, '*Northanger Abbey* and *Sense and Sensibility*', in Edward Copeland and Juliet McMaster, eds, *The Cambridge Companion to Jane Austen,* Cambridge (2011 edition), pp. 21–38.

King, Gaye, 'The Jane Austen Connection', in Bearman, ed. (2004), pp. 163–77.

King, Helen, *The Disease of Virgins,* New York (2004).

Kirkham, Margaret, *Jane Austen: Feminism and Fiction,* Brighton (1983).

L'Estrange, A.G., *A Life of Mary Russell Mitford, Related in a Selection from her Letters to her Friends,* London (1870).

Lane, Maggie, *Jane Austen's Family,* London (1984).

——, *A Charming Place: Bath in the Life and Novels of Jane Austen,* Bath (1988).

——, *Jane Austen and Lyme Regis,* Chawton (2003).

Lank, Edith, 'List of Annotations in the Bellas Copy of Lord Brabourne's *Letters of Jane Austen*', *Persuasions Online,* vol. 29, no. 1 (winter, 2008).

Laski, Marghanita, *Jane Austen and her World,* London (1969).

Lathom, F., *The Midnight Bell: A German Story Founded on Incidents in Real Life,* n.p., (1798; 1823 edition).

Laurence, Anne, *Women in England, 1500–1760,* London (1994).

Le Faye, Deirdre, 'Fanny Knight's Diaries: Jane Austen through her Niece's Eyes', *Persuasions Occasional Papers,* no. 2 (1986).

——, ed., *Jane Austen's Letters,* Oxford (1995; 1997 edition).

——, ed., *Reminiscences of Caroline Austen,* Jane Austen Society (1996).

——, 'Mr Austen's Insurance Policy', *The Jane Austen Society Report,* Chawton (1999), p. 26.

——, 'Lord Brabourne's Edition of Jane Austen's Letters', *The Review of English Studies,* New Series, vol. 52, no. 205 (2001), pp. 91–102.

——, *Jane Austen's Outlandish Cousin,* London (2002).

——, *Jane Austen: A Family Record,* Cambridge (2004).

——, *A Chronology of Jane Austen and her Family,* Cambridge (2006; 2013 edition).

——, 'The Austens and the Littleworths', *Jane Austen Society Collected Reports (1986–1995),* pp. 64–9.

——, 'James Austen's Poetical Biography of John Bond', *Jane Austen Society Collected Reports (1986–1995),* pp. 243–7.

Lefroy, Helen and Gavin Turner, eds., *The Letters of Mrs Lefroy: Jane Austen's Beloved Friend*, Winchester (2007).

Lefroy, Thomas, *Memoir of Chief Justice Lefroy*, Dublin (1871).

Lewis, Theresa, ed., *Extracts from the Journals and Correspondence of Miss Berry from the Year 1783 to 1852*, London (1810; 1866).

Libin, Kathryn L., 'Daily Practice, Musical Accomplishment, and the Example of Jane Austen', in Natasha Duquette and Elisabeth Lenckos, eds, *Jane Austen and the Arts*, Lehigh University Press (2014), pp. 3–20.

Long, Bridget, '"Regular and Progressive Work Occupies my Mind Best": Needlework as a Source of Entertainment, Consolation & Reflection', in Alice Dolan and Sally Holloway (eds), *Emotional Textiles* special issue, *Textile: The Journal of Cloth & Culture*, vol. 14, no. 2 (2016), pp. 176–87.

Macdonald, John, *Travels, in various parts of Europe, Asia and Africa*, London (1790).

Macdonald, Mairi, '"Not unmarked by some eccentricities": The Leigh Family of Stoneleigh Abbey', in Bearman, ed. (2004), pp. 131–62.

Malcolmson, A.P.W., *The Pursuit of the Heiress*, Belfast (2006).

Manco, Jean, 'Pulteney Bridge', *Architectural History*, vol. 38 (1995), pp. 129–45.

Mandal, A.A., 'Making Austen Mad: Benjamin Crosby and the Non-publication of *Susan*', *The Review of English Studies*, New Series, vol. 57, no. 231 (2006), pp. 507–25.

Markham, Sarah, 'A Gardener's Question for Mrs Leigh Perrot', *Jane Austen Society Collected Reports (1986–1995)*, pp. 213–14.

Marshall, John, *Royal Naval Biography, or, Memoirs of the Services*, London (1824).

Michaelson, Patricia Howell, *Speaking Volumes: Women, Reading, and Speech in the Age of Austen* (Stanford, 2002).

Mitford, Mary Russell, *The Works of Mary Russell Mitford*, Philadelphia (1846).

——, *Our Village*, Oxford (1982).

More, Hannah, *Strictures on Female Education*, London (1799).

Moritz, Karl Philipp, *Travels in England in 1782*, Bremen (2010 edition).

Morris, Christopher, ed., *Selections from William Cobbett's Illustrated Rural Rides*, Waltham Abbey (1992).

Moss, William, *An Essay on the Management and Nursing of Children*, London (1781).

Mullan, John, *What Matters in Jane Austen* (London, 2012).

Murray, Christopher John, ed., *Encyclopedia of the Romantic Era, 1760–1850*, London (2004).

Nicolson, Nigel, *Godmersham Park, Kent, Before, During and After Jane Austen's Time*, Alton (1996).

Nokes, David, *Jane Austen: A Life*, London (1997).

Norman, Andrew, *Jane Austen: An Unrequited Love* (The History Press, 2009).

Oldfield, John, 'Removing the Myths from Jane Austen and Lyme Regis', *Dorset*, no. 43 (April–May 1975), pp. 6–11.

Oliver, Vere Langford, *The History of the Island of Antigua*, Antigua (1896).

Olsen, Kirstin, *Daily Life in 18th-Century England*, Westport and London (1999).

Oulton, Wally Chamberlain, *The Traveller's Guide; or, English Itinerary*, London (1805).

Parissien, Steven, *George IV: The Grand Entertainment*, London (2001).

Patterson, A. Temple, *A History of Southampton 1700–1914*, Southampton Records Series vol. XI (University of Southampton, 1966).

Pearson, Mowbray, ed., *Flitting the Flakes: The Diary of J. Badenach, a Stonehaven Farmer, 1789–1797*, Aberdeen (1992).

Pevsner, Nikolaus, 'The Architectural Setting of Jane Austen's Novels', *The Journal of the Warburg and Courtauld Institutes*, vol. 31 (1968), pp. 404–22.

Piggott, Patrick, 'Jane Austen's Southampton Piano', *Jane Austen Society Collected Reports (1976–1985)*, The Jane Austen Society (1989), pp. 146–9.

Pinchard, John, *The Trial of Jane Leigh Perrot, taken in Court by John Pinchard*, Taunton (1800); *Grand Larceny, Being the Trial of Jane Leigh Perrot*, Oxford (1937).

Pryme, Jane Townley and Alicia Bayne, *Memorials of the Thackeray Family*, London (1879).

Richardson, Alan, 'Reading Practices', in Janet Todd (ed.), *Jane Austen in Context* (Cambridge, 2005), pp. 397–405.

Roberts, George, *The History and Antiquities of the Borough of Lyme Regis*, London (1834).

Roberts, Warren, *Jane Austen and the French Revolution*, London (1979).

Robinson, John Robert, *The Last Earls of Barrymore, 1769–1824*, London (1894).

Robinson, Mary (writing as Anne Frances Randall), *Letter to the Women of England on the Injustice of Mental Subordination*, London (1799).

Russell, Lord John, ed., *Memorials and Correspondence of Charles James Fox*, London (1853–7).

Sabor, Peter, ed., *The Subscription List to Frances Burney's Camilla*, Montreal (2003).

——, ed., *The Cambridge Edition of the Works of Jane Austen – Juvenilia*, Cambridge (2006).

——, ed., *The Cambridge Companion to Emma*, Cambridge (2015).

Scott, George Ryley, *The Story of Baths and Bathing*, London (1939).

Selwyn, David, ed., *Jane Austen: Collected Poems and Verse of the Austen Family*, Manchester (1996).

——, ed., *The Complete Poems of James Austen, Jane Austen's Eldest Brother*, The Jane Austen Society (2003).

——, *Jane Austen and Children*, London (2010).

Shields, Carol, *Jane Austen*, London (2001).

Silliman, Benjamin, *A Journal of Travels in England, Holland and Scotland*, New York (1810).

Simond, Louis, *Journal of a Tour and Residence in Great Britain During the Years 1810 and 1811*, New York (1815) and Edinburgh (1817).

Smith, E.A., *George IV*, London and New Haven (1999).

Smith, Erin J., 'Dancing in a New Direction: Jane Austen and the Regency Waltz', *Persuasions Online*, vol. 30, no. 2 (spring 2010).

Smith, Lisa, 'The Moon and Epilepsy in the Eighteenth Century', *The Sloane Letters Blog* (23 May 2013); http://www.sloaneletters.com/the-moon-and-epilepsy/

Southam, B.C., ed., *Jane Austen: The Critical Heritage*, London and New York (1979).

Southam, B.C., *Jane Austen and the Navy*, National Maritime Museum (2005 edition).

——, 'Jane Austen and her Readers', *Collected Reports of the Jane Austen Society (1966–1975)*, pp. 76–86.

Spence, Jon, *Becoming Jane Austen*, London (2003; 2007 edition).

——, ed., *Jane Austen's Brother Abroad: The Grand Tour Journals of Edward Austen* (Jane Austen Society of Australia, 2005).

Sutherland, Kathryn, ed., *J.E. Austen-Leigh: A Memoir of Jane Austen and Other Family Recollections*, Oxford (2002).

——, *Jane Austen's Textual Lives*, Oxford (2005).

Takei, Akiko, '"Your Complexion Is So Improved!" A Diagnosis of Fanny Price's "Disease"', *Eighteenth-Century Fiction*, vol. 17, no. 4 (July 2005), pp. 683–700.

Tanner, Tony, *Jane Austen*, Harvard (1986).

Terry, Judith, 'Seen But Not Heard: Servants in Jane Austen's England', *Persuasions*, no. 10 (1988), pp. 102–16.

Todd, Janet, ed., *Jane Austen: New Perspectives*, London and New York (1983).

——, ed., *Jane Austen in Context* (Cambridge, 2005).

Tomalin, Claire, *Jane Austen*, London (1997).

Townsend, Terry, *Jane Austen's Hampshire*, Wellington, Somerset (2014).

——, *Jane Austen and Bath*, Wellington, Somerset (2015).

Troide, Lars E. and Stewart J. Cooke, eds, *The Early Journals and Letters of Fanny Burney*, vol. v, *1782–1783*, Quebec (2012).

Tucker, G.H., *A Goodly Heritage: A History of Jane Austen's Family* (Manchester, 1983).

Turner, Barbara Carpenter, *Winchester*, Southampton (1980).

Uglow, Jenny, *In These Times: Living in Britain Through Napoleon's Wars, 1793–1815*, London (2014).

Upfal, Annette, 'Jane Austen's Lifelong Health Problems and Final Illness: New Evidence Points to a Fatal Hodgkin's Disease and Excludes the Widely Accepted Addison's', *Med Humanities* (2005), vol. 31, pp. 3–11.

Vick, Robin, 'Jane Austen's House at Chawton', *Collected Reports of the Jane Austen Society (1986–1995)*, Chawton (1997), pp. 388–91.

——, 'More on Sophia Sentiment', *Jane Austen Society Report*, Chawton (1999), pp. 15–17.

——, 'Mr Austen's Carriage', *The Jane Austen Society Report*, Chawton (1999), pp. 23–5.

——, 'Steventon Prepares for War', *Jane Austen Society Report*, Chawton (1999), pp. 28–30.

——, 'Deane Parsonage', *Collected Reports of the Jane Austen Society (1986–1995)*, vol. 4, p. 343.

Vickery, Amanda, *The Gentleman's Daughter*, London and New Haven (1998).

——, *Behind Closed Doors*, London and New Haven (2009).

Walker, Linda Robinson, 'Why was Jane Austen Sent Away to School at Seven? An Empirical Look at a Vexing Question', *Persuasions Online*, vol. 26, no. 1 (winter, 2005).

Wall, Cynthia, 'Gendering Rooms: Domestic Architecture and Literary Acts', in Harold Bloom, ed., *Jane Austen* (2009).

Walshe, Natalie, 'The Importance of Servants in Jane Austen's Novels', *Persuasions Online*, vol. 35, no. 1 (winter 2014).

Ward, Valentine, *The Stage: A Dangerous and Irreconcilable Enemy to Christianity*, Aberdeen (1819 edition).

Warner, Jill and Pam Bennett Gupta, *The Bennetts of Lyme Regis, 1762–1911*, Wimborne (1997).

Warner, Richard, *Excursions from Bath*, Bath (1801).

Weigall, Lady Rose, ed., *A Brief Memoir of the Princess Charlotte of Wales*, London (1874).

White, Charles, *A Treatise on the Management of Pregnant and Lying-in Women*, London (1791 edition).

Wilkes, Sue, *A Visitor's Guide to Jane Austen's England*, Barnsley (2014).

Williams, William, *Essay on the Mechanic of Oil Colours*, Bath (1787).

Wilson, Harriette, *The Game of Hearts: Harriette Wilson's Memoirs*, New York (1955 edition).

Wilson, Kim, *At Home with Jane Austen*, New York, London (2014).

Wilson, Margaret, *Almost Another Sister: Fanny Knight, Jane Austen's Favourite Niece,* Kent (1998).

Withers, Tom, ed., Reginald Fitz Hugh Bigg-Wither, *A History of the Wither Family,* Victoria, BC, Canada (2007).

Wrigley, E.A. and R.S. Schofield, *The Population History of England 1541–1871*, Cambridge (1981).

Wrigley, E.A., et al., *English Population History from Family Reconstitution, 1580–1837,* Cambridge (1997).

Wyndham, The Hon. Mrs Hugh, ed., *Correspondence of Sarah Spencer, Lady Lyttelton, 1787–1879,* London (1912).

Notes

Introduction

1. An editorial paragraph by Richard Bentley, reproduced by Henry Austen in his 'Memoir of Miss Austen', in J.E. *Austen-Leigh: A Memoir of Jane Austen and Other Family Recollections*, ed. Kathryn Sutherland, Oxford (2002) p. 154.
2. Fanny Palmer letters, Morgan Library, PML MA4500 A9338.P174 (3), quoted in Deborah Kaplan, 'Domesticity at Sea', *Persuasions*, no. 14 (1992), p. 119.
3. Caroline Austen, 'My Aunt Jane Austen: A Memoir', in Sutherland (2002), p. 174.
4. Henry Austen, 'Biographical Notice of the Author', in Sutherland (2002), p. 137.
5. David Nokes, *Jane Austen: A Life*, London (1997), p. 353.

Chapter 1

1. Sutherland (2002), p. 14.
2. Edward Brabourne, 1st Lord, ed., *Letters of Jane Austen in Two Volumes*, London (1884), vol. 1, pp. 35–6.
3. Sutherland (2002), p. 14.
4. Richard Arthur Austen-Leigh, *Austen Papers, 1704–1856*, Colchester (1942), pp. 64–7, letter from Tysoe Saul Hancock to his wife, Philadelphia Austen Hancock, Calcutta (23 September 1772).
5. Deirdre Le Faye, *A Chronology of Jane Austen and her Family*, Cambridge (2006; 2013 edition), p. 36.
6. Anna Austen Lefroy, quoted in Hampshire Record Office, MS 23M93/85/2, Fanny Caroline Lefroy unpublished Family History (unpaginated).
7. Hampshire Record Office, MS 23M93/85/2.
8. Hampshire Record Office, Deane Parish Register, quoted in Le Faye, *Family Record* (2004), p. 12.
9. *Reading Mercury* (13 June 1768), p. 4, column 2, quoted in Robin Vick, 'Deane Parsonage', *Collected Reports of the Jane Austen Society (1986–1995)*, vol. 4, p. 343.
10. Kent History and Library Centre MS 18M61/BOX/C, bundle of unnumbered documents, Edward Randall to (presumably) Thomas Knight (26 February 1764).
11. Sutherland (2002), p. 21.
12. Ibid., p. 11.

13. Quoted in Le Faye (2004), p. 10.
14. Sutherland (2002), p. 15.
15. For Mary Leigh's novels, see Claire Harman, *Jane's Fame*, Edinburgh (2009), p. 26.
16. Shakespeare Birthplace Trust Record Office, MS 671/677, fols 1–2.
17. *The Lady's Magazine*, London (1808), vol. 39, p. 110.
18. Hampshire Record Office, MS 23M93/85/2.
19. Ibid.
20. Austen-Leigh (1942), pp. 22–4, letter from Rev. George Austen to Mrs Walter, Steventon (8 July 1770).
21. Hampshire Record Office, MS 23M93/85/2.
22. Le Faye (2004), p. 3.
23. Ibid.
24. Ibid., p. 10.
25. Hampshire Record Office, MS 21M65/B4/1/1, fol. 309 Richard Wright, rector 1720–27 (16 August 1725).
26. Ibid.
27. William Cobbett, *Rural Rides*, London (1830), p. 100.
28. Cobbett (1830), pp. 582, 585.
29. Helen Lefroy and Gavin Turner, eds, *The Letters of Mrs Lefroy: Jane Austen's Beloved Friend*, Winchester (2007), p. 81.
30. John Gillies, *Memoirs of Rev. George Whitefield*, Middletown (1839), p. 20.
31. Sutherland (2002), p. 23.
32. Bellas MS, quoted in Le Faye (2004), p. 13.
33. Sutherland (2002), p. 23.
34. Christopher Morris, ed., *Selections from William Cobbett's Illustrated Rural Rides*, Waltham Abbey (1992), p. 84.
35. Deirdre Le Faye, 'Mr Austen's Insurance Policy', *The Jane Austen Society Report*, Chawton (1999), p. 26.
36. Sutherland (2002), p. 23.
37. Anna Lefroy, quoted in Hampshire Record Office, MS 23M93/85/2.
38. Sutherland (2002), p. 23.
39. http://www.bbc.com/news/uk-england-hampshire-20678244
40. Hubback MS, quoted in Le Faye (2004), p. 20.
41. Anna Austen Lefroy, quoted in Hampshire Record Office, MS 23M93/85/2.
42. Mary Lloyd Austen pocketbook, quoted in Le Faye (2013), p. 305.
43. Debbie Charlton, leader of the 2011 Steventon Rectory archaeological investigation, gave me a verbal summary of her findings and showed me several of the finds during a tour of the site in 2016. The results are due to be published as Debbie Charlton, *Archaeology Greets Jane Austen, By Unearthing Her Birthplace and First Home,* Basingstoke (forthcoming).
44. Quoted in *The Gentleman's Magazine,* vol. 222 (1867) p. 150
45. Hampshire Record Office, MS 8M62/14, f. 269v (March 1792).
46. Anna Austen Lefroy, quoted in Hampshire Record Office, MS 23M93/85/2.
47. Collins (1995), p. 65.
48. *The Parliamentary Register*, London (1802), vol. 17, p. 478.
49. Deirdre Le Faye, 'James Austen's Poetical Biography of John Bond', *Jane Austen Society Collected Reports (1986–1995)*, p. 244.
50. Ibid.

51. Ibid., p. 243.
52. Brabourne (1884), vol. I, p. 151.
53. R.W. Chapman, ed., *The Works of Jane Austen*, vol. VI, *Minor Works*, Oxford (1954), p. 129.
54. Austen-Leigh (1942), pp. 24–6, Mrs George Austen to Mrs Walter, Steventon (26 August 1770).
55. Austen-Leigh (1942), pp. 28–30, Mrs George Austen to Mrs Walter, Steventon (6 June 1773).
56. 'Verses to Rhyme with "Rose"', in Selwyn (1996), p. 21.
57. Sutherland (2002), p. 31.
58. Lefroy (2007), p. 40.
59. Sutherland (2002), pp. 186–7.
60. Anna Austen Lefroy, quoted in Hampshire Record Office, MS 23M93/85/2.
61. James Woodforde, *The Diary of a Country Parson, 1758–1802*, Norwich (1999), p. 387 (10 June 1799).
62. Hampshire Record Office, MS 8M62/14 f. 269r (March 1792).
63. Anna Lefroy (20 July 1869), National Portrait Gallery Archive, quoted in Le Faye (2004), p. 21.
64. Hampshire Record Office, MS 23M93/85/2.
65. David Selwyn, ed., *The Poetry of Jane Austen and the Austen Family*, Iowa City (1997), p. 28.
66. Anna Lefroy, National Portrait Gallery Archive, quoted in Le Faye (2004), p. 21.
67. Ibid.
68. Sutherland (2002), p. 23.
69. Austen-Leigh (1942), pp. 24–6, Mrs George Austen to Mrs Walter, Steventon (26 August 1770).
70. Austen-Leigh (1942), p. 72, Tysoe Saul Hancock to Philadelphia Austen Hancock, Calcutta (9 August 1773).

Chapter 2

1. Austen-Leigh (1942), pp. 31–2, Mrs George Austen to Mrs Walter, Steventon (20 August 1775).
2. Walter Johnson, ed., *Gilbert White's Journals*, Boston (1931), p. 115.
3. Johnson (1931), p. 116.
4. Tom Withers, ed., Reginald Fitz Hugh Bigg-Wither, *A History of the Wither Family*, Victoria, BC, Canada (2007), p. 61.
5. Austen-Leigh (1942), pp. 32–3, Rev. George Austen to Mrs Walter, Steventon (17 December 1775).
6. Ibid.
7. Ibid.
8. Ibid.
9. Maria Eliza Ketelby Rundell, *A New System of Domestic Cookery*, Exeter (1808), p. 268.
10. *Reading Mercury*, vol. XXXIX, no. 2048 (27 April 1801), p. 2.
11. Charles White, *A Treatise on the Management of Pregnant and Lying-in Women*, London (1791 edition), p. 131, p. 6.
12. Woodforde (1999), p. 275 (14 January 1792).

13. Austen-Leigh (1942), pp. 32–3, Rev. George Austen to Mrs Walter, Steventon (17 December 1775).
14. Annette Upfal, 'Jane Austen's Lifelong Health Problems and Final Illness: New Evidence Points to a Fatal Hodgkin's Disease and Excludes the Widely Accepted Addison's', *Med Humanities* (2005), vol. 31, pp. 3–11; p. 4.
15. Samuel and Sarah Adams, *The Complete Servant*, London (1825), p. 257.
16. William Moss, *An Essay on the Management and Nursing of Children*, London (1781), p. 44.
17. John Huxham, *The Nurse's Guide*, London (1744), p. 16.
18. Huxham (1744), p. 41.
19. Emily J. Climenson, ed., *Passages from the Diary of Mrs Philip Lybbe Powys*, London (1899), p. 157.
20. Sutherland (2002), p. 23.
21. G.H. Tucker, *A Goodly Heritage: A History of Jane Austen's Family* (Manchester, 1983), pp. 18–19.
22. Sutherland (2002), p. 24
23. Moss (1781), p. 59.
24. Park Honan, *Jane Austen: Her Life*, London (1987; 1997 edition), p. 143.
25. Sutherland (2002), p. 39.
26. Joanne Bailey, *Parenting in England 1760–1830*, Oxford (2012), p. 246.
27. Austen-Leigh (1942), pp. 22–4, Rev. George Austen to Mrs Walter, Steventon (8 July 1770).
28. Henry Austen, 'Biographical Notice of the Author', in Sutherland (2002), p. 139.
29. Ibid.
30. Anna Lefroy, 'Recollections of Aunt Jane', in Sutherland (2002), p. 160.
31. Sutherland (2002), p. 19.
32. Marilyn Butler, 'Austen, Jane (1775–1817)', *Oxford Dictionary of National Biography*, Oxford University Press (2004; online edition, January 2010).
33. Anna Lefroy, 'Recollections of Aunt Jane', in Sutherland (2002), p. 157.
34. Sir Egerton Brydges, *The Autobiography, Times, Opinions and Contemporaries of Sir Egerton Brydges* (London, Cochrane and M'Crone, 1834), vol. 2, p. 41.
35. Anna Lefroy, 'Recollections of Aunt Jane', in Sutherland (2002), p. 160.

Chapter 3

1. Honan (1987; 1997 edition), p. 17.
2. George Austen to Frank Austen, quoted in John Henry Hubback and Edith Charlotte Hubback, *Jane Austen's Sailor Brothers*, London (1906), p. 20.
3. Sutherland (2002), p. 26.
4. David Spring, 'Interpreters of Jane Austen's Social World: Literary Critics and Historians', in Janet Todd, ed., *Jane Austen: New Perspectives*, London and New York (1983), p. 60.
5. Margaret Hunt, *The Middling Sort*, Berkeley (1996).
6. Adams (1825), p. 5.
7. Francis William Austen's *Memoir* of his own life, in the possession of his family, quoted in Le Faye (2004), p. 56.
8. James Austen, *The Loiterer*, no. XXIX (15 August 1789), p. 1.

9. Vere Langford Oliver, *The History of the Island of Antigua*, Antigua (1896), vol. 2, p. 296.

10. Austen-Leigh (1942), pp. 28–31, Mrs George Austen to Mrs Walter, Steventon (6 June 1773), pp. 30–1, Mrs George Austen to Mrs Walter, Steventon (12 December 1773).

11. 'Epistle to G. East Esq.r', in Selwyn (1996), p. 25.

12. Le Faye (2004), p. 45.

13. Caroline Austen, in Sutherland (2002), p. 173.

14. See Warren Roberts, *Jane Austen and the French Revolution*, London (1979), pp. 13–14.

15. Caroline Austen, in Sutherland (2002), p. 173.

16. Quoted in Honan (1987; 1997 edition), p. 74.

17. Hampshire Record Office, MS 23M93/85/2.

18. Austen-Leigh (1942), pp. 132–4, Eliza de Feuillide to Philadelphia Walter, Orchard Street (22 August 1788).

19. Ibid.

20. James Austen, *The Loiterer*, no. 1 (31 January 1789).

21. Christine Grover, 'Edward Knight's Inheritance: The Chawton, Godmersham, and Winchester Estates', *Persuasions Online*, vol. 34, no. 1 (winter 2013).

22. Hampshire Record Office, MS 23M93/85/2.

23. Sutherland (2002), p. 16.

24. Ibid., p. 13.

25. Hampshire Record Office, MS 23M93/85/2.

26. Quoted in Le Faye (2004), p. 44.

27. Ibid., p. 108.

28. Honan (1987; 1997 edition), p. 127; Le Faye (2013), p. 33.

29. Jon Spence, ed., *Jane Austen's Brother Abroad: The Grand Tour Journals of Edward Austen* (Jane Austen Society of Australia, 2005). Spence points out the barbed, Jane-ish qualities of Edward's prose.

30. Quoted in Spence (2007), p. 35.

31. Frank's Memoir, quoted in Le Faye (2004), p. 65.

32. Sutherland (2002), p. 17.

33. Ibid., p. 36.

34. Quoted in Le Faye (2004), p. 65.

35. East India Company's Court Books and Minutes, 1808 and 1810, in Honan (1987; 1997 edition), p. 69.

36. Frank Austen's note of 14 January 1796, quoted in Hubback (1906), p. 29.

37. Uglow (2014), p. 174.

38. Sutherland (2002), p. 17.

39. Jane's niece Fanny Knatchbull, in a letter published in *The Cornhill Magazine*, vol. 163 (1947–9), pp. 72–3.

40. Edward Hall, ed., *Miss Weeton: Journal of a Governess*, Oxford (1939), vol. 1, pp. 6–7.

41. Sutherland (2002), p. 16.

42. Hubback (1906), p. 2.

43. Austen-Leigh (1942), pp. 26–7, Mrs. George Austen to Mrs Walter, Steventon (9 December 1770).

44. Austen-Leigh (1942), pp. 22–4, Rev. George Austen to Mrs Walter, Steventon (8 July 1770).

45. John Andree, *Cases of the Epilepsy, Hysteric Fits, and St Vitus's Dance*, London (1746; 1753 edition), p. 6.

46. Ibid., p. 1.
47. Lisa Smith, 'The Moon and Epilepsy in the Eighteenth Century', *The Sloane Letters Blog* (23 May 2013); http://www.sloaneletters.com/the-moon-and-epilepsy/
48. Andree (1753), pp. 26, 30.
49. Ibid., p. 6.
50. James Austen, *The Loiterer*, no. XXIX (15 August 1789).

Chapter 4

1. Le Faye (2004), p. 10.
2. Hampshire Record Office, MS 23M93/85/2.
3. Bridget Long, '"Regular and Progressive Work Occupies my Mind Best": Needlework as a Source of Entertainment, Consolation & Reflection', in Alice Dolan and Sally Holloway, eds, 'Emotional Textiles' special issue, *Textile: The Journal of Cloth & Culture*, vol. 14, no. 2 (2016), pp. 176–87; 185.
4. Henry Austen, 'Biographical Notice of the Author', in Sutherland (2002), p. 139.
5. *Reading Mercury*, vol. XXXIX, no. 2048 (27 April 1801), p. 2.
6. Caroline Austen, 'My Aunt Jane Austen: A Memoir', in Sutherland (2002), p. 171.
7. Henry Austen, 'Biographical Notice of the Author', in Sutherland (2002), p. 139.
8. Hannah More, *Strictures on Female Education*, London (1799), pp. 20–1; Kathryn L. Libin, 'Daily Practice, Musical Accomplishment, and the Example of Jane Austen', in Natasha Duquette and Elisabeth Lenckos, *Jane Austen and the Arts*, Lehigh University Press (2014), pp. 3–20.
9. *Reading Mercury*, vol. XXXIX, no. 2048 (27 April 1801), p. 2.
10. Ibid.
11. 'Lines written at Steventon', in David Selwyn, ed., *The Complete Poems of James Austen, Jane Austen's Eldest Brother*, Chawton (2003), pp. 70–7, lines 116–18.
12. Sutherland (2002), p. 16.
13. Lord Byron, *Letters and Journals*, ed. Leslie A. Marchand, 13 vols, London (1973–94), vol. 8, p. 15 (6 January 1821).
14. F. Lathom, *The Midnight Bell: A German Story Founded on Incidents in Real Life*, n.p. (1798; 1823 edition), vol. 1, p. 21; vol. 2, p. 35.
15. Hampshire Record Office, MS 8M62/15, f. 102v (1795).
16. Henry Austen, 'Biographical Notice of the Author', in Sutherland (2002), pp. 140–1.
17. Le Faye (1995; 1997), p. 373.
18. Le Faye (2004), p. 58.
19. BL Add MS 59874.
20. Peter Sabor, ed., *The Cambridge Edition of the Works of Jane Austen – Juvenilia*, Cambridge (2006), p. 181.
21. Sutherland (2002), p. 71.
22. Honan (1987; 1997 edition), p. 75.
23. Annette Upfal and Christine Alexander, eds, *Jane Austen's The History of England and Cassandra's Portraits*, University of New South Wales (2009).
24. Jan Fergus, *Jane Austen: A Literary Life*, Basingstoke and London (1991), p. 38.

25. Mrs Austen 'Epistle to G. East Esqr.', in Selwyn (1996), p. 25.
26. Clergyman William Holland (1812), quoted in Roy and Lesley Adkins, *Eavesdropping on Jane Austen's England*, London (2013), p. 65.
27. Quoted in Don Herzog, *Poisoning the Minds of the Lower Orders* (Princeton, 1998), p. 258.
28. More (1799), p. 106.
29. Anon., 'On Female Education', *Quarterly Journal of Education*, vol. 8, no. 16 (October 1834), pp. 214–45; p. 215.
30. Hubback (1906), p. 20.
31. Adams (1825), p. 13.
32. Ibid., p. 14.
33. Eric Gillett, ed., *Elizabeth Ham By Herself 1783–1820*, London (1945), p. 19.

Chapter 5

1. Sutherland (2002), p. 43.
2. Butler (2004; 2010).
3. Anna Lefroy, 'Recollections of Aunt Jane', in Sutherland (2002), p. 160.
4. Linda Robinson Walker, 'Why was Jane Austen Sent Away to School at Seven? An Empirical Look at a Vexing Question', *Persuasions Online*, vol. 26, no. 1 (winter 2005).
5. 'To the AUTHOR of the LOITERER', letter from 'Sophia Sentiment', *The Loiterer*, no. ix (28 March 1789).
6. Louis Simond, *Journal of a Tour and Residence in Great Britain During the Years 1810 and 1811*, Edinburgh (1817), vol. 2, p. 298.
7. Upfal (2005), p. 5.
8. Sophia Kelly, ed., *The Life and Times of Mrs Sherwood*, London (1854), p. 92.
9. Ibid., p. 94.
10. Ibid., p. 91.
11. Ibid.
12. Ibid., p. 98.
13. *The Reading Chronicle* (31 July 2011), 'Mummified hand of St James is returned'.
14. Le Faye (2004), p. 52.
15. John Keay, Julia Keay, Christopher Hibbert and Ben Weinreb, *The London Encyclopaedia*, London (1983), p. 673.
16. *The Lady's Magazine* (1774), pp. 147–8.
17. *The Gentleman's Magazine* (1797), p. 983, quoted in Le Faye (2004), p. 51.
18. Kelly (1854), p. 92.
19. Ibid.
20. Ibid.
21. Edmund Burke, *A Philosophical Inquiry into the Origin of Our Ideas of the Sublime and Beautiful* (1792 edition), p. 174.
22. Francis Paget Hett, ed., *The Memoirs of Susan Sibbald, 1783–1812*, London (1926), pp. 44–5.
23. Kelly (1854), p. 103.
24. Ibid., p. 99.
25. Ibid., p. 103; sale advert in the *Reading Mercury* (24 February 1894).

26. Richard Valpy, ed., *William Shakespeare, The Second part of King Henry the Fourth, altered from William Shakespeare as it was acted at Reading School in October 1801*, Reading (1801).

27. Paula Byrne, *Jane Austen and the Theatre*, London (2002), p. xi.

28. Mr Austen's account, Hoare's Bank 23, f. 117, quoted in Le Faye (2013), p. 108.

Chapter 6

1. Elizabeth Jenkins, 'Some Notes on Background', in *Reports*, vol. 3 (1976–85), pp. 152–68.

2. Jon Spence, *Becoming Jane Austen*, London (2003; 2007 edition), p. 11.

3. TNA IR 1/18/146; Claire Tomalin, *Jane Austen: A Life*, London (1997), pp. 16–17.

4. John Cleland, *Fanny Hill: or, Memoirs of a Woman of Pleasure*, London (2001 edition), p. 101.

5. Ibid., pp. 106, 108.

6. Mark Bence-Jones, *Clive of India*, London (1974), p. 220, Clive to Margaret (24 August, 21 September 1765).

7. Nokes (1997), p. 28.

8. Lefroy (2007), p. 52.

9. Bence-Jones (1974), p. 220, Clive to Margaret (24 August, 21 September 1765).

10. Austen-Leigh (1942), pp. 64–7, Tysoe Saul Hancock to Philadelphia Austen Hancock, Calcutta (23 September 1772).

11. BL Add MS 29125, fols 13–14, Warren Hastings to Hancock, Fort St George (5 November 1769).

12. BL Add MS 29236, fol. 7, Tysoe Saul Hancock to Philadelphia Austen Hancock (10 February 1771).

13. BL Add MS 29236, fol. 9, Tysoe Saul Hancock to Philadelphia Austen Hancock (28 August 1771).

14. Austen-Leigh (1942), pp. 24–6, Mrs. George Austen to Mrs Walter, Steventon (26 August 1770).

15. Austen-Leigh (1942), pp. 73–4, Tysoe Saul Hancock to Philadelphia Hancock, Calcutta (3 September 1773).

16. Sutherland (2002), p. 28.

17. Austen-Leigh (1942), pp. 109–13, Elizabeth de Feuillide to Philadelphia Walter, Paris (7 May 1784).

18. Austen-Leigh (1942), pp. 88–92, Elizabeth Hancock to Philadelphia Walter, Paris (16 May 1780).

19. Ibid.

20. Austen-Leigh (1942), pp. 117–19, Elizabeth de Feuillide to Philadelphia Walter, Guyenne (23 May 1786).

21. Deirdre Le Faye, *Jane Austen's 'Outlandish Cousin'*, London (2002), p. 133, Eliza to Philadelphia Walter, London (13 December 1796).

22. Austen-Leigh (1942), pp. 99–105, Elizabeth de Feuillide to Philadelphia Walter, Paris (27 March 1782).

23. Le Faye (2002), p. 51, Mr Woodman to Warren Hastings (26 December 1781; 7 August 1781).

24. Austen-Leigh (1942), pp. 99–105, Elizabeth de Feuillide to Philadelphia Walter, Paris (27 March 1782).

25. Le Faye (2002), pp. 65–6, Elizabeth de Feuillide to Philadelphia Walter, Château de Jourdan (25 July 1785).

26. Austen-Leigh (1942), pp. 113–17, Elizabeth de Feuillide to Philadelphia Walter, Château de Jourdan (17 January 1786).

27. Le Faye (2002), p. 80, Philadelphia Walter to James Walter (19 September 1787)

28. Le Faye (2004), p. 57.

29. Austen-Leigh (1942), pp. 130–1, Philadelphia Walter to James Walter, Seale (23 July 1788).

30. Ibid.

31. Le Faye (2002), p. 75, Mrs Austen to Philadelphia Walter (31 December 1786).

32. Austen-Leigh (1942), pp. 147–50, Eliza de Feuillide to Philadelphia Walter, Steventon (26 October 1792).

33. Austen-Leigh (1942), pp. 88–92, Elizabeth Hancock to Philadelphia Walter, Paris (16 May 1780).

34. Le Faye (2002), p. 97, Eliza to Philadelphia Walter (7 January 1791).

35. Sutherland (2002), p. 28.

36. Reading Mercury, vol. XXXIX, no. 2048 (27 April 1801), p. 2.

37. Le Faye (2002), p. 80, Philadelphia Walter to James Walter (17 September 1787).

38. Austen-Leigh (1942), pp. 126–8, Eliza de Feuillide to Philadelphia Walter, Orchard Street (16 November 1787).

39. Austen-Leigh (1942), pp. 128–9, Eliza de Feuillide to Philadelphia Walter, Orchard Street (23 November 1787).

40. Anne Fremantle, ed., The Wynne Diaries, Oxford (1935–40), vol. 3, p. 247 (22 February 1806).

41. Quoted in Byrne (2002), p. 25.

42. Valentine Ward, The Stage: A Dangerous and Irreconcilable Enemy to Christianity, Aberdeen (1819 edition), p. 35.

43. Byrne (2002), p. xiii.

44. James Austen, 'Epilogue to the Sultan', in Selwyn, ed. (1996), p. 40.

45. Susannah Centlivre, The Wonder: A Woman Keeps a Secret! n.p. (1747), p. 3.

46. James Austen, 'Epilogue to the Comedy of The Wonder, acted at Steventon 26th: & 28th: December: 1787. Spoken by a Lady in the character of Violante', in Selwyn, ed. (2003), pp. 20–1.

47. Letter from Anna Lefroy, in Sutherland (2002), p. 183.

48. Letter from Caroline Austen, in Sutherland (2002), p. 193.

49. David Tunley, ed., Songs by Henri Reber (1807–1880), Six Romances Populaires (1849), Six Melodies de Victor Hugo (1855), and Five Other Songs by Edouard Lalo (1823–1892), London (2013), p. xliii.

50. Gillett (1945), p. 27.

51. Austen-Leigh (1942), pp. 130–1, Philadelphia Walter to James Walter, Seale (23 July 1788).

52. Sutherland (2002), p. 19.

53. Robin Vick, 'More on Sophia Sentiment', Report of the Jane Austen Society (1999), pp. 15–17; p. 17.

54. Letter of Caroline Austen, in Sutherland (2002), p. 185.

55. Hampshire Record Office, MS 23M93/85/2.

56. Brydges (1834), p. 40.

57. Le Faye (2004), p. 47.

58. Brydges (1834) vol. 2, p. 40.

59. Sutherland (2002), p. 50.

60. Mrs Lefroy's obituary in the *Reading Mercury* (24 December 1804).

61. Brydges (1834), vol. 2, pp. 40–1.

62. Family letter, quoted in Lefroy (2007), p. 8.

63. Lefroy (2007), p. 147.

64. Brydges (1834), vol. 2, p. 41.

65. For example, it was tactless of Sir Egerton to write that 'even the most brilliant abilities are too apt to sink into indolence in the inactivity of the country', in *Arthur Fitz-Albini, a novel*, London (1798), pp. 17–18.

66. Lars E. Troide and Stewart J. Cooke, eds, *The Early Journals and Letters of Fanny Burney*, vol. v, *1782–1783*, Quebec (2012), p. 24 (1782).

67. Harman (2009), p. 33.

68. Jan Fergus, 'The Professional Woman Writer', in Edward Copeland and Juliet McMaster, eds, *The Cambridge Companion to Jane Austen*, Cambridge (2011 edition), p. 2.

69. Mary Robinson (writing as Anne Frances Randall), *Letter to the Women of England on the Injustice of Mental Subordination*, London (1799), p. 95.

70. Peter Sabor, ed., *The Subscription List to Frances Burney's Camilla*, Montreal (2003).

71. Robinson (1799); Jocelyn Harris, *A Revolution Almost Beyond Expression*, Newark (1997), p. 24.

72. You can now find all the *Juvenilia* photographed and transcribed online at the wonderful website janeausten.ac.uk, or else beautifully edited in Peter Sabor, ed., *The Cambridge Edition of the Works of Jane Austen – Juvenilia*, Cambridge (2006), p. 106. See also Linda Bree, Peter Sabor and Janet Todd, eds, *Jane Austen's Manuscript Works*, Toronto (2013).

73. Adkins (2013), p. 61.

74. Harman (2009), p. 14.

75. http://www.janeausten.ac.uk/manuscripts/blvolfirst/Front_(left)_pastedown_(reverse).html

76. http://www.janeausten.ac.uk/facsimile/blvolfirst/iv.html

77. Sutherland (2002), p. 132.

Chapter 7

1. All three are in *Northanger Abbey*; Joan Austen-Leigh, 'Jane Austen: The French Connection', in *Persuasions*, no. 20 (1998), pp. 106–18; p. 110.

2. Penny Gay, '*Emma* and *Persuasion*', in Copeland and McMaster (2011 edition), p. 59.

3. Joyce Hemlow, ed., *The Journals and Letters of Fanny Burney (Madame D'Arblay)*, Oxford (1973), vol. 3, pp. 9–12 (Fanny Burney to Mrs Waddington, 19 September 1793).

4. James Austen, *The Loiterer*, no. IX (28 March 1789).

5. Lord John Russell, ed., *Memorials and Correspondence of Charles James Fox*, London (1853–7), vol. 2, p. 361, to R. Fitzpatrick (30 July 1789).

6. Edmund Burke, *Substance of the Speech . . . In the Debate on the Army Estimates*, London (1790), p. 23.

7. Anna Seward, in *The Gentlemen's Magazine* (spring 1793), vol. 63, part 1, p. 108 (Miss Seward to Miss Williams (17 January 1793).

8. Woodforde (1999), p. 286 (26 January 1793).
9. Quoted in Uglow (2014), p. 28.
10. Francis Abell, *Prisoners of War in Britain, 1756 to 1815*, London (1914), p. 263.
11. Ann Gore and George Carter, eds, *Humphry Repton's Memoirs*, Norwich (2005), p. 118.
12. Helena Kelly, 'Austen and Enclosure', *Persuasions Online*, vol. 3, no. 2 (spring 2010).
13. Hampshire Record Office, MS 21M65 E1/4/2601, Henry Austen to the Bishop of Winchester (5 November 1816).
14. Woodforde (1999), p. 347 (10 May 1796).
15. Quoted in Uglow (2014), p. 32.
16. Clive Caplan, 'Jane Austen's Soldier Brother', *Persuasions*, no. 18 (1996), pp. 122–43.
17. Quoted in Uglow (2014), p. 38.
18. What's said to be 'Jane's' cockade is on display today at Lyme Regis Museum.
19. Austen-Leigh (1942), pp. 168–72, Eliza Austen to Philadelphia Walter, Ipswich (16 February 1798).
20. Austen-Leigh (1942), pp. 130–1, Philadelphia Walter to James Walter, Seale (23 July 1788).
21. Le Faye (2002), p. 104.
22. Austen-Leigh (1942), pp. 138–40, Eliza de Feuillide to Philadelphia Walter, Margate (7 January 1791).
23. Austen-Leigh (1942), pp. 145–7, Eliza de Feuillide to Philadelphia Walter, n.p. (7 June 1792).
24. Austen-Leigh (1942), pp. 123–6, Philadelphia Walter to James Walter, Seale (19 September 1787).
25. Austen-Leigh (1942), pp. 147–50, Eliza de Feuillide to Philadelphia Walter, Steventon (26 October 1792).
26. Austen-Leigh (1942), p. 323, appendix on Comte de Feuillide.
27. Austen-Leigh (1942), pp. 321–3, appendix on Comte de Feuillide.
28. Robin Vick, 'Steventon Prepares for War', *Jane Austen Society Report*, Chawton (1999), pp. 28–30; Hampshire Record Office, MS Q22/1/2/5/10.
29. Lefroy (2007), p. 139.
30. Ibid., p. 144.
31. BL MS 2394, fol. 3, reproduced in Le Faye (2002), p. 155.
32. Patricia M. Ard, 'George Austen's Absence from Family Life: The Shifting Biographical Response', *Persuasions Online*, vol. 34, no. 1 (winter 2013).
33. Le Faye (2004), p. 100.
34. Fanny Caroline Lefroy, daughter of Ben and Anna, recorded these notes in her edition of Lord Brabourne's *Letters of Jane Austen*, vol. 2, p. 100, as published in Edith Lank, 'List of Annotations in the Bellas copy of Lord Brabourne's *Letters of Jane Austen*', *Persuasions Online*, vol. 29, no. 1 (winter 2008).

Chapter 8

1. Austen-Leigh (1942), pp. 141–3, Eliza de Feuillide to Philadelphia Walter, Orchard Street (1 August 1791).
2. Austen-Leigh (1942), p. 144, Eliza de Feuillide to Philadelphia Walter, Orchard Street (14 November 1791).

3. Ibid.
4. Alexander Hamilton, *A Treatise on the Management of Female Complaints*, Edinburgh (1813), p. 29.
5. Carol Shields, *Jane Austen*, London (2001), p. 24.
6. Sutherland (2002), p. 71.
7. Hampshire Record Office, MS 23M93/85/2.
8. Sutherland (2002), p. 27.
9. Ibid., p. 28.
10. The Reverend William Jones, quoted in Collins (1993), p. 30.
11. Pierce Egan, *Walks Through Bath*, Bath (1819), p. 22.
12. Troide and Cooke (2012), p. 64.
13. Hampshire Record Office, MS 71M82/PR3.
14. A.P.W. Malcolmson, *The Pursuit of the Heiress*, Belfast (2006), p. 135.
15. Nokes (1997), p. 156.
16. Austen-Leigh (1942), pp. 158–60, Elizabeth de Feuillide to Philadelphia Walter, n.p. (3 May 1797).
17. Ibid.
18. Ibid.
19. Ibid.
20. Le Faye (2004), p. 199.
21. Hampshire Record Office, MS 23M93/85/2.

Chapter 9

1. E.A. Wrigley, et al., *English Population History from Family Reconstitution, 1580–1837*, Cambridge (1997), p. 143.
2. Adams (1825), p. 16.
3. Austen-Leigh (1942), pp. 168–72, Eliza Austen to Philadelphia Walter, Ipswich (16 February 1798).
4. Austen-Leigh (1942), p. 168, Elizabeth de Feuillide to Warren Hastings, Manchester Square (28 December 1797).
5. Le Faye (2013), p. 203.
6. Sutherland (2002), p. 70.
7. Nokes (1998), p. 246.
8. For a remarkably full analysis of 'Jane Austen's pelisse' see Hilary Davidson, 'Reconstructing Jane Austen's Silk Pelisse, 1812–1814', *Costume*, vol. 49, no. 2 (2015), pp. 198–223. DOI: 10.1179/0590887615Z.00000000076.
9. Sutherland (2002), p. 70.
10. Le Faye (2004), p. 165.
11. Caroline Austen, 'My Aunt Jane Austen: A Memoir', in Sutherland (2002), p. 169.
12. Caroline Austen, in Sutherland (2002), p. 171.
13. Upfal (2005), pp. 4, 6.
14. E.A. Wrigley and R.S. Schofield, *The Population History of England 1541–1871*, Cambridge (1981), p. 254; Deborah Kaplan, *Jane Austen Among Women*, Baltimore and London (1994), p. 26.
15. *The Gentleman's Magazine*, London (1798), p. 168.

16. Kent History and Library Centre, MS U1015 C115/5, Sir Richard Hardinge to Thomas Papillon (5 February n.y.).

17. Deirdre Le Faye, 'The Business of Mothering: Two Austenian Dialogues', *Book Collector* (1983), pp. 296–314; Byrne (2002), p. 27. (NB some scholars dispute whether the dialogues are really by Jane.)

18. Letter of Catherine Hubback, daughter of Frank Austen, in Sutherland (2002), p. 190.

19. Kirstin Olsen, *Daily Life in 18th-Century England*, Westport and London (1999), pp. 36–8.

20. Donna Andrew, *Aristocratic Vice: The Attack on Duelling, Suicide, Gambling, and Adultery in Eighteenth-Century England*, Yale (2013).

21. Henry Fielding, 'Tom Thumb', in *Cawthorn's Minor British Theatre*, London (1806), p. 38.

22. National Maritime Museum, Frank Austen's log of the *London* (27 August 1798), quoted in Honan (1987; 1997 edition), p. 160.

23. William Hayley, 'The Mausoleum', in *Plays of three acts: written for a private theatre*, London (1784), p. 368.

24. Anna Lefroy, 'Recollections of Aunt Jane', in Sutherland (2002), p. 157.

25. Chapman (1954), pp. 113–14.

26. Adams (1825), pp. 66–7.

27. Black and Le Faye (1995), p. 38.

28. 'A Receipt for a Pudding', in Selwyn, ed. (1996), pp. 32–3.

29. Maggie Black and Deirdre Le Faye, *The Jane Austen Cookbook*, London (1995), p. 38.

30. Ibid., p. 36.

31. Hampshire Record Office, MS 23M93/85/2.

32. Austen-Leigh (1942), pp. 248–50, Cassandra Elizabeth Austen to Mrs Whitaker, Chawton (18 August 1811).

33. 'Miscellaneous Observations', p. 1, in Maria Eliza Ketelby Rundell, *A New System of Domestic Cookery*, Exeter (1808).

34. Mary Russell Mitford, *The Works of Mary Russell Mitford*, Philadelphia (1846), p. 49.

35. Linda Robinson Walker, 'Why was Jane Austen Sent Away to School at Seven? An Empirical Look at a Vexing Question', *Persuasions Online*, vol. 26, no. 1 (winter 2005).

36. Deirdre le Faye, 'The Austens and the Littleworths', *Jane Austen Society Collected Reports (1986–1995)*, p. 66.

37. Adams (1825), p. 10.

38. Ibid., p. 12.

39. Natalie Walshe, 'The Importance of Servants in Jane Austen's Novels', *Persuasions Online*, vol. 35, no. 1 (winter 2014).

40. Walshe (winter 2014).

41. Mowbray Pearson, ed., *Flitting the Flakes: The Diary of J. Badenach, a Stonehaven Farmer, 1789–1797*, Aberdeen (1992), p. 155 (15 February 1793).

42. John Gregory, *A Father's Legacy to his Daughters*, Boston (1832), p. 40.

43. James Townley, *High Life Below Stairs: A Farce of Two Acts*, London (1759), p. 44.

44. Anna Lefroy, 'Recollections of Aunt Jane', in Sutherland (2002), p. 157.

45. Constance Hill, *Jane Austen: Her Homes and Her Friends*, London (1902), p. 27.

46. Akiko Takei, '"Your Complexion Is So Improved!" A Diagnosis of Fanny Price's "Disease"', *Eighteenth-Century Fiction*, vol. 17, no. 4 (July 2005), pp. 683–70.

47. Helen King, *The Disease of Virgins*, New York (2004).
48. John Gregory, *A Father's Legacy to his Daughters*, 1774, Boston (1832), p. 23.
49. William Cowper, in *The Connoisseur*, vol. 4, Oxford (1767 edition), p. 226.
50. Robin Vick, 'Mr Austen's Carriage', *The Jane Austen Society Report*, Chawton (1999), pp. 23–5; Le Faye (1995), p. 20 (17–18 November 1798).
51. Hampshire Record Office, MS 23M93/62/2/1a, Mrs Austen to Mary Austen (30 November 1796).
52. Julia Kavanagh, quoted in B.C. Southam, ed., *Jane Austen: The Critical Heritage*, London and New York (1979), vol. 1, p. 10.

Chapter 10

1. Letter of Caroline Austen, in Sutherland (2002), p. 185.
2. Kaplan (1994), p. 157.
3. John Mullan, 'Psychology', in Janet Todd, ed., *Jane Austen in Context* (2005), p. 381.
4. Ibid., p. 382.
5. The Lady's Monthly Museum (1799), quoted in G.J. Barker-Benfield, *The Culture of Sensibility*, Chicago (1992), p. 359.
6. Robinson (1799), p. 90.
7. Tony Tanner, *Jane Austen*, Harvard (1986), p. 75.
8. Hampshire Record Office, MS 8M62/15, f. 65r (5 December 1794).
9. For the role of real estate in Georgian marriage, see Amanda Vickery, *Behind Closed Doors: At Home in Georgian England*, New Haven and London (2009).
10. Cynthia Wall, 'Gendering Rooms: Domestic Architecture and Literary Acts', in Harold Bloom, ed., *Jane Austen* (2009), p. 111.
11. Hampshire Record Office, MS 8M62/15, f. 6r (13 August 1792); f. 103r (29 April 1795).
12. Hampshire Record Office, MS 8M62/14, f. 192r (17 October 1791).
13. Hampshire Record Office, MS 8M62/15, f. 10v (23 July 1792).
14. Anna Lefroy, quoted in Sutherland (2002), p. 213.
15. Hampshire Record Office, MS 8M62/15, f. 101v (2 March 1795).
16. Anna Lefroy, quoted in Sutherland (2002), p. 213.
17. Le Faye (2004), p. 74.
18. Hampshire Record Office, MS 23M93/85/2.
19. Hampshire Record Office, MS 8M62/15, f. 64v (20–30 January 1794).
20. Hampshire Record Office, MS 8M62/14–15; Edward Copeland, '*Persuasion*, The Jane Austen Consumer's Guide', *Persuasions*, no. 15 (1993), pp. 111–23.
21. Hampshire Record Office, MS 8M62/15, f. 65r (4 June 1794).
22. Hampshire Record Office, MS 23M93/85/2.
23. Ibid.
24. Anna Lefroy, 'Recollections of Aunt Jane', in Sutherland (2002), p. 157.

Chapter 11

1. Letter of Caroline Austen, in Sutherland (2002), p. 186.
2. A.G. L'Estrange, *A Life of Mary Russell Mitford, Related in a Selection from her Letters to her Friends*, London (1870), vol. 1, p. 305.

3. Le Faye (2002), p. 89, Eliza to Philadelphia Walter (22 August 1788).
4. Le Faye (2002), p. 95, Eliza to Philadelphia Walter (11 February 1789).
5. James Fordyce, *The Character and Conduct of the Female Sex*, London (1776), p. 14.
6. Austen-Leigh (1942), pp. 147–50, Eliza de Feuillide to Philadelphia Walter, Steventon (26 October 1792).
7. *Reading Mercury*, no. 1617 (14 January 1793), p. 1.
8. *Reading Mercury*, vol. XXXVII, no. 1971 (4 November 1799), p. 2.
9. Austen-Leigh (1942), pp. 273–4, Jane Leigh Perrot to James Edward Austen (6 September 1826).
10. Black and Le Faye (1995), p. 36.
11. *Reading Mercury*, no. 598 (28 June 1773), p. 3.
12. Henry Austen, 'Biographical Notice of the Author', in Sutherland (2002), p. 139.
13. Le Faye, ed. (1996), p. 13.
14. Lefroy (2007), p. 48.
15. http://austenonly.com/2010/07/05/the-interesting-history-of-white-soup
16. Lefroy (2007), p. 30.
17. Thomas Lefroy, *Memoir of Chief Justice Lefroy*, Dublin (1871), p. 13.
18. Brydges (1834), vol. 2, p. 40.
19. Lefroy (1871), p. 7.
20. Samuel Richardson, essay in *The Rambler in Four Volumes*, London (1784 edition), no. 97 (19 February 1751), p. 255.
21. Sutherland (2002), pp. 10–11.
22. Henry Fielding, *The History of Tom Jones, a Foundling*, London (1763 edition), vol. 2, p. 160.
23. Honan (1987; 1997 edition), p. 108.
24. Professor Jeanice Brooks, personal communication. See also her team's research on 'The Austen Family's Music Books', summary at http://www.southampton.ac.uk/music/research/projects/austen_family_music_books.page
25. Quoted in Honan (1987; 1997 edition), p. 107.
26. Quoted in Sutherland (2002), p. 221.
27. Letter of Caroline Austen, in Sutherland (2002), p. 186.
28. Ibid.
29. Spence (2007). Mr Spence carried me a good distance, but finally lost me with his claim that when Jane had a dream about Sir Thomas Williams, it *really meant* that she was still dwelling upon another Thomas, Tom Lefroy.
30. Joan Klingel Ray 'The One-Sided Romance of Jane Austen and Tom Lefroy', *Persuasions Online*, vol. 28, no. 1 (winter 2007).
31. Lefroy (1871), p.14.
32. Ibid., p. 8.
33. Ibid., pp. 14–15.
34. Ibid., p. 22.
35. Ibid., p. 30.
36. Jane Townley Pryme and Alicia Bayne, *Memorials of the Thackeray Family*, London (1879), p. 163.
37. Sutherland (2002), p. 48.
38. Le Faye (2004), p. 278.

Chapter 12

1. Wall (2009), p. 92.
2. Chapman (1954), plate facing p. 242.
3. Henry Austen, 'Biographical Notice', in Sutherland (2002), p. 138.
4. Anna Lefroy, 'Recollections of Aunt Jane', in Sutherland (2002), p. 158.
5. Harman (2009), p. 28.
6. Uglow (2014), p. 142.
7. Henry Austen, 'Biographical Notice of the Author', in Sutherland (2002), p. 11.
8. Ibid., p. 140.
9. St John's College Oxford Library, MS 279. View it online at https://stjohnscollegelibrary.wordpress.com/2014/06/25/jane-and-george-austen-letters-ms-279/
10. Sutherland (2002), p. 105.

Chapter 13

1. Zechariah Cozens, *A Tour Through the Isle of Thanet*, London (1793), p. 253.
2. Christine Grover, 'Edward Knight's Inheritance: The Chawton, Godmersham, and Winchester Estates', *Persuasions Online*, vol. 34, no. 1 (winter 2013).
3. Le Faye, ed. (1996), p. 24.
4. Cozens (1793), p. 253.
5. Hampshire Record Office, MS 23M93/85/2.
6. Quoted in Le Faye (2004), p. 140.
7. Le Faye, ed. (1996), p. 20.
8. Marianne, daughter of Edward Austen, quoted in Hill (1902), p. 202.
9. 'Godmersham Park Library Catalogue' (1818–c.1840), 2 vols, Chawton House Library, Chawton, Hampshire.
10. Gillian Dow and Katie Halsey, 'Jane Austen's Reading: The Chawton Years', *Persuasions Online*, vol. 30, no. 2 (spring 2010).
11. Kent History and Library Centre, MS U.951/C.102/1, E.F.C. Austen to Miss Chapman (20 March n.y.).
12. One set is at Lyme Regis Museum, the other at the Jane Austen House Museum. The two rival sets, both 'said' to be Jane's, illustrate the difficulty in proving which surviving artefacts really were hers; possibly both were.
13. Anna Lefroy, 'Recollections of Aunt Jane', in Sutherland (2002), p. 158.
14. Woodforde (1999), p. 99 (15 April 1778).
15. *Kentish Weekly Post or Canterbury Journal*, no. 2990 (20 September 1808), p. 1.
16. Le Faye (1986).
17. *The Cornhill Magazine*, vol. 163 (1947–9), pp. 72–3.
18. Austen-Leigh (1942), pp. 266–8, Mrs George Austen to Mrs James Austen, Chawton (27 April 1820).
19. Adams (1825), p. 6.
20. Ibid., p. 8.
21. Judith Terry, 'Seen But Not Heard: Servants in Jane Austen's England', *Persuasions*, no. 10 (1988), pp. 102–16.
22. Brabourne (1884), vol. 2, pp. 127–8.
23. Bailey (2012), p. 250.

24. Adams (1825), p. 272.
25. Quoted in David Selwyn, *Jane Austen and Children*, London (2010), p. 78.
26. Mary Wollstonecroft, *Thoughts on the Education of Daughters*, London (1787), pp. 70–1.
27. Le Faye (1986), p. 7.
28. Kent History and Library Centre, MS U951/F24/2 (26 June 1805).
29. Le Faye (2013), p. 324.
30. Gay (2011), p. 61.

Chapter 14

1. Honan (1987; 1997 edition), p. 5.
2. Adkins (2013), p. 245.
3. Quoted in Jones (2014), p. 51.
4. *Reading Mercury* (19 August 1793).
5. Lefroy (2007), pp. 97–8.
6. Richard Southey, *Letters from England; by Dom Manual Alvarez Espriella* (1807; 1836 edition), p. 5.
7. Sutherland (2002), p. 50.
8. Caroline Austen, 'My Aunt Jane Austen: A Memoir', in Sutherland (2002), p. 171.
9. Vickery (1998), p. 11.
10. Letter of Anna Lefroy, in Sutherland (2002), p. 184.
11. Carol Houlihan Flynn, 'The Letters', in Copeland and McMaster (1997), pp. 97–110; p. 100.
12. Reproduced in Chapman (1954), p. 243.
13. Sutherland (2002), p. 27.
14. Ibid., p. 59.
15. Austen-Leigh (1942), pp. 291–2, Jane Leigh Perrot to James Edward Austen (19 January 1835).
16. Honan (1987; 1997 edition), p. 169.
17. Egan (1819), p. 31.
18. Ibid., p. 48.
19. Simond (1815), p. 15.
20. Egan (1819), p. 66.
21. Ibid., p. 68.
22. Ibid., p. 66.
23. Friedrich Graf von Kielmansegge, *Diary of a Journey to England in the Years 1761–1762*, London (1902), p. 121.
24. Elizabeth Canning, quoted in Day (2006), p. 179.
25. Peter Sabor, ed., *The Cambridge Edition of the Works of Jane Austen – Juvenilia*, Cambridge (2006), p. 193.
26. Anon., *The Improved Bath Guide*, Bath (1809 edition), p. 56.
27. 'By a Society of Ladies', *The Lady's Monthly Museum*, London (1798), vol. 1, p. 289.
28. William Rowley, *The Gout Alleviated*, London (1780), p. 38.
29. Egan (1819), p. 56.

30. Christopher Anstey, *The New Bath Guide: or Memoirs of the B-R-D Family*, London (1766 edition), p. 15.
31. John Macdonald, *Travels, in various parts of Europe, Asia and Africa*, London (1790), p. 382.
32. Benjamin Silliman, *A Journal of Travels in England, Holland and Scotland*, New York (1810), vol. 2, p. 24.

Chapter 15

1. Hampshire Record Office, MS 8M62/14, fols 268v–269r (March 1792).
2. *Reading Mercury*, vol. XXXIX, no. 2048 (27 April 1801), p. 2.
3. Hampshire Record Office, MS 23M93/85/2.
4. Sutherland (2002), p. 50.
5. Anna Lefroy, 'Recollections of Aunt Jane', in Sutherland (2002), p. 157.
6. Sutherland (2002), p. 50.
7. Ibid.
8. Letter of Caroline Austen, in Sutherland (2002), p. 185.
9. Hampshire Record Office, MS 23M93/85/2.
10. Ibid.
11. Ibid.
12. Nokes (1997), p. 221.
13. Hampshire Record Office, MS 23M93/85/2.
14. Ibid.
15. Maggie Lane, *A Charming Place: Bath in the Life and Novels of Jane Austen*, Bath (1988), p. 53.
16. Le Faye (2013), p. 256.
17. *Reading Mercury*, vol. XXXIX, no. 2048 (27 April 1801), p. 2.
18. *Reading Mercury*, vol. XXXIX, no. 2068 (14 September 1801), p. 2.
19. Le Faye, ed. (1996), p. 57.
20. Quoted in Le Faye (2004), p. 190.
21. Sutherland (2002), p. 67.

Chapter 16

1. Silliman (1810), vol. 2, p. 24.
2. Sutherland (2002), p. 26.
3. Nokes (1997), p. 122.
4. Anna Austen Lefroy, quoted in Hampshire Record Office, MS 23M93/85/2.
5. Julia Prewitt Brown, *Jane Austen's Novels: Social Change and Literary Form*, London (1979), p. 157.
6. Clive Caplan, 'Jane Austen's Banker Brother: Henry Thomas Austen of Austen & co., 1801–1806', *Persuasions* (1998), no. 20, pp. 69–90; p. 70.
7. Caplan (1996), p. 140.
8. Silliman (1810), vol. 2, p. 24.
9. Simond (1815), p. 16.
10. Ibid., p. 16.

11. Lane (1988), p. 43.
12. Samuel Gale, *Tour Through Several Parts of England . . . Being the Third Volume of the Bibliotheca Topographica Britannica*, London (1705; 1790 edition), pp. 21–2.
13. Tobias Smollett, *Humphrey Clinker*, Edinburgh (1820 edition), p. 47.
14. Christopher Anstey, *The New Bath Guide: or Memoirs of the B-R-D Family*, London (1766 edition), p. 42.
15. John Doran, *A Lady of the Last Century*, London (1873), p. 21.
16. Egan (1819), p. 53.
17. *The Times* (11 December 1799), quoted in Sarah Jane Downing, *Fashion in the Time of Jane Austen*, Oxford (2010), p. 42.
18. Le Faye (2013), p. 300.
19. Frances Bamford, ed., *Dear Miss Heber*, London (1936), p. 71.
20. Egan (1819), p. 51.
21. John Cam Hobhouse, *The Wonders of a Week at Bath*, London (1811), p. 24.
22. *The Bath Chronicle*, vol. 44, no. 2054 (7 May 1801), p. 2.
23. *The Bath Chronicle*, vol. 44, no. 2056 (21 May 1801).
24. Jean Manco, 'Pulteney Bridge', *Architectural History*, vol. 38 (1995), pp. 129–45, p. 130.
25. *The Bath Herald* (15 November 1800), p. 3.
26. Obituary of the Countess of Bath, *The Athenaeum*, London, vol. 4 (July–December 1808), p. 176.
27. Michael Davis, 'Jane Austen in Bath: 4 Sydney Place', *The Jane Austen Society Report for 1997*, pp. 28–34.
28. *Bath Chronicle*, vol. 50, no. 2367 (7 May 1807), p. 3; vol. 53, no. 2529 (9 August 1810), p. 3.
29. Simond (1815), vol. 1, p. 50.
30. Richard Warner, *Excursions from Bath*, Bath (1801), pp. 9–10; Le Faye (2013), p. 265.
31. Lane (1988), p. 35.
32. R. Campbell, *The London Tradesman*, London (1747), p. 104.
33. William Williams, *Essay on the Mechanic of Oil Colours*, Bath (1787), p. 45.
34. James Ayres, *Building the Georgian City*, London and New Haven (1998), p. 226.
35. Anon., *The New Bath Guide*, Bath (1799), p. 45.
36. Austen-Leigh (1942), pp. 174–6, Eliza Austen to Philadelphia Walter, Upper Berkeley St. (29 October 1801).

Chapter 17

1. Austen-Leigh (1942), pp. 174–6, Eliza Austen to Philadelphia Walter, Upper Berkeley St. (29 October 1801).
2. Gillett (1945), p. 44.
3. William Coombe, illustrated by Thomas Rowlandson, *The Tour of Dr Syntax, in Search of the Picturesque: A Poem*, London (1812), p. 48.
4. John Feltham, *A Guide to All the Watering and Seabathing Places*, London (1813 edition), pp. 283–4.
5. Augustus B. Granville, *The Spas of England and Principal Sea-Bathing Places*, London (1841), p. 476.

6. Fanny Burney, *Diary and Letters of Madame D'Arblay*, London (1854), vol. 5, pp. 27–8.

7. Brydges (1834), vol. 2, p. 41.

8. Ibid.

9. 'Remarks on the Coast of Kent' (12 August 1803), quoted in Uglow (2014), p. 363.

10. John Robert Robinson, *The Last Earls of Barrymore, 1769–1824*, London (1894), p. 174.

11. Mrs James Harris (1771), in Robert Douch, ed., *Visitors' Descriptions of Southampton*, Southampton Papers, no. 2, Southampton (1961), p. 17.

12. Sutherland (2002), p. 29.

13. Letter of Caroline Austen, in Sutherland (2002), p. 188.

14. Hampshire Record Office, MS 23M93/85/2.

15. Ibid.

16. Sutherland (2002), p. 192.

17. Edith Lank, 'List of Annotations in the Bellas Copy of Lord Brabourne's *Letters of Jane Austen*', *Persuasions Online*, vol. 29, no. 1 (winter 2008).

18. Norman (2009), p. 118.

Chapter 18

1. Letter of Caroline Austen, in Sutherland (2002), p. 187.

2. Nikolaus Pevsner, 'The Architectural Setting of Jane Austen's Novels', *The Journal of the Warburg and Courtauld Institutes*, vol. 31 (1968), pp. 404–22; p. 406.

3. Tom Withers, ed., Reginald Fitz Hugh Bigg-Wither, *A History of the Wither Family*, Victoria, BC, Canada (2007), p. 115.

4. Ibid., p. 115.

5. Ibid.

6. Caroline, daughter of Mary Austen, quoted in Le Faye (2004), p. 137.

7. Ibid.

8. Ibid.

9. William Hayley, *A Philosophical, Historical and Moral Essay on Old Maids*, London (1786 edition), p. 7.

10. Anne Laurence, *Women in England, 1500–1760*, London (1994), p. 56.

11. Mary Russell Mitford, *Our Village*, Oxford (1982), p. 4.

12. Le Faye, ed. (1986), p. 7.

13. Hayley (1786 edition), p. 8.

14. Hall (1939), vol. 1, p. 178 (17 July 1809).

15. Edith Lank, 'List of Annotations in the Bellas copy of Lord Brabourne's *Letters of Jane Austen*', *Persuasions Online*, vol. 29, no. 1 (winter 2008).

16. Hampshire Record Office, MS 23M93/85/2.

17. Quoted in Le Faye (2004), p. 137.

18. Caroline, daughter of Mary Austen, quoted in Le Faye (2004), p. 137.

19. Lefroy (2007), p. 69.

20. Withers (2007), p. 61.

21. Ibid.

22. Le Faye (2004), p. 137.

23. Caroline, daughter of Mary Austen, quoted in Le Faye (2004), p. 138.

24. E.J. Clery, 'Gender', in Edward Copeland and Juliet McMaster, eds, *The Cambridge Guide to Jane Austen*, Cambridge (1997), pp. 159–75; p. 164.
25. Hayley (1786 edition), p. 13.
26. Hampshire Record Office, MS 23M93/85/2.
27. Louisa Knight, quoted in Jenkins (1989), p. 166.
28. John Halperin, 'Jane Austen's Lovers', in *Studies in English Literature, 1500–1900*, vol. 25, no. 4 (autumn 1985), pp. 719–36; p. 731.
29. Sutherland (2002), p. 157.
30. Ibid., p. 70.
31. Quoted in Vickery (1998), p. 40.
32. Jane Austen, 'To Miss Bigg', in Selwyn, ed. (1996), p. 7.
33. William Austen-Leigh, *Jane Austen, Her Life and Letters: A Family Record*, New York (1914 edition), p. 92.
34. Hampshire Record Office, MS 23M93/85/2.
35. Le Faye (2004), p. 138.
36. Catherine Hubback, daughter of Frank Austen, in Sutherland (2002), p. 191.
37. Caroline, daughter of Mary Austen, quoted in Le Faye (2004), p. 138.

Chapter 19

1. Sutherland (2002), pp. xiii–xlviii.
2. Keymer (2011), p. 29.
3. Ibid., p. 31.
4. Lane (1988), p. 62.
5. A.A. Mandal, 'Making Austen Mad: Benjamin Crosby and the Non-publication of *Susan*', *The Review of English Studies*, New Series, vol. 57, no. 231 (2006), pp. 507–25; p. 513.
6. Hampshire Record Office, MS 23M93/62/2/3/1, Mrs Austen to Mary Lloyd Austen (July 1811).
7. *The New Bath-Directory*, Bath (1805), p. 19.
8. Selwyn (1996), p. 30.
9. Keymer (2011), p. 25.
10. Ibid., p. 26.
11. Mandal (2006), p. 522.
12. Keymer (2011), pp. 24–5.
13. Ibid., p. 22.
14. Ibid., p. 24.

Chapter 20

1. Roberts (1834), p. 180.
2. Feltham (1813 edition), p. 284.
3. Harriette Wilson, *The Game of Hearts: Harriette Wilson's Memoirs*, New York (1955 edition), p. 384.
4. Feltham (1813 edition), p. 284.
5. Hemlow (1972), vol. 1, p. 25, Fanny Burney to Mrs Phillips (8 August 1791).

6. George Roberts, *The History and Antiquities of the Borough of Lyme Regis*, London (1834), p. 163.
7. Wilson (1955 edition), p. 386.
8. Feltham (1813 edition), p. 282.
9. Maggie Lane, *Jane Austen and Lyme Regis*, Chawton (2003), p. 7.
10. John Fowles, *A Short History of Lyme Regis*, Lyme Regis Museum (1991), p. 10.
11. Fowles (1991), p. 17.
12. Roberts (1834), p. 173.
13. Fowles (1991), p. 23.
14. Lane (2003), p. 35.
15. Hemlow (1972), vol. 1, p. 25 Fanny Burney to Mrs Phillips (8 August 1791).
16. Anna Lefroy letter (8 August 1862) at The National Portrait Gallery, quoted in Le Faye (2004), p. 142.
17. Hemlow (1972), vol. 1, p. 25, Fanny Burney to Mrs Phillips (8 August 1791).
18. Wilson (1955 edition), p. 384.
19. Edmund Burke, *A Philosophical Inquiry into the Origin of Our Ideas of the Sublime and Beautiful* (1792 edition), p. 184.
20. Robin Jarvis, 'Hydromania: Perspectives on Romantic Swimming', *Romanticism*, vol. 21, issue 3, p. 250.
21. Wilson (1955 edition), p. 384.
22. Rowland Brown (1857), p. 64.
23. Plan of 1824 at The Lyme Regis Museum, reproduced in Lane (2003), p. 40.
24. Lane (2003), p. 42.
25. Feltham (1813 edition), p. 283.
26. Roberts (1834), p. 183.
27. Hill (1902), p. 143.
28. Advert for J. Hiscott's Boarding and Lodging-House, in Lyme Regis Museum.

Chapter 21

1. Quoted in Lane (1988), p. 73.
2. Sutherland (2002), p. 15.
3. Townsend (2014), p. 52.
4. Le Faye, ed. (1996), p. 6.
5. Sutherland (2002), p. 49.
6. Ibid., p. 50.
7. Lefroy (2007), p. 159.
8. Withers (2007), p. 63.
9. I am much indebted to the medics of Twitter, as this paragraph pools the responses of nine of my followers with medical training.
10. Deirdre Le Faye, *Jane Austen's Letters*, Oxford (1995; 1997 edition), p. 381.
11. Kent History and Library Centre, MS U951/F.24/2, Fanny Knight's diary (27 January 1805).
12. Le Faye (2013), p. 306.
13. Le Faye (2004), p. 146.
14. Quoted in Le Faye (2004), p. 241.
15. Tomalin (1997), p. 175.

16. Vickery (1998), p. 8.
17. Butler (2004; 2010).
18. Austen-Leigh (1942), pp. 234–5, Henry Thomas Austen to Frank Austen, Bath (28 January 1805).
19. Le Faye, ed. (1996), p. 9.
20. Austen-Leigh (1942), pp. 235–6, Henry Thomas Austen to Frank Austen.
21. Austen-Leigh (1942), pp. 234–5, Henry Thomas Austen to Frank Austen, Bath (28 January 1805).
22. Austen-Leigh (1942), pp. 235–6, James Austen to Frank Austen, Steventon (30 January 1805).
23. John Marshall, *Royal Naval Biography, or, Memoirs of the Services*, London (1824), vol. 2 (part 1), p. 278.
24. Ibid., p. 279.
25. Hubback (1906), p. 155; also Southam (2005 edition), p. 95.
26. *The New Bath-Directory*, Bath (1805).
27. Quoted in Townsend (2015), p. 125.
28. Le Faye (2004), pp. 152–3.
29. Hampshire Record Office, MS 23M93/62/2/2, Mrs Austen to Mary Lloyd Austen (10 April 1806).
30. Peter Hore, *The Habit of Victory*, National Maritime Museum (2005), p. 202.
31. Sir Leslie Stephen, ed., entry on Sir Richard Keats (1757–1834) in the (old) *Oxford Dictionary of National Biography*, London (1892), vol. 30, p. 290.
32. Hubback (1906), p. 176.
33. Ibid., p. 175.
34. Kent History and Library Centre, MS U951/F24/1, Fanny Knight's diary (11 October 1804).
35. Horace Walpole and P. Cunningham, eds, *The Letters of Horace Walpole, Earl of Orford* (1877–80), vol. 5, p. 19 (22 October 1766).

Chapter 22

1. Edward Cooper, *Practical and Familiar Sermons*, London (1805).
2. Repton (1840), p. 162.
3. Shakespeare Birthplace Trust, (SBTRO), MS DR18/31/884a, Mary Leigh, MS of Family History of the Leighs of Adlestrop (1788) (p. 27 of transcript version).
4. *The Morning Post*, no. 11,052 (19 July 1806), p. 3.
5. Hampshire Record Office, MS 23M93/85/2.
6. Mairi MacDonald, '"Not unmarked by some eccentricities": The Leigh Family of Stoneleigh Abbey', in Robert Bearman, ed., *Stoneleigh Abbey: The House, Its Owners, Its Lands* (Stoneleigh Abbey, 2004), p. 141.
7. SBTRO, MS DR 671/36, 'Papers concerning the accounts rendered by the committees of the estate of Edward Lord Leigh, a lunatic' (1772–82).
8. Le Faye (2004), p. 155.
9. MacDonald (2004), p. 155.
10. Le Faye (2004), pp. 155–6.
11. SBTRO, MS DR 18/17/32/41.
12. SBTRO, MS DR 18/17/32/52.

13. Ibid.
14. SBTRO, MS DR/18/17/32/53 (30 July 1806).
15. Hampshire Record Office, MS 23M93/62/2/4, copy of a letter from Cassandra Austen to Mary Austen (13 August 1806).
16. Ibid.
17. Ibid.
18. Ibid.
19. Le Faye, ed. (1996), p. 21.
20. Hampshire Record Office, MS 23M93/62/2/4, copy of a letter from Cassandra Austen to Mary Austen (13 August 1806).
21. Nikolaus Pevsner, 'The Architectural Setting of Jane Austen's Novels', *The Journal of the Warburg and Courtauld Institutes*, vol. 31 (1968), p. 408.
22. Le Faye, ed. (1996), p. 22.
23. Ibid.
24. Hampshire Record Office, MS 23M93/62/2/4, copy of a letter from Cassandra Austen to Mary Austen (13 August 1806).
25. Ibid.
26. Ibid.
27. Ibid.
28. Ibid.
29. Lars E. Troide and Stewart J. Cooke, eds, *The Early Journals and Letters of Fanny Burney*, Montreal (2012), vol. 5, p. 23 (1782).
30. Hampshire Record Office, MS 23M93/62/2/4, copy of a letter from Cassandra Austen to Mary Austen (13 August 1806).
31. Ibid.
32. Ibid.
33. Letter in possession of Joan Austen-Leigh, quoted in Gaye King, 'The Jane Austen Connection', in Bearman, ed. (2004), pp. 163–77; p. 173.
34. SBTRO, MS DR18/17/32/150, draft letter from Joseph Hill to Edward Cooper (4 October 1806).
35. Letter in possession of Joan Austen-Leigh, quoted in Gaye King, 'The Jane Austen Connection', in Bearman, ed. (2004), pp. 163–77; p. 173.
36. Harman (2009), p. 57.
37. SBTRO, MS DR 671/56 (1806).
38. SBTRO, MS DR 671/677, Agnes Leigh's memoir of her family (1910), p. 30.
39. Victoria Huxley, *Jane Austen and Adlestrop*, Adlestrop (2013), p. 148.

Chapter 23

1. William Gilpin, *Observations on the Western Parts of England*, London (1798; 1808 edition), p. 352.
2. Feltham (1813 edition), p. 454.
3. Ibid., p. 455.
4. Philip Brannon, *The Picture of Southampton, or Strangers Handbook*, Southampton (n.d., early 1840s), p. 94.
5. Simond (1817), vol. 2, pp. 298–9.
6. Ibid., p. 298.

7. Mrs James Harris (1771) in Douch (1961), p. 16.
8. Feltham (1813 edition), p. 461.
9. Brannon (n.d., early 1840s), p. 16.
10. Feltham (1813 edition), p. 457.
11. Ibid., p. 460.
12. Ibid., pp. 459–60.
13. Patterson (1966), p. 103.
14. Kent History and Library Centre, MS U951/F24/1 (10 October 1804).
15. *Hampshire Chronicle*, vol. XXXII, no. 1664 (20 January 1806), p. 1.
16. Sutherland (2002), p. 65.
17. Brannon (n.d., early 1840s), p. 16.
18. Feltham (1813 edition), p. 452.
19. Sir Henry Englefield, *A Walk through Southampton*, Southampton (1805), p. 28.
20. Adams (1825), p. 62.
21. Simond (1817), vol. 2, pp. 298–9.
22. Lord Glenverbie (1813), quoted in Peter James Bowman, *The Fortune Hunter: A German Prince in Regency England* (2010), p. 24.
23. Arthur Jeffery, *Jane Austen in Southampton*, City of Southampton Society (Southampton, n.d.), pp. 11–12; Bowman (2010), p. 23.
24. Bowman (2010), p. 23.
25. Lord Glenverbie (2013), quoted in Bowman (2010), p. 24.
26. Lord Granville Leveson Gower (first Earl Granville), *Private Correspondence, 1781–1821* (1917), vol. 2, pp. 79, 409.
27. Sutherland (2002), pp. 66–7.
28. It is reproduced in Patrick Piggott, 'Jane Austen's Southampton Piano', *Collected Reports of the Jane Austen Society (1976–1985)*, The Jane Austen Society (1989), pp. 146–9; p. 147.
29. Adams (1825), p. 3.
30. Kent History and Library Centre, MS U951/F24.4 (29 April 1807).
31. Terry Castle, 'Sister-Sister', a review of Le Faye, ed., *Jane Austen's Letters*, Oxford (1995), in *The London Review of Books*, vol. 17, no. 15 (3 August 1995), pp. 3–6; John Mullan, *What Matters in Jane Austen*, London (2012), pp. 24–5.
32. Kent History and Library Centre, MS U951/F24.4 (29 April 1807).
33. Sutherland (2002), p. 17.
34. The Hon. Mrs Hugh Wyndham, ed., *Correspondence of Sarah Spencer, Lady Lyttelton, 1787–1879*, London (1912), pp. 45–6.
35. Austen-Leigh (1942), p. 249, Cassandra Elizabeth Austen to Mrs Whitaker (18 August 1811).
36. *Hampshire Chronicle* (3 June 1807), quoted in Patterson (1966), p. 114.
37. Kent History and Library Centre, MS U951/C106/8 (1807).
38. Kent History and Library Centre, MS U951/F24/5 (10 October 1808).
39. Kent History and Library Centre, MS U951/C107/12 (18 February 1809).
40. Kent History and Library Centre, MS U951/C108/13.
41. Sarah Markham, 'A Gardener's Question for Mrs Leigh Perrot', *Collected Reports of the Jane Austen Society (1986–1995)*, p. 214.
42. William Galperin, *The Historical Austen* (Philadelphia, 2003), p. 38.
43. Le Faye (2006; 2013 edition), p. 347.
44. *The Gentleman's Magazine*, vol. 92, part 1 (London, 1822), p. 91.

45. Ibid.; Patterson (1966), p. 115.
46. Nokes (1997), p. 353.

Chapter 24

1. Selwyn (2003), p. 87.
2. Sutherland (2002), p. 67.
3. Robin Vick, 'Jane Austen's House at Chawton' (1995), *Collected Reports of the Jane Austen Society (1986–1995)*, p. 389.
4. Ibid., p. 390.
5. Caroline Austen, in Sutherland (2002), p. 168.
6. Ibid., p. 167.
7. Hampshire Record Office, MS 79M78/MB211, p. 36 (9 November 1809); p. 61 (2 July 1810).
8. Hampshire Record Office, MS 79M78/MB211, p. 39 (22 October 1809); p. 43 (29 November 1809).
9. Sutherland (2002), p. 69.
10. Caroline Austen, 'My Aunt Jane Austen: A Memoir', in Sutherland (2002), p. 168.
11. *Hampshire Chronicle*, vol. XXVI, no. 1395 (7 July 1800), p. 1.
12. *Hampshire Chronicle*, no. 976 (7 November 1791), p. 2.
13. Washington Irving, *The Works of Washington Irving*, New York (new edition, 1860), vol. 2, *The Sketch-Book*, pp. 234–5.
14. *A Narrative of the Life of Richard Titheridge, a Native of Alresford, Better Known in Winchester and Southampton by the Name of Dickey Dung Prong*, London, John Fletcher (1835), p. 2.
15. *Hampshire Chronicle*, no. 1026 (22 October 1792), p. 3.
16. *The Sporting Magazine*, London (1793), vol. 2, p. 189.
17. Caroline Austen, 'My Aunt Jane Austen: A Memoir', in Sutherland (2002), p. 168.
18. Sutherland (2002), p. 67.
19. Caroline Austen, 'My Aunt Jane Austen: A Memoir', in Sutherland (2002), p. 168.
20. Hampshire Record Office, MS 79M78/MB211, p. 74 (4 April 1811).
21. Le Faye (2004), p. 175.
22. Caroline Austen, 'My Aunt Jane Austen: A Memoir', in Sutherland (2002), p. 165.
23. Hampshire Record Office, MS 23M93/85/2.
24. Nokes (1997), p. 373.
25. Sutherland (2002), pp. 18–19.
26. Caroline Austen, 'My Aunt Jane Austen: A Memoir', in Sutherland (2002), p. 171.
27. Ibid.
28. See, for example, Vickery (2009), pp. 272–3.
29. Woodforde (1999), p. 92 (29 March 1777).
30. Brabourne (1884), vol. 2, p. 365 (26 October 1809).
31. Caroline Austen, 'My Aunt Jane Austen: A Memoir', in Sutherland (2002), p. 172.
32. Ibid.
33. Le Faye, ed. (1996), p. 46.
34. Caroline Austen, 'My Aunt Jane Austen: A Memoir', in Sutherland (2002), p. 168.
35. Hampshire Record Office, MS 23M93/85/2.
36. *Reading Mercury*, vol. XXXIX, no. 2048 (27 April 1801), p. 2.

37. Le Faye (2004), p. 218.
38. Le Faye (1995; 1997 edition), p. 176.
39. Jones (2014), p. 32.
40. Hall (1936), vol. 1, p. 126 (14 November 1808).
41. L'Estrange (1870), vol. 1, p. 305.
42. Le Faye (2004), p. 199.
43. Anna Lefroy, 'Recollections of Aunt Jane', in Sutherland (2002), p. 158.
44. Caroline Austen, 'My Aunt Jane Austen: A Memoir', in Sutherland (2002), p. 169.
45. Louisa Knight, quoted in Jenkins (1989), p. 166.
46. Le Faye (2004), p. 199.
47. Quoted in Sutherland (2002), p. xlvi.

Chapter 25

1. Henry Austen, 'Biographical Notice of the Author', in Sutherland (2002), p. 140.
2. Fergus (1991), p. 131.
3. Harman (2009), p. 38.
4. Fergus (2011), p. 9.
5. Ibid., p. 7.
6. Jan Fergus, 'Composition and Publication', pp. 1–16, in Peter Sabor, ed., *The Cambridge Companion to Emma*, Cambridge (2015), p. 6.
7. Kathryn Kayne, https://regencyredingote.wordpress.com/2011/10/07/the-making-of-regency-books
8. Jane Austen, 'When stretch'd up on one's bed', in Selwyn, ed. (1996), p. 15.
9. Le Faye (2004), p. 189.
10. Letter of D.G. Boyle, in Sutherland (2002), p. 196.
11. Harman (2009), p. 53.
12. Hampshire Record Office, MS 23M93/85/2.
13. Fergus (2011 edition), p. 3.
14. Bronte Parsonage Museum, MS BSIXSou.1837-03-12.
15. Henry Austen, 'Biographical Notice of the Author', in Sutherland (2002), p. 140.
16. Austen-Leigh (1942), pp. 264–6, Mrs George Austen to Jane Leigh Perrot (4 January 1820).
17. Caroline Austen, 'My Aunt Jane Austen: A Memoir', in Sutherland (2002), p. 165.
18. Brian Southam, 'Jane Austen and her Readers', *Collected Reports of the Jane Austen Society (1966–1975)*, p. 84.
19. Clery (1997), pp. 159–75.
20. Kaplan (1994), p. 198.

Chapter 26

1. Sutherland (2002), p. 81.
2. Marianne, daughter of Edward, quoted in Hill (1902), p. 202.
3. Le Faye (2004), p. 241.
4. Sutherland (2002), p. 81.
5. Ibid., p. 82.

6. Caroline Austen, 'My Aunt Jane Austen: A Memoir', in Sutherland (2002), p. 173.

7. Ibid., p. 171.

8. Sutherland (2002), p. xvi.

9. See fantastic photos of the original, BL MS Egerton 3038, online at http://www.janeausten.ac.uk/facsimile/blpers/index.html

10. Sutherland (2002), p. 79.

11. Le Faye (2004), p. 190.

12. Spence (2007 edition), p. 191.

13. Sutherland (2002), p. xli.

14. Ibid.

15. The original is in The Morgan Library and Museum New York, MS MA 1034.1.

16. Sutherland (2002), pp. 98–9.

17. L'Estrange (1870), vol. 1, p. 300.

18. Southam (1979), vol. 1, p. 6.

19. *The British Critic*, London (March 1818), n.s., vol. 9, pp. 296–7.

20. Charlotte Brontë to George Henry Lewes (12 January 1848) in George Henry Lewes, 'A Word about *Tom Jones*', in *Blackwood's Edinburgh Magazine*, vol. 87 (March, 1860), pp. 331–41.

21. Virginia Woolf, *A Room of One's Own*, London (1929), pp. 101–2, 104.

22. Le Faye (2002), p. 128, Eliza to Philadelphia Walter (7 November 1796).

23. Henry Austen, 'Biographical Notice of the Author', in Sutherland (2002), pp. 139–40.

24. Caroline Austen, 'My Aunt Jane Austen: A Memoir', in Sutherland (2002), p. 174.

25. Reverend F.W. Fowle to Caroline Austen (9 January 1870) in Sutherland (2002), p. 194.

26. Alan Richardson, 'Reading Practices', in Todd, ed. (2005), pp. 397–405 (p. 403); Patricia Howell Michaelson, *Speaking Volumes: Women, Reading, and Speech in the Age of Austen* (Stanford, 2002), pp. 180–215.

27. Annabella Milbanke to her mother (1 May 1813), quoted in Malcolm Elwin, *Lord Byron's Wife*, New York (1963), p. 159.

28. L'Estrange (1870), vol. 1, p. 305.

29. Sutherland (2002), p. 10.

30. Caroline Austen, 'My Aunt Jane Austen: A Memoir', in Sutherland (2002), p. 169.

31. Ibid., p. 174.

Chapter 27

1. Jenkins (1989), p. 168.

2. Kent History and Library Centre, MS U951/F24/9, Fanny Knight's diary, written on the notes side of the journal spanning 6–8 December 1812.

3. Kent History and Library Centre, MS U951/C106/7 (30 August 1807).

4. http://www.chawtonhouse.org/?page_id=55548

5. Terry Townsend, *Jane Austen's Hampshire*, Wellington, Somerset (2014), p. 132.

6. Kent History and Library Centre, MS U951/C106/7, Fanny Knight to Miss Chapman (30 August 1807).

7. Kent Library and History Centre, MS U951/F24/4 (23 September 1807).

8. Kent Library and History Centre, MS U951/F24/10 (21 April 1813).

9. Caroline Austen, 'My Aunt Jane Austen: A Memoir', in Sutherland (2002), p. 165.
10. John White of Chawton, quoted in George Holbert Tucker, *A History of Jane Austen's Family*, Sutton (1998), p. 164.
11. Le Faye, 'The Austens and the Littleworths', *Collected Reports of the Jane Austen Society (1986–1995)*, p. 67.
12. Quoted in Le Faye (2004), p. 202.
13. *The Cornhill Magazine*, vol. 163 (1947–9), pp. 72–3.
14. Le Faye (2004), p. 211.
15. Hampshire Record Office, MS 23M93/85/2.
16. Theresa Lewis, ed., *Extracts from the Journals and Correspondence of Miss Berry from the Year 1783 to 1852*, London (1866 edition), vol. 3, p. 332 (16 March 1823).
17. Le Faye (2004), p. 199.
18. Le Faye, ed. (1996), p. 27.
19. Adams (1825), p. 41.
20. Le Faye, ed. (1996), p. 21.
21. Lewis (1865 edition), vol. 2, p. 434 (1810).
22. Spence (2007 edition), p. 171.
23. Quoted in Le Faye (2004), p. 259.
24. Roberts (1979), p. 206.
25. Jocelyn Harris, 'Pride and Prejudice and Mansfield Park' in Edward Copeland and Juliet McMaster, eds, *The Cambridge Guide to Jane Austen*, Cambridge (1997), pp. 159–75, 47.
26. Byrne (2002), p. 39.
27. Paula Byrne, *The Real Jane Austen: A Life in Small Things*, London (2013), p. 222.
28. Ibid, p. 25.
29. See Nicholas Dames, *Amnesiac Selves: Nostalgia, Forgetting, and British Fiction, 1810–1870*, Oxford (2001), p. 64.
30. Spence (2007 edition), p. 191.
31. Jenkins (1989), p. 166.

Chapter 28

1. Hampshire Record Office, MS 23M93/85/2.
2. Le Faye (2004), p. 111.
3. Kent History and Library Centre, MS U951/F24/10 (15 May 1813).
4. Prewitt Brown (1979), p. 158.
5. Anna Lefroy, 'Recollections of Aunt Jane', in Sutherland (2002), p. 159.
6. Kent History and Library Centre, MS U951/ F24/2 (5 July 1805).
7. Hampshire Record Office, MS 23M93/85/2.
8. Quoted in R.W. Chapman, ed., *Jane Austen's Letters to Her Sister Cassandra and Others* (Oxford, 1959 edition), p. 568.
9. Kent History and Library Centre, MS U951/ F24/7 (13 February 1810).
10. Kent History and Library Centre, MS U951/ F24/7 (17 February 1810).
11. Kent History and Library Centre, MS U951/ F24/7 (20 February 1810).
12. Kent History and Library Centre, MS U951/C106/2, Fanny Knight to Miss Chapman (15 March 1807).

13. Anna Austen Lefroy 'On Reading a Letter' (December 1809) in Selwyn, ed. (1996), p. 57.
14. Kent History and Library Centre, MS U951/C107/15.
15. Kent History and Library Centre, MS U951/ F24/7 (1 May 1810).
16. Kent History and Library Centre, MS U951/ F24/7 (4 May 1810).
17. Hampshire Record Office, MS 23M93/85/2.
18. Anna Lefroy 'Recollections of Aunt Jane', in Sutherland (2002), p. 159.
19. Hampshire Record Office, MS 23M93/85/2.
20. Sutherland (2002), p. 119.
21. Chapman (1954), p. 436.
22. Kent History and Library Centre, MS U951/ F24/8 (see April–May 1811).
23. Kent History and Library Centre, MS U951/ F24/8 (12 June 1811).
24. Kent History and Library Centre, MS U951/F24/10 (6 June 1813).
25. 'I hope, my Anna', in Selwyn, ed. (1996), p. 34.
26. Le Faye, ed. (1996), p. 40.
27. Jan Fergus, 'The Professional Woman Writer', in Copeland and McMasters, eds (2011 edition), p. 12.
28. Ibid., p. 16.
29. Letter to Amelie Opie (October 1813), quoted in Fergus (1991), p. 188.
30. William Gifford to John Murray (21 September 1815), quoted in Jan Fergus, 'Composition and Publication', pp. 1–16, in Peter Sabor, ed., *The Cambridge Companion to Emma*, Cambridge (2015), p. 8.
31. Ibid.
32. Letters, p. 294 (20/21 November 1815).

Chapter 29

1. Simond (1815) vol. 1, p. 184.
2. Nikolaus Pevsner, 'The Architectural Setting of Jane Austen's Novels', *The Journal of the Warburg and Courtauld Institutes*, vol. 31 (1968), p. 414.
3. Henry Hole (1802), quoted in Adkins (2013), pp. 245–6.
4. Egan (1819), p. 3.
5. Karl Philipp Moritz, *Travels in England in 1782*, Bremen (2010 edition), p. 13.
6. Louise Allen, *Walking Jane Austen's London*, Oxford (2013).
7. Hill (1902), p. 207.
8. Silliman (1810), p. 283.
9. Karl Philipp Moritz, *Travels in England in 1782*, Bremen (2010 edition), p. 38.
10. Laura Boyle, 'The Harp as a Status Symbol' (20 June 2011); https://www.janeausten.co.uk/the-harp-as-a-status-symbol/
11. Le Faye (2004), p. 186.
12. Deirdre Le Faye, 'Jane Austen's Laggard Suitor', quoted in Le Faye (2004), p. 192.
13. Letter of D.G. Boyle, in Sutherland (2002), p. 196.
14. Le Faye (2004), p. 186.
15. Henry Austen, 'Memoir of Miss Austen', in Sutherland (2004), p. 150.
16. Kent History and Library Centre, MS U951/F24/10 (1 May 1813).

Chapter 30

1. 'To Miss J. Austen', James Edward Austen-Leigh, in Selwyn, ed. (1996), p. 61.
2. Caroline Austen, 'My Aunt Jane Austen: A Memoir', in Sutherland (2002), p. 175.
3. Sutherland (2002), p. 92.
4. Ibid.
5. Le Faye (2004), p. 71
6. Hampshire Record Office MS 8M62/15, fols 64v; 71r.
7. Steven Parissien, *George IV: The Grand Entertainment*, London (2001), pp. 120–1.
8. The Hon. Mrs Hugh Wyndham, ed., *Correspondence of Sarah Spencer, Lady Lyttelton, 1787–1879*, London (1912), p. 104.
9. Caroline Austen, 'My Aunt Jane Austen: A Memoir', in Sutherland (2002), p. 176.
10. Earl of Malmesbury, ed., *Diaries and Correspondence of James Harris, First Earl of Malmesbury*, London (1845), vol. 3, p. 211.
11. Linda Colley, *Britons*, New Haven and London (1992), p. 265.
12. *The Times* (20 September 1820).
13. Parissien (2001), p. 260.
14. 'To Miss J. Austen', James Edward Austen-Leigh, in Selwyn, ed. (1996), p. 61.
15. Le Faye (1995), p. 307, James Stanier Clarke to Jane Austen (21 December 1815).
16. Adkins (2013), p. 232.

Chapter 31

1. Fergus (2011 edition), p. 14.
2. *Gentleman's Magazine* (September 1816), vol. lxxxvi, pp. 248–9.
3. *Monthly Review* (July 1816), vol. lxxx, p. 320.
4. Fergus (2011 edition), p. 14.
5. Chapman (1954), vol. vi, pp. 437–8.
6. Accounts from the John Murray Archives were displayed at the Jane Austen House Museum in 2016.
7. Quoted in Le Faye (2004), p. 216.
8. Le Faye, ed. (1996), p. 39.
9. Le Faye (2004), p. 217.
10. Ibid.
11. Le Faye, ed. (1996), p. 47.
12. David Selwyn, ed., *The Complete Poems of James Austen*, The Jane Austen Society (2003), p. 71.
13. Le Faye, ed. (1996), p. 47.
14. *The Times* (10 Sept. 1807), quoted in Clive Caplan, 'The Brewery Scheme is Quite at an End', *Report of the Jane Austen Society* (2010), pp. 92–6.
15. Hampshire Record Office, MS 23M93/85/2.
16. Quoted in Caplan (1998), p. 73.
17. Caplan (1998), p. 85.
18. Quoted in ibid., p. 86.
19. Hampshire Record Office, MS 23M93/85/2.
20. Sutherland (2002), p. 16.

21. Hampshire Record Office, MS 23M93/60/2/12, Jane Leigh-Perrot to James Austen (31 January 1819).
22. Le Faye (2004), p. 234.

Chapter 32

1. I had the privilege of handling the original at the Jane Austen House Museum.
2. Woodforde (1999), p. 125 (28 February 1782).
3. Le Faye, ed. (1996), p. 11.
4. Kent History and Library Centre, MS U951/F24/10 (18 July 1813).
5. Kent History and Library Centre, MS U951/F24/10 (24 July 1813).
6. Oscar Faye Adams, *The Story of Jane Austen's Life*, Madison (1891), p. 176.
7. Sutherland (2002), p. 106.
8. Ibid.
9. Caroline Austen, 'My Aunt Jane Austen: A Memoir', in Sutherland (2002), p. 177.
10. Ibid., p. 175.
11. Hampshire Record Office, MS 23M93/85/2.
12. Caroline Austen, 'My Aunt Jane Austen: A Memoir', in Sutherland (2002), p. 178.
13. Hampshire Record Office, MS 23M93/85/2.
14. Upfal (2005), p. 10.
15. Le Faye (2013 edition), p. 441.
16. Christopher John Murray, ed., *Encyclopedia of the Romantic Era, 1760–1850*, London (2004), p. 722.
17. Upfal (2005), p. 10.
18. Mentioned by @JaneAustenHouse.
19. Noted by Spence (2007 edition), p. 214.

Chapter 33

1. Quoted in Le Faye (2004), p. 259.
2. Gay (2011), p. 63.
3. John Mullan, 'Psychology', in Todd, ed. (2005), p. 385.
4. Letter of D.G. Boyle, in Sutherland (2002), p. 196.
5. Le Faye (2004), p. 267.
6. Prewitt Brown (1979), p. 168.
7. Quoted in Le Faye (2004), p. 243.
8. Arthur M. Axelrad, *Jane Austen's Sanditon: A Village by the Sea*, Bloomington (2010), p. 64; pencilled section visible at http://www.janeausten.ac.uk/manuscripts/sanditon/b2-38.html.
9. Wally Chamberlain Oulton, *The Traveller's Guide; or, English Itinerary*, London (1805), vol. 2, p. 912.
10. Antony Edmonds, *Jane Austen's Worthing*, Stroud (2013), pp. 44–5.
11. *Brighton Gazette*, no. 686 (5 October 1837), p. 3.
12. Oulton (1805), vol. 2, p. 912.
13. *Brighton Gazette*, no. 333 (5 July 1827), p. 3.
14. Lefroy and Turner (2007), p. 81.

15. Sir Walter Scott, unsigned review of 'Emma' (1815), *The Quarterly Review*, vol. xiv, London (second edition, 1821), p. 189; Keymer (2011), p. 21.
16. This is persuasively argued in Edmonds (2013).
17. Austen-Leigh (1942), pp. 291–2, Jane Leigh Perrot to James Edward Austen (8 March 1835).
18. TNA PROB 1/78, 'Will of Jane Austen Proved 27 April 1817'; Le Faye (1995; 1997 edition), p. 339 (27 April 1817).
19. Caroline Austen, 'My Aunt Jane Austen: A Memoir', in Sutherland (2002), p. 179.

Chapter 34

1. For well-informed speculation that Jane might have occupied a different building on College Street also owned by Mrs David, see Keiran Phelan's article at http://literarywinchester.co.uk
2. Le Faye (2004), p. 221.
3. Caroline Austen, 'My Aunt Jane Austen: A Memoir', in Sutherland (2002), p. 179.
4. Hill (1902), p. 254.
5. Townsend (2014), p. 137.
6. Barbara Carpenter Turner, *Winchester*, Southampton (1980), p. 132.
7. Tom Beaumont Jones, *The English Heritage Book of Winchester*, London (1997), p. 111.
8. Hayley (1786 edition), p. 7.
9. Carol Houlihan Flynn, 'The Letters', in Copeland and McMasters, eds (1997), pp. 97–110.
10. Sutherland (2002), p. 18.
11. Caroline Austen, 'My Aunt Jane Austen: A Memoir', in Sutherland (2002), pp. 179–80.
12. Ibid., p. 182.
13. Ibid., p. 181.
14. James Austen, in W. Austen-Leigh, *Jane Austen, Her Life and Letters: A Family Record*, New York (1965), p. 392; Le Faye (2004), p. 251.
15. National Maritime Museum, Greenwich, Charles Austen's diary (1817), AUS/109, quoted in Le Faye (2004), p. 252.
16. Caroline Austen, 'My Aunt Jane Austen: A Memoir', in Sutherland (2002), p. 182.

Chapter 35

1. Letter of James Edward Austen-Leigh, in Sutherland (2002), p. 190.
2. Jane Austen, 'Written at Winchester on Tuesday the 15th July 1817', in Selwyn, ed. (1996), pp. 17–18.
3. Harman (2009), p. 79.
4. Caroline Austen, 'My Aunt Jane Austen: A Memoir', in Sutherland (2002), p. 182.
5. James Austen, in W. Austen-Leigh, *Jane Austen, Her Life and Letters: A Family Record*, New York (1965), p. 392.
6. Henry Austen, 'Biographical Notice of the Author', in Sutherland (2002), p. 138.
7. Mrs Austen to Anna Austen Lefroy, quoted in Hampshire Record Office, MS 23M93/85/2.

8. Hampshire Record Office, MS 23M93/62/1/8, Mary Austen Diary (18 July 2017).
9. Caroline Austen, 'My Aunt Jane Austen: A Memoir', in Sutherland (2002), p. 175.
10. Le Faye (1995; 1997 edition), p. 344 (20 July 1817).
11. Letter of Caroline Austen, in Sutherland (2002), p. 187.
12. Frederick Bussby, *Jane Austen in Winchester*, Winchester (1973), p. 6.
13. *Hampshire Chronicle*, vol. XLIV, no. 2254 (21 July 1817), p. 4.
14. TNA IR 59/4, AUSTEN, Jane (1817).
15. Fergus (2011), p. 16.
16. Castle, (1995), pp. 3–6.
17. The intriguing theory of researcher Lindsay Ashford was reported in Alison Flood, 'Jane Austen Died from Arsenic Poisoning', the *Guardian* (14 November 2011); Ferris Jabr, 'Was Jane Austen Poisoned by Arsenic? Science May Soon Find Out', *Scientific American* (5 December 2011).

Chapter 36

1. Robinson (1799), p. 91.
2. Selwyn (2003), p. 87.
3. Argument made in Harman (2009), p. 82.
4. Harman (2009), p. 86.
5. Sutherland (2002), p. 91.
6. Honan (1987; 1997 edition), p. 117.
7. Deirdre Le Faye, 'Lord Brabourne's Edition of Jane Austen's Letters', *The Review of English Studies*, New Series, vol. 52, no. 205 (2001), pp. 91–102; p. 92.
8. Sutherland (2002), p. 18.
9. Ibid., p. 17.
10. Ibid., p. 48.
11. Jenkins (1989), p. 168.

Epilogue

1. Le Faye, ed. (1996), p. 57.
2. Anon., *Hampshire Notes and Queries*, vol. 1, Winchester (1883), p. 10.
3. Hill (1902), p. 258.
4. Caroline Austen, 'My Aunt Jane Austen: A Memoir', in Sutherland (2002), p. 168.
5. Deirdre Le Faye, 'The Austens and the Littleworths', *Collected Reports of the Jane Austen Society (1986–1995)*, p. 68.

Index

Picture Acknowledgements

Alamy: 3 below left/Chronicle, 4 above left/TravelCollection, 6 below/Stewart McKeown, 9 below/Lebrecht Music and Arts Photo Library, 11 above left/Jane Tregelles, 12 above/Archimage, 12 below/UrbanLandscapes, 14 below/Richard Donovan, 15 centre right/Heritage Image Partnership Ltd, 15 below/Steve Vidler, 16 below/travelib prime.'Astley's Amphitheatre' from August Pugin and Thomas Rowlandson's *Microcosm of London*, 1808: 8 below. Jane Austen's House Museum Hampshire UK: 3 above right, 6 above left and centre right. James Edward Austen-Leigh *A Memoir of Jane Austen*, published by Richard Bentley, 1870: text page 5 (Steventon Parsonage), 13 above right. Bridgeman Images: 1 below (painting by Paul Sandby/private collection photo © Christie's Images), 2 above right (National Portrait Gallery/De Agostini Picture Library), 3 below right (watercolour by George Engleheart/private collection photo © Christie's Images), 7 below right (Jane Austen Society on loan to Chawton House Library UK), 8 above (painting by Rolinda Sharples © Bristol Museum and Art Gallery UK), 10 and 11 below (John Claude Nattes *Bath, Illustrated by a Series of Views*, 1806), 14 above (watercolour by Cassandra Austen/private collection), text page 229 (*A Quiet Moment* pen and ink on paper by John Harden/Abbot Hall Art Gallery Kendal Cumbria UK). British Library London UK/© British Library Board All Rights Reserved/Bridgeman Images: 2 above left and below left, 5 above left and centre left, 13 below. © Chawton House Library Hampshire UK/Richard Knight: 7 below left (Edward Austen's suit on display at Chawton House Library, chawtonhouselibrary.org). Constance Hill *Jane Austen Her Homes & Her Friends,* 1902: 2 below right, 3 above left, 7 above (*The Wellings Silhouette* 1783), text page 289 (the parlour in College Street, Winchester). Historical Picture Archive/Corbis via Getty Images: text page 151 (Milsom Street Bath/ John Claude Nattes *Bath, Illustrated by a Series of Views*, 1806). J. H. Hubback and Edith C. Hubback *Jane Austen's Sailor Brothers*, 1906: 5 below, 16 above. Courtesy of Lyme Regis Museum: 9 above (print from *Lyme Regis, A Retrospect* by C. Wanklyn, 1927). © By permission of Lyme Regis Museum: 9 centre (detail from George Cruickshank's *Hydromania, or a Touch of the Sub-Lyme and Beautiful − The Beach at Lyme Regis*, 1819). Private collections reproduced with permission: 1 above left, 11 above right, 15 above. G.F. Prosser *Select illustrations of Hampshire* 1833: 4 below left. Lucy Worsley: 1 above right, 4 centre right, 12 centre right.